Leviathan

James Byron Huggins

OLIVER
NELSON

THOMAS NELSON PUBLISHERS
Nashville • Atlanta • London • Vancouver

Dedicated
to
Jan Dennis
and
family

Published in Nashville, Tennessee, by Thomas Nelson, Inc.

Scripture quotations are paraphrases from THE NEW KING JAMES VERSION of the Bible, Copyright © 1979, 1980, 1982, Thomas Nelson, Inc., Publishers.

Library of Congress Cataloging-in-Publication Data

Huggins, James Byron.
    Leviathan : a novel / by James Byron Huggins.
    p.   cm.
    ISBN 0-7852-7709-9 (hardcover)
    ISBN 0-7852-7263-1 (paperback)
    I. Title.
PS3558.U346L48   1995
813'.54—dc20
                                                                95-11061
                                                                    CIP

Printed in the United States of America

3 4 5 6 7 — 01 00 99 98

Acknowledgments

No true novel is the work of an author. At a novel's best moments, it contains the grace of Almighty God, who alone gives skill and discernment. Yet it also contains the work of others, their contribution of ideas, criticism, and insight. Others who helped in ways that can hardly be described or even, sometimes, remembered.

Jan Dennis of Jan Dennis Books conceptualized *Leviathan* and gave the book its truest, highest, and best meaning. He made *Leviathan* what I wanted it to be but could not conceive, alone. And for his insight and judgment and discernment on all matters of right and wrong, for knowing truth and substance, I owe a substantial debt.

Second, I thank Frank Cohee, Jr., a great Christian man and internationally recognized scientist, who first explored and created the process of Electromagnetic Chromosomal Manipulation. Frank deserves all the credit for scientific and genetic ideas captured within these pages, and their possible effects upon our lives. Without Frank's God-given genius and ideas, this book could not have been written.

Also, I want to thank Cindy Bond for her patient and exacting editorial judgment in polishing the final manuscript, and Larry Applebaum for his creative criticism of the story line, character development, and design. Further, I thank Anna Quinn at Thomas Nelson for her skillful assistance in all matters of editing and publication, an exceedingly hard job which is often underappreciated but is absolutely invaluable to both publishers and writers. I thank Bruce Zabel for everything he has done, for his sacrifice of time, his patience and endless work. And, as always,

I thank Bill Jenson for his longtime support and encouragement and friendship.

Most of all, I thank my wife and two children who so patiently endured my long hours and the hard task of writing. Without them in my life, I say truthfully, I fear I would have nothing to say.

Prologue

Endless ice, measureless night, was before him.

And at the rim of the world, where the pale moon crested on early darkness, ice mountains floated over the deep, borne by glacial rivers, a rising night. Like frozen fangs the ice towers rose above the sea, shredding the horizon with shadows of white.

Snow swept over freezing waves that broke heavily against the red limestone shore where he stood. And green ice slates spun slowly in the rising tide like frozen storm clouds in a gale, drifted closer, and closer, until they too broke upon the slabs, where the wind lifted frost from the heaping ice, settling it again upon the land, and the man.

Alone in the freezing sleet, the man wrapped his cloak, rough and hoary with frost, more tightly about his gigantic form, staring into the gale.

Colossal in the gloom, he towered almost eight feet above the shore. His long red beard and hair, thick and heavy and raggedly cut, were solid and white with ice. But his face was indifferent to the cold, his gaze unblinking. His arms, folded over a deeply muscled chest, were thick and heavy, and he was titanically massive—the image of a Teutonic frost giant of old, or a Viking sea king loosed from the corridors of time to stand once more against the merciless gale, defying the conquering cold.

His horse, saddled and blanketed against the storm, stood close beside him; a heavy-maned Icelandic breed born for the cold, to endure the bitter North. For a long time now it had stood faithfully in the dusk, waiting beside the man as he watched the night descend. It was accustomed to the long and bitter stand. But tonight it shuffled steadily with unusual, nervous strength, seeking to retreat from the approaching gloom.

Frowning, the red-bearded giant turned to the stallion. His voice was gentle, soothing. "Easy, Tanngrisner." He wrapped a huge arm around the stallion's thick neck. "What is it that you see, old friend? What is it that frightens you?"

The great stallion stomped to break free its ice-sleeved hooves, moving slightly back from the shore. Angrily it shook sleet from its mane.

A broad smile creased the man's face, causing ice to crack on the ragged beard. "Are you afraid of the storm, brother?" His tone grew jestful. "Or is it *Ragnarok* you fear? The last great battle between evil and good?" He laughed again, at himself. "There is nothing to fear, old friend. Ragnarok is only a story. A story told to bright-eyed children, who still have hope . . ."

Smile fading, the man turned to the sea, his voice gentler. "No, Tanngrisner, we will find no battle here. Here there is only ice, and rock, and sea. And . . . dreams of what might have been."

Tanngrisner impatiently shook its head, retreating from the shore despite the man's great strength. And surrendering compassionately to the stallion's uneasiness, the man went gently with it, leading by a weathered rein.

"Yes, yes . . ." he said, falling in beside Tanngrisner's gait, moving from the shore. "You are wiser than I, because I stand in the ice, like a fool, when we could be warm. But it has always been my foolishness that I search too long . . . and dream too much . . ."

Before them, massive and moon-white upon the shore, stood the tower. Smooth and cylindrical, it erupted like a polished ivory tusk from the shattered red stones, stretching beyond view to the night sky. Tightly constructed from huge granite blocks, the tower was utterly impervious to the cold and ice. And a wide portal stood open, framed by light within.

Inside the thick walls, they both knew, comfortable flames would be carefully banked, repelling the outside world. And the stallion would find its place on the lower level, safe and protected from the wind to feed and sleep, while the man climbed the long stairway to inhabit his place, closer to the stars, in the upper chamber.

"Come," he muttered. "The world is cold . . . and dark."

A sudden blast shattered a slashing ice wave against the red shore and the man spun, staring. As if unexpectedly awakened from a frightful sleep, he stood, scowling deeply. Without looking again at the stallion, he controlled its fearful shuffle.

"Steady, Tanngrisner, steady now . . ."

But the man could not turn his eyes from the night, or from watching. And whether it was there or not, he could not be sure, but he thought he saw something on the horizon that had not been there before. He squinted, searching, but the distance was too great, the shadows too uncertain. But it seemed like, yes, like something was out there, something rising . . .

Like a serpent, from the sea.

His breath froze in his chest as he watched.

For where the haggard moon lay upon the sea, the night appeared to thicken, gathering, as if to mark the unnatural creation of a long and bitter darkness. And the pale circle of light, overcome by the fangs of ice, was vanishing in narrow slivers as if the moon itself were being slowly devoured by an irresistible, unearthly evil.

An evil that devoured. Piece by piece . . .

Chapter 1

Bloodred warning lights blazed as the cavern's shock alarm was triggered, frantically launching wounded computer personnel into emergency stabilization procedures.

Echoing through the underground facility like a nuclear blast, the fantastic heat-concussion still trembled the steel-plated walls of the reinforced Observation Room.

Terrified beyond rational thought, shocked scientists abandoned their stations to charge explosively into nearby corridors while others desperately held their place in the flame-tinted chamber. Unintelligible commands bellowed as workers tore extinguishers from walls and blindly emptied foam onto electronic panels that smoldered and arced with sparks, shattered by the stress.

Noxious gray smoke clouded the room, the remains of seared steel paneling and insulation. Then emergency ventilation units, activated automatically by the alarm, kicked in and a strained wind rushed through the room, clearing the fumes as fresh air flooded through connecting ducts. In moments the choking grayness dissipated, leaving those who had held their stations to stare dumbly at the Plexiglas shield. Fire extinguishers hung forgotten in their hands.

Writhing and swirling in superheated flame on the far side, the six-foot-thick Plexiglas shield continued to disintegrate, inch by inch, before their eyes. Spirals of serpentine flame twisted slowly, hypnotically, mesmerizing with blue-white circles that had already begun to radiate heat into the monitoring chamber, consuming, devouring . . .

On the floor of the Observation Room, Dr. Peter Frank groaned and rolled awkwardly to his side, trying painfully to reorient himself. Stunned, he remembered nothing for a moment, only volcanic white light filling the room in an electric eruption, blinding thunder with human bodies flung like rags at the unbelievable power surge . . .

Wiping a smear of blood from his eyes, Frank found conscious control, numbly shaking his head. Then with a supreme effort of will, he struggled to his knees. Unsteadily he gained his feet.

Wide-eyed, he stared at the spiraling flames on the Plexiglas before tearing his attention from the glowing aftermath of the holocaust. With rapidly gathering control he gazed down at the smoldering panels, youthful eyes darting with increasing speed along the flashing red lights, searching until he found a small microphone. Instantly he shouted into the computer—

"Shut the heat shield!"

No response.

Frank grabbed the computer's microphone. "GEO! This is Dr. Frank with a voice command! Shut the heat shield now!"

Nothing happened.

Behind him a handful of personnel screamed and broke, running.

Without any expression on his sweating face, Frank rapidly ran his hands over the control panel to override auditory command. He repeated the same procedure three times, glancing up wildly as globs of melting Plexiglas fell away, flames consuming a vengeful path into the Observation Room.

No response from the computer; flames writhed on the other side of the Plexiglas . . .

Stunned by the sight, Frank gripped the sides of the computer's optical sensor matrix, glaring at the fast-approaching holocaust, his breath thin and panicked.

"We've lost contact with GEO," he whispered, breathless,

watching the blue spirals on the Plexiglas. "We've lost contact with the computer. We can't lower the heat shield . . ."

No one moved—disbelief, shock all that remained.

Desperately Frank snatched a portable computer access unit from his belt and immediately jammed the connector into the panel. In seconds he hit an override command to circumvent the shattering hardware. The control panel's fiber-optic matrix blinked erratically; the heat shield failed to descend.

Disintegrating sheets of Plexiglas slid away.

The Observation Room began to overheat.

"Nothing works," Frank muttered, unable to hide his emotion, hands flying over commands. "We don't have thermones for the fire. Nothing! This is unbelievable . . . unbelievable . . ."

Frantically he hit one command after another, his face aglow with the crimson light, sweat visible on his forehead as the thinning plastic in front of him melted away. Then, abruptly and unexpectedly, the control panel's subprocessing unit locked in light, backup power somehow finding a path through the shattered circuits. Frank hit commands as quickly as he could, commanding, commanding . . .

"Come on," he whispered, unable to contain himself even though voice control was gone. His fingers flew over the unit. "Come on, GEO! Listen to me! Shut the door, shut the door . . ."

Suddenly there was a harsh thundering on the burning side of the Plexiglas, a continuous gray mist filling their view. Flames vanished instantly beneath the fog.

"We've got thermones!" Frank shouted, emotional. "We've got nitrogen thermones! It works! It works!"

Moving his hands over the portable access unit, he quick-programmed a new routine to lower the heat shield and in seconds a grating sound released itself in the wall above them, the niobium-titanium wall descending to seal the void where the Plexiglas fell away.

A vault lock reverberated through the room.

With trembling hands and whitened face, Frank stepped slowly, unsteadily back from the alloy shield. He stared at the wall for a moment as if he couldn't remember where he was, what he was doing. Red emergency lights in the monitor room continued to glow, backup modes functioning despite the impact of the phenomenal blast on the electrical system. Finally, glassy-eyed, he turned to the Observation Room. Only two of the dozen staff scientists remained.

"It didn't get out," he said, pale with sweat.

No response.

A gray-haired man, decades older than Frank himself but centuries behind his understanding of the project, collapsed heavily into a chair. He raised a white, trembling hand to smooth back sweat-plastered hair and leaned forward, head hanging low, clearly exhausted. The other remaining scientist, a raven-haired woman in her early twenties, the sleeve of her lab coat still smoldering where flames had erupted from the computer panel, turned away, trembling quietly. Without even acknowledging that she had heard the comment, she leaned her head against the wall, breathing deeply, firmly grasping a steel support beam, regaining control.

"It didn't get out," Frank repeated, almost apologetic. "It's still locked in the Containment Cavern. And I'm flooding the cavern with nitrogen, to put it to sleep. It didn't . . . it didn't get out."

"What happened in here!"

The irate voice had erupted from the military figure who appeared suddenly in the doorway.

Wearing green utility fatigues swirling with smoke from the corridor beyond, the lean presence in the entry dominated the room. The man glared at the foam-covered computer terminals and the overturned printouts, coffee cups, fire extinguishers, and chairs. Then through the fading vapors he nervously centered on Frank, repeating the question with impatient authority.

"Doctor! I asked you a question! What happened?"

Frank pointed to the niobium-titanium wall. Said nothing.

For the first time since he had entered, Colonel Carl Chesterton switched his glare to the alloy shield. Hesitant, he slowly walked into the room, his right hand settling on the .45-caliber semiautomatic on his belt. He froze in front of the optical control panel, staring with silent fear before he turned toward Frank. His voice was low, harsh.

"Did it—"

"No," Frank answered, a thin, dark-haired man who looked too young for the position. "It didn't get out."

As if from reflex, Colonel Chesterton's gaze wandered between the scientist and the reinforced wall. Then with a conscious effort he seemed to collect himself, solidifying into a more commanding bearing. He focused again on Frank, locked into a calmness.

"Did it cause all this?" he asked, frowning uneasily.

No expression. "Yes."

Controlled rage hardened Chesterton's voice. "Well . . . is it still locked in the Containment Cavern, Doctor? Or did it melt one of the doors?" He stared. "Maybe you should let me know. Before we discover that we're in a world of hurt."

Without missing a beat Frank reached out and switched on a screen that had somehow escaped the chaotic foaming. The monitor blinked unsteadily in red, then orange, flickering.

"The viewing camera inside the Containment Cavern is shielded from heat," he said. "It should have survived the blast. If it's still working, we'll be able to see it on the monitor."

Unsteadily the monitor continued to flicker, hazy and uncertain, before it honed into a gray clarity. Then, as the image cleared, Frank released a dismal laugh, disoriented or stunned.

"Yeah, it's in there," he said, amazement fading into cold observation. "See for yourself."

Chesterton was already leaning in front of the screen, staring intently into the haze. Sweat beaded his forehead, his neck. He squinted as he studied the blurred image. "Where?" he muttered. "Where is it?"

"It's right in front of you."

"No, Doctor. It's not in there."

"Look closer."

Chesterton leaned toward the screen, his eyes roaming from one side to the other, searching. Then he suddenly stepped back, a startled curse catching in his throat. A grim hate passed over his face as he lifted a trembling hand, pointing to the screen.

"All right," he said. "Shut it off. It's in there."

Frank continued to stare at the screen. "I never saw it coming," he said, scientific discipline entering to make his voice almost emotionless. "I guess it was a mistake, but I just never saw it coming. None of us did." A long pause. "I mean, we all knew it had some kind of potential for this. But this was just . . . just unreal."

Silent, Chesterton stared coldly at the screen.

"That blast was at least ten thousand degrees," Frank said, a confused expression. "And the whole attack just came from nowhere. It hadn't made any threatening movements. It didn't uncoil. There was no increase in heart rate. One minute it was just sitting at the far end of the cavern. Staring at us. And then it just charged forward—" He raised his hands to describe a terrific image. "—and then *fire*! Everywhere! Nothing but fire!"

Lowering his hands, Frank quietly joined Chesterton in staring at the screen once more, watching the horrific bestial face hatefully and purposefully poised in front of the camera.

Captured on the monitor, a pair of glowing green eyes glared at them, unable to see through but somehow sensing their presence and blinking with a dark, malicious intelligence—soulless, unmerciful, calculating. A thick row of armored scales, black and green on the sloping forehead, bled off the top half of the screen, the lower half of the screen glinting in jagged white jaws that hung distended, smiling . . .

Mocking.

"It was testing the strength of the Containment Cell," Frank commented, continuing to stare.

Chesterton was grim. "And why is that, Doctor?"

The scientist dismally shook his head, as if the answer were obvious.

"It's hungry."

Chapter 2

Struggling to light a large black bowl pipe with long pulls from a match, the gray-haired old man sat down at the conference table, casually waving the tiny flame into a thin spiral of smoke.

"I understand that we remain in danger," Dr. Jason Hoffman commented encouragingly. "But I believe we are fortunate not to find ourselves in immediate peril."

"We're *fortunate* not to find ourselves dead!" Colonel Chesterton fumed, leaning on the table with both forearms. "That's something all of you need to realize, Doctor. And let me add that we are not out of the woods. At least, not yet."

Hoffman gazed over a broad, flat nose. "Yes, Colonel, I agree. I agree wholeheartedly. But, still, we are not presently in peril." He nodded curtly to the far end of the table. "Thanks to Peter."

Frank, tired and sweaty and still shaking from the terrifying ordeal, said nothing. Silently he pressed his hands flat against a computer printout to still their trembling from residual adrenaline.

Chesterton leaned forward, a hard edge in his voice. "Look, Dr. Hoffman, I don't mean to be disrespectful. But it is my obligation to inform you that we are not in a good defensive condition. We have sustained a catastrophic systems failure. We have very little automatic control, which means that the security vaults remain unstable." His face grew tightened. "No one knows what will happen if that creature does something like this again. The shock might completely shut down the electrical system. It could even open the containment vaults. There's just no way to know."

"I understand, Colonel," Hoffman responded through a haze of pipe smoke. "Frank, does GEO remain on-line?"

Frank nodded. "Yes. GEO's redundant computer core is magnetically shock-suspended to protect it from the island's natural seismic activity. So that protected it from the impact with only temporary field distortion in the neural net. Right now it's performing self-diagnosis on all subprocessors and dedicated terminal nodes. It'll finish reconfiguring secondary Cray class units, reprogramming setup standardization, and reestablishing orbital satellite net links. But the system is 75 percent dedicated in reconfiguring and self-diagnosis, and those operations are taxing our already strained power supply. There's still about another two hours of processing remaining."

"I understand," replied Hoffman. "How long before the control panel is repaired?"

"Twenty-four hours," Frank answered. "We have replacement parts, but we have to get that electrical line repaired first. And we'll have to use somebody from the surface to do it. My people aren't qualified."

"I see." Hoffman frowned over his pipe. "Well, Colonel? Is it possible to use someone from the surface personnel to repair the line?"

A sullen pause, and Chesterton nodded. "Yeah, I think so. Jackson Connor can do it. He's a master electrician, a mechanic, and foreman of the civilian support crew. He knows construction, engines, whatever, so there's not much he can't handle. In fact he's probably the only man on the island who's qualified to handle it by himself. But he doesn't have the necessary security clearance to enter the Containment Cavern."

"Meaning he does not know the exact nature of the experiment," Hoffman confirmed.

"No," Chesterton replied. "Connor doesn't know what we

. . . what they . . . have created in the cavern. And there would probably be, uh, danger if he did discover what's in there."

"What kind of danger?" Hoffman asked quickly, focusing.

"Connor is a cautious man, Doctor. He does his job and he does it well. But if Connor thinks that his men are being unnecessarily endangered, he can be very, very hard to deal with."

An alarming silence settled.

"Then you will, of course, ensure that Mr. Connor does not become concerned for the safety of his men," Hoffman replied. "Something that will happen immediately if he somehow gets a look inside the Containment Cavern. We certainly . . . no, no . . . we certainly cannot afford a breach of security at this critical moment."

Chesterton paused, spoke. "I think I can handle him, Doctor. I'll just tell him that we overloaded the line, and that should take care of it. And the fire doors of the Containment Cell are shut, so he can't see what's in there."

The old man nodded. "Good. Yes . . . very, very good. And how long do you think it will take Mr. Connor to complete repairs?"

"Connor knows his job, Doctor. But this won't be easy. It'll take him at least a couple of hours."

"Very well." Hoffman was gazing at his smoldering pipe. "Then it is a risk we can tolerate." He paused. "And now, Colonel, what other security precautions are we taking?"

"I've ordered all vaults transferred to manual control," Chesterton answered, jaw setting solidly. "I've stationed men at every exit of the Containment Cavern with LAW rockets and M-60s and they've got a standing green light to open up with everything they've got if that thing even looks sideways at them. And,"—he turned to look at Frank—"I will not be allowing anyone to open any more fire doors for observation purposes."

"I can't do that anyway, Chesterton," Frank replied. "The heat blast melted the Plexiglas."

"What I'm saying here, Doctor," Chesterton stressed, "is that no one is going to raise another fire door at the Containment Chamber. Not ever. Because we had a close call today and we got lucky. So as of right now, I'm ordering all further tests done by camera. We can't risk that thing escaping. And tomorrow I'm contacting Washington for additional men and equipment to shore up the Containment Cavern. And I'm strongly suggesting that we maintain a holding pattern on further tests until adequate safety measures are installed."

Hoffman nodded his head. "Yes, Colonel, I agree. I agree wholeheartedly. We should postpone all further tests until we can guarantee the safety of our lives. We are at a . . . a critical stage."

With a dead-silent gaze that shifted as quickly as a hawk, Frank glanced to the only man who hadn't contributed.

Dressed in expensive casual clothes but carrying a pleasant air of cooperation, Operations Director Spenser Wayne Adler was reclined in his habitual position of customary dispassionate concern. Frank expected the posture, had even grown somewhat seduced by it, just as everyone else. But he knew better than any of them how badly Adler wanted the project carried to completion. Knew just as well that the operations director would not allow anything to stand in the way of final testing.

Although Adler was indisputably in charge of the underground facility, the project, and the Ice Station located on Grimwald Island above them, he wore his position without condescension. Yet he still seemed like a man who would always be in charge, no matter where he stood. Well into his sixties, Adler's deep face revealed a keen and confident intellect. And even at his advanced age he seemed to retain a formidable physical strength. His hair was a dramatic white, making him seem lordly, even overpowering, a mesmerizing effect accented even more by his hypnotic, ice-blue eyes.

In all, he held an imperial presence, the presence of a man who seemed genuinely born to both natural ability and station. But Frank suspected that Adler's regal bearing may come as much from his superior attitude and six-foot-six height as anything else.

Frank remembered that Adler had been a collegiate heavyweight boxing champion at Oxford in the early fifties. A real street fighter, someone had told him once, and Frank felt himself grimace at the thought. Somehow the knowledge always made him uncomfortable.

"Well, I'm pleased that no one was killed in this incident," Adler said in his deep, resonant voice. "It would have been a great . . . a *great* tragedy . . . for any lives to have been lost. And we've certainly come too far to have this brilliant achievement marred."

Together they stared at him. Frank was as still as a statue, his face betraying nothing.

"Soon, gentlemen," Adler continued, "we will stun the scientific world. Because what we have accomplished in this cavern may very well have altered the nature of life as we know it. I commend you all. And that is the very reason why we must press on. Steadily and safely, to be sure, yes, but we must press on to our goal. Only two more tests remain to be done tomorrow and—"

"Tomorrow?" interjected Chesterton. "Mr. Adler, I'm sorry if I didn't make myself clear. I said we should delay. Let me restate it. I'm ordering a delay on all tests until we can guarantee that this creature can't escape the Containment Cavern."

Adler raised a hand. "Yes, yes, Colonel. I know how you must feel. Especially after today. But we were all aware of the risks involved. And after careful consideration, I've decided that we must—"

"*Mister* Adler," Chesterton stressed, muscular forearms flexing without effort, "let me clarify something for you."

Adler stared, frowning.

"There is no question that your company, Stygian Enterprises, owns this facility and funds this billion-dollar project," Chesterton continued. "And it is not within the bounds of my authority, nor do I possess any desire, to terminate the experiment. But the United States Government—and I am the United States Government—is in absolute charge of security." Chesterton paused, frowning. "Understand me, Mr. Adler. I am not a flexible man. My orders are not flexible. I am required to ensure that there is no penetration of this underground facility by hostile forces, that the personnel at this station are shielded from harm, and that this creature does not escape the Containment Chamber. I have three platoons of Rangers to achieve this objective and I will achieve it. But it is going to take at least two months to make adequate preparations. First, we have to cement all the corridors leading into the Containment Cavern. And my men aren't qualified for that work. Connor and his civilian ground crew will have to do it."

Adler's brow furrowed. "Cement?"

"Yes, Mr. Adler, cement. That thing can melt steel. It might even be able to melt titanium. But it can't melt cement. A nuclear weapon can't even melt cement. Once that creature is safely sealed inside cement walls, this place will be secure again. Then you can run all the tests you want."

Frank felt a distance from the conversation. He watched the ceiling lights that had begun blinking more steadily. It seemed like the electrical system was slowly recovering from the shock wave.

There was a silent conflict of wills until Adler finally nodded. "Very well, Colonel," he submitted. "I recognize, and defer to, your ultimate authority in these matters. But once adequate safety measures have been completed, I will insist that we finish all tests."

Frank decided it was time. "I think there's something else we need to consider, Mr. Adler."

A receptive smile. "Yes, Doctor?"

"We're entering a crucial stage with this creature that is obviously beyond predictability." Frank didn't blink as he spoke. "For example, this attack today was completely unexpected. This creature should never have done anything like this. An attack against the Containment Cell is completely outside its programming. So I think . . . I think that we should make a hard decision."

Adler's brow lifted. "What kind of decision, Doctor?"

"The data we've received from quantitative analyses are far beyond any anticipated results," Frank said. "Our equipment isn't even capable of measuring this kind of . . . of power. Even now, this thing's physical speed is tenfold any projections. So let me stress, Mr. Adler: We are dealing with a very, very dangerous creature. A creature that is far more dangerous than anything that has ever lived. We don't know its true potential. I don't think it even knows its true potential. But it will. Because it's neurally programmed to test itself more and more as it nears maturity. And as it begins to detect increases in its cybernet levels, it will begin searching for ways to expend the extra energy. And that is a significant threat." Frank stared, took a breath. "With the creature's newfound ability for projected combustion, combined with its rapidly increasing strength and speed and this unexplainable hostility against facility personnel, a tragedy could occur."

"What kind of tragedy, Doctor?"

"The creature could escape," Frank answered. "It might even become . . . uncontrollable."

"And then, Doctor?"

Frank waited, staring. He shifted, speaking with an almost frightening resignation. "I suppose that it would kill everything on Earth, Mr. Adler."

Adler seemed struck. "So," he responded finally, "you are saying we should terminate the life of the creature?"

"I'm saying, Mr. Adler, that the experiment is already a success," Frank answered. "Those final tests were designed only to determine if the creature is strong enough to withstand heavy weapons fire and to see if it is smart enough to defeat humans in combat. But after what we saw today, I think that we all agree that it's capable of doing both."

"I disagree, Doctor." Adler shook his head impatiently. "What the beast accomplished was impressive, yes, but it proved nothing. We do not yet know if it is strong enough to sustain heavy weapons fire. It has not yet been hit by heavy weapons fire. Nor, despite this creature's great success at defeating holograph targets, can we prove that it is smart enough to defeat humans in combat. And these are two capabilities which must be, ah, undisputable before this experiment is labeled a success."

Frank was adamant. "Believe me, Mr. Adler, that creature is strong enough to survive anything. Even artillery fire. And it's as smart as anything can get. It's even smarter than us." The scientist's face tightened. "Sir, the only thing powerful enough to defeat this creature is a nuclear weapon. That's something we need to get on the table. And that's why we need to call this experiment off and label this a success before anybody else gets hurt."

"I concur," Dr. Hoffman broke in, glaring from beneath bushy white eyebrows. "I believe the hour is upon us to terminate the project, Mr. Adler. It is clear that this creature has served its purpose, and that is the reasonable goal of any scientific endeavor. To allow this beast to live any longer would be acting irresponsibly. Lives are already at risk. But to continue will only invite a tragedy of colossal proportions."

Adler's face was concentrated. "Gentlemen, I respect your joint opinions. But I must insist that we complete these final two tests. And we must complete them as quickly as possible. We need both videotape and computer analysis by GEO to document that this creature can survive an actual military attack from heavy weaponry and that it is tactically smart enough to defeat military combat units." He paused, staring. "Let me remind you, gentlemen, that Stygian Enterprises has a substantial investment in this project. A billion-dollar investment. And a decision to terminate the life of the creature before the final two tests are completed and this system can be sold would be a very serious matter for the company."

Hoffman broke in. "But you own Stygian Enterprises, Mr. Adler. It is a decision that you are capable of making."

"I am only one among many, Doctor," Adler responded coldly, staring. "I do not control the company. I would need the approval of the Executive Council before I could terminate this experiment."

Hoffman released a puff of pipe smoke. "So for the sake of procedure, you are willing to put the lives of over a hundred men and women at risk? Listen to me! We have created on this island and under your supervision"—he pointed with the pipe—"the most terrifying beast to ever walk the face of the earth! I personally do not believe that anything equal to it has ever existed. Just think, man! What if this creature should escape the Containment Chamber? I tell you quite literally that no one inside this facility would survive. It would kill us all. Easily. And if it somehow made it to the surface of the island, the men and women of the support crew would be caught completely off guard. And they would certainly be attacked because the creature's food consumption level is dramatically accelerated, commensurate with its metabolism. It requires at least a thousand pounds of meat every two hours in order to survive and—"

"I'm familiar with the statistics, Dr. Hoffman," Adler interrupted. "And I don't want any of you to misunderstand me. I also place a high value on human life." His tone hardened. "But we have a job to do, gentlemen. And without the final two tests to measure this creature's ability to survive heavy weapons fire and its ability to defeat humans in a military conflict, this experiment remains a failure." His teeth gleamed. "And if failure is the curtain that closes this facility, gentlemen, I can assure you there will be no more funding whatsoever for Electromagnetic Chromosomal Research. Because this billion-dollar exercise, fully funded by Stygian Enterprises, will be viewed as a complete waste of expenditures." He nodded. "I can assure you of that."

A discordant silence blanketed the bunker. Frank noticed that the overhead lights had ceased blinking. Fresh air was flowing through the ducts. The room was cooler. Systems were on-line.

"Two more tests," Adler continued, a nod. "Two more tests and then we'll have the data we require. Colonel Chesterton, you may have this support foreman repair the electrical line. And I will make arrangements through the company for filling the Containment Cavern corridors with cement. It shall be done as quickly as possible."

Chesterton stared. "I think I should take care of the cement, Mr. Adler. It's part of my—"

"Yes, Colonel," Adler gestured sharply, "it is part of your job. But the United States Government does not fund this experiment. And cementing the Containment Cavern will cost Stygian a great deal of money, so it is something that I will have to authorize. And then you can supervise the procedures." He paused. "Is this acceptable to your demands?"

A pause, and Chesterton nodded.

"Very well then. It's decided." Adler rose, gathering his files. "We shall make safety adjustments, and this creature shall live until we complete the final two tests. Our respective obligations shall be fulfilled; and then, and only then, gentlemen, will we receive authorization to destroy this creature and perform an autopsy."

No one spoke as Adler crossed the room. But when he reached the door, he turned abruptly back. His face, rigidly cold and implacable, allowed no room for misunderstanding.

"Leviathan lives, gentlemen. It lives until it's time for it to die."

Chapter 3

Connor smiled as he watched Chesterton's approach through the storm window of the warehouse. Walking stiffly, Chesterton crossed the wide expanse of wind-frozen tundra until he quickly opened the door and closed it even more quickly behind him. He stood for a moment in the warmth, as if he'd been shocked. He had a look of severe impatience.

Connor laughed out loud. "What'd your people blow up this time, Chesterton?"

"We've got a big problem, Connor," he replied, walking forward. "There's a 1,000-amp line that's been burned up. We've got circuit breakers blown all over the place."

Chesterton glanced at a bright-eyed four-year-old boy sitting contently on the bulldozer's tread. Barely three feet tall, the child was contentedly consuming a large candy bar, fingers and face coated with chocolate.

"Well," the Colonel smiled, "how are you doing today, Jordan?"

Jordan nodded politely. "Fine."

"Is that a good candy bar?"

"Yes, sir. Daddy gave it to me."

"Well, it sure *looks* like a good candy bar," Chesterton said, leaning forward. "Think you might share a bite with me?"

Jordan paused, staring seriously. Then he stretched out the half-consumed candy bar in a chocolate-covered hand and

Chesterton laughed easily. "That's all right, partner." He patted the pocket of his coat, whispering, "I've got a few of 'em hidden in my coat."

Jordan received the news without blinking and returned to his snack while Connor picked up a rag, wiping hydraulic fluid from his hands. "How did your people burn up a 1,000-amp line, Chesterton?"

"You *could* call me Colonel, Connor."

"I *could* call you a lot of things, Chesterton," Connor responded with a slight smile. "But before we get personal, why don't you tell me how your people burned up a 1,000-amp line?"

"Good grief, Connor, I don't know. Do I look like an electrician? It was overloaded. It surged. It did whatever electrical lines do when they blow. I think they were trying some kind of experiment with lasers or something, and they just blew the thing up."

Connor dropped the rag over an engine line and gathered a handful of tools. "Did you see it blow?" he asked.

"No."

"Then you were a lucky man."

Chesterton leaned back, staring. "I figured that much, Connor." He paused. "But now that these preliminaries are over, can we get on with fixing the thing? We're on a schedule."

Dropping tools in a leather pouch, Connor nodded. "All right. I'll send a crew down in a few minutes."

"No." Chesterton shook his head. "We can't use a regular crew on this. It's a highly classified area, and everybody below is already nervous about it. They expressly said they don't want a crew poking around the damage. You'll have to handle this one by yourself."

Something in Chesterton's voice made Connor turn. Staring for a long moment, he leaned a shoulder against the bulldozer. "So I need to do it myself, huh?"

"That's right."

Studious, Connor glanced again at Jordan and the boy looked up, continuing to munch happily. With a laugh Connor reached down to tousle the light brown hair. But when he looked back to Chesterton, his face hardened; something focused sharply between the two of them.

Chesterton blinked.

"I've never seen a 1,000-amp line burn up before, Chesterton. I've never even heard of a 1,000-amp line burning up." Connor paused. "Just how much power was it pulling?"

"Connor," Chesterton replied, harder, "I have no idea how much power that thing was pulling. But I assume that it was a lot. And now, if you don't mind, we need to get on with fixing the thing."

Raising his chin, Connor gestured to a large, two-story stone building behind them. "Did you know that that building was built ten years ago when Norway tried to turn this place into a loading port? And all they used was 440 wiring. That's all they needed."

"I know about Grimwald Island, Connor. And I'm not sure whether the history of this place is relevant to what we need to be doing."

With a shrug, Connor picked up the leather electrician's belt. "I just wasn't sure if you knew as much about this island as I do, Chesterton. I wasn't sure if you knew—"

"Connor," Chesterton broke in, "believe me, I know everything there is to know about Grimwald Island." He paused. "This place is one hundred fifty square miles of land with three hundred miles of coastland. It's located ninety miles east-northeast from Iceland and approximately fifty miles inside the Arctic Circle. It's got a forty-mile gap between the south coast and the north coast and a sixty-mile gap between the east and west coasts. It's mostly mountain but it's got some valleys and four freshwater lakes. The highest peak is 7,792 meters, and it's got a wheelbarrow load of arctic bear, wolf, elk, and seal that make for real good hunting. But we don't have any time to hunt any of them because we're always working. And nobody's ever managed to colonize this place because the winters are too hard and the ground can't keep the cattle or sheep alive. There's nobody here now but us."

"And Thor," replied Connor.

Chesterton stared. "Who?"

"Thor."

Confusion gave way to amazement.

"He lives in the tower on the other side of the island."

Chesterton was already nodding. "Yeah, yeah, all right. I forgot about him. The big guy. But what does any of this have to do with anything? I came up here with a simple request"—he shook his head to express wonder at how a simple request could get so sidetracked—"and you start asking me about the history of Grimwald Island and some old lighthouse keeper and—"

"A line of 440 can handle a lot of power," Connor said, locking eyes. "But a 1,000-amp line can handle a whole lot more, Chesterton. More power than you can probably even imagine. It would take an absolutely unbelievable power surge to burn one up."

"Yeah?" Chesterton replied. He hesitated a long time, abruptly still. "What kind of power are we talking? A million volts, maybe?" He stared strangely. "Maybe more?"

"It'd take a *lightning* bolt, Chesterton." Connor noticed a faint trembling in Chesterton's hands. His face seemed suddenly pale. "That's the kind of power we're talking about. The kind of power that can vaporize steel."

"You still don't have total clearance," Chesterton said as they stepped into the elevator. "So just go by the drill, Connor. Don't mess with anything that's not involved in the job."

Without replying, Connor casually held the ribs of the cage. Maybe it was Chesterton's overly rigid control or maybe it was something else, but Connor somehow already knew the answer to his question.

"So where's the problem at?"

"It's at the Observation Room located beside the Containment Cavern." Chesterton was staring into the darkness beneath them. "We've got a line burned out."

Connor smiled. "Yeah. You said that."

Chesterton glanced up, expressionless, and turned away. Connor studied him for a moment more but found nothing in the disciplined face and tried to shift his mind to something else. He watched the white chalk walls of the elevator shaft sliding past them and remembered how this cavern formation was created.

Created shortly after volcanic activity thrust Grimwald Island through the crust of the Norwegian Sea to tower high in the Arctic Circle, the sprawling maze-cave was almost the only one like it in this region of the world. Not formed solely as a result of volcanic activity, it had been burned out of the island's heart by hydrogen sulfide gas rising from nearby oil reserves. As the hydrogen sulfide reached the ocean floor, it reacted with oxygen, creating sulfuric acid that ate through the limestone of Grimwald Island to form a complex labyrinth of tunnels, over twenty miles of them.

The cavern itself was a far-ranging complex of passages and cathedral openings deep inside the island, beneath sea level. Although some of the tunnels were merely narrow crevices, most were immensely wide, even wide enough to accommodate heavy equipment, trucks, dozers, whatever was needed for extensive construction. And Connor knew there were at least twenty major caverns, the deepest and largest cavern being over 4,000 feet across with a 600-foot ceiling.

One of the chambers housed the living quarters for the thirty supervisory and science personnel who managed the research project. Another was a barracks for military personnel, while still another was a command center that housed military operations. And one cavern held an elaborate supercomputer known as GEO, a powerful multiprocessing creation of artificial intelligence that oversaw all aspects of the secret research operation.

Another cavern, deemed the power plant, was dedicated to an electrical generator system that linked the underground laboratory with a powerful Norwegian power cable laid across the Atlantic floor. That was where Connor spent most of his time, breaking down the incredible voltage of the line so the power could be used in substations located in the rest of the facility.

The entire cavern was a maze of high-voltage wires. But the most troublesome section was the Containment Cavern, a place Connor had rarely seen since his early days on Grimwald. Although Connor didn't know exactly what the cathedral-sized chamber was designed to contain, he knew there was a sophisticated computer room adjoining it. And he knew that the cavern itself was heavily reinforced by niobium-titanium fire walls.

It also housed a strangely designed sphere—more like one sphere balanced concentrically inside another—wired to create an electromagnetic pulse above a 500,000-volt cooling platform.

Shrouded in secrecy, the sphere had been delivered during a secret midnight landing of a C-130, and Connor wasn't surprised that they would be having more problems with the mystery machine. When it arrived almost a year ago, he had installed it himself, quickly and efficiently completing circuit tests, wiring, and backup systems. Connor had never asked any questions about the purpose of the sphere. But in his bones, he remembered, it had always troubled him. And not because of its strange power demands or unexplainable electromagnetic design. But because its purpose had, from the very first, been cloaked in such nervous silence, and remained so even today.

A nagging concern began to tug at Connor as they descended deeper into the cavern, sloping at a sharper and sharper angle. And he wondered why, in the last six months, they had not needed him to repair the troublesome thing. Perhaps, the thought came to him with disturbing intensity, because it had been functioning perfectly.

Without revealing his mind, Connor wondered what they might have done with the sphere. But after a moment he knew that he'd manage only the wildest uneducated guess. He had no idea what it was truly designed to accomplish, had never possessed an idea, even when he installed it. He was an electrician, a welder. He knew metals and construction and had a general understanding of just about anything mechanical. But he wasn't a scientist. And whatever the thing was, it was definitely high science.

With a frown Connor gazed at the passing, prodigious formations of calcite, their huge rounded columns rising toward the surface. And little by little he realized the air was falling utterly still. It was something he had never gotten used to.

Always, it seemed to him, the cave was like some super-

natural subterranean netherworld with air so motionless it felt like
outer space might feel, if space had a constant temperature of 71
degrees and a humidity level of 100 percent.

No one could endure the thick, humid heat of the cavern
without the strategically positioned large-capacity dehumidifiers
that made the place livable, machines that Connor and his men
also maintained. But because of the unbearable working conditions for welding and wiring, pain-soaking exercises that made the
cavern an endless marathon of mental toughness, Connor's crew
had hatefully dubbed it "the Inferno."

Though originally created by acidic gas, the Inferno was void
now of corrosive fumes. Whatever colossal power had created the
underground cavern was claimed by another time. But ventilators
had been installed to ensure that the atmosphere remained nonpoisonous, though the ventilators couldn't begin to match the
cave's natural force of expiration. For at the cavern entrance, over
1,000 feet above them, wind howled from the tunnel to the surface
at over seventy miles per hour. It was nature's way of stabilizing
the cavern's internal atmospheric pressure with the surface.

Connor recalled how a company called Stygian Enterprises
had purchased the site several years ago for private research. And
yet, though Stygian owned the facility and the cavern, the complex
itself was designated as a United States Arctic Research Station
and operated under the protection of the United States Army.

Once construction had been completed in the cavern, Connor arrived to begin a three-year stint as foreman of the civilian
support crew. Although he didn't know the exact purpose of the
laboratory, he didn't care. He only knew that Grimwald Ice
Station was a semimilitary installation and that the tax-free hourly
salary was more than twenty times what he could have earned in
the States. And for the money—money that would change the life
of his family forever—Connor had chosen to briefly endure the
arctic climate. Then one month after he arrived, a team of twenty-
odd scientists and supervisory personnel landed to inhabit the
cavern's living quarters.

Connor suspected that they had initiated classified research
with the sphere, but he didn't ask questions. He didn't know, and

he didn't want to know. He was determined to do his job and finish his three-year contract as easily as possible. Then he'd leave this godforsaken place and buy a nice house and a good-sized chunk of land where he could live in peace. Maybe Montana, he thought often enough. Or Wyoming. Or maybe he would return to Kentucky, where he was born. But it would be a place where his family could live safely. Yet the thought of safety only reminded Connor again of Grimwald, and how this dark and dismal place had never truly known any peace at all. And probably never would.

Norway's doomed attempt to colonize the island had failed miserably, partly because of Grimwald's harsh weather and inhospitable terrain, but also because of the superstitious dread Norwegians and Icelanders reserved for it. The Scandinavians passionately labeled the island as haunted and cursed and with unbending stubbornness refused to settle it.

Many even said that Norway's impetuous attempt to colonize the island ten years ago failed more from a soul-draining sense of doom than the actual difficulties of surviving. And until that settlement had collapsed beneath the relentless haunting terror possessed by Grimwald, the only inhabitable structure had been a mysterious and formidable tower founded on the far north side, a smooth, cylindrical fang of imperial white granite that erupted from a slate-red peninsula.

The tower, eternally white with frost, was mysteriously constructed in A.D. 900 by a single, unknown Viking warrior who had defied all curses and fears and demons to make a grim stand on Grimwald's hostile shore. Although the nameless warrior's fate was never known, was ultimately claimed by the dark nightvales of Grimwald's forests, his tower had endured—a lasting testament to his iron courage and spirit and strength.

Built by hand from hand-hewn blocks of solid granite, each weighing over a quarter ton, the tower was as impervious to storm after a thousand years as it had ever been. Upon observation its strength was obvious, for it had clearly been built to stand forever, as if created for the purpose of resisting the cold, cold hate of winter until the world's winter finally passed.

Now, Connor knew, the tower served as the curious home of Thor Magnusson, a mysterious, red-bearded Norwegian giant who was a scholar of literature, poetry, and language. Although Thor was, in truth, a gigantic, colossal brute of a man, towering almost eight feet and possessing unimaginable physical strength, he was also a compassionate companion. Connor had learned quickly that though his tower was cold and lonely, Thor possessed a generous, warmhearted soul.

After they had become friends, Connor had listened for long, long nights as Thor eloquently recited passages of Latin, Greek, and Hebrew, translating them into perfect English and in turn drawing parallels in effortless German, Italian, and a host of European languages.

Thor's grasp of history and philosophy, also, was comprehensive and unforced, as though he had learned the lessons from heart and drew genuine pleasure in remembering them. It had not taken long for Connor to decide that Thor had been something of a teacher, or even a scholar, before he began his lonely sojourn on Grimwald.

Connor thought often of it—such a loving, strong, gentle giant of a man so mysteriously exiled to this lonely Arctic island where there was only storm and ice and hateful cold. And although Connor realized that Thor's habitation of the tower was a strange and disturbing thing, he never had the heart to ask him the reason for it.

Nor had Thor offered to tell.

Chapter 4

Crimson shadows walked stiffly through the reddish glare of the midnight sun, the summer sun, moving with organized purpose across the wide-ranging Ice Station.

Cloaked in a white bearskin, Thor sat motionless upon his stallion, Tanngrisner, gazing over the facility from the mountaintop. His long red hair hung loose, falling beneath the polar fur that draped his mammoth chest and shoulders. His beard was tinged with wide flakes of snow that struck and froze beneath his careful, searching eyes.

Only a moment ago, missing nothing that his gaze passed, Thor saw his good friend, Jackson Connor, descending into the cavern. He had been closely accompanied by the military commander.

Yes, Thor thought, *the soldier called Chesterton.*

He frowned.

He had traveled all day across Grimwald Island, covering the forty-mile ride from the north coast to the south on Tanngrisner's strong legs, riding the dry glacier riverbeds. He had passed beneath the mountainous highlands, the dark nightvales of woodland concealed from the sea as he searched—for what he did not know—only to find the end of his journey here, at this mysterious Ice Station that he still did not fully understand.

Always, always this had been to him a place of cruel machines ravaging the frozen earth, of dark planes landing in the night to deliver mysterious equipment, of harsh spotlights piercing the night snow and cold breath piercing the light.

Thor remembered the Ice Station's creation, only five years past. He remembered how he had sat stiffly upon this very ridge, stoically ignoring the cold while he watched them labor at its birth, wondering at what manner of tower they were building to God. And night after bitter night he had been ceaselessly mystified. Nor did he know why it troubled him so.

An answer to his uneasiness had never come, though in the end he had found an unexpected friend, a good friend, a friend that a good man might know once in a lifetime.

Almost a year ago it had happened, at the beginning of early light as Thor dozed tiredly beneath a thick overhang of rock, forgetful of his watch, a small fire kindled at his feet. Coming with strangely quiet steps up the mountain path, the man had surprised him. Almost before Thor could open his eyes, the man was poised, motionless, close beside him.

Shaggy red hair frosted with night, large frame cloaked in his white bearskin, Thor had risen titanically to his feet, towering a high head and shoulders over the man who had, at first, seemed as startled as Thor himself.

Silent, they stood face to face in the harsh white light. Thor had waited, grim and even embarrassed that his hiding place had been discovered. He had not known what to say, or what to expect.

Calmly the man had glanced at Thor's sleeping bag and the large, scoped rifle laid to the side. Then he had focused again on Thor, taking his time. Finally he turned his head to look down over the installation, nodding at the view.

"Doing some hunting?" he had asked, not seeming to notice, or care, about Thor's discomfort.

And it was in that moment that Thor had measured the spirit before him, had somehow sensed that indefinable quickening that fast-joined the hearts of good men, that mysterious force that forged friends in the chaos of war or brought strangers together in strange lands as each somehow knew and understood the other with little more than a glance. And Thor had decided that the man commanded a solid heart, possessed a soul as discerning and knowing as his own.

"Yes," Thor replied, also smiling, gazing down on the man from his gigantic height. "I hunt here often."

Nodding, the man extended his hand. "Yeah, well, as far as I'm concerned, you can hunt any place you want. They don't own this island. They just own what's inside the fence."

Thor had laughed, warmed.

"Connor," the man had said. His name was Jackson Connor.

Compared to Thor's mythic height and stature, Connor was as nothing. But in truth he was of average height and build. And he carried himself with a quiet solidness, like a man who has survived hard years by the strength of his back and will. His smooth-shaven face was brown-weathered, leathered by the freezing wind. But his most prominent feature was the solid, craggy edges of his chin, forehead, and jaw—edges that seemed to reflect a hardened attitude to everything around him.

At times, Thor could easily see him as suspicious, unfriendly, and even hating of the world. But Thor could also see him as someone who simply wanted a bitter world to be different, but had learned he could not change it so had crusted himself over with a bitter armor instead. Thor knew, almost from the first, that the man was something else inside, something softer and more understanding and somehow far gentler than his hardened exterior would ever reveal. Even as he, himself, was.

He had a wife and a son, he said, answering Thor's questions, which grew friendlier and more intimate as an hour of easy conversation passed. And yes, he said, they lived in one of the homes inside the installation. His son, Jordan, was four years old, he said in a proud father's voice that told Thor even more. His wife's name was Beth, and his eyes grew soft and comfortable as he mentioned her. She also was employed by Stygian Enterprises, as a civilian supervisor of the groundside Communications Center.

"Come on down to the house," Connor had said at the last, seeming to tire of the relentless, bracing wind that Thor rarely noticed anymore. "It's cold up here. And Beth will want to meet you." He laughed. "If we're nice enough to her, she might even make us some coffee."

Thor had glanced at the installation. "They will allow me inside the perimeter?"

"Yeah, they'll let you in," Connor replied, not seeming to care about security. "I'll tell whoever's interested that you're cleared. The top part of the base isn't a big deal, anyway. It's just the underground section that's off-limits." He shook his head, looking out over the Ice Station. "Yeah, they're doing some kind of research down there . . ."

Thor focused on him. "I know this island, Connor. I have been here for many, many years. And I know this: There is nothing in that cavern but darkness." He waited. "Nothing good can come from it."

Connor had frowned before he shook his head. "Probably not, Thor." He stared a moment, silent. "But those decisions are beyond my pay grade. I just work here."

And so it began—a friendship where Thor would descend often from the mountain, bellowing greetings to the installation's ground personnel who seemed to relish their boring routines being broken by the appearance of this boisterous, gigantic Viking-shape with red hair and beard flowing and cloaked in a white bearskin. Eagerly welcomed inside to shatter the monotony, Thor would give children and women long rides around the compound on Tanngrisner's broad back, fearlessly and tunelessly singing Nordic dirges that carried without restraint to the far side of the perimeter. Eventually he would dramatically sweep out again into a long sunset, waving a dramatic, theatric farewell.

Connor and Beth had laughed at the antics, and Jordan loved him, content to sit for hours on his tree-trunk leg as Thor created spellbinding tales of great adventures, of legendary heroes of old and their ancient battles with mythic beasts. Or of frightening, epic journeys by men who dared to venture to mysterious lands where they discovered magical rings and fantastic treasures, hidden on the far side of darkness. Then he would, as ever, leave with the red dawn that never seemed to truly depart.

Memories . . .

Sleet slashed him and Thor winced.

A sea wind whispered, rising from the ice tide over the edge of the blackened ridge, and the cold brought Thor again to the present. He blinked against the dark tide, focusing his mind once more. He felt a night wind pass through his spirit and perceived a fear that disturbed him, a fear that made him sense that something . . . that something had ended . . .

Ice-green eyes hard against the wind, Thor wondered at the sensation. Then he grimly turned his mind from it before it gained a foothold in his soul, before it corrupted him with fear. He knew deep in his heart what was coming; yes, coming beneath the wind and the darkness and the sea. Knew it as surely as he knew his own life, and death.

"Come, Tanngrisner," he frowned, easing the proud stallion forward. "Let us go down and see our friend. One last time . . ."

After tiredly shedding his cold weather gear at the bottom of the elevator shaft, Chesterton set off at what seemed a familiar pace, walking the brightly illuminated alloy grill that networked the cavern. Wordless, Connor fell in behind him.

It was a long journey, and Connor took notice that never once did Chesterton look up at the fantastic, inverted forests of stalactites, the brilliant white gypsum columns, or fist-sized calcite cave pearls that filled the far recesses of the floor. One hour later they reached the Observation Room, located beside the deepest cavern.

"Remember," Chesterton said, staring intently, "just do your job, Connor. Don't mess with the control matrix. Don't mess with anything at all. This room is as classified as it can get."

Connor shook his head as he stepped onto the dull, polished floor. A thick steel door was open, propped against the wall by a chair. But as he entered the room he looked up, abruptly pausing.

Though it had been cleaned, the room showed obvious signs of a fantastic explosion. Cautiously, Connor took a light-footed step into the room, as if he were walking over a live wire. He glanced at Chesterton, now standing quietly in the center, staring grimly at the flame-blackened paneling.

In front of the twenty-foot-long row of computer terminals, Connor saw that the fire door was emergency sealed, solid as an anvil. But above the control panel, a long section of steel paneling had been essentially vaporized, the remaining edges molded in the shape of water pouring up at the top, down at the lower edge. Looking upward into the section, Connor also saw a broken length of 1,000-amp wiring, one end melted to the south wall, the other melted to the north wall, twenty feet between the two junctions. Unable to contain his amazement, Connor turned to Chesterton.

"How many people got killed in here?"

Chesterton shook his head. "Just do your job, Connor. Whatever happened in here is classified."

Connor looked back at the wall. Then he pushed down on the computer panel, testing, and leaped lightly atop it. He stood, gazing more closely into the melted section of steel before he walked to the south edge, peering at the blackened wire.

"Is this power line shut off, Chesterton?"

A solid nod. "It's off."

"You sure?"

"Yeah, Connor, it's off. I'm sure."

"Uh-huh."

Connor picked up a long piece of plastic. He stood five feet away and lightly touched the wire. Nothing happened. So he stepped closer, prying less timidly with the shaft at the thick, unbending stick. The wire moved slightly. Then he took out a screwdriver, walking up. He stuck the point behind the burned end and jerked hard on the insulated section once, twice, three times until it loudly tore loose.

Chesterton shifted. "Do you have to make so much noise, Connor?"

With faint anger, Connor looked down. "What?"

"I said: Do you have to make so much noise?"

Connor gazed wonderingly at the empty room, down again. "We disturbing somebody, Chesterton?"

Frowning, Chesterton focused on the fire door. "Just do the job as quietly as possible."

A moment of silence and Connor turned away, working at the wire until he had pulled two extra feet of its length from the wall. He turned the end in his hands, studying the wire, the steel panels. He saw that a small hole was burned in the exterior wall, the insulation blown away from the far side of the wiring, and the closer side of the thick 1,000-amp wire was melted. He studied the combination for a long time, finally leaping from the platform.

"It's got to be spliced," he said.

Chesterton didn't even reply.

Connor gazed back up at the wall. "You see that wire, Chesterton?'

Disagreeable. "No."

Carefully, Connor pointed. "You see how the far strands of copper are blasted deep into the wire while the strands on this side are melted?"

Chesterton didn't look up. "No, sir. And I don't care to. I've already told you. I'm not an engineer and it's not my job."

"Well, look closer."

As if profoundly irritated with the dilemma of the conversation, Chesterton glanced at the wire. "All right, Connor, I can see it. Now can you do your job?"

Connor smiled. "Yeah, I can do it. But answer a question for me. Do you know how something like that could happen?"

Chesterton's teeth gleamed in a grimace. "No, Connor. I don't."

"Then I'll tell you," Connor said, smile fading. "It doesn't."

Chesterton was impatient, but he didn't raise his voice. His naturally assertive nature of expressing authority had apparently been overcome by a compelling passion for quiet. "What do you mean, 'it doesn't happen'? It happened. I'm looking at it."

"No, Chesterton, it doesn't happen. Not by itself."

Chesterton's angry gaze went distant again.

Stepping closer, Connor's aspect was suddenly conspiratorial. "What have your people been doing down here, Chesterton? What happened on the other side of that fire door?"

"Nothing," Chesterton said, shaking his head. "And your people haven't been put in danger, Connor. It was a simple accident and you need to fix it."

With somberness, Connor nodded. "I'm sure it was, Chesterton. But let me tell you something. If—"

"Save it."

A shake of his head, and Connor continued. "Look, Chesterton, I don't know if anybody got killed in here when that wire broke, but that wire is not your problem. Whatever is on the far side of that wall is your problem. That's what caused this accident."

"And how can you know that?"

"There's a small hole melted in the steel wall," Connor replied, a nod. "It's been sealed by the fire door. But it's there. It looks like it was done with an arc weld burning at maybe nine or ten thousand degrees. The flame punched a hole in the steel and then it hit the electrical line. The insulation was blown away from the far side, grounding out the wire, and then the circuit left the line and went through the wall. That's what knocked out the steel paneling. It depends on how much power the line was pulling at the time, but it probably looked like a bolt of lightning going through this room."

Chesterton was angry. "Why are you telling me this, Connor? You think we don't know all this?"

"Because I can replace the wire, Chesterton," Connor said, anger hardening his tone. "But I'm telling you this up front. Your military boys don't need to try any welding down here. This is a sensitive environment and sensitive equipment, and somebody can easily get killed. I don't care what kind of secrets you've got in that cavern, you need to let my people handle the construction work."

Chesterton's jaw locked.

"Just fix it, Connor," he said somberly. "And try to fix it so it can't happen again."

Chapter 5

Spenser Wayne Adler, imperial and commanding in his private office near the Observation Room, turned to Frank with an indulgent aspect, smiling benignly—an aged and wise grandfather patiently enduring the foolishness of his young and unwise grandson.

"I hope you understand my reasons for overruling you at the meeting, Dr. Frank," he began, as if the incident were thoroughly settled and merited only the vaguest defense.

Frank shrugged. Said nothing. He still felt as if he were in a state of shock, and he had no compulsion to tell Adler anything at all, although he knew where the conversation was going.

"I appreciate your concerns," Adler continued. "Truly, I do. I am not an unsympathetic man. But you must have more faith in our ability to control the beast. The incident today was an aberration." Adler's confidence was completely unforced. "I'm certain that it won't happen again. Especially with a few additional safety measures."

"Well, I'm not certain that it won't happen again, Mr. Adler. I don't think you even realize what we're dealing with here. I don't think anybody does, really. Except me."

Adler appeared unsurprised, even pleased.

"Indeed," he smiled, "and that is the reason I summoned you, Doctor. There is no need to remind you that I have only been with this project for three months, while you have worked on it for years. I was assigned to the island only when the creature began this remarkably successful stage of development, and until then Dr. Hoffman was, ah, directing the operation. And I have not altered the line of command." He waved vaguely. "I have simply added another level of supervision. Surely such a fantastic scientific achievement as this merits as much supervisory personnel as possible, don't you agree?"

Silent, Frank waited.

"I want to know the latest data concerning Leviathan's development." Adler smiled. "I understand computers, but I prefer personal input from the source. It is an ultimately superior method for evaluating data."

Frank stared a moment, spoke rapidly. "Leviathan is now sixteen feet tall and thirty-five feet long with fifteen feet of that in its tail. Its weight is approximately 12,000 pounds, and it seems to have reached its maximum size. Internal resting body temperature is 326 degrees without the temperature rise ignited by kinetic energy release for—"

Adler abruptly lifted a hand. "Excuse me, Doctor. Explain this creature's ability to release kinetic energy to me again, and the relationship of the energy release with Leviathan's body temperature. I'm still not certain that I understand it."

A reluctant pause, and Frank spoke. "Leviathan has vertebrae disks that continually contract, Mr. Adler, building unreleased potential chemical energy in semimuscular non-Newtonian fluid sacs located between the vertebrae themselves. The vertebrae sacs also contain high catalyst molarity enzymes and menantinic, an enzyme that increases hemoglobin levels and euthrocytes in the blood stream. When Leviathan releases the enzymes and they are absorbed by specific muscle tissue that is already at peak tension in preparation for the event, a chemical reaction converts the tension into explosive kinetic energy where—"

"Like a dolphin," Adler confirmed.

"Yeah," Frank continued. "Like a dolphin does before he leaps from the water. A dolphin stores kinetic energy in its spine and then releases it all at once, propelling itself forward with greater force than it could have generated by simple muscular contraction."

"Yes, I see," Adler gestured. "Good. Go on."

Frank stared a moment. "But with Leviathan, the kinetic release of stored energy is electro-neural and chemical in nature and therefore highly exothermic. When the reaction reaches a critical stage it increases the creature's surface temperature from its normal 326 degrees to slightly over 600 degrees in the first 76 hundreths of a second."

"Incredible . . ." Adler muttered, looking away. "Absolutely incredible." He focused on Frank. "But how does the creature survive such an intense temperature? I don't understand this. How can its blood not boil at such intolerable heat?"

"Water boils at 212 degrees Fahrenheit," Frank said, "unless it's under pressure. And the more pressure the water is under, the higher the temperature has to be before it will boil. Leviathan's blood pressure is approximately 300 over 270. So that's enough pressure to keep the water in its blood from boiling or evaporating at 326 degrees. And any blood damaged by excessive heat shock is quickly being replenished with high doses of menatopoietic in the blood stream, which is regulated by the upgraded hypothalamus in the cerebral cortex. Besides, Leviathan's mutated cellular makeup is altered sufficiently to place the heat vaporization point well outside of kinetic energy release parameters. The native cellular structure of Leviathan's vascular system is almost equal to copper or bronze in tensile strength, so the veins and tissues sustain the stress pretty easily."

"Absolutely incredible," Adler repeated, amazed out of character. "But surely . . . surely when the creature's internal temperature reaches 600 degrees during the . . . ah . . . ah . . ."

"Kinetic energy release."

"Yes," Adler nodded, "during the kinetic energy release. Yes. Surely then the creature's blood would boil. It would die."

"No," Frank shook his head, "Leviathan's blood doesn't boil because the internal rise in body temperature only lasts a split second. And that's not long enough to superheat its entire circulatory system. Although a split second is more than long enough for . . ."

Adler appeared to struggle with his enthusiasm. "Long enough for what, Doctor?"

Frank hesitated. It seemed to him that the answer was obvious, considering the purpose of the project. Then he decided that Adler had asked the question simply so he could enjoy the answer. "Long enough to launch an attack, Mr. Adler," he replied. "Just like it's neurally programmed to do."

Adler smiled. "And what is the speed of Leviathan's attack?"

Frank felt an internal distance from the discussion. "Normally Leviathan charges at approximately 95 miles per hour, using only its hindlegs. We've timed its attacks from one end of the cavern to the other. But with the kinetic energy release, it can cover approximately 1,000 feet at 145 miles per hour on all four legs before it exhausts the catalytic enzymes and adrenaline in its bloodstream. Then it has to move at normal speed for the rest of the attack. But a peripheral danger of the kinetic energy release is that Leviathan's surface temperature of 600 degrees will cause anything in its immediate physical proximity to burst into flames. Even if it doesn't touch anything. The shock of the ambient temperature suddenly increasing to over 600 degrees Fahrenheit will cause all low grade materials to shatter instantly, creating a virtual sphere of destruction. There's just . . . there's just too much heat."

Adler's eyes had widened. "And this . . . this kinetic release of energy is what caused the fire we had in the cavern this afternoon?"

"No," Frank responded. Adler's ignorance of the creature's true potential was almost frightening. "Today's fire was caused by Leviathan's ability to ignite the carpasioxyllelene gel."

"Yes!" Adler exclaimed suddenly, before settling both hands again on his chair. He nodded. "Yes. That is it. Go on, Doctor."

Frank sighed. "At some point in the tenth week of development," he continued, "when I was using the nerve-input interpretative stimulus to upgrade its central neural net in the cerebral cortex with tactical data and initiating automatic reprinting of echo-memory on new brain cells, Leviathan developed gel sacs in the roof of its mouth and the front of its neck."

"The carpasioxyllelene," Adler contributed.

"Yes. One of the sacs contains carpasioxyllelene. The other sac contains another organic substance, still unknown to us, that reacts with it. Alone, each chemical is useless. But when they are misted together in an oxygen atmosphere, they become highly flammable and react against each other to initiate explosive combustion. By rerouting muscles in its neck to provide pressure to the gel sacs, Leviathan can spray both chemicals at once from its mouth. Just like a pit viper sprays venom from its mouth to blind prey. And, like I said, when the chemicals mist together in an oxygen atmosphere they ignite. Explosively."

"How long can it sustain this combustion?"

Frank hesitated, as if the question had never occurred to him. "I . . . don't really know for certain. Today is the first time Leviathan ever did it. And I wasn't even sure that it could. I don't even think *it* knew that it could, until it tried. And I've been a little busy since then, so I haven't run any computations." He squinted. "But . . . it looked like Leviathan sprayed the gel approximately 300 feet with a temperature of maybe . . . 12,000 degrees. More than enough to melt steel if it's focused for a few seconds."

Motionless, Adler stared. "Surely you overestimate."

Frank leaned back. An apocalyptic vision of hellish flames exploding against the Plexiglas shield passed before him.

"Look, Mr. Adler, you really need to understand what we're dealing with here. This type of chemical combustion is similar only to plasma arc welding. It produces extremely high temperatures. Sometimes as much as 18,000 to 20,000 degrees. It's a type of welding used on high nitrogen metals that are innately resistant to ionization."

Not appearing to notice the slight, Adler continued, "And do you think that the creature can sustain the combustion long enough to melt steel? Or titanium? Or even a niobium-titanium alloy?"

Frank shook his head. "It can't melt niobium-titanium alloy. Niobium-titanium doesn't even have a melting point because it's created in a magnetic matrix where the molecules are electromagnetically converged to form a high nitrogen content. But 12,000 degrees can certainly melt steel. Leviathan has a capacity for about twenty gallons in each individual sac. With both sacs combined, that's forty gallons of gel that it can utilize. That much gel will probably allow it to sustain a significant level of combustion at a twenty percent oxygenated atmosphere for as long as five minutes. But then the sacs would be exhausted and Leviathan would need time to regenerate carpasioxyllelene pressure."

"How much time?"

"A couple of hours, probably."

Pacing, Adler turned away. "This is absolutely incredible. Truly, this is something completely unknown to science."

"No," Frank replied, finding some pleasure in taking a little wind out of Adler's sails. "It's not unknown to science at all. The bombardier beetle in South America does the same thing. It sprays two chemicals that mist together to create quinine. And the quinine bursts into flames upon contact with oxygen. The beetle can fire about twenty bursts before exhausting itself, and scientists have known about it for years. It's just that we've never seen the same external combustion process on this scale."

Adler walked to the side. He cupped his chin before turning back. "And is there any possibility that the creature will melt the vault of the Containment Chamber?" he asked.

"No."

"But can it break down the doors? Is that possible?"

Strangely, Adler seemed more concerned for the creature than for the staff. Frank was struck by the sensation. "Yes," he replied, staring, "it's possible that it could break them down. We never counted on having to contain anything like this."

"But we are taking precautions?"

Frank nodded.

For a moment Adler stared. "Yes? Can you continue, Doctor?"

"I've replaced the oxygen in the cavern with nitrogen. Leviathan will sleep as long as it's in a nitrogen atmosphere."

Turning fully, Adler dropped his hand to his side. "But . . .

but will the creature not suffocate? Does it not need oxygen to breathe?"

"No, Mr. Adler, Leviathan won't suffocate. Leviathan has a lung capacity of 270 liters, almost equal to that of a killer whale. And it filled itself with oxygen as soon as it sensed the presence of the nitrogen. Just like it's neurally programmed to do. Right now it's gone into something like hibernation, where it'll stay until its epidermic sensors detect the presence of an oxygen atmosphere again."

"And how long can it survive in hibernation?"

"We don't know."

Adler tilted his head.

"GEO calculates that it can go at least eight weeks," Frank responded wearily. "But it can probably go a lot longer. Maybe as long as eight months. There's no way to know because I've never had to put Leviathan to sleep in a nitrogen atmosphere before. But it will survive for quite awhile. And, by the way, Mr. Adler, this brings me to something I wanted to tell you."

Adler looked unconcerned. "Yes, Doctor?"

"I'm going to run the tests in a ninety percent nitrogen atmosphere," Frank said, solid. "Even after we cement the corridors, I'm not going to give Leviathan enough oxygen to ignite the gel again. And we're not going to give it enough oxygen to get its strength up. We'll test it, but we'll keep it weak. Maybe at a quarter strength." He paused. "I'll run the tests for you, Mr. Adler. But I'll run them *my way*. I'm not going to risk the lives of everybody on this island."

"I see," Adler replied, a touch of scorn. "And you will not move from this? You are insistent?"

"Yes."

"What is your justification?"

Frank leaned back. "We've known for some time that Leviathan had developed phenomenal strength. That's why I never completed neural programming a full-blown Hunter-killer Mode. Leviathan was becoming too dangerous." He hesitated. "Until today Leviathan never gave the faintest indication that it would attack the cell. But now the situation has changed. And we can't trust that Leviathan won't force its way out of the holding area. That's why I'm going to keep it in a high nitrogen atmosphere. If Leviathan is not operating at full strength, it won't be able to defeat the Containment Chamber."

Adler was motionless. "But how accurate will the tests be?"

"Leviathan will attack food targets as we put them out," Frank replied. "It will be moving more slowly than it's capable of moving, but GEO will do calculations of its speed based on the increased nitrogen level. So in the end, we'll have pretty accurate estimates on how it would have done in an oxygenated atmosphere." He nodded. "That's the best you're going to get from me, Mr. Adler."

"I see." Adler smiled. "Yes, I see. And you will not be dissuaded?"

"No," Frank replied, staring hard. "You have to try and understand something, Mr. Adler. Leviathan is *not supposed* to be in full-blown Hunter-killer Mode. Which it appears to be in. It *should not* be attacking the cell or trying to escape. The neural programming for an absolute Hunter-killer Mode was never completed. This is the mystery we're dealing with. And I don't like mysteries."

"But you created the creature, Doctor," Adler said, frowning. "You should not be surprised at any development at all. After all, the entire purpose of your neural programming was to bring the creature into a Hunter-killer Mode."

"But I never *finished* the Hunter-killer Mode in its neural network!" Frank reiterated, angry. "That's what I'm trying to get you to understand! Leviathan is not supposed to be reacting this way. It's not in its neural programming!"

"Then why is it reacting this way, Doctor?"

A pause, silence.

And Frank abruptly bowed his head, rubbing his eyes. "I don't know, Mr. Adler," he replied, calmer. "It's got to be something . . . something genetic. Leviathan has always been genetically unpredictable."

Adler stared a moment. "All right, Doctor," he said slowly, "I understand your argument. And you may have your way. You may keep the creature in a high nitrogen atmosphere in order to reduce its strength. I only wish you to complete the tests as well as possible under the current conditions."

Frank leaned back again, uncertain.

"Please, don't look so surprised," Adler continued, smiling. "I am not an unreasonable man. I realize that this creature is extremely dangerous. I probably understand a great deal more than you realize." He seemed to enjoy his abrupt display of knowledge, as if it displayed his power as well.

"I understand quite well, Doctor, how you used the electromagnetic pulse focused through the sphere to genetically alter what was once a Komodo dragon. I understand how the amino acids in the dragon's dual-strand DNA chromosomes were molecularly altered by the pulse to replicate in a mutated form. Your formula to determine the amount of power necessary to accomplish the task was fairly simple: M equals E squared times T-I."

He smiled, almost laughing. "M is the manipulation-mutation of amino acids in the chromosomes, E is the electromagnetic energy pulse wave, and T-I is the niobium-titanium intensification required for enhancing electron transference. Of course each factor had to be perfected individually before it was inserted into the formula. But it is the combination that achieves the desired effect.

"And to prevent current loss you used the niobium-titanium superconductors with a 50,000-ampere charging field. The current was stored magnetically in a battery thirty meters long and 3.5 meters wide, discharging an electromagnetic pulse echoed through the center of the sphere every 25 hundreths of a second.

"When the dragon was three weeks old, cellular impact began on tissues—first with compressed air, then sand, then larger objects that caused a rapid mutation of high-tensile armored scales. And when the creature was four weeks old, you magnetically supported its regenerative abilities, enhancing endocrine systems and tripling the molecules used for mitosis, or healing."

Frank didn't move. "It was a little bit more complicated than that, Mr. Adler."

"But of course it was, Doctor," the old man returned. "I speak only in layman's terms. Yet the truth remains. You gave the dragon a phenomenally enhanced healing factor, an ability to survive virtually any wound. At five weeks, the healing factor was permanently set and a computer-aided Neural Control Program was bioelectronically installed. Or in other words, Doctor, you planted the seeds of the infamous Hunter-killer Mode, the instinct to hunt and kill every other living creature on the face of the earth.

"You used cyberspace functions in GEO to remove the locus that produces a-calcium calmodulin kinase, the chemical which would have allowed Leviathan to recognize fear, and in this way made it into a creature without any fear whatsoever. Only a cold and calculating instinct to kill. Then you neurally encoded tactical and strategic military data directly onto its cerebellum, which was in turn inlaid at ten weeks of age.

"Then, in one of your most remarkable alterations, you increased brain synapse current levels until Leviathan's mind speed was at least five times faster than a human's. Also, the creature's newly generated brain cells, cells which have no memory at all, are continuously overlaid with an electronic echo-pulse from the chip which gives them instant memory. That is how Leviathan can never forget the Hunter-killer Mode or any of its tactical knowledge." He paused. "I applaud you, Doctor. You deserve it."

Frank was unimpressed. He didn't need accolades.

"You're pretty caught up on the creation process, Mr. Adler," he said slowly. "Can you tell me how Leviathan developed the rest of its altered weapons system? Including the ability to generate an inhibitor and catalyst to cause combustion?"

"No," Adler replied, a slight laugh. "Why don't you tell me?"

"Because Leviathan is innately polyploidal in its genetic makeup, Mr. Adler."

The old man said nothing, waiting.

"Meaning," Frank continued, "that we discovered late in the process that Leviathan had more than the usual number of chromosomes for a Komodo dragon. A great many more chromosomes, actually. Some of which we still can't identify. They don't match the molecular encoding of any identified vertebrate. And their unexpected structure created unexpected mutation."

Confusion registered on Adler's severe face. "Exactly what kind of chromosomal structure are we discussing, doctor?"

Tired, Frank shook his head. "I don't know. I determined that it was just some kind of recessive genetic pattern . . . *remembered* and made dominant by the chromatic manipulation process waves. Some kind of . . . genetic code that nature somehow piggybacked inside random members of this species for thousands of years. It was deeply submerged but it survived in the chromosomal makeup of the Komodo dragon. And the electromagnetic manipulation didn't actually alter this particular dragon's chromosomal makeup as much as it ignited the rapid development of this unidentified, recessive genetic code."

Adler's interest spiked. "Thus the explanation for why you renamed the project 'Leviathan' at the fifth week of development?" he asked, keenly alert.

Dismal, Frank nodded.

"So . . . a biblical reference," Adler smiled. It was not a question, and his expression made it clear that there was no need for an answer. *Yes*, the smile said, *I know of these things. I am not an ignorant man.*

A lengthy pause and Frank nodded, simply to end the conversation. He had long ago passed the point where he wanted to leave. And the overbearing Adler finally granted his wish. He rose.

"I congratulate you on your success, Doctor," he said. "You have reached a great achievement. And truly, there is no immediate foretelling where your research will lead. You may very well have changed the world as we know it." Without effort he shifted into his paternal mode. "Yes, Electromagnetic Chromosomal Manipulation may herald the dawn of a new and superior lifeform on the earth. In the near future it may be used to alter living organisms so that they cannot age, cannot die. It may cure cancer. Or eliminate an entire host of crippling genetic disorders."

With tired, dead eyes, Frank focused on the director.

"Or make living weapons of war," he said flatly.

Connor wiped sweat from a dirt-grimed brow as Chesterton led him along the steel walkway. Exhausted, he was irritable and hot and still frustrated by the secret atmosphere of the Observation Room. But now the job was done, and Chesterton was leading him back toward the elevator shaft.

Moving for some irrational reason in the same bizarre silence they had maintained in the Observation Room, they passed the cavern's Command Center. But as they neared the doorway two men walked out of the portal, shadowed in darkness.

Connor instantly recognized one of them as the young, hotshot scientist who was supposedly running the project, Peter Frank. He didn't know the older man, but his words immediately reached Connor.

"Leviathan will be tested when—"

"*Hey*!" Chesterton yelled, glaring. The two men turned abruptly, and Chesterton turned to Connor, then back to the older man.

Connor stepped into the middle of the walkway, sensing the seriousness of the situation and moved by some primal impulse to hold his own ground. He evenly held the older man's gaze.

A silent moment passed, Connor watching them all, waiting for them to make the first move. Then, slowly, the older man walked forward, holding Connor's gaze until he stood fully in the walkway, blocking the path. Connor estimated the white-haired man was at least six inches taller and very obviously in charge. There was something faintly ominous about how he barred the walkway.

"What did you hear, Mr. Connor?" he asked, supremely confident.

Sullen, Connor lowered his gaze, momentarily looking past the man to see Peter Frank standing in the doorway, mouth open, hands hanging limp at his sides. He seemed afraid. And Chesterton was stoic, accustomed to the sight of men throwing their weight in the paths of others. But Connor also saw a poised readiness in

Chesterton's stance, as if he thought he might have to physically intervene.

Connor looked up. But this wasn't his place and he didn't want any part of it. Without blinking, he held the mesmerizing gaze of the older man as he spoke. He didn't bother to make his voice friendly.

"I didn't hear anything."

"No," the old man smiled, teeth gleaming, as if the answer had never been in doubt. "Of course you didn't."

Chapter 6

Bellowing and piled atop with a dozen burly workmen, Thor momentarily staggered on the crest of the hill. With one arm pinned by four men and another two-hundred-pound wrestler perched on his shoulders, the giant Norseman struggled ferociously to hold his ground.

A dozen men heaved together, pushed against him, over a ton of hardened muscle straining violently to knock Thor off balance, to topple him from the top of the low hill.

Laughing manically, face as red as his wild red beard, Thor crouched to plant his booted feet in place. Then, reaching down with a tree-trunk arm, he began peeling his attackers off like children or pulling them forward over his shoulders to hurl them down the tundra-mound where they would slide to a muddy halt only to launch themselves up the hill again, sweating and smiling, to rejoin the fray.

Connor heard the commotion as he stepped off the elevator, instantly smiling. Catching the spirit of the contest, he moved around the side of the facility to see Thor, a solid and unshaken King of the Hill, holding off his challengers who were mostly airborne or straining without effect to overcome his stance. Loud bets and cheers were cast from a divided crowd.

"C'mon, Thor!" someone yelled. "Just ten more seconds!"

Struck by the voice, Connor looked into the crowd and saw Beth enthusiastically clutching a fistful of money and laughing as she called out the last seconds. His son, Jordan, was jumping up and down, cheering.

"Five! . . . Four! . . . Three!"

Thor roared and laughed, effortlessly lifting a behemoth electrical worker, Tom Blankenship, high over his head. Framed by the midnight sun, his titanic arms extended to hold Blankenship aloft, Thor commanded the mound like a fortress, his lower body submerged in bodies and arms and legs that seemed to be straining against solid granite, a mountain. Connor winced as he saw Blankenship's uplifted, fear-stricken bearded face, the wide eyes staring down the hill where he would be hurled as . . . "Two! . . . One! . . . It's over! It's over!" Beth screamed, joining Jordan in jumping up and down. "Thor won! He won! He beat all of you!"

Atop the hill, bodies instantly fell away, slumping over the tundra. Some of the attackers rolled onto their backs, holding their hearts, staring in a daze at the sky. Connor saw Thor lift his bearded face, laughing at the still terrified Blankenship who might even yet be airborne down the hill. Then with a mirthful grin that made his white teeth gleam, Thor suddenly set Blankenship back on his feet.

Connor laughed as Thor enthusiastically clapped Blankenship's massive arm, towering a full head and shoulders taller even than the worker, apparently congratulating. But Connor couldn't hear their words because of the joyous riot erupting among the winners.

"We won! We won!" Beth was repeating over and over again, hugging Jordan who jumped gleefully up and down, clapping his hands. Several others, apparently those who had put money on Thor, were all hugging each other. Amused, Connor began to wonder just how much money had been wagered on the match.

With a smile he walked forward and Beth saw him, smiling back with delight. "Hey, babe," she laughed. "We won!" She lifted Jordan to his feet. "Tell Daddy how much money we won!"

Jordan grabbed the money, too many one-dollar bills to hold in his four-year-old hand. "Daddy! We won!" he laughed, his face alight with sheer joy. His light brown hair was tousled.

"Yeah, I can see that," Connor smiled. He walked up to lift the boy from Beth's arms. "How you doing, buddy?" he asked. "Are you having a good time today?"

"Yeah," Jordan smiled, hugging Connor's neck for a long, hard moment before he leaned back. "And me and Mommy just won a bunch of *money*!"

Connor grinned and delivered a light kiss to Beth. Maybe it was Beth's joy or maybe it was the red-glowing sun, but whatever he had brought from the cavern fell away at her smile. And Connor realized, with Beth's slim figure silhouetted against the red midnight sun, how truly beautiful she was. Even without makeup, with her hair uncombed and windblown, she was still striking. Her dark Italian eyes and olive skin were from her distant heritage, and her thick, brown hair fell beneath her shoulders. Her face and neck were strong and smooth, her body still as strong and toned as when they married ten years ago. She was wearing faded blue jeans, a pair of black boots, and a red and black checkered lumberjack shirt.

Connor leaned forward, examining the money in Jordan's hand, looked again. "So, uh, how much did we win?"

Beth's face twisted, satisfied. Then she laughed and made a fist, whooped a football cheer. "Fifty dollars! Yes, yes, yes! Right, Jordan?"

"Yes! Fifty dollars!" the boy laughed, smiling into Connor's face. Connor was suddenly inspired to hold his son closer as defeated betters shambled past, returning to their jobs. Then Thor towered at the base of the hill and Connor turned to him.

The gigantic Norseman was literally covered in mud, his leather jacket and pants plastered where tundra-soiled arms and hands had strained to upset his unshakable stand.

Thor's sleeveless arms were unbelievably muscular and huge, stout pillars of granite-hard strength that fell from the sides of a gigantic barrel chest. He seemed even more enormous than usual. Sweat dripped from his face, still red from the strain. He was smiling hugely.

Connor knew Thor had met the challenge for mere sport, to provide some slight excitement to the lives of the families working at the township. Just as Connor knew that the victory, or even a defeat if it had come, meant nothing to the good-natured giant.

"They almost had you there for a moment," Connor said somberly, gazing up at the red-bearded face.

Thor scowled. "Eh?"

"Oh, Connor," Beth laughed as she took Jordan from his arms.

"Yeah. I saw it clear as day," Connor continued, shaking his head compassionately. "That was close, boy. They just about sent you down that hill like a big ol' fat dogsled on greased lightning. Good thing they didn't succeed, huh?"

A narrow smile had crept across Thor's face.

"Yes . . ." he rumbled. "Yes, now that you say it, I perceive that my great strength is almost gone. Gone to exhaustion. It is a good thing . . . you have a refrigerator."

Connor looked up sharply. "What?"

Beth laughed more loudly as she turned to the house.

"Leviathan sleeps until we cement the corridors leading out of the Containment Chamber," Frank said, signing a clipboard. "Just make sure that the nitrogen level in the Containment Chamber remains at one hundred percent!"

Because the nervous instruction wasn't given to anyone in particular, everyone stared.

Frank felt the concentration, just as he had felt it so often of late. It was a gathering of frightful, accusing glares. "Just making sure that everyone knows," he smiled casually, feeling the force of the focus.

No one moved.

Frank lifted a hand. "Look, I want everybody to relax. You all know that it's not going to wake up until we give it oxygen. And even then, we're only going to give it just enough to move around. It will barely be able to walk, so there's nothing to worry about."

After a moment, everyone turned to their work.

Shaking his head, Frank turned away, focusing on Dr. Hoffman. The old man appeared to be suffering a grave loss of energy. He held a cold pipe in a stiff hand. But he seemed to feel Frank's attention, looking up from a computer monitor.

"You are certain that the creature must have a high oxygen atmosphere to ignite the carpasioxyllelene, Peter?"

"Yeah, Dr. Hoffman, I'm certain. It'll sleep until we give it a little air. It's not going to be attacking the cell." Hoffman's eyes were vacuous behind his glasses. He turned back to stare at the monitor.

At the far end of the cavern a dark, solidly coiled mass lay unmoving, thick armor plates overlapping so tightly that not even air could pass between the seals. Even in sleep, it appeared deadly. There were no vital areas of the body exposed, and there was no breathing, no movement. Vaguely, Frank could see ominous, foglike vapors created by its superheated body temperature rising from the stone floor, hovering like a death shroud.

"We should not continue," Hoffman said flatly.

Clearly, he had determined that the experiment had run its course and that they had reached the point where both sanity and professional responsibility required them to terminate it. Frank didn't reply. He knew that Adler would continue the experiment with or without them. And danger levels were too high to risk Adler flying in new scientists—pompous yes-heads with no idea of the creature's true potential—to run the program.

Hoffman continued, "Perhaps we will not be able to perform the tests, anyway. Perhaps the explosion this morning injured the creature. Perhaps it is even dying."

"I don't think so, Doctor."

Hoffman looked up. "But how can you be certain, Peter? That was a . . . a tremendous explosion! How can we be certain that the beast is not injured, or even dying, from the trauma?"

Frank placed a hand on the older man's shoulder. Then he slowly lifted a jet-black wireless headset from the countertop, placing it over his head as lab workers scurried past, moving in new equipment.

"GEO, identify my voice," he spoke softly into the headset.

He paused before continuing. "Yes, it's Dr. Frank. I want you to switch to the intercom system for reply."

A split second later the computer's eerily soft, impersonal voice came over the speaker, a screened black circle built into the wall. Wired directly into the next generation neural net dual-multiprocessor, the speakers were located throughout the entire cavern for alarms, paging, or for Frank's vocal communication with GEO.

"Affirmative. Communicating through intercom system."

Frank met Hoffman's gaze. The old doctor's lip trembled slightly as Frank spoke. "GEO, give me the current physiological stats on Leviathan."

"Leviathan maintains heart rate of five beats per minute. Respiration remains at zero. Internal temperature remains constant at 400 degrees, and mitosis is locked in biofeed loop on outer armor epidermis."

Hoffman looked down, a slight shudder going through his chest. Frank continued, speaking into the headset. "GEO, what is your evaluation of Leviathan's condition?"

"Leviathan has initiated Hibernation Sequence."

"Why?"

"Leviathan has determined that cavern atmosphere contains high probability death factor. Leviathan will continue Hibernation Sequence until atmosphere is no longer poisonous."

"And what will be Leviathan's actions on termination of the Hibernation Sequence?"

"Leviathan will begin altering physiological demands for oxygen and will begin kinetic energy release process. It will also begin contracting muscular areas of mouth and throat to prime expulsion of flammable gel. Leviathan will increase epinephrine level and begin contraction of muscle ligatures to enhance physical strength by 25 percent. Then Leviathan will initiate thermal sensors according to neural program parameters."

A disturbing thought passed like a ghost across some instinctive recess of Frank's mind as the computer replied. Slowly standing erect, he stared at the titanium fire door, following the dim impression, wondering why it had taken him so long to make the connection.

"GEO," he began quietly, "why did Leviathan attack the Observation Room this morning?"

"Insufficient data exists to answer that question."

Frank had anticipated that. "GEO, do you think Leviathan was attempting reconstitution when it attacked the Observation Room this morning?"

"Leviathan is fed one thousand pounds of sustenance in the form of raw beef every two hours. It is not logical for Leviathan to attack Observation Room for reconstitution."

"Then—" Frank closed his eyes, focusing. "—what other logical purpose could Leviathan have for attacking the Observation Room?"

"Insufficient data exists to—"

"Terminate answer."

Frank leaned forward. "GEO, I want you to calculate the following premise: Determine if it is numerically possible for Leviathan's polyploidal chromosomes to have taken the initial neural programming to mature evolution of a Hunter-killer Mode without the assistance of Dr. Frank."

A long silence shrouded the room before the computer replied. *"Yes. It is numerically possible for Leviathan's polyploidal DNA to have genetically completed the Hunter-killer Mode without the assistance of Dr. Frank. It is theoretically possible that Leviathan has genetically promoted itself to a mature Hunter-killer Mode without control parameters."*

Frank bowed his head, thinking he should have known. He asked the next question only for confirmation. "GEO, according to initial programming performed by Dr. Frank, what would Leviathan logically conclude as the ultimate purpose of a genetically completed Hunter-killer Mode?"

"Dr. Frank knows the parameters of Hunter-killer Mode. Dr. Frank created Leviathan."

A dark tide was rushing over Frank's consciousness, sight and sound forgotten. "I know, GEO. But I want you to answer the question. What would Leviathan conclude as the final purpose of its own independently completed Hunter-killer Mode?"

"Leviathan would logically conclude purpose of Hunter-killer Mode to be complete elimination of unfriendly organisms."

Abruptly Frank sensed that everyone in the Observation Room had stopped working. Somehow touched by the corporeal focus he turned, saw a dozen pale faces staring at him. He licked his lips, knowing a quick nervousness, a transmitted fear that burned into him, feathering his heartbeat. He felt his breath increase, faster, and he was almost as surprised as everyone else when he asked his next question.

"GEO, would Leviathan distinguish at all between friendly and nonfriendly organisms?"

"It is not probable that Leviathan would differentiate between friendly and nonfriendly organisms. It would attempt to—"

"Terminate answer," Frank said quickly, taking a deep breath. "GEO, if Leviathan has brought itself into a Hunter-killer Mode, what is the best course of action?"

Instantly the computer replied.

"Do not awaken."

Chapter 7

Like I need a *computer* to tell me that!"

Frank turned to see Chesterton standing in the doorway. The colonel stood for a second before he walked forward, focusing on everyone, on no one. He paused in front of Frank.

"I just knew . . ." Chesterton said, shaking his head. "I just *knew* that you people couldn't control that thing."

Frank was motionless. His eyes darted from Chesterton to the computer panel. "But this . . . this wasn't supposed to happen, Chesterton. Leviathan's neural enhancement wasn't *supposed* to promote itself into a Hunter-killer Mode!" He looked up. "I mean, if this thing is in a Hunter-killer Mode, it's going to want to kill . . . to kill everything . . ."

Chesterton stared, grim.

"I never counted on this," Frank whispered, bowing his head. "I never counted on any of this . . ."

"Well you'd better count on it, Frank." Chesterton grimaced. "Because things have now and forever changed. And because I'm in charge of this place, I'm telling you right now that there's not going to be any more tests. At all." He hesitated, surrendering a little of his hardened tone. "But . . . try and calm down a little, son. This isn't something we can't overcome. I've been through worse."

Turning to the fire wall, Chesterton placed his hands on his hips. "Still, though, we're going to have to take some serious

precautions. And that means I'm going to shut down this operation until I can find a way to permanently secure that thing inside
that cavern."

"How are you going to do that?"

"Honestly, Doctor, I don't know." Chesterton continued to
stare at the fire wall. "That thing is sixteen feet tall and thirty-five
feet long and is without question the meanest, most vicious thing
to ever walk the face of God's green earth. It's got claws and teeth
that are as hard as diamond. It's armored like a tank, and it's
strong enough to rip the hull out of a battleship. So containing it
ain't gonna be easy. But then again, it's *never* been easy. We'll just
have to do it. Or die trying." He turned back. "And if all else fails,
Frank, we've always got the fail-safe."

Frank's hand tightened on the computer chair.

Chesterton continued, "But no matter what happens, Doctor, we've got to contain that thing inside that cavern. And we've
got to kill it inside that cavern." He stared down. "And you can
tell Adler that this experiment is officially over. As officially over
as it's gonna get."

His mind spinning, Frank whispered, "But I don't think that
you can hold it, Chesterton. Not if Leviathan really wants to get
out. That cavern was never designed to hold anything like this."
He trembled. "I don't think that *anything* can hold it. Or stop it."

"Well, you're wrong about that, Frank. Because that fail-safe
of yours can stop it. Dead in its tracks." Chesterton turned again,
studying the titanium fire wall. "But you've got a point. And . . .
maybe you did too good a job, son. Maybe even better than they
wanted you to do." He paused. "One thing is certain, though.
That thing is going to sleep as long as you've got it in a nitrogen
atmosphere. And nobody is going to be waking it up. Not for
anything. And in the morning, I'm going to get on the horn to the
Pentagon and obtain more men to mount a company-sized defensive perimeter that can—"

But Frank was no longer listening. Because with Chesterton's
words, a horrible thought had settled over him, a black shroud of
a thought that had blocked out everything else. And the scientist
turned away, staring blindly at the wall as if he could even now

see the black-scaled monster rising from the cavern floor, flames kindled in its mouth, hell-hating eyes glowing like coals. It was a revelation that came from Frank's back, unexpected and unseen, moving through him like a superheated soul to pass out the blackened wall.

Too good a job . . .

"Oh, no," he whispered.

Releasing some of his tension, Chesterton was still going. "—and in a few months, we'll have cemented the corridors so that it can never escape to kill everything that walks or crawls on the face of the—"

Frank broke him off, touching the headset with a trembling hand.

"GEO," he said quickly, a gathering fear in his voice, "use analysis of Leviathan's numbered molecular DNA strands to calculate if it is numerically possible for polyploidal chromosomes to achieve the following mutation: Determine if Leviathan can replicate an immunity factor to a nitrogen-based atmosphere."

Frank's quiet command brought a horrified Hoffman to his feet. Chesterton suddenly paled, pausing from his doomsday drum to stare, mouth tight and grim. In a moment the computer replied.

"Presuming accuracy of assumption that Leviathan has genetically self-promoted Hunter-killer Mode to evolution by mutation of polyploidal chromosomes, it is certain that Leviathan has achieved dual-strand polyploidal DNA of sixteen billion, two-"

"GEO, I don't want to hear the calculation. I just want the conclusion. Is it numerically possible for Leviathan's polyploidal DNA chromosomes to continue mutation until it achieves an immunity to nitrogen?"

A pause.

"If Leviathan's DNA has reached Hunter-killer Mode by self-mutation, it is numerically possible for Leviathan to replicate mutated polyploidal DNA to make a nitrogen-based atmosphere nonpoisonous."

Frank closed his eyes. He had never expected this. It had been one of the unknowns. But now, in this single surreal moment, he knew that everything had changed. Would never be the same. He spoke distinctly into the headset. "GEO, I want you to extrapolate from this morning's attack and tell me how much longer, from this second, it would take Leviathan to attain an immunity to nitrogen."

Hushed breathing could be heard in the room.

"Leviathan would require an additional ten hours, fifteen minutes and thirty-two seconds to replicate sufficient dual-strand DNA to achieve an immunity to nitrogen," came the calm reply.

Lab techs reacted, clutching. Frank's mind had accelerated to computer speed. He asked quickly, "Will Leviathan be able to generate flame in a nitrogen atmosphere?"

"No. Oxygen level must exceed twenty—"

"Terminate answer," Frank interrupted, unable to wait for the computer's response. "Will Leviathan have full-strength use of all other weapons in a nitrogen-based atmosphere?"

A blood-hot wind, dark.

"Yes."

Frank was already moving for the room.

"I've got to talk with Adler," he whispered, sweating.

As he neared the door, Frank recognized the deep, rich fear that liquefied his entire body and he fiercely resisted the overwhelming need to rush, not wanting to spur panic. But as the doorway loomed up, he felt himself rising higher on his feet, moving lighter into it, and as he cleared the frame with the hallway open and white with air before him, he gave in.

Running.

Thor belched loudly over his empty plate, rubbing the corners of his mouth to smooth out the mustache of his bright red beard. He nodded to Beth, gesturing with his usual theatric flair.

"A finer meal I have never tasted," he laughed, leaning back in his chair to place both hands on his expanded gut. With an air of supreme contentment he patted his ample waist, gazing at Connor.

"My strength is returning," he smiled.

"Uh-huh," Connor replied, leaning his chin on a hand. "You

sure you had enough? I mean, I could go kill a steer or something if you need some more. There's some big ol' mountain goats up in the hills that—"

"No, no," Thor replied, gesturing. He glanced slowly to the window; the long red sunset had faded to black. "Perhaps, yes, on my next trip, we shall hunt one of the longhorns. But for now, I think, we should proceed to coffee."

Connor blinked, turned to Beth. "Darlin', you better put on the *big* pot."

"I've already started it," Beth smiled, placing dishes in the industrial-sized sink. She turned back as she began washing. "Hey, Thor, I've always wanted to ask you something. How come your parents named you Thor? Isn't that the name of a Viking god or something?"

Thor nodded, working studiously with a toothpick. "Yes, it is the name of the Norse god of thunder," he commented, clearly eager to speak forth now that dinner was complete.

Connor leaned back, smiling slightly. He knew that Thor, starved as he was for someone to talk with, would dominate the conversation for the better part of the night.

"It has always been a common and popular name in Norway," he continued. "I have two uncles by the same name, Thorson and Thorwulf. And my father's name was also Thor."

"Is that where you were born? Norway?"

"Yes," Thor said, picking at a stubborn gap in his teeth. "I was born in the Northland, where there are few people. My family were sheepherders. I was raised in the Lofoten Isles located between the Norwegian Sea and the Vest Fiord."

Beth looked up. "On the sea? It must have been awfully cold."

"No." Thor shook his head. "Not so cold. Here, so close to Iceland, we are in the southbound Arctic current that comes down from the Pole. It is a cold current. An iceberg current. But Norway is far to the east. It is located beside a northbound current coming up from the Atlantic. It is a warm current, so the Norwegian coast is well above freezing. It only becomes cold when you go inland to the fiords, where the sea wind cannot warm the air. Then it is much like this place. Very harsh. Very cold."

Connor spoke. "Why were there so few people in the . . . uh, the . . ."

"Lofoten Islands."

"Yeah. The Lofoten Islands."

"It is a brutal land." Thor frowned. "The closest village is Harstad, over 120 kilometers away." He gestured with the toothpick. "It was a hard life, I tell you. We were forced to make everything for ourselves. Our houses, clothes, lamps, fuel, saddles, and bridles. Whatever we had, we made from the land. Our boots were sealskin stuffed with sedge grass."

Screaming gleefully, Jordan ran into the room, still wet from a bath. He crashed wildly against Connor, crawling quickly and with fierce determination into his lap. Connor laughed, hugging the small naked body, wiping the wet brown hair from the childish eyes.

"Time for bed, Jordan," Beth called from the kitchen.

"But I don't *want*—"

"Jordan," Connor repeated, attempting to appear stern and unbendable. "You heard what your mother said."

Jordan stared back at him, seeming to weigh Connor's conviction, deciding he could risk a protest. "But Thor is here and . . . and . . . and Thor always tells me a *stooorrry*."

Thor laughed gustily.

"Thor can tell you a story on his next visit," Beth said, wiping her hands as she walked forward. "Now give Daddy and Thor a hug. I'm going to read to you and then we'll tickle feet. Thor can visit you again tomorrow, and then he can tell you a big, long story." She cast a weighty glance at Thor. "A *big* story. Just like he always does."

Thor smiled as Connor wrapped his arms around the tiny form, and then Jordan leaned back, staring intently at his father. "Are we still going fishing tomorrow?" he asked.

With a laugh, Connor replied, "Yeah, boy. Of course we're going fishing. I promised you that we'd go fishing, didn't I?"

"Uh huh."

"And don't I always keep my promises?"

Jordan smiled. "Yeah. You always keep your promises."

Laughing, Connor hugged him a moment. "Okay. Now it's time for bed. But tomorrow you and me are going fishing. And Thor will even come back and tell you a story. So give Thor a big bear hug and say good night."

Jordan descended to the floor and walked around his chair, vanishing for a moment in Thor's gentle, massive arms. Then the child leaned back, gazing into the bearded face. "You'll come back tomorrow after we go fishing and tell me a story?"

Thor held the tiny hands, gazing down. "For sure, boy. I'll even come back tomorrow and tell you a long, long story about a magical sword and a great king who used the sword to destroy a terrible beast." Thor nodded seriously. "It is one of my best stories."

"Okay," Jordan said, enduring the disappointment of not hearing the adventure this minute. He turned to give Connor a kiss.

"Nite-nite," Connor said.

"Nite-nite."

Beth smiled and picked him up and in a moment had disappeared into the back of the stone house. Connor rose from the table and went to the kitchen, returning a moment later with two large containers of coffee. Thor nodded gratefully and reached out to drain half of his with a long swallow. When he set it down, he cast a glance at the door where Jordan had vanished.

"He is a good boy," he rumbled, a faint smile.

"Yeah," Connor replied. "He's a good boy. He's the love of my life. I don't know what I'd do without him."

"You will do well with him," Thor nodded. "You promise, and you keep your promise. Not an easy thing in these days."

"Yeah," Connor replied. "But keeping my promises to him isn't hard. I love him. He means everything to Beth and me. To tell you the truth, Thor, I never really wanted to bring a child into this sorry world. It just sort of happened. But it's been really good."

Motionless, Thor stared into the doorway. "Maybe Jordan

will change the world," he said finally. "Maybe that is the reason he is here."

"Thor . . ." Connor said, staring. "There aren't any reasons for things. Things happen, and there's no reason, no purpose. I think that we've had this discussion before."

Thor laughed heartily. "Let's have it again."

Shaking his head, Connor looked away. "I don't believe like you do, Thor. I never have." He paused. "You believe in good and evil. God and Satan. You believe in hope and faith and the rest of it. But I don't. I don't believe in anything. Nothing but my family. That's all there is for me."

"A family is a great thing," Thor said.

"I really don't care to change the world, Thor," Connor continued, looking up. "I just want to get away from it. When I finish this job, we're going to go someplace where Jordan can grow up like a kid should be allowed to grow up. And it'll be a long way from a city, I'll tell you that. A long way from any people at all."

"And what will you do when you reach this place in the sun?" Thor asked, his voice harder.

"Live in peace," Connor replied. "Live a decent life."

"Yes. That would be a good thing also. To live a peaceful life. A good life." Thor paused. "Do you know what a good life would be for me?"

Connor smiled. "Yeah, but I think you're going to tell me anyway."

Accepting the lack of invitation, Thor went on solemnly, "Yes, I will be glad to tell you. And you will be glad you asked. Because it is a philosophy full of insight and meaning." He smiled, almost laughing. "And the heart of it is this, my friend: I would live a life to change the world for good. A life where I made a good difference in the life of one, or in the lives of many. Where I faced great battles like a man. With courage and strength. Doing what is right. And I would win, in the end."

For a moment Connor said nothing, impressed by the un-abashed seriousness of Thor's speech. "That's a pretty tall order, Thor," he answered, touching the rim of the coffee mug. "But to want that, you've got to believe in good and evil or something beyond this world. And I don't."

"All men believe in good and evil." Thor looked up. His ice-green eyes didn't waver. "Even you, Connor. But you think that only man is evil. And yet all the civilizations that have ever held kingdoms on the earth have written of an evil that is beyond man. Just as they all have written of a last, great battle that will occur between good and evil. A battle that is yet to come."

"You really believe that?" Connor asked. He searched Thor's open eyes. "Do you really believe that there's going to be a last battle between good and evil?"

"Yes," Thor answered, "and I believe in more than that. I believe that if a man is a man, he will live his life for good, making war with evil. Because that is part of the battle to come."

Connor was silent. Unmoving.

"My ancestors called it *Ragnarok*," Thor continued, leaning forward. The table and chair creaked beneath his weight. "It was to be the last battle on the earth between good and evil. According to tradition, it would begin with a winter three years long. Then there would be a collapse of morality, with greed ruling the hearts of men. And finally, a great falling away of faith with men's hearts turning to selfishness and all manner of sin." He paused, frowning. "It is the Nordic representation of Armageddon."

Connor's eyes narrowed. He was silent.

"In truth," Thor continued, "the entire Scandinavian mythology, and many other mythologies of the North, can be traced to Celtic roots, which can in turn be traced to the Hittites or other Mesopotamian tribes that immigrated into the North in 1500 B.C., fleeing the occupation of Israel in Canaan. Tribes that knew well the story of the Hebrew God and the Serpent."

"And how can you know this?"

"By discipline, and by applying my mind to history," Thor replied with a smile. "I learned long ago that the North was settled by the Asiatic 'broadheads' who immigrated across Europe during the late Stone Age or early Iron Age. Tribes that eventually crossed the sea to settle Norway in the first century."

"Yeah," replied Connor, "but the tribes who settled Norway

in the first century were pretty distant descendants of the tribes who immigrated to Britain in 1500 B.C., Thor. It seems like they would have had a hard time remembering the stories of the Old Testament or the Hittites or whatever. A thousand years is a long time for people to remember anything."

"Memory lives longer than man," Thor replied steadily. "Superstition survives stone monuments. Look at Stonehenge. The people who built it, and even the altar itself, are gone. But the superstition remains. I tell you the truth; the original beliefs of the tribes who settled Europe in 1500 B.C. were remembered by their descendants, though in altered form. And what the Vikings passed by oral tradition closely paralleled the Hebrew cosmology and even pieces of the long-vanished Hittite mythology."

Connor grunted. "Give me an example."

"Like Thor himself, the Norse god of thunder who fought with an iron hammer to defend Asgard from evil. Is it any coincidence that the Hittites also had a god of thunder, named Tarku, who fought with an iron hammer to defend heaven and hurled lightning from his hand?" He stared intently. "An ancient Hittite image carved in stone at Tel-Engidi reveals Tarku of the Hittites waving his hammer over slain horses, bringing them back to life. In Norse mythology, Thor also waves his hammer over his goats, bringing them to life. I tell you, this is no coincidence."

Connor had never really thought about it, and he was faintly surprised that he had never come across anything like it before since he had read widely and enjoyed reading. But this was an alien theory to him, as alien as anything he had ever heard.

"And there is more." Thor held forth like a schoolteacher starved from teaching. "You will remember that Satan was the fallen angel who deceived man into betraying God. While Loki, the evil god of Norse mythology who deceived man into rebelling against Odin, the father of all Norse gods, is only a parallel of Satan. The Norse story of man's rebellion is only a reflection of the Old Testament story of Eden.

"Loki told man that he could become immortal if he would find true life by submitting to his unrestrained passions. And this is the argument Satan used in the Garden of Eden, and an enduring tenant of mythology. In almost all societies of the ancient world, a battle between immortal good and evil is recorded, with man caught between the two forces, destined to serve one or the other."

Connor's gaze was concentrated. "And that's what makes you think there's good and evil, Thor? And that a man should choose between them?"

"It is part of what makes me believe," Thor said, thoughtfully stroking his red beard. "A man must believe what is reasonable to believe. He must open his mind and see."

"Well," Connor began, "I don't think that a lot of people actually see this kind of thing, Thor."

"The past suffers the present," Thor replied, abruptly grim. "Men try to change history to agree with their needs, but truth does not change. Neither truth, nor heroism, nor courage. Today, men say that we live in an age without good or evil; therefore, we live in an age without heroes. They say that a man should live only for himself, for whatever is right in his own eyes. They say the age of heroes has passed."

Connor scowled. "Thor, it's hard to agree anymore on what's right or wrong. Everybody has their own opinion on just about everything. So it's obviously hard to agree on heroism." He paused. "I mean, what's a hero really supposed to be, anyway? Someone who saves somebody's life?"

"It is a simple thing," Thor rumbled. "A hero is someone who stands upon truth, to the end."

"Someone who stands on *truth*?" Connor asked, eyes widening. "What does truth have to do with heroism?"

"Truth and heaven are beyond man's changing, Connor. Just as evil and hell are beyond man's changing. To fight for the cause of truth, one must fight for the cause of heaven."

Connor was silent. But he was used to this; all conversations with Thor eventually went into the deep.

"And I believe more than this," Thor mumbled, gazing up. "I believe that each man, at his last chance to know truth, faces his own Ragnarok. His own battle with Armageddon. And all of a man's life comes together to meet it. His past, his present, and his future. Whether such a man lives or dies, it will be his greatest hour, the hour when he sees the true measure and light of his life, and knows the destiny of his soul." Thor's face hardening like age-old Arctic ice. "This is where all our lives will end. When we stare the old serpent in the eyes . . . and make our final stand."

Connor said nothing, staring, and after a moment Thor blinked. His eyes slowly became less intense. "A lofty ambition, is it not?"

"Yeah, partner, it is," Connor replied quietly, staring sadly. "But it sounds like something you could do. Better than anybody I've ever known."

Thor laughed shortly, glancing down. "And you also, my friend. Because you may believe as you believe, Connor. But I think that it is your destiny also to advance onto that field. To overcome evil with your own good strength, and God's strength."

Silence lasted between them.

"I don't believe in miracles, Thor," Connor replied stoically.

Thor laughed. "I do, my friend."

Moved by Thor's words to cross a line he had never crossed, Connor was compelled to ask, "Were you once a priest?"

"I am still a priest." Thor nodded, frowning.

"Then what are you doing here?" Connor knew that whatever he might hear could change their relationship forever, and he almost resisted the question. But somehow, spellbound by the moment, he had to know.

Thor leaned forward in his chair, elbows on his knees. "It is a longer story than you would care to hear," he began. "But I can tell you that I was a priest of a small Norwegian village located near the coast of Sweden. There was much . . . *evil* . . . in a village so small. And many of my flock were enslaved by it, even against their will. It was an organized evil, and powerful; an evil nurtured by the hand of man but bred by the hounds of hell. As father of my flock, I told my people that they were no longer compelled to serve it. I placed them under the protection of the church and under my personal protection as well." He became mournful. "In the end it was a fiendish battle, a battle which I narrowly won. And the evil and murderous son of a very powerful man was killed in the struggle. Not by my hand, for certain, but he was killed just the same. And his father blamed me for his death, so powerful men sought my life in revenge. So the Holy Father, in his wish to protect me, removed me from my church and my world until it would be safe for me to return. It was a decision made out of love, and I was told that it was only for a short time. He placed me on this island with only his knowledge of my whereabouts until my enemies no longer sought to kill me." Thor grew more quiet. "I was grateful for his benevolence. But in removing me from the forefront of the battle, the Holy Father removed me from life, as well. I have been here five years. And I don't know when I will return."

Connor noticed he hadn't moved as Thor spoke. Shifting, he cleared his throat. "So you're not going to be here forever?"

"Forever?" Thor twisted his head, once more releasing a mysterious frown. "No, my friend. Not forever."

A sudden knock at the door broke the solemnity. Caught in a vaguely catastrophic mentality by Thor's speech, Connor was on his feet, expecting anything. He opened the door to find his assistant foreman breathing heavily and frosted with crystalline sea spray. The man spoke quickly and then Connor closed the door, coming back to sit at the table. His brow hardened.

"What is it?" Thor rumbled.

"A plane," Connor said quietly, staring back at the door. "He said a C-130 landed five minutes ago on the airfield with about twenty guys who looked like scientists. He said there were also about forty MPs with them, all dressed in black and loaded up with weapons like a SWAT team or something. He said they went down to the cavern. I think it scared him."

Thor scowled. "What does it mean?"

"I don't know," Connor replied. "But I don't think it's good. A lot of the guys have been uneasy lately. They think they've heard sounds coming from the Containment Cavern. They couldn't say what it was. They just said that whatever it was didn't sound *happy*. But I've managed to calm them down, so far. I've told them to just relax and do their jobs." Connor shook his head, finally focusing on Thor. "You know a lot about languages, don't you?"

"Yes. I studied at the University of Paris. I am a student of all languages."

For the slightest moment Connor stared at the red-bearded face, hesitating to compromise whatever small security clearance he had received to do his job. Decided to go against it.

"Have you ever heard the word *leviathan*?"

Thor leaned back, a disturbance surfacing. "Yes," he said quietly. "I know the word."

Connor waited. "What does it mean?"

"It is a word almost lost to time," Thor replied, his tone submerged in Nordic coldness. "It is the ancient name for Dragon."

Chapter 8

B ut there is no way to be certain," Adler commented, settling behind his desk. "Surely, Dr. Frank, you have no means of being certain that Leviathan will achieve an immunity to nitrogen. You don't even have any way to be certain that Leviathan has entered this . . . this . . ."

"Hunter-killer Mode," Frank said, breathless.

"Yes, yes," Adler said, nodding, "this infamous Hunter-killer Mode. If you wish to make presumptions, Doctor, you could presume that Leviathan's attack this morning was the result of a natural tendency to obtain food. We can all presume anything we please. But science demands data! We cannot leap beyond available facts."

"I *know* this creature, Mr. Adler!" Frank slammed his hand onto the desk. "I know how it thinks! It would *never* have attacked the cell this morning unless some instinct prompted it."

"And that instinct could have been for *food*," Adler responded. "It could also have been sheer bestial anger at being contained in the cavern! It could have been any number of things!"

"But it wasn't any number of things!"

"Has GEO confirmed your presumptions?"

"No, it doesn't work like that. GEO can only monitor Leviathan's body statistics like its heart rate, blood pressure, temperature, brain activity, or whatever. The program chip that was designed to control Leviathan was never implanted, and it wouldn't do any good to implant it now because Leviathan's DNA has completed the instinct that the control chip was supposed to project."

"What do you mean?" Adler stared.

"Forget it, Mr. Adler. It's complicated."

"Yes, of course, Doctor." Adler smiled. "But I am a complicated man. Explain it to me."

Frank swore softly. "The part of Leviathan's brain that would have been controlled by the mission control chip has already been overcome by Leviathan's Hunter-killer Mode instinct. It's like . . . like someone who has a weak eye when they're a child. If nothing is done to make that eye fuse the proper nerve connections to the brain, then that eye will always be weak. There won't be anything physically wrong with the eye itself, but the visual part of the brain that would have controlled that eye will be taken over by the other eye, the strong eye. And when that happens, it can't be reversed. The nerves are fused and that's it."

Frank paused, catching a breath. "Leviathan can never be controlled, Mr. Adler! The part of Leviathan's brain that could have been controlled has already fused to something more powerful. It's been taken over by the Hunter-killer Mode. It's an instinct-reflex that regulates synapses."

"Yes, I see," mumbled Adler, nodding. "So all GEO can do is track Leviathan, tell us where it is. But as of this moment, Leviathan controls itself." He leaned back, cradling the back of his head in his hands. "Yes. And just what do you propose we do, Doctor?"

"I propose that we totally abandon the island and initiate GEO's nuclear fail-safe."

Adler was suddenly upright. "Surely you fail to understand what you are saying."

"I understand exactly what I'm saying," Frank rasped. "GEO has a nuclear fail-safe. It's built into the lowest center of the cavern, and it's strong enough to vaporize this entire island. It's designed to trigger itself if Leviathan ever activates the detectors at the island perimeter or if Leviathan is ever escaping without authorization into the ocean. You know that that was a safety measure I insisted on from the beginning, and I got it."

"But Leviathan hasn't escaped," Adler retorted. "GEO . . . GEO cannot simply activate the—"

"I can activate the fail-safe," Frank replied. "I can't deactivate it once it has begun. But I can push the button."

"Doctor, Doctor, please, you are not thinking logically. If Leviathan must be terminated, we should simply allow Chesterton to—"

"Chesterton doesn't stand a chance and he knows it," Frank said, leaning back. "If Chesterton and his men ever opened up with their weapons, Leviathan would come out of hibernation like a rocket. You don't know what you're dealing with, Adler." Frank purposefully dropped the *mister*. "There is *nothing* in this cavern that can stop Leviathan except the fail-safe."

Adler rose to his feet. "I will not sanction the nuclear vaporization of a billion-dollar experiment! Particularly since Leviathan is still asleep in the Containment Cavern, and we have no means whatsoever of knowing with any certainty that it is in this so-called Hunter-killer Mode!" He placed his knuckles on the desk, leaning into it. "That is the end of this discussion!"

Silence.

"I'm going over your head, Adler," Frank replied finally. "I'm going to Stygian Enterprises on this, and I'm going to tell them your judgment is unsound. I'm going to tell them that you are unsound, that you're being criminally irresponsible! I'm going to tell them that you're unnecessarily putting the lives of everyone in this installation at stake—the project itself at stake—because you can't realize the danger we're in!"

Unexpectedly, Adler smiled.

Air in the doorway shifted and Frank turned, realizing instantly. He saw the host of implacable and disciplined faces staring knowingly at the contest of wills. He recognized men who presumed themselves to be far more responsible and far more advanced in this arena of science. There were at least ten of them in the room already. More were gathered outside. And their focus on Frank was condemning. Disappointed.

"As you can probably guess," Adler said, leaning back from his aggressive position, "I had anticipated this on your part, Doctor. So after our meeting this morning I placed calls to the United States Government and Stygian Enterprises. As of this moment we have a new science team, Doctor. And Colonel Chesterton has also received orders to be relieved of command."

"I want to talk to the company myself," Frank said coldly.

"I'm afraid the lines of communication have now been encrypted," Adler responded. "So there will be no civilian or military communications from this facility without the proper code, which only myself and Colonel Chesterton's replacement possess. I informed the company that the sensitivity of the project at this critical moment mandated additional security measures."

Frank's head tilted. "So you're saying I can't talk to the company?"

"What I'm saying, Doctor"—Adler moved around the desk, distinctly pugilistic despite his age—"is that I am now singly in charge of this facility's communications. Please understand, this is a sensitive situation. We stand on the brink of a brilliant triumph. And I know even better than you why we must follow through as soon as possible."

Frank glanced at the faces behind him, at Adler. "What are you going to do?"

"I'm going to complete the tests," Adler replied, smiling. "And I am going to complete them on schedule, just as I've been ordered to do. Rest assured, Doctor, they will all be done with adequate safety measures. But they will, indeed, be done. Then we will finally see what kind of power Leviathan truly possesses."

Frank felt himself surrendering to the situation. He shook his head dismally, nothing else that he could feel.

If you wake that thing up it's going to kill you, Adler," he said. "It's going to kill every one of us."

"All ancient civilizations documented encounters between man and leviathans," Thor said in the patient tone of a scholar.

"Early historians record that leviathans were beasts of unequaled power and rage, supreme on the earth in strength."

Connor frowned, silent.

"First," Thor began, "I'll tell you what Job, the oldest book in the world, says about Leviathan. Then we will proceed from one text to another, examining the evidence."

With a smile Connor said, "You sound like a scientist, Thor. You're talking about this leviathan, or dragon, like it was a real thing."

"It was real." Thor nodded simply.

Connor held Thor's ponderous gaze. He tried to sound respectful when he finally spoke. "You're saying that dragons were real creatures? I mean, like fire-breathing and the whole nine yards?"

"I only repeat what history records," Thor replied. "But I believe that a dispassionate analysis of history can reveal hidden science." He sniffed, moving past Connor's skepticism. "Now, the forty-first chapter of the book of Job, a brilliantly written historical exegesis of science and culture despite servile objections of critics, records that Leviathan ruled both the sea and the land. It says that Leviathan was unequalled on the earth for physical power, and that it was armored with scales the size of shields, each overlapping the other so tightly that air couldn't pass between them. Job says that Leviathan's heart was hardened as a lower millstone, its skin utterly impervious to weapons. Arrows and lances had no effect against it, and its strength could shatter iron or bronze like straw. Its eyes glowed like a red dawn, and fire was kindled in its mouth. It could set coals ablaze with a blast of its breath and—"

Connor sat up. "What did you say?"

Anticipating skepticism, Thor nodded curtly. "Yes. It was known to breathe fire," he added.

A silence passed, Connor seeing in his mind the steel plate melted into shreds beyond the wiring. He thought about confiding it. Decided to wait.

"Sorry," he said quietly. "Go on."

"Historically," Thor continued without hesitation, "the

largest and most powerful of all the leviathans was the Heraldic Dragon. But the entire species of leviathan was apparently a family of closely related creatures, some more powerful than others. The lesser leviathans were known as wyverns, amphepteres, or guivres. And the prehistoric plesiosaur may have also been incorrectly included in the species, but the plesiosaur was not a true leviathan. It was simply an ocean creature which, by all the evidence, survives to this day. The rest of the leviathans, however, were smaller and weaker images of the Heraldic Dragon. But the Heraldic Dragon was the greatest of all leviathans. It was unchallenged in size and strength and was said to have defeated entire armies in battle."

"Just how big *was* this thing?" Connor asked.

"It is unknown. Apparently the size of Heraldic Dragons could vary. Many of the largest dragons were observed in England, India, and North Africa. In the ancient world, Africa was infamous for large leviathans. And during the height of the Roman Empire, when Rome controlled North Africa, there was even a Roman Legion that engaged a leviathan in battle."

"When?" Connor asked. He had a need for specifics.

Thor didn't hesitate. "In A.D. 67 the Roman historian Octavus Livy wrote that he personally witnessed a savage and bloody battle between a single leviathan and the Eighth Roman Legion, led by General Scipio Regulus. The battle occurred in what is now Libya and lasted for almost a week. Livy wrote that over three thousand Roman soldiers were killed in the encounter."

Connor stared a moment. "That's incredible. The Romans were disciplined fighters." He paused again. "What started the battle?"

"Livy writes that the leviathan attacked the Legion without warning," Thor answered. "There was no reason, no provocation. Apparently, Leviathan was a beast of unnatural hostility. That agrees with other historical accounts of its temperament. But once the battle was engaged, it was a battle to the death. Livy recorded that the Legion fought effectively against it, but the leviathan was heavily armored and couldn't be wounded. Eventually, recognizing a complete defeat of his six thousand men at hand, General Regulus ordered a desperate retreat. The surviving Roman soldiers then built siege engines, like catapults, for hurling heavy stones. Afterwards, they attacked the leviathan again and eventually cornered it in a small canyon, where they crushed it with repeated blows."

"So leviathans were prone to attack people?" Connor asked, uneasy.

"Apparently, yes," Thor replied, brooding. He had become more Icelandic as he continued, darker and more somber. "In the eleventh century it was recorded by Byliny, a respected Ukrainian historian, that a leviathan had terrorized the steppes of Western Russia for decades. It was called Gorynych and was supposedly responsible for slaughtering a large number of villagers. It was finally killed after a savage monthlong battle with a legendary Ukrainian hunter named Dobrynja, who hunted the beast down and killed it to avenge his brother's death."

"Just one man?" Connor broke in. "A single man killed a leviathan?"

Thor shook his head. "I believe, from the oldest and most accurate description of the beast, that what Dobrynja slew was a wyvern and not the biblical Leviathan or mythical dragon." A pause. "It was obviously not a creature equal to the size of the leviathan that attacked the Roman Army in North Africa. That leviathan was almost certainly the heraldic dragon, and no single man who ever lived could defeat such a beast in combat."

A pause to gather his thoughts and Thor went on, "But other battles between foreign armies and the leviathans, or heraldic dragons, are recorded in the historical documents of India, England, France, China, Japan, Mesopotamia, Egypt, and Africa as late as the eighth century. They were recorded by dispassionate historians who had virtually no contact with one another and sought only to leave an accurate record of their times. All of the descriptions of heraldic dragons agree in general, but some commentators noted unusual aspects of the creatures that others did not."

Connor's brow hardened, concentrated. "Like what?"

Thoughtful, Thor seemed to search his memory. "In *Historia Naturalis,* written in 1701, it's recorded that a powerful heraldic dragon was killed on Vatican Hill in 1669 during a savage fight with the army of Rome. It was a bloody engagement because the Romans, no matter how hard pressed, could not very well retreat from their own city and retain their pride. They were forced to stand their ground, to the last man. It is recorded that the brutal conflict lasted an entire day and reportedly reduced the standing militia of Rome to a skeletal crew. And upon the creature's slow and bloody death, it was examined by the Regulaus-Cassium, prefect of the city. Overall, the surviving description, also recorded by numerous scholars, fits the biblical Leviathan or the heraldic dragon. But the leviathan slain on Vatican Hill was also recorded to have had webbed feet."

"Webbed feet?" Connor asked, frowning. "For swimming?"

"Many leviathans were said to have had webbed feet," Thor continued dispassionately. "And many were said to have had wings."

Connor was expecting that. "For flying, I suppose."

With a nod Thor replied, "In 793 at the monastery of St. Cuthbert, located on the rocky island of Lindisfarne on England's western coast, over a hundred monks witnessed what they said was a flying leviathan. It had large, dark wings like black leather, and soared low over the monastery throughout the entire sunset. Then it was joined by other flying leviathans. Witness accounts say the sky was eventually filled with them. They said the air was alive with their shadows until the sun was finally gone."

"I suppose they didn't kill anybody," Connor commented drily, taking another sip of coffee. "Sounds like they were cruising for food."

"I don't believe the cautious monks gave them a chance." Thor smiled. "But on the French isle of Saint Marguerite a flying leviathan, apparently similar to the biblical Leviathan, was said to have killed over three thousand villagers and seamen and even English knights throughout the Middle Ages. During that period of history it was known as the Tarasque. Incorrectly, I think. I believe it was confused with another leviathan that was said to have inhabited the Rhone River in France throughout the thirteenth century. Its name was Drac, and it was infamous for the blood it shed. The French town of Draguignan was named after it. But I think that Drac's most vicious attacks were launched against the village of Beaucaire. Many, many people were recorded to have been slain there in its repeated attacks. At least a dozen armies went on campaigns against it, desperate to end its reign of terror. If you doubt me, the specific campaigns are recorded by the French and early Germanic historians Ocino, Ragnarold, and Umberto of Guineve. Thousands of soldiers were killed by Drac in the battles, which lasted over a century."

Connor found himself waiting. "Well, did they kill it?"

"No." Thor shook his head. "All the armies were defeated. Eventually, it is speculated, the dragon died of old age. It would have been well over a hundred years old. But long life is characteristic of reptilian creatures. Even today some reptiles are known to live for well over a hundred years. And many leviathans were reported to have lived for centuries."

Connor's eyes narrowed. "Could that be accurate history, Thor?" he asked with careful respect. "I mean, it seems . . . fantastic."

"It is foolish to doubt the integrity of men who were regarded by their peers to be utterly trustworthy," Thor commented. "People can scoff only so much at accumulated history before they must bow to intelligent debate. Objectivity must have its place. There are far too many incidents of trustworthy persons witnessing similar sights to disbelieve all accounts. It flies in the face of logic and reason to mindlessly classify everything written about Leviathan as myth or superstition or hysterical paranoia. There is a time when we must trust the reliable, well written accounts of those who were recognized to be scholars and wise men of their time and hold those accounts as the best and most accurate window to the past, regardless of our prejudices."

He chewed a corner of his mustache a moment, adding, "In the Cathedral of Canterbury there is a contemporary chronicle that speaks of a savage fight between two leviathans. It occurred on Friday, September 26, 1449, between the English county borders of Suffolk and Essex and was witnessed by an entire township. It lasted for an hour and stunned witnesses by the ferocity of the conflict. One leviathan was black, the other red. And at the end of the hour-long battle, the black leviathan, badly wounded, retreated into its lair.

"Two of the most respected Englishmen of the fifteenth century, John Steel and Christopher Holder, were present at the scene. Afterwards they gave their unemotional endorsement to verify the account." He paused. "Steel and Holder were known throughout all of England as strong men of superior intelligence and judgment. In all other areas of history, they are revered as such. It is only in this one account that modern men disbelieve them. And why? Because modern men do not wish to believe that leviathans existed. But Steel and Holder were not prone to lie. They would have had no reason to lie. And history repeats itself in this, over and over.

"In 1942 the German U-boat *Reichland* torpedoed a Norwegian trawler near the Scottish coast. Upon the torpedo's impact, the U-boat crew witnessed what they later recorded as a great sea serpent of unknown species violently breaching the surface of the ocean. It was witnessed by the U-boat captain and commanding officers, all intelligent men who also had absolutely no reason to lie. They said it was not a whale or similar to any other known mammal. It was a beast of tremendous size, possibly over sixty feet in length with a long neck and tail and a long, wedged head.

"And in 1966 two British paratroopers rowing across the Atlantic in a survival test were awakened. John Ridgeway, one of the crewmen, looked out from the boat and clearly saw what he described as a creature of enormous size, like a serpent, poised over them with its head held high above the waves. Then the creature dove deep and was gone."

Pausing, Thor took another sip of coffee, set the mug down carefully. He focused once more on Connor. "Ridgeway was an experienced soldier, a trained observer. He was held in the highest esteem by his peers, also hard men who only respected other men of superior strength and judgment. He wrote later that he had seen all manner of creature on the trip. Whales, dolphins, flying fish. But he reluctantly had to admit that there was only one explanation for what this thing could have been. A sea serpent. And he was correct. He could only say what he saw with his own eyes. He also had no reason to lie."

Connor was silent, staring at the red-bearded face. He had listened a long time, and he was amazed at Thor's command of this branch of history, ancient and modern.

"You seem to know an awful lot about this creature," Connor said, curiosity coming through. "How come?"

Thor was still leaning forward. He had not moved. "The Leviathan is one of the great legends of my people," he replied.

"But this thing isn't legend. It was real, wasn't it?"

"Yes. But there is also much legend. And among my people there is a story told often to me when I was a boy."

"What story?"

"A story told to me by my grandfather," Thor responded, his eyes focusing distantly. "A story the old man would tell me often, to teach me the meaning of courage and strength."

Connor said nothing, waiting.

"My grandfather was a good man," Thor continued, a slow nod. "Though he died when I was only three or four, I remember him well. I remember his heart." He turned to the window. "He was a strong man, even for my people. Even taller than I am, and heavier. He had never been defeated in cannon throwing at the games until the year of his death. But he was already old when I was a child."

He hesitated, smiling. "He was young once, I suppose. But I only remember him with his long white hair and white beard flowing like a snow mound from his head. Always strong. Mythic. A giant who reminded me of the heroes of old. He could appear a hard man, and revealed little to the world. But his heart . . . his heart was great."

A silence passed.

"He would come to me often when I was a child," Thor said softly. "Or I would crawl onto his lap at night as he sat beside the window, gazing out over the gray sea. It was only then, when we were alone in the gray evening, that he would show me his heart. When there was no one else who might mock his secret words." The gigantic Norseman paused somberly. "Yes. Then he would talk freely, and speak of heroes of old, of love and honor and strength. He would tell me the old stories of our people. Men who fought great battles and won. Men who saw evil as evil and good as good, and who fought for what they believed. It was his dream, he told me late one night when the sun was low, to die as they had died. Doing battle with evil. Giving angry blow for angry blow to finish the fight, overcoming with his last breath."

Thor looked down, frowning.

"Often enough, he told me the same story," he continued. "The story of *Ragnarok*. Dusk of the gods. And I would listen with a child's wide eyes."

Connor waited. "*Ragnarok*? The last battle between good and evil?"

A nod, and Thor continued, "Yes. It is the story of Asgard and a leviathan named Jormungand who would rise from the sea at the end of time." He paused. "Jormungand was the Midgard Serpent, the most terrible of all the evil creatures of the deep. It was horrible and strong, and all of Asgard trembled at the sight of it. But there was a single Norse god, the strongest and the one who held the most generous and noble heart, who refused to tremble before it. He was angered that the Serpent dared to threaten the lives of the innocent. So alone he arose from his throne, took up his hammer, and went forth to do battle against it.

"On the great ice field beside the sea, they met. Never before had the world witnessed such a conflict. Long was the battle, and uncertain. It continued for a day and a night.

"Asgard's strongest defender struck the Midgard Serpent again and again, hard blows that would have shattered mountains. But Jormungand would not die. Instead it coiled around the titan and struck with its killing venom, venom that had burned mountains and valleys alike into dust. Eye to eye and shoulder to shoulder, in thunderous blows they struck, grappling to the last, carrying the grim battle to a grim death. On and on it went, seeming to last forever until both were all but dead in the grip of the other, the strongest heart alone destined to overcome. In the long and terrible end the Norse god staggered to his feet, rising up and raising his hammer high. Then he brought it down once more to deliver a last, thunderous blow, finally crushing the head of the beast. And the Serpent died."

Connor was captured by Thor's somber aspect.

"The god staggered back nine steps," he whispered, "the battle won. But he was also dying, defeated by the Serpent's venom. His great, heroic strength, strength that many thought had been inexhaustible, was gone forever. It had been the price for his victory. And, knowing the fingers of death were curling around him, he lifted his hammer high and drove it into a mountain, burying it deep into the earth to leave a testament of his courage. Then, succumbing at last to the Serpent's poison, the titan fell to the ground and died."

Connor waited, watching the brooding face. "So it's strength of heart that won the battle," he said, breaking the strange but comfortable silence. "Strength of heart. Courage."

"Yes." Thor nodded. "Strength of heart. Courage. Love. Honor." He smiled narrowly. "It's only a story, a myth of my people. But truth does not change, I think."

Silence.

Thor bent his head, somber. "It is a story that meant much to me when I was a child," he continued, a light laugh. "And perhaps it still does. Perhaps that's why I believe each man has his own destiny with *Ragnarok*. A worthy death delivered to him by God only if his life, his courage, and his heart have earned it for him."

A vague fear settled over Connor. "What's it like, living your life like that?"

Thor smiled. "It is a gray, lonely place, my friend. But any place can feel like home . . . if you stay long enough."

Silent, Connor met the resolute gaze.

Thor rose, gazing down a moment. "I will return to the tower tonight by the old riverbed." He smiled. "It is a long ride, but I feel a need to be alone tonight . . . in the cold. Beneath the stars. But I will come back later tomorrow and tell Jordan a story." He smiled. "Perhaps I will tell him the story of Jormungand and Ragnarok."

Thor seemed to shrug off the aspect of gloom as he turned from the table, the crest of his shaggy head only slightly lower than the eight-foot ceiling. As he opened the door, Connor again found his voice.

"Hey, Thor."

The giant turned in the doorway, waiting. Connor saw that the darkness outside was blocked out by his titanic form, overcome by the red-bearded face, the Nordic image of strength.

"You never said which Norse god it was that Jormungand killed," Connor added, staring.

Thor hesitated, smiling faintly.

"It was Thor," he said, smile fading beneath a suddenly somber gaze. "It was Thor that Jormungand killed."

Vaguely disturbed by the late-night conversation with Thor, Connor walked silently into Jordan's room, uncertain of the reason for his fear or why he wanted to make sure his boy was secure and warm.

And as he bent to pull the covers higher, Connor sensed Jordan gazing up at him. Connor smiled, sitting down on the bed and laying an arm across the tiny figure. There was a moment of warm silence.

"We're friends, ain't we?" Jordan whispered.

Connor laughed lightly, nodding. "Yeah, buddy, we're friends. We're best friends."

Jordan stared, smiling.

"I tell you what." Connor bent slightly closer. "When we go fishing tomorrow, we'll try and catch one of those real big trout. Then we'll clean it with our knives and cook it for supper!"

Jordan laughed. "Yeah! That would be fun!" Then he paused, adding quietly, "I always want to be with you, Daddy."

Connor stared, shaken, not knowing what to say. It took him a moment to recover from the four-year-old's words. Then he leaned forward and spoke, "And I always want to be with you, buddy."

Jordan stared up, serious.

"I've got a good idea," Connor whispered. "Maybe you and me could have a secret sign? Something that just the two of us know about? How's that? Is that a good idea?"

Jordan smiled. His eyes widened.

"All right, let's do this," Connor said, raising his hand, fingers spread to the air. "Do you think we can keep this sign as a secret?" He whispered, "It's got to be something that just you and me know about!"

Jordan laughed, raising his hand.

Gently, Connor placed their hands together. "All right, then. When I hold up my hand, it'll mean I'm always thinking about you! And when you hold up your hand, it will mean that you're always thinking about me! How do you like that for a sign?"

Jordan grinned and pressed his hand firmly against Connor's. "Yeah. I like that."

"Okay," Connor continued. "That's enough for right now. Because you need to go nite-nite. Then in the morning we'll go fishing, and Thor is going to come back in the afternoon and tell you a big story."

A pause with bright, wide-awake eyes staring up. "Daddy, are we ever going home? Because Mommy says that . . . She says that this isn't our real home. She says we've got a real home."

Stunned, Connor hesitated. "Yeah, buddy. Sure, sure we're going home. Just as soon as I finish my job."

"But where is it?"

"Where's what?"

"Home," Jordan whispered. "Where's home?"

With a sad gaze, Connor leaned forward. "Well, our real home is real, real far away from here. You don't remember it because you were just a baby when you were there. You weren't a big boy like you are now. But it's in the mountains where it's warm and where there's grass and trees and streams. It's where you can throw rocks in the streams and play in the woods. And where you can have a dog, and a cat, and maybe we can even build a tree house! And we'll all be together! You and me and Mommy!"

Jordan's wide eyes stared. "I hope we can go home real soon."

Connor nodded, touching the small face in his weathered hand. "We will, buddy. I promise."

"You promise?"

"Yeah. I promise."

Jordan smiled. "And you always keep your promise."

Connor gazed down, gently placed a hand on his son's chest. "Yeah, buddy, I always keep my promise."

Chapter 9

His face was as lifeless and white as the belly of a dead fish, the stark hair cut almost to his scalp. Although his manner was calm, his fists were tight, like a man holding back a pathological urge to strike. It was an uncommon look for a scientist.

"Now," Sol Tolvanos whispered, leaning over Frank. "I am ordering you to turn over control of GEO to my people! Either that or you will be placed under military arrest!"

Frank shook his head. "GEO isn't going to obey you," he answered, refusing to look up from his seat. "And neither will I."

Shouting, the Russian slammed his hand onto the table, snatching up an ashtray. In a rage he flung the thick glass plate to the tile floor where, to Frank's sharp astonishment, it didn't shatter. It hit the floor and bounced high into the air, straight up, spinning like a Frisbee to land on the desk again, where it spun for another second, settling in the same place it had been. For a split second even Tolvanos seemed shocked.

Frank used it. "If you're such a brilliant physicist, Tolvanos, you should be able to figure GEO out all by yourself." He smiled. "After all, it's only a computer, isn't it?"

"Don't insinuate that I am a fool, Doctor," Tolvanos muttered, staring through opaque white eyes. "I know that GEO is a unique entity. And I admit, reluctantly, that it is the peak of artificial intelligence. An actual learning computer with its own independent neurally copied network personality. A machine, certainly. But almost a living being." He paused. "Yes, Dr. Frank, I know everything about GEO."

Frank's face went cold as a gravestone.

"And I must say"—Tolvanos shook his head—"that it was rather ghoulish of you to electromagnetically copy your dead wife's neural web for the Logic Core. Isn't that a bit, ah, Frankensteinish? Even for you?"

With a slow blink Frank looked up. "Rachel designed GEO," he heard himself say. "She was the one who invented neural networking. It seemed like the right thing to do."

"Really?" Tolvanos replied. "If I didn't know better, Doctor, I would say that you copied your wife's neural network so that you could continue to have her at your side." He paused. "How unfortunate that her untimely death prevented her from seeing GEO's ultimate completion. An automobile accident, wasn't it? Yes, truly unfortunate. Especially since she did, indeed, possess a brilliant mind. She might have been proud of you."

Frank's face was whiter. "I'm sure she is," he said.

Tolvanos stared down. "And now I ask you again, Doctor. Will you not do your job as a professional? Will you not surrender voice control of GEO to my team?"

"No," Frank returned the tone. "I won't. GEO belongs to me."

Adler was sitting sorely to the side. "Frank, your behavior is completely without justification. It is childish, petulant, and inexcusable, and you are making me regret ever signing you on to the project!"

"I hate it."

Frank tried to resist the fatigue, but they had been pressuring him for over an hour in an argument that began in Adler's office and proceeded to the Observation Room to find Hoffman and Chesterton gone and GEO locked in self-diagnosis. Tolvanos had ordered Frank to surrender voice control. Frank had refused. A stalemate. Things had heated up quickly.

Frank knew that Tolvanos had been, until recently, the leading researcher in Russia's illegal development of germ warfare, a science outlawed since the United Nations Treaty of 1972. Now, with the Soviet Union essentially defunct, the Russian was a freelance researcher working for the private defense industry, selling his skills to the highest bidder.

And his skills were, indeed, in high demand. Primarily because, in the secretive community of germ warfare, Tolvanos was a legend.

He deserved the reputation. He had achieved devastating and exceedingly deadly success in highly contagious viral infections that could cause long, lingering suffering before an utterly unalterable death.

It was the work of genius because Tolvanos's viral weapons were far more effective than simple nerve gas agents that merely killed. Not only did his shifting antigen viruses eliminate the effectiveness of a single soldier, but the long incubation period exposed even more soldiers, ambulatory personnel, nurses and doctors in critical care of the ailing patient, in turn infecting them also to kill on an increasing geometric curve.

Almost from the start of Leviathan, Stygian Enterprises had requested Tolvanos's presence and input, but Frank had refused to let the Russian join the effort. He had even threatened to back out and work for similar projects under development by the Germans and Japanese if Stygian didn't accede to his demands. In the end the company had blinked, cutting Tolvanos out of the loop. It was something the Russian physicist had never forgotten or forgiven.

Now, however, he was back to claim his share of the game. And to claim his share of the profit that Stygian would make for selling Leviathan to the American government. Frank knew Tolvanos wasn't insane, just utterly committed to furthering his own game plan.

Sweat on the Russian's skin gleamed like glass on white satin. "I do not play games, Doctor," he whispered. He shook his head ominously, as if the words should be sufficient for an intelligent man. "I am a man of science, Frank. So I do not play games in this arena. There is far too much at stake. And if you are half as intelligent as I perceive you to be, you should know that resistance to my will is futile."

Frank laughed, but he was wishing fervently that Chesterton would arrive and put these people in their place. But Frank had a bad feeling about that, too, observing the stranger in the dark green Army uniform. Although Frank didn't understand rank, he knew the broad gold insignia on the collar indicated something serious. Just as the twenty men behind him in SWAT-type black fatigues indicated something serious. This project was, after all, guarded by the United States Army. Chesterton could always be outranked.

Adler rose from his chair. "Frank," he leaned over the computer chair, "why won't you cooperate? I have already told you that we will take every possible precaution."

Frank stalled for Chesterton's imminent arrival. "Cement the cavern corridors like Chesterton said to do, and then I'll run all the tests you want. But not until then."

"I am not a fool, young man!" Adler growled. "I know that you will never agree to test the creature yourself. You irrationally believe that it is too dangerous. But you overestimate Leviathan's power! You don't even understand your own creation! So I only ask you to turn over what is not yours to keep. You do not own the computer! You do not own GEO! You designed it, yes, and programmed it, but it was bought and built by Stygian Enterprises. And despite your mutinous actions, Frank, we will eventually find a way to circumvent the Voice Control System. I simply want to avoid the unnecessary expenditure of manpower which will further delay tests."

Frank caught something in Adler's voice.

"Why is it so important that we test immediately?" he asked. The old man hesitated. But Frank knew the answer, knew it immediately, and knew it all went back to the beginning of the project when, as Frank had understood, the American government decided to develop the ultimate biological military deterrent. Originally the plan was coded "Project: Doomsday," and was later altered to "Project: Leviathan."

Yes, the title had changed, but not the purpose: *The Purpose of Project Doomsday, by Executive Order, shall be to create the ultimate biological military deterrent, a controllable biological weapons system ultimately unstoppable against any standing army but which does not result in biological or radioactive poisoning of the atmosphere or subjugated territories.*

Nor had America been the only nation to think of using Electromagnetic Chromosomal Manipulation for such a purpose.

There was first this facility, run by Stygian Enterprises, the private defense contractor that had bought Frank's services. Then there was a Japanese company, Yashima Cyberspace Technology, which also stood on the threshold of ECM success. And finally, a West German company located in Frankfurt.

For the past year it had been an around-the-clock race to determine who would be the first to develop the biological warfare technology, the ultimate military deterrent.

"What has Yashima done?" Frank asked, centering on Adler.

The old man gazed down. "What Yashima may or may not have done is none of your concern, Doctor."

"I think it is."

Tolvanos spoke. "They have broken through to the other side, Dr. Frank."

Frank focused on the indifferent face.

"Yes," Tolvanos continued, solemn, "they have beaten you, Doctor. They have done what you could not do. Yashima has demonstrated without question that a vertebrate can be genetically and ultimately enhanced for purposes of total war."

Frank searched the white eyes. "What do you mean? What did Yashima do?"

"Yashima crossed the void, Doctor," the Russian replied. "They used ECM to genetically alter a superior beast of prey and they succeeded. Succeeded tremendously, I might add."

Frank held a defiant silence.

"Dr. Tolvanos," Adler began, shifting nervously, "I don't think—"

"Yes, Doctor," the Russian physicist continued coldly. "Until yesterday Yashima Technology was the sole possessor of a thoroughly tested weapon of war created by Electromagnetic

Chromosomal Manipulation." And the Russian said silently: *You have failed, Dr. Frank. You have failed because I was not working at your side.*

Frank wasn't touched. "I asked you a question, Doctor. What exactly did Yashima do?"

A pause, and Tolvanos laughed harshly, retreating from any semblance of respect. "Yashima created the world's first genetically enhanced beast of prey, Doctor. A beast specifically created and genetically altered so that its single reason for existing would be to wreak havoc on an army. That is *exactly* what Yashima did."

"You're lying."

"No," Tolvanos replied, shaking his head. "Hardly, Doctor. I never lie about such things. The Japanese successfully altered a lion, I think it was, into something the world has never seen. And never wanted to see, I assure you. A singularly vicious creature, according to our most reliable intelligence reports. It weighed well over two thousand kilos and was of a rather startling transformation of structure. It did not so much resemble a lion, in the end, I think. It was almost like a god, or something from another world. It was vastly, almost unbelievably intelligent. Strong beyond belief. And with a superior weapons arsenal that included thermal senses and night vision. Means-testing on its claws and fangs revealed a level of hardness that surpassed diamond molecularly molded around steel cores. Not one-tenth so powerful as Leviathan, no, but still strong and armored enough to survive light weapons fire. In truth, a creature of phenomenal power." He frowned. "Now, fortunately for us, it is gone. Along with Yashima's computers, records, everything else. The result of a sudden and tragic accident."

A hushed silence dominated the Observation Room.

"What kind of accident, Tolvanos?"

"An explosion, Doctor," the Russian replied. "It seems that someone from Stygian Enterprises sabotaged the facility with what may have been the largest nonnuclear explosion in the history of the world." His stare was utterly devoid of emotion. "Suddenly . . . no more research facility. No more creature. No more nothing."

Frank turned to stare at Adler. "I can't believe you people did that," he whispered. "Chesterton will absolutely kill you when he finds out about this. He is going to go absolutely ape-crazy ballistic."

Trembling, Adler whirled, glaring at Tolvanos. "Dr. Tolvanos! I believe enough has been said about whatever . . . ah . . . *accidents* may have—"

"So it is clear, Doctor," Tolvanos continued, "America is currently losing the arms race. I am employed by the American government through Stygian Enterprises to ensure that such does not happen."

"You work for the Russians, Tolvanos," Frank muttered.

"Oh no, Doctor," the Russian replied. "Please, do not be mistaken. My previous national loyalties have nothing to do with my current loyalties." He paused, laughing lightly. "You yourself can remember how, ah, generously the German rocket scientists of World War II, who were only days from perfecting the V-2 which would have burned England to dust and changed the fate of the war, were received by your own government. They were lauded as heroes, and American cities, streets, and civic centers were named after them. But if these same scientists had succeeded in fully developing the V-2 rocket before 1944, Germany would have decisively won the war. And within a few more years, Hitler would have possessed the intercontinental ballistic missile along with the hydrogen bomb that it would deliver. Then, to be cruel, Hitler would have crossed the Atlantic to invade American soil. And quite probably would have won." He paused.

"But after the Allied invasion at Normandy, the war was lost," he added. "And Hitler's famed V-2 rocket scientists were offered American citizenships and received into NASA and every other private and military enterprise with open arms. Because military and monetary expertise overrule all other command-ments, Doctor. Or sins. And for that reason, Frank, I am commit-ted to ensuring that your government is the first and only country to possess the power of Leviathan. I would have preferred to have worked beside you. But you refused. So the situation eventually worked to my advantage. You defied the mandate of the project, refusing to cooperate, so you have been outcast. And now I alone possess the power of the Dragon."

"So what are you saying?" Frank asked. "You're saying that we have to rush the tests and confirm Leviathan's true potential so Stygian can close their deal with the government?" He shook his head, arguing the point in desperation. "But why can't other nations share the technology? Other nations share atomic weapons, and everyone uses treaties to control their use! The same could be done with Leviathan!"

"No, no, Doctor." Tolvanos frowned. "What I am saying is that the time has come for you to reluctantly accept the truth." He paused, an exasperated professor staring upon a disappointing student. "We have surpassed the age of treaties, Frank. And you are far, far too intelligent not to realize it. Neither America, nor the powers which control America, can any longer risk the tenuous security of treaties. That is the truth which your moral blindness has prevented you from recognizing from the beginning." Tolvanos hesitated, frowning. "The simple truth that has evaded you, Doctor, is this: America can, and will, use Leviathan to control the entire world. That is why America does not wish for any other country to have its equal."

Frank stared at the Russian. "But . . . but how are they going to do that? If America ever used Leviathan against any country that possessed a nuclear arsenal there would be an immediate nuclear response!"

"And how could that be, Doctor?" Tolvanos posed, pausing as if he were willing to wait forever for an answer. "Leviathan is simply a beast. It would come from the sea and return to the sea. No one would know that America was responsible for the atrocity. Leviathan would rise from the ocean as the beast of ancient lore to destroy a single city, army, nation, or even a targeted individual. And absolutely nothing on the face of the earth, save a nuclear holocaust, could stop it." He paused. "No nation would ever call down a nuclear holocaust upon itself. So they would be left with conventional defenses which would, of course, be wholly inefficient. And eventually, within a few short years, the entire world could be brought to the feet of the very men who control the Dragon."

Frank closed his eyes. "I'll talk," he said simply. "I swear to you, I'll talk. I won't let you do this."

He felt Tolvanos staring upon him, almost sympathetically. "No, Doctor. I doubt . . . very seriously . . . that you shall talk."

Frank looked up hard. "You're crazy, Tolvanos. You people can kill me if you want. I know you can. But it won't make any difference because Leviathan *can't be controlled*! Leviathan has brought itself into its own Hunter-killer Mode, and it *cannot* differentiate between friendly and nonfriendly organisms! Don't you get it? Leviathan's unstable DNA promoted itself ahead of programming, and it doesn't have any program parameters to limit prey. It's not going to work with anybody! If Leviathan ever gets out of that cavern it's going to kill every living thing on the face of the earth! Everything! Including us! Because Leviathan actually believes with all its heart that it has to kill every other living thing on the planet in order to survive! It's something that can't be corrected! It's too late to undo what's been done!"

"I don't agree with you, Doctor," Tolvanos said. "And I will tell you that I am not, as you say, *crazy*." He stared down. "*Crazy* is a man who throws away his life because he will not finish an experiment that will be finished with or without his help."

Adler spoke. "The situation is out of your hands, Doctor."

"Nothing is out of my hands!" Frank shouted, glaring. Tolvanos had taken his headset, but Frank knew that the panel microphone of GEO was still activated. "Nothing! All I have to do is tell GEO to wipe out everything in her memory and the backups, and then you won't have anything but an uncontrollable creature. And you'll *never* be able to find the right formula to repeat the genetic transformation of another Komodo dragon. It'll be *gone*!"

Tolvanos froze and Adler paled, sweat gleaming on his face. Instantly Frank realized that they had never anticipated this movement. They had been caught completely off guard.

A long moment passed as Frank gazed over the edge, his entire life's work almost gone with a single command. Then slowly, entreatingly, Adler lifted a hand. "Listen, son," he began, "let's discuss this rationally. I respect you, Frank. Truly, I do. You're . . . a great scientist. Certainly you don't think I would ever go against your—"

"What is going on in here?"

Frank felt a long withheld breath leave his chest as a livid Chesterton—followed by a big black man, Lieutenant Barley—stalked into the room. They were followed closely by two Rangers.

Shocked by Chesterton's vivid anger and Barley's glaring, warrior aspect, Tolvanos's science team parted like water to leave a wide and cautious wake. As Barley came through the door he sharply turned his head toward the two soldiers behind him.

"Secure it!" he snapped.

Instantly the Rangers divided solidly to either side of the exit, M-16s frozen at port arms. Their intent was immediately clear: Absolutely no one, armed or unarmed, was leaving this room. Dead or alive.

Tolvanos and Adler stepped backward toward the control matrix as Chesterton halted beside Frank, glaring down, and Frank saw a quick suspicion flicker in the dark eyes. Somehow, Frank knew that Chesterton understood, had even expected this. Then Chesterton turned with a menacing frown toward Tolvanos. His voice was low.

"And just who are you?"

Adler gathered himself, spoke distinctly: "Dr. Tolvanos is . . . uh, replacing Frank as head of the science team, Colonel. In fact, all the members of Frank's team have been replaced. I believe the strain has become too much for them."

"*Nobody's* replacing *anybody* as long as I'm around, Mr. Adler. This isn't musical chairs at a Halloween carnival. We're running a secure facility here, and I'm still in charge of who comes and goes."

A voice came from the side, entering the debate. "I am afraid that you are not ultimately in charge, Colonel. Not any longer."

Imperious, the portly man in the dark green uniform had spoken for the first time. And Frank focused on him; the man was well into his fifties and much shorter than Chesterton, his short black hair heavy with gray. Behind him, the black-clad soldiers stepped forward.

"I must remind you, Colonel Chesterton," he added, somewhat cautiously, "that this project remains under Executive Command. And I inform you that I am now your commanding supervisor."

Chesterton stared, his eyes flickered over the insignia. "Blake?" he asked, peering. "Colonel Blake of the National Security Agency?"

Blake nodded.

Implacable, Chesterton shook his head. "This facility doesn't answer to the NSA, Blake. It's under Pentagon control."

"Not any longer, Colonel Chesterton."

"What do you mean?" Chesterton's voice hardened. "What do you mean that it's not under Pentagon control any longer? Who gave the NSA authority to take over my operation?"

Blake stepped forward, removing papers from inside his uniform. He handed them to Chesterton with a solemn air, clasping both hands patiently behind his back as Chesterton read. He was forced to wait a long time. Finally Chesterton looked up.

"I don't like this, Blake."

"That is an Executive Order, Chesterton."

"Neither the NSA, the CIA, the Director of Central Intelligence, nor any subordinate of the DCI has the authority to control an Army weapons system," Chesterton said, dead steady. "Not unless they do it according to Act 186-4 of the Senate Intelligence Oversight Committee of 1976, which requires that the United States Army supervises and maintains and ultimately controls the use of all such weapons systems."

"Act 186 has no relevance to this situation because it has not yet been demonstrably proven that Leviathan is a weapons system, Colonel Chesterton. That Executive Order grants me the authority to oversee all further research. And further, in case you have forgotten, I *am* a colonel in the United States Army."

"Blake, you can rest assured. That thing *is* a weapons system."

"But tests have not proven that to be a fact, Chesterton."

A long pause and Chesterton growled, "Well, this may be an Executive Order, Blake, but I'll need to confirm it before any of you take a single step in this facility."

Blake responded with force. "That paper comes from the highest level, Colonel. The very, very highest level. And in case you didn't notice, it's been initialed by your own superiors in the Pentagon." Blake lifted his chin, pushing it forward. "I formally advise you, Colonel Chesterton, that you are relieved of duty."

"Am I?" Chesterton snarled, stepping into it. "Barley!"

Barley snapped his head to the door. "Lock and load!"

Instantly the two Rangers loudly chambered rounds into the M-16s, faces dead calm. And Barley's aspect became utterly dangerous. He placed a hand solidly on the Beretta pistol at his waist, standing behind Chesterton like granite.

Blake stepped back and shouted to the black-clad MPs. "Lock and load!"

Chambered rounds thundered across the room from the MPs, and Frank felt his head go light. Then with a movement too quick to follow Barley had jerked out his pistol and thumbed the hammer back instantly to place the barrel point-blank against the nose of the MP lieutenant.

With the touch Barley's finger had taken all the slack from the trigger of the semiautomatic, and the MP's face went stark white. His hands dropped limply from his weapon.

Barley's voice was so low it was almost inaudible.

"You'll be the first," he whispered to the MP, a cold nod.

The MP lieutenant nodded, raising his hands to his sides. Then he gestured quickly, almost frantically, to the rest of the black-clad soldiers who were obviously not regular Army or they wouldn't have surrendered, and they also lowered their weapons.

Implacable and vengeful and terrible, Chesterton stepped forward until he was face to face with Blake. Frank suddenly realized that if anybody got killed, Barley would put the MP lieutenant at the head of the crowd. And Chesterton would personally take out Blake, no matter what else happened in the room.

Chesterton's angry voice rumbled in the tense silence. "You

want to go head to head with me, Blake? You want to see who's really been relieved?" Blake blinked, his face white. Took another step backward.

"Be . . . b-b-be assured, Colonel Chesterton, that . . . that I-I-I've been informed of your credentials!" Blake drew a quick breath. "I know very well that you're . . . that y-y-you're West Point. Fourth in your class. Just as I know that y-y-you demanded . . . very, very adamantly demanded . . . to command a Special Force Battalion during Vietnam."

Chesterton frowned, eyes darkening.

"Your decision was certainly noble, Colonel," Blake continued, standing more solidly. "And I know that you . . . ah, personally led your battalion to more campaign victories than any other commander of the Vietnam era. Ultimately even gaining control of the Mekong during '68." Blake's chin lifted. "But your stubborn decision to remain in combat, Colonel, also . . . ah, also stalled your career. Your determination to command the soldiers of a Special Forces Battalion in the Vietnam Conflict was—"

"It was a *war*, boy. Not a *conflict*."

Blake hesitated. "Yes, of course . . . but, ah, your stubborn determination to command a Special Forces Battalion during the . . . the *war* . . . removed you from a circle of career-minded candidates." Blake paused. "Candidates who laid the groundwork for advancement while you were out of the country. And, just to remind you, Chesterton, you are still a Lieutenant Colonel, an 06. While I am an 05. A full bird. So I have the rank, Chesterton. And an Executive Order. And the authority of the Pentagon! So I believe you should carefully consider just how much you are willing to defy!"

Blake glanced at the others, who seemed mesmerized by the conflict.

"I am not sure that this is even the best place for this discussion, Chesterton. But the fact remains that those orders were issued from the Executive Office and signed by your own chain of command! And, regardless of your personal objections, you are still under Pentagon control!"

Silence.

"You know," Chesterton said slowly, eyes hardening like black diamonds, and just as impenetrable, "I've never liked working with any of you guys, Blake. Because I know that whenever Black Ops takes command of good soldiers, then good soldiers get killed. I saw it in Vietnam. I saw it in Beirut. Somalia. Panama. It's always the same story. You desk-riding goons don't know the job, and you're too stupid to admit it. But some civilian who's been appointed to a Cabinet post always gives you a command."

Blake laughed. "Certainly, Colonel, someone with your consummate credentials will not disobey orders from the highest level. After all, you and I are part of the military machine."

"I'm not a machine, Blake." Chesterton leaned even farther forward, eye to eye. "I'm a gentleman and a professional soldier in the United States Army. And I have a duty to defend my men and protect my government's interests."

"As do I," Blake responded flatly.

"No you don't, Blake. You work for those clowns in the NSA who send good men to their deaths because they don't have the foggiest idea what real war is all about. You fight a war with polls and toothpicks and little flags. You have no idea what it's like to share the same foxhole and food and ammo as your men just so you can turn a hostile sector into your backyard. You don't know what it's like to watch your men die. Or what it's like to write their mammas back home to tell them the only boy they'll ever have in their entire life just died like a man."

"We're both soldiers, Colonel," Blake responded. "We are expendable assets of our government."

Chesterton's teeth gritted. "*None* of my men are expendable, Blake. And I'm going to need confirmation on this!"

"You shall have it, Colonel," Adler said, stepping forward. "In the morning we shall open communications with the Pentagon so that you can confirm whatever—"

"Open communications?" Chesterton shouted. He looked like he would strike Adler without any hesitation at all. "What do you mean 'open communications'? I've got three platoons of Rangers, and I've got the authority and equipment to communicate with my superiors whenever I deem it necessary and prudent."

"Not any longer, Colonel," Adler returned, implacable. "Colonel Blake can explain the situation."

Utterly hostile, Chesterton turned to Blake. "Well, Blake? I need an explanation right now."

"To ensure security, communications are now coded," Blake responded quickly. "They are coded with an NSA encryption known only to Mr. Adler and myself. So this facility's communications link has now been switched to an NSA satellite which comes in range every four hours. And I sincerely hope that this will not be, ah, a source of tension between us. It is only a temporary procedure."

"You're pushing it, Blake. You are on very, very dangerous ground."

Blake swayed. "The Army is like a machine, Colonel. It is a machine of men. You know that, and I know that. So we do as we are told. We do as we are told or the machine breaks down. And orders, in the end, are orders. Especially when they are issued from the highest office in the land."

A slow acknowledgment settled over Chesterton. Frank saw it coming and tried to stop it. "Don't let them do this, Chesterton!" he interjected. "They're going to wake up Leviathan!"

Chesterton gazed down, frowning. And without even looking, Barley knew what Chesterton had decided. The big lieutenant slowly lowered his pistol from the face of the MP commander, still staring the man in the eye.

"Everything is under control, Colonel Chesterton," Adler said, forceful again. "You are, after all, a professional. You are part of the, ah, machine. The simple truth is that you are under orders from your own government to submit to Colonel Blake's command. But I do assure you, for your own peace of mind, that we will use every possible security measure." He turned to gesture. "Dr. Tolvanos is the leading man in this field, and he understands the creature quite well. But first I suggest that you remove Dr. Frank, at least temporarily, from the Observation Room. He appears to be overstressed. Then we can discuss this matter more thoroughly and iron out any details that might concern you. Afterwards we—"

Frank rose, startling everyone. "GEO acknowledge my voice!" he said quickly.

"NO!" Adler bellowed and leaped forward with Tolvanos screaming beside him. Frank sensed a dozen bodies leaping on him from behind.

"Voice identification confirmed as Dr. Frank," came the soft reply that somehow penetrated the screams.

"GEO!" Frank screamed, defensively raising his hands. "Erase all—" Adler's fist slammed into the side of his head, rocketing him back into grappling arms that pulled him to the ground, muffling him, burying his voice beneath shouts that tore through the Observation Room like a bomb blast.

Stunned, Frank caught, *"GEO does not understand Dr. Frank's command. GEO requests that Dr. Frank repeat command for implementation."*

It was the last thing Frank heard, shocked by the sight of Adler's snarling face above him, the huge white fist coming down again to . . .

Blackness.

Connor gently stroked Beth's long brown hair, soft and luxurious tendrils that he combed back from her forehead with his fingers. They lay in the blue-sheeted bed, side by side, bathed in the gray-white light of an early dawn. Sleep had never come to him through the long night.

He had stared at the ceiling for hours, remembering what Thor had said, thinking it through over and over while thin shadows, indistinct and snakish, crawled across the ceiling. He had watched the shadows a long time, becoming more aware of Beth's head on his chest, thinking more and more of Jordan sleeping blissfully, helplessly, in the adjoining room. He was responsible for their safety, the thought came to him again and again. But he couldn't understand why he was so worried.

Leviathan, the older man had said. But what did it mean?

Connor wondered at what relation the name might have to the project hidden in the cavern. *What have they done? Surely they couldn't have—no, that is impossible,* he told himself, again and again. *That is completely impossible.* But what did it mean? What was Chesterton so afraid of? Were Beth and Jordan in danger? And what should he do about it? *Was* there anything he could do? It had been a cacophony of questions through the slow, dark night. Unanswered questions, questions that plagued him with guilt and confusion, and even more guilt. Then he felt soft brown eyes staring at him through the gloom.

"Are you still awake?"

"Yes," Connor replied. "I couldn't sleep."

Beth's face was shadowy in soft white light as she turned to him, lifting herself onto an elbow. Her other forearm rested across his chest. She stared at him, inches away.

"What is it?" she whispered.

Connor touched her cheek, smiling. "It's nothing."

"Yes, it is." Awakening quickly. "It's something."

Connor sniffed, leaning his head back against the pillow. She continued to stare at him. "It's nothing, really," he said softly. "I was just thinking of maybe leaving this place a little early. Maybe quitting."

Even in the dark he could read the surprise on her face. "Well, you know I'd love that," she replied. "And Jordan would love it. He's never even known what a real home is. But I'm more interested in why you suddenly want to leave. What's disturbing you?"

"I'm just tired of this place," Connor said easily. "I'm thinking that maybe we've already got enough money to buy us a place. Maybe even a farm. Somewhere in the country. A place where Jordan can have a real life. Maybe it's time we moved on."

"Are you serious? We'll just leave?"

"Sure," Connor said, smiling. "We'll just leave. They can always find somebody else to do my job. I don't mean anything to them. They've got lots of money."

She laughed. "Well then, when I go into work I might as well get on the NAV-COM satellite hookup with New York. I'll need to make contact with Mother back in Kentucky and let her know we're coming."

Connor looked narrowly. "Your mother?"

Beth's laugh was beautiful. "Come on, Connor. You know that you love her. The two of you get along great. And we wouldn't have to live with her for that long, anyway. Maybe a couple of months. And living on a real farm would be great for Jordan." She stared. "He doesn't need to stay here any longer, anyway. This is no place for a little boy."

"Yeah, I know. I worry about him a lot."

"I know you do. And sometimes . . . sometimes I think that you worry too much. Jordan *knows* how much you love him, Connor. He knows that you love him more than anything else in the world. You're always telling him, and showing him. And he remembers all of it. I don't think there's ever been a little boy who had a more loving father."

Connor stared at the ceiling. He was touched, and yet something cut deep into his heart with the words. The shadows leaped suddenly to life, crawling, writhing. Connor felt his face harden, knowing that whatever had haunted him through the long night was awakening more and more with the approaching dawn, or day.

Beth's gaze narrowed. "What is it? You're worried about something."

"No," Connor responded quietly, shaking his head. "I'm not worried about anything. I'm just getting tired of this place. The ice. The cold. Nothing to do but work. Jordan doesn't have anybody to play with. And I'm pretty certain that we've made enough money to buy us a little place. Maybe not the kind of place we really wanted. But good enough. And I can always find another job when we get back to the States. Make up the rest."

Silence.

"Would you ever worry about Thor?" she asked finally, falling into her tendency to talk of friendships whenever he mentioned moving. "He'll be all alone without you as a friend."

"Thor will be all right," Connor said softly. "He told me some things last night. He's not going to be here forever. He'll probably be leaving this place pretty soon, too."

"He seems very lonely."

Connor was silent a moment. "He is, I think."

"But why? You're his friend and he visits you all the time. It doesn't seem like . . . like he should be so lonely."

Connor remembered the conversation, the depth and almost mythic power that had been captured in the ice-green eyes, the noble visage. "Thor's lonely," he said, "because there's no one else like him."

Beth grimaced. "That's so sad. He's such a wonderful person."

"Yes," Connor said softly, gently removing her hand from his chest. He sat upon the edge of the bed. "Yes, he is."

"Are you getting up already?" she asked.

"Yeah. I need to get started."

"But you haven't slept all night. You can't go all day without sleep."

Connor smiled back. "I'll be all right, Beth. I'm just going to get an early start. There's something I've got to do."

"What?" She was suspicious. "What do you have to do?"

"Nothing important," he said, smiling down. He gently kissed her cheek. "I've just got to go down into the cavern to check something out."

Chapter 10

Frank saw everything clearly after a few moments of staring at the ceiling. What at first appeared to be a hazy black cloud became more and more vivid, foggy lines tightening until the individual ceiling tiles took on a normal aspect. With a groan he put a hand to his temple and slowly sat up, angrily enduring the increasing pain.

Chesterton was sitting in a chair, staring down at him. His face was impassive. "You all right, Doctor?" he asked.

Frank felt for the communication headset at his waist.

"They took it," Chesterton added. "I'm sorry for what happened in the computer room, Frank. I jumped in and threw Adler off. Manhandled him pretty good, I think. And the rest of 'em too, for whatever it's worth. I didn't spend six years in Vietnam for nothing. But you'd already been hit." He paused. "You're something like a prisoner, Doctor."

"Something like?" Frank looked up with the words. He grimaced at another jolt of pain. "What does that mean, Chesterton? Does that mean I'm actually a prisoner in this place?"

"That's about the size of it, Frank. But it wasn't my call. Blake's running the show now, and I don't like any of it. But I have to take orders. And they're coming from way, way up the chain." He was plainly apologetic. "I really don't have any choice, Frank."

"Are you a prisoner too?"

Chesterton shook his head. "Nobody makes me a prisoner, son. They'll die if they try. But we've been put on a bad detail to secure the perimeter of the Containment Chamber and the front gate." He stared. "Blake's so-called MPs, which are really just some kind of covert CIA goon squad, are controlling the rest of the cavern. Within twelve hours they'll have relieved all my men. They're flying in more CIA mercenaries from the States. This place is being taken away from Army jurisdiction. From my jurisdiction."

Frank looked around the room. There were no speaker-receivers where he could communicate with GEO. He looked up at the ceiling again, as if checking to see if it was still there.

"Have they done the tests yet?" he asked, focusing on Chesterton.

"No. But I think they've circumvented GEO. It won't unlock completely because it's still asking about you. But they've sort of disconnected a Cray and they're rigging it up to run the Observation Room. I think they managed to turn off the Voice Control System."

"Have they flooded the cavern with oxygen?'

"No." Chesterton shook his head. "Not yet."

"Then you've got to stop them before they do, Chesterton." Frank tried to rise, leaned back suddenly on both hands. "This situation is out of control, Colonel. Stygian Enterprises or . . . or the CIA or the NSA or whoever, blew up a Japanese facility because they had succeeded with ECM. Tolvanos admitted it. He was . . . he was even proud of it."

A long pause, and Chesterton nodded. "Then it'll go before a Senate Intelligence Committee, Frank." His voice was thoughtful. "But I can't really deal with it right now. Right now I've got enough to deal with. I've got to stabilize a very bad situation."

"What time is it?"

"About 0-dark thirty."

"No, really, I need to know what time it is."

Chesterton didn't look at his watch. "It's four in the morning."

Frank spoke with difficulty. "Leviathan will achieve an

immunity to nitrogen in less than six hours, Chesterton. We've got to get off this island as fast as we can."

Silent for a moment, and Chesterton finally shifted. His voice dropped lower as he began, "And just what would you have me—"

Tolvanos entered the room, staring suddenly at Chesterton. Adler was beside the Russian, turning slowly to Chesterton. "Are we disturbing something, Colonel?" he asked.

"No," Chesterton replied. "You're not disturbing anything at all. Dr. Frank here was just waking up."

"Good," Tolvanos said, walking forward. His face was ghastly, a smiling corpse. "I would like to catch you up on events, Doctor. Things have proceeded nicely since we overrode GEO's Voice Control. Shortly we will begin final tests."

Frank caught the image of Adler smiling down, trying unsuccessfully to hide admiration of his pugilistic work: *No*, Frank thought dimly, *there is no more need for illusions.*

"Just wait a few hours, Tolvanos," Frank said, closing both eyes. "In a few hours Leviathan is going to wake up on its own. Then you can give it the last test of your life."

"The creature is enclosed in nitrogen, Doctor. It will be doing nothing until I allow it."

"Unless it develops an immunity to nitrogen."

"That is impossible."

"No, it's not impossible. With Leviathan nothing is impossible."

"It is impossible, Doctor," Tolvanos stressed. "Nitrogen in its purest form is a poisonous element. To any creature."

"Unless . . ." Frank began.

Tolvanos was still. "Yes, Doctor?"

"You're so smart, you figure it out," Frank replied, opening one eye.

Tolvanos's smile never reached his pale eyes. "I see. You wish to mock me. Well, I do not play games, Doctor. I am a scientist. Leviathan will sleep until I choose to wake it up. Which will be very, very soon."

Frank laughed, casting Chesterton a glance.

"Nitrogen molecules pass over a fibrous potassium water membrane that might have developed around Leviathan's lungs," he said, abruptly dropping his hand to stare at a frozen Tolvanos. "A large portion of the nitrogen reacts with potassium to make KNO_3. Potassium nitrate. A harmless chemical that's found in everyone. Then the stored oxygen inside Leviathan begins a measured reaction with the remaining level of nitrogen in its blood system to thin the nitrogen even more until the blood is oxygenated to one-half normal atmosphere. Or about 18 percent oxygenated. Enough for Leviathan to operate at full strength."

"Unlikely, Doctor," Tolvanos replied slowly. "And even if Leviathan could accomplish such a phenomenal mutation, it could not continue active movement forever. The beast would need the cleanly oxygenated air in its lungs for the process. The 270 liters of stored air would not last very long with the creature operating at full strength. And even the potassium nitrate, normally harmless, would eventually accumulate to a fatal level."

"Leviathan could continue long enough to rupture a door of the Containment Cavern, Tolvanos. That would give it all the oxygen it needed. Enough oxygen to ignite the carpasioxyllelene. It would clean its blood of the potassium nitrate after it escaped."

"I see no evidence that it can accomplish such a task," the Russian replied angrily. "How can you presume that the creature has the propensity for such a fantastic mutation?"

Frank laughed. "A wild guess."

"Well, I do not guess, Doctor," Tolvanos retorted. "Nor am I irresponsible as you so transparently infer. I am an accomplished scientist, just as yourself. Our major difference, Dr. Frank, is that you are restrained by a highly developed personal code of honor. While I am not so restrained." He paused. "Be assured, Doctor. I am not an evil man, and circumstances of our earlier meeting may have cast me in an improper light. But I felt provoked by your obstinance and I . . . I admit that I am sometimes too committed to my objective. It is a fault. But I tell you now that you have my genuine respect, and that I regret this event. Your prodigious, extraordinary brilliance commands international admiration, including mine. It would have been an honor to have worked beside you, Dr. Frank, instead of against you."

Frank's head was bowed, his face expressionless.

Tolvanos stared a moment, as if waiting. Then he turned and walked away, dragging a strangely submissive Adler in tow. Chesterton watched them vanish through the door, his face stoic. When they were fully gone he looked back at Frank, and Frank saw a flicker of serious intent narrow the colonel's dark eyes. He moved on it.

"You've got to do something, Chesterton," he whispered. "You've got to do something before they kill all of us."

Dr. Jason Hoffman shouted, staring at the monitor. Behind him science personnel whirled, watching, as if they expected the older man to fall from his chair before the computer panel.

Hoffman was pointing to the screen. "Did you see!" he gasped. "It-it-it *moved!*"

Immediately he was surrounded by science personnel who stood staring at the screen. But the creature was as still as the stone surrounding it. There was no shifting of the reptilian form, no cracks visible between the heavy black armor plates. Nothing could be seen but hardened scales, the muscular tail coiled tightly over the feet and long, serpentine neck.

"It *moved!* . . . I swear to you!" Hoffman whispered. "It . . . it is beginning to awaken!"

For a time everyone continued to watch, but nothing more occurred. Then they patted the old man compassionately on the shoulders before moving back to their stations. But Hoffman continued to stare, as if mesmerized, watching and knowing, knowing somehow that it was coming, had always been coming . . .

Bearing a thick coil of 440 wire, Connor strode up a cavern walkway projecting a severely overworked, harassed expression. In moments he encountered an Army lieutenant, a tall, stoic man whom Connor knew to be smart, fair, and competent.

Lieutenant Barley walked forward, lean and muscular and disciplined, the epitome of a professional soldier. Because he was both polite and efficient, Connor had always held Barley in high respect. The man smiled warmly as Connor walked up.

"What's up, Connor?"

"You guys are about to be walking around in the dark," Connor said.

"What's wrong?"

"You got two circuit breakers that are about to blow near the Containment Chamber." Connor removed two large breakers from his belt. "These have to go in or that 440 line is going to burn up and you'll be using flashlights."

Barley straightened. "Are you sure?"

"What do you mean?"

"I just mean, are you sure? We've got a new commander down here, Connor. Somebody named Blake. A real hard case. And he's got a bunch of doofus CIA MPs with him. He says nobody goes in, out, whatever. We got kind of a bad situation."

Connor wondered about Chesterton but let it pass. "Well, you're about to have a bad situation in the dark," he said, lifting the line again. He turned away. "You can tell that to Blake."

"Hold on, hold on," Barley said quickly. He paused, concentrating. "All right. Go on. But I'll have to tell Blake about it, Connor. Those are the orders. It's a tight situation down here. Even for us."

"Whatever, Barley. But I gotta change those breakers pretty quick. They're not going to stand the strain much longer."

Moving wide to the side, Barley replied, "Yeah, all right. But you be careful down there. And you need to stay away from the cavern, man. It's totally off-limits."

"I don't even need to go near the cavern," Connor replied as he moved forward. "The breaker box is up in Beta Passage. That's over two hundred yards from the cavern."

"All right." Barley said. "But be careful, Connor. If you run into a squad of Blake's MPs just have them raise me on the A-unit. I'll deal with them."

Connor waved, walking away. In ten minutes he was at the

breaker box to put his real plan in action. He haphazardly scattered electrical tools on the steel walkway. Then he reached into the breaker box, hesitated, and shut off the main power switch.

Instantly total darkness descended through the cavern, and panicked shouts echoed along the hallways. Connor ran fast, knowing his way even in the dark. He took a hundred strides to get close to the Containment Cavern's steel door and then he dropped beside a wall, watching the activity.

Military flashlights bounced, piercing the liquid blackness as soldiers took aim on a single defensive spot. It took Connor only three seconds to determine their point of concern.

Then he quickly spun and ran back up the tunnel as the pager system boomed with a call for emergency electrical assistance. He reached the box and hit the switch, and the corridor was flooded with light. He heard boots clattering on the walkway, approaching, and began the last phase of his act, dropping to the ground and rolling.

Barley and two soldiers came charging down the corridor. They were carrying flashlights and rifles, moving with purpose. Connor waved to them and shouted, grimacing theatrically in an expression of extreme pain. Frantically he lifted a hand, signaling.

"It's hot!" he screamed. "Don't get any closer!"

"What!" Barley shouted, stopping in place along with the entire team. They stood more than twenty feet away.

Face twisted, Connor rose, bending to one side. Making a great and dramatic display of trembling hands, he took out a high-powered circuit tester, a formidable black box that had been the scariest thing he could come up with for the stunt. Then he glanced ominously at the soldiers, the steel walkway. "If you get hit with the current, try to reach the calcite," he warned. "If you get off quick enough, it might not kill you."

Choosing not to wait for that, two of the soldiers jumped onto the calcite. But Barley nervously held his ground. "What is it?" he whispered.

Connor answered, "A wire grounded out." Tentatively, he reached into the box, touching a circuit.

"Don't kill yourself, Connor!"

"The circuit grounded into the walkway," Connor gasped, moving with infinite caution. "I got hit pretty bad. I don't know if this new breaker is going to be enough . . . or *not!*"

Connor felt in the box, narrowly watching Barley shift. The lieutenant's hands were tight on the M-16. Finally, Connor released a breath. "It's gonna hold," Connor said, turning and leaning against the wall as Barley ran up, grabbing his arm. The lieutenant's muscular face glistened with sweat.

"You gonna be okay, Connor?"

"Yeah. I got off it pretty quick. I've been hit with a 440 before . . . but . . . but I think it hurt me this time."

Barley glanced with cautious distance into the box. Looked back at Connor. "Is it fixed?"

"Yeah. I think so."

"Thank God," Barley said, "I thought that . . ." He cast an angry glance toward the Containment Cavern before looking abruptly at Connor, but Connor ignored it. He left the coil of wire lying on the ground, walked away.

"I've got to get checked out," he said, moving painfully up the tunnel. Overcome by his own theatrics, he fell into a slight limp. "I don't like the way that felt."

"Yeah," Barley said, glancing again at the box. "Do whatever you need to do, man."

Connor waved, walked away. Wounded.

But he knew now what he needed to know. He had seen the guns, the sandbags, the rest. An entire platoon of heavily armed soldiers moving frantically to throw themselves down with a desperate aim. But they hadn't been aiming up the tunnel, as if to keep something out. They had been aiming dead at the cavern's steel-reinforced door.

To keep something in.

Connor entered the Ice Station's Communications Center to find Beth angry and concentrated, leaning over a computer panel. Her dark eyes were focused, her mouth grim.

"Beth," he whispered, "we need to talk. I've got to—"

"Not now, Connor." She didn't even look up. "Something has happened to the communications link with SAT-COM." She typed quickly into a computer keyboard: HTTP://WWW.FED. WORLD.GOV.*.*

The screen displayed: ACCESS DENIED.

A silent curse twisted her lips. "What is going on here? We can't contact anybody!" She turned to glare at the four assistant civilian dispatchers. "Did any of you perform a systems scan for a viral interface?"

Heads were shaken. Apparently, everyone was as confused as she was. When Beth turned back to the computer screen her mind was visibly racing behind her dark Italian eyes.

"Beth, listen to me for—"

"Just a second, Connor." She typed quickly: HTTP:// SAT.COM. WEA-REP.*.*

Reply: ACCESS DENIED.

Beth leaned back, staring down. "This is all wrong. Why can't we get a National Weather System report? What has hit this system?" A subdued pause. "This is just absolutely not right, Connor."

"Beth," he said, reaching out to gently grip her arm, "we have to talk right now!"

A deep, calculating expression that was almost no expression at all settled over her face before she nodded. Then she leaned over the machine again, typing with infinite care: C: DOWNLOAD ALL INCOMING KEYBOARD STROKES FOR SATELLITE RELAY: DURING LAST 24 HRS .A.B.C

A short pause, then a PC began blinking continuously. Connor had no idea what she had done. When she turned to Connor she was solid and concentrated, but he still saw a faint flash of fear.

"What's happening, Connor? Somebody or something has shut down the entire Communications Center. We can't talk to anyone. Anywhere. And no one can talk to us. We can't even talk to the cavern."

Connor leaned forward. "Beth, I think we're all in serious danger. Something is very wrong in the cavern."

She stared, blinked. "What?"

Because Connor knew she was strong enough to handle almost anything, he said it plainly. "Beth, I think that those idiots have created something down there that is very, very dangerous. And it's out of control. That's why they've shut down the Communications Center. They've probably put some kind of lockout code inside the relay because they're afraid that the ground crew is about to discover what's going on, and one of us will panic and call for help. Then the whole world is going to know what's going on here."

Beth's teeth gritted as she shook her head. "But . . . but shutting down this Communications Center is stupid, Connor! All the phone lines in the cavern are routed through this place! If someone's tampered with the satellite relay they couldn't help but shut down the—" Without a second's hesitation she snatched up a phone, listening. Set it down again. Her face was almost pale. "It's dead. All the lines are dead."

Connor glanced over her shoulder to see the assistant dispatchers working without result to clear up the system. His voice was low. "We've got to get off this island, Beth. As fast as we can."

She glanced out the window of the center, toward the dock. "Can we use one of the boats?"

"No. I've already been down there. The cruisers are being guarded by those MPs, but I managed to get on board with the excuse that the cruisers held dangerous chemicals that needed electrical maintenance. But while I was there I found that the ships have been mechanically disabled. It's simple stuff, really—could probably fix it in an hour. But I can't get an hour. They'll arrest me if I try. And none of my men can fly one of the military choppers."

"Which leaves us with what?"

"The North Atlantic Sea Patrol," Connor responded. "They can get here inside two hours if we can contact them. They'll bring a cruiser big enough to get all of us off the island."

Bowing her head, Beth was motionless for a moment. Then

she looked up, dark fire flashing in her eyes. "Then I'm going to try and break this code and send out a distress, Connor. I'm going to contact the Sea Patrol for an emergency airlift of this facility."

"How are you going to do that?"

She glanced contemptuously at the panel, shook her head. "I don't know what these fools have done, Connor. But I guarantee you they can't outthink me. I'm not going to let them put my child in this kind of danger! I'll smash this security code to pieces." She studied it. "But it might take time. Maybe more time than we have. We've got to have another plan, Connor. You've got to reach Thor's tower and use his shortwave. It's not linked to this system and it might connect with Iceland."

Connor frowned. "Beth, Thor's tower is on the north coast of the island. That's almost forty miles away. Even if I take a Jeep down the dry glacier road and don't wipe out in Funstaf Ravine, it's still a two-hour drive. A lot could happen before I get back to—"

"That doesn't matter, Connor!"

Connor grimaced, staring. "All right, Beth. I'll go for the tower. But I don't want you going head to head with these military maniacs while I'm gone. Do you understand? I want you to do everything low-key!"

Beth glanced at the communications terminal, and her voice almost cracked with rage. "Yeah, Connor. I'll be discreet. I'm downloading incoming keystrokes during the last twenty-four hours to see what happened." She paused. "If these people are monitoring the system they could still get wise to what I'm doing. But that's just a risk we've got to take." She looked up at him. "Both of us."

Connor leaned forward. "Just be careful, Beth. Stay calm and very, very careful. Don't lose your temper. And don't let anyone else know what you're doing."

Her face was steady against his chest. "I won't," she whispered.

Connor kissed her on the forehead.

"I'll be back in four hours. Two hours over and two hours back. Send someone in your crew to take Jordan from the day care center and keep him at the house. Make up some excuse to cover it."

Beth nodded, raising her face to reveal an essence that was intuitive and intimate and frightening. Her voice was a low whisper that Connor had learned long ago to deeply respect.

"Something horrible is coming, Connor. I can feel it."

Connor nodded, grim.

"I'll be back as soon as I can."

Connor left the Communications Building in a thinly veiled rush. He wanted to warn the crew, but he wasn't sure what kind of panic it would cause or what kind of military retaliation would be executed so he said nothing, playing for discretion.

Without speaking to anyone at all, Connor climbed into a Jeep and he immediately gunned the engine. But as he put the vehicle in gear he was somehow touched, touched by something close, deep, and familiar, and he looked carefully across the Housing Complex to see . . .

Jordan.

His small son was standing alone in the crimson light, a lonely, solitary shape poised on the steps of the small day care center. He stared at Connor and smiled, raising his hand into the air, fingers spread wide, *I always want to be with you.*

Pain twisting his face, Connor raised his hand to the air to hold it high and strong, and he saw Jordan laugh, smiling in joy. Then Connor looked down, ignited by a silent rage that blazed white-hot in his heart into a single dominating thought: *If they do anything to harm my boy, I'll kill them. I'll kill every one of them.*

The Jeep's engine was wild and hoarse and roaring as Connor went through the open gate.

But the rage came from Connor's soul.

Chapter 11

Connor's Jeep slid to a stop at the base of Thor's tower.
Connor took the steps three at a time to enter the cylindrical chamber at the top without announcement

Dressed in a coarse woollen white shirt, Thor sat behind a crude oak desk with a fire roaring in the hearth. The giant Norseman held a long, feathered ink pen in his hand, parchment spread on the table before him. He regarded Connor's entrance without surprise.

"We're in serious trouble," Connor said.

Thor nodded. "I know."

Connor didn't know how to receive that answer so he moved on. "When they put you here on the island, didn't they leave you a shortwave radio so that you could call for help?"

"Yes." Thor replied quickly. "A radio. It is not much. But it is strong enough to access the North Atlantic Sea Patrol maritime frequencies."

"Good. We've got to get off this island as fast as possible. All of us. We don't have any time to waste."

Thor was immediately on his feet and Connor saw that he was wearing his customary leather pants and sealskin boots. Without hesitation the giant moved to a large chest, opening the top. He lifted a dusty, very primitive-looking radio from within. He set it on the desk and ran a wire to the single electrical outlet bracketed to the stone wall, plugging it in.

"I will start the generator," Thor rumbled, moving to the door. "I use it for light sometimes."

Connor pulled up a chair and sat down in front of the radio, a 1960s-era shortwave. He read the frequency band—3,000 kilohertz. "Great," he muttered. "It doesn't get any weaker than that."

He heard the gas-operated generator start up in the lower level of the tower, and he twisted the power output to maximum, watched the power red-line. He opened the receiver, twisting the signal dial to test frequencies. He received only a haze of static crackling, overloading. In another moment Thor came through the doorway, watching expectantly.

"Does it usually sound like this?" Connor asked, sweating in the heat of the room.

"No." Thor shook his head. "I used it once when I broke my leg in a fall. It was not like that."

For another long moment Connor twisted the dials, receiving nothing but haze. "This isn't right," he said. "They must be using some kind of electromagnetic countermeasure. They're jamming the signal."

"Yes. They would do that." Thor paused. "Tell me what I can do."

"We need a boat," Connor whispered. He flipped the radio on its face, quickly removing the screws on the back. "I've got to get Beth and Jordan and the rest of my crew off this island. And you too. Something is very wrong in that cavern, and I don't think any of us are safe here." A pause. "I know we're not."

Connor tossed the back of the radio aside like a Frisbee.

Thor asked, "If they are jamming the frequency, what can you do?"

"Blast through it. That's the easiest way to defeat it. All they're doing is throwing a lot of cross-current electromagnetic activity into the air. But we've got something on our side. We're pretty far from the Ice Station and we've got the mountains between us and the base, so that's going to cut off some of their signal. But then again, this old radio doesn't have much power." He glanced around. "Do you have any wire?"

118 JAMES BYRON HUGGINS

"Wire?" Thor scowled.

"Yeah, wire."

"What kind of wire?"

"Any kind of wire."

Without a word Thor turned, descending the stairs. And Connor was working on the back of the radio again, removing a transistor. He uncoiled the wire wrapped around the loopstick, stretching two feet of it from the back. Then he looked around Thor's chamber, saw an empty aluminum foil package. Quickly he wrapped the foil tightly around the loopstick wire and tore off another piece of foil to connect both transistors. He knew that the aluminum around the transistors would allow for a slightly higher flow of electricity, and the aluminum wrapped around the loopstick would intensify the frequency.

Trying to recall everything he had learned about shortwave radios during electronics school, Connor removed the mesh cover from the microphone and disconnected the ground and hot wires. Then he used his knife to strip the insulation from the hot wire and attached it to the handle of Thor's cast-iron frying pan. Last, he stripped the insulation from the ground wire and laid the wire to the side. Now, he knew, whenever he touched the ground wire close to the iron handle beside the hot wire, there would be a short, intensified blast of Morse code. And that was exactly what he needed, because where electromagnetic jamming could confuse a multiplexing frequency like a voice, a single-pulse frequency like Morse code could usually be blasted through. Thor entered the chamber, holding an old coil of electrical wiring in his hands. His face was amazed, as if he had shocked himself by finding it.

"That's good enough," Connor said. Instantly he began stripping the rubber insulation from the dusty coil of 14-gauge wire.

"What are you doing?" Thor whispered intensely, bending forward.

"I'm setting up a broad wave antenna. They used to call it a whip antenna in the old days."

"Why?"

"Because a whip antenna will throw a hard signal in a

straight direction instead of just sending it out all over the place. The whip will give the Morse code better range and power." Connor glanced out a long rectangular window. "Which direction is Reykjavik?"

"It is there." Thor pointed inland.

Connor stared. "What?"

Thor nodded. "Yes, Connor. Reykjavik is to the south. We must broadcast back over the island and the mountains in order to reach it. We will have to broadcast through the Ice Station and the jamming. If we put the signal straight out to the ocean, we will be sending it into the Arctic Circle."

For a moment Connor was silent. In his urgency he hadn't even thought of that. "What about oil tankers?" he asked. "Or ice breakers? Would we reach one if we sent the signal into the Arctic Circle?"

"Only in the spring. Icebergs make the area too dangerous for shipping this time of year."

A grimace contorted Connor's face. Without another word he bent the wire in half, leaving two ten-foot strands. He attached the center of the V to the unwired loopstick and the capacitor. Thirty seconds later he had stretched out the two bare lines of wire to attach them to the bookcase beside the opposite side of the chamber. The antenna was aimed over the mountains and Ice Station.

"All right," he said quickly. "Go downstairs and crank up the generator to full blast."

"All the way to 220 volts?"

"Yeah. Turn it up all the way."

With a curt nod Thor vanished and Connor twisted the dial to the Maritime Emergency Frequency, a channel reserved by international law for sea disasters. Then he lifted the ground wire, holding it by a piece of rubber insulation that he had saved from the antenna. All dials on the radio maxed out, and Connor heard the generator roaring even louder on the lower level. Instantly he began sending the SOS signal, three quick beeps and three long followed by three quick. He continued it for thirty seconds before pausing.

Thor stood in the doorway.

Connor listened intently, motionless. The scent of overheating circuits filled the room and he sent the signal out again, quicker this time, hitting the ground wire as clearly as he could manage before listening to the receiver. With a loud humming, a thin spiral of smoke drifted up from the capacitor. Connor heard a crackling and then there was a faint response of Morse code, almost undetectable beneath the jamming static.

"We got 'em!" Connor yelled.

"Give them our location!" Thor said, staggering a step into the room.

Quickly Connor hit the ground wire against the steel and then an explosion shattered the shortwave, transistors blowing shards of glass into the air with a white-green blast of electric flame. Connor had instantly let go of the wire to throw his forearm across his face, and Thor yelled, leaping to the side to snatch the plug from the outlet.

Stunned silence; the harsh scent of burned circuits blackening the air. Waves crashed along the shore as Thor gazed down on the shortwave. He said nothing as Connor lowered his forearm, both of them watching the still glowing circuits of the capacitor fading quickly from orange to gray, to black. Still staring at the radio, Connor stood up. He was motionless for a second before he caught a deep breath.

"Well . . . that's it," he said.

Thor grimaced. "We can bring Beth and Jordan to the tower. I will protect them until you can find a means of transport. They will be safer here than at the Ice Station."

Connor was abruptly struck by the fact that Thor had never asked what the danger was. He looked intently at the red-bearded face and then, drawn by a strange, changing focus, he noticed a gigantic, double-bladed battle-ax hung high above the stone fireplace.

Twin-bladed, each crescent slab of sharpened steel as wide as Connor's chest, the battle-ax seemed to glow, strange and subdued, with a fantastic war scene exquisitely engraved upon the side, a scene that intrigued Connor despite everything else that was happening.

Connor felt an eerie sensation as he studied the image, the image of a great, fiery dragon with wings as wide as the universe itself, viciously locked in battle with a heroic, winged figure that grimly held the dragon's hideous head, struggling breath to breath.

Wrestling in the stars, the two gigantic warrior figures were exquisitely embroidered into the side of the battle-ax with uncountable smaller figures battling beneath them.

Despite Connor's rush, he was struck by the image and the vague feeling of power it invoked. There was something distinctly ancient and forgotten in the scene, something that gave an . . . Old Testament sensation. Connor blinked to shake himself from the distraction as Thor leaned over him. The giant's hand had settled on his shoulder.

"We will discover what the danger is," the Norseman rumbled. "Perhaps it is not what we think, my friend. That would be . . . unlikely. A man's imagination can do many things."

"Maybe," Connor replied, turning his attention from the ax. "But I'm not taking any chances with my family. So you stay here and I'll bring Beth and Jordan this afternoon. I want them here until I can get all of us off this island."

"I will make arrangements. They will be comfortable."

"I'll be back in four hours." Connor moved to the door, pausing. "And keep an eye out, partner. I've got a real bad feeling about this."

A doubled guard stood at the gate when Connor reentered the Ice Station. Although the entrance was usually a perfunctory ritual, this time the Rangers motioned for Connor to step down from the Jeep. Connor readily complied. They directed him into the guard's shack, where Barley was waiting. The muscular lieutenant looked morose, depressed.

Connor stared at him.

"Well, what is it, Barley?"

Barley shook his head. "This place has gone weird, Connor. I don't know how else to say it."

"What do you mean?"

"Blake is really messed up, man. He went ballistic when he received a report of your fixin' the breaker box. I ain't never seen anything like it. It was unreal. Things are tight in the cavern, buddy. That's no joke."

"That's not my problem, Barley. That's military."

"You're right about that," he replied. "But there's something else. Blake wanted to know where you went when you left the base. He was zooming, Connor. Like he was on drugs or something. Just crazy. And there was some kind of rat-faced Russian dude with him. And . . . I hate to tell you about this, man, but we had a wild scene at the Communications Center. And Beth was right in the middle of it."

Connor said nothing, freezing on Barley.

Barley raised his hands. "I didn't have anything to do with it, Connor! I wasn't even there!"

"What happened, Barley?"

The lieutenant shook his head, as if shocked. "It was wild, Connor. It went down about an hour ago, when Blake and that inbred Russian goon came up to the surface with his squad of MPs. They went straight to the Communications Center and accused Beth of doing something with the computer system. Like I said, I wasn't there, but I heard that it was a real ugly confrontation. That crazy Blake was in Beth's face and Beth wouldn't back down. She told 'em off, boy, and I heard it was ugly. Then the Russian made a move like he was going to do something to Beth, so she smashed him across the face with a keyboard. Sent him flying."

Barley paused, took a deep breath. "And then it was pure pandemonium, man. I mean pure pandemonium. Blake was screaming for more MPs, for all his MPs, but Beth wasn't going anywhere! And then the fight was on! And to make it even worse, a bunch of your electrical guys saw Blake beating up on Beth and they went ballistic! Your boys grabbed chains and two-by-fours and four-by-fours and everything else they could find and charged into the Communications Center to help her." He hesitated, fatigue on his face. "Before it was over, fifty of your construction guys went nose to nose with almost all of Blake's MPs and, son, let me tell you something. It was a no-holds-barred, full-blown, head-bustin', backbreaking fiasco from beginning to end. The Communications Center is absolutely demolished. And I honestly think that your guys would have won in the end if Blake hadn't pulled out his .45 and fired a full clip into the ceiling."

Barley took a deep breath. "Then everybody stopped fighting. I guess it was because they thought somebody'd been killed. I hear that Blake swore he'd plant the next man that lifted a hand against an MP. And that pretty much ended the head-bashin'. After that, everybody was placed under arrest. There's about fifty people laid up in the groundside medical center, most of them military." Barley paused, staring. "Blake's MPs were put on stretchers, man. And . . . and Blake took Beth down into the cavern, Connor. In handcuffs."

Connor was dangerously still. His eyes locked like lasers on Barley. "Was Beth injured?"

"No," Barley replied quickly. "Beth wasn't hurt, man. She might have . . . she might have gotten a few bruises and scratches . . . because she was right in the thick of it. But she's not hurt. I had a few minutes to meet with her in the Housing Cavern before I came topside, and she looked okay. But she made me promise that I'd fill you in on everything when you came back from Thor's place."

Connor nodded. "I appreciate it, Barley. How many of my men are hospitalized?"

"Ten of them are in topside medical with broken bones, and thirty more are locked up in the warehouse." Barley paused. "I didn't really have any choice, Connor. Those were Blake's orders. And the rest . . . the rest are really, really mad, man. It is absolutely not safe for the military to walk around this place. I'm telling you the truth. This island is about to explode."

"What about Blake's MPs?"

"Well, like I said, almost all of them came up to deal with the riot in the Communications Center, and they pretty much got wiped out. Your guys demolished them."

"So who's in charge of security of the cavern?"

"Blake." Barley nodded. "Blake has assumed command over the three platoons."

"And Chesterton?"

"He's been given an Executive Command to step down. He turned over command to Blake."

"So Chesterton's not in charge anymore?"

"No." Barley looked away, dejected. "Chesterton ain't in charge no more. It's just Blake."

Connor's face was hard. "Well . . . if Beth is in the cavern, who's watching Jordan?"

Barley nervously licked his lips. "Blake took Jordan down into the cavern with him, Connor. And I don't know any reason for—"

With a savage curse Connor had already turned, slamming the door outward so hard that it struck the wooden wall of the shack and stayed there. Then Connor was running, Barley and the two guards hastening to keep up as he made a dead direct line for the cavern entrance.

Chapter 12

A rapturous pleasure, almost sensuous, flowed from the eyes of Dr. Sol Tolvanos as he leaned over the Observation Room panel. His fish-white face glistened with a thin sheen of sweat, and his lips moved minutely as if mouthing silent awe, or praise.

On the monitor the massive black scales of Leviathan could be seen through the vaporous shroud spiraling lazily up from the cavern floor. Enormous in the gray gloom, the heavily armored Dragon remained in a motionless hibernation.

"Initiate the test," Tolvanos whispered to the computer specialists. "Begin a slow decrease of the nitrogen level to allow a 20 percent oxygen mixture. And lower cavern temperature to 32 degrees Fahrenheit. Prime nitrogen thermones for quick extinguishing."

The computer matrix blinked with the commands.

"Are you quite certain," Adler asked, trembling, "that you can control the creature?"

"Of course I am certain, Mr. Adler," the Russian replied, not looking up from the monitor. "It is, after all, only an animal. It is not a god. Any competent scientist retains the ability to control his creation. Or kill it. Anything less is nonsensical."

Adler stared at the screen, sweat beading his forehead.

"Yes . . . yes, of course."

Connor was the first man off the elevator, Barley and two guards following. And the first thing Connor saw were Army Rangers decked in full combat gear, rifles at port arms.

"Stand down!" Barley ordered, moving up beside Connor. "I've got it under control!"

Without hesitation the soldiers obeyed, and Connor understood how solidly Barley commanded his men. It was obvious that Barley held as unbreakable a control over the men as Chesterton himself.

"Beth and Jordan are being held in the Housing Complex," Barley said, breathless as they moved. "And listen, Connor. Blake also ordered Frank's science team held there, too. That crazy colonel has turned this entire cavern into some kind of prison."

"What about the rest of Blake's MPs?"

"Most of Blake's people are in the hospital or guarding the warehouse or the docks, Connor. But I think that two of them are in the Observation Room, just to keep the area secure."

"So only two of Blake's people are still in the cavern?"

Barley nodded. "Just the two in the Observation Room. But you've got to remember, Connor, Blake has assumed command of the platoons. And I'm taking a big chance right now. I'm supposed to have you under arrest. Like Beth and Jordan and the rest of Frank's team."

Connor suddenly released his anger, turning fully. "How could you let them do this, Barley?"

"I'm sorry, Connor. Those were the orders."

"That's no excuse," Connor responded, teeth clenched. "You know what they've got in that Containment Cavern." His voice was accusing. "How could you let them bring Beth and Jordan down here with that thing ready to tear down those doors?"

"Those were the orders, Connor!" Barley shouted. "This place is still under military law! If I disobey Blake I'll just be put in the brig like everybody else in this place!"

"Well tell me this," Connor said, leaning forward. "Does Chesterton know that Blake has dragged my family down here?

Does Chesterton know that two innocent civilians have been placed under military arrest in the middle of a combat zone?"

"No," Barley shook his head. "Chesterton doesn't know that Beth and Jordan have been hauled down here. He's been busy at the Containment Cavern. Real busy."

"Yeah, I figure he has, Barley. Because Chesterton doesn't think that he can contain that thing. And neither do you."

Barley was silent.

Grim, Connor said, "Raise Chesterton on the horn."

"Connor, Blake has ordered all radio contact through him. And the way they've screwed up the communications system of this place, we can't even call from cavern to cavern on the phones. All we've got are A-units, and they barely work inside these walls!"

"Get Chesterton on the horn, Barley!" Connor snarled. "Tell him that Blake has dragged Beth and Jordan down here! Then tell him that I'm down here, too, and that I'm about to do something massive."

Barley stared, hesitating. "Blake will hear the transmission, Connor. And Chesterton has been relieved of command! Don't you get it? Don't you understand? Chesterton isn't in charge anymore! And Blake is crazy! I'm telling you, man, he's—"

"Just do it, Barley!"

A long pause, and Barley finally raised his A-unit. "Squad Leader One to Top Dog."

A moment later Chesterton's angry voice came over the radio. It took Barley thirty seconds to explain the situation, and when he finished he lifted his finger from the "send" button to hear the response. Connor also listened, wondering how Chesterton would receive the news.

Chesterton never replied.

A half hour later Connor entered the Housing Complex to see Frank's science team sitting in circles. Startled, many of them stood as he entered. Connor knew that he appeared enraged and dangerous and out of control, but he didn't care. He scanned the entire complex, not finding Beth or Jordan. He turned angrily to Barley.

"Where are they?"

Barley demanded an immediate answer from the two Rangers stationed in the cavern, and seconds later Connor entered the complex to see Beth sitting against a far wall, gently cradling Jordan in her arms. Jordan saw him as soon as he entered, leaping instantly to his feet.

"Daddy!" he screamed, running quickly through a maze of chairs. Connor ran forward and caught his son in his arms. He searched the boy's face, searched his body for any signs of injury, found none. He was obviously tired, but unharmed. Then Beth was beside him and Connor looked, identifying faint scratches and bruises on her face and arms.

"Are you hurt, Beth?"

She shook her head sharply. "No. I'm mad, but I'm not hurt."

Connor nodded and turned to Jordan.

"Are you doing okay?" he smiled.

Jordan nodded. "Yeah. Are you okay?"

With a smile Connor replied, "Yeah. I'm just fine, boy." He continued to hold Jordan in his arms. The four-year-old was patting him on the back with the attitude that everything was fine now, just fine, fine, everything was fine . . .

With burning eyes Beth focused on him. "A lot happened, Connor. And I feel . . . I feel like it's all my fault."

"Tell me what happened, Beth."

A pause, and she spoke, "I found out that they'd set up a code that prevented interfacing with any satellite system. So I copied all the incoming keyboard strokes during the past twenty-four hours on a high density disk—"

"Why?"

She sighed. "Because the keyboard strokes will contain the code." A pause. "Anyway, I began deciphering the encryption, and twenty minutes later that ape-crazy Blake came up to the surface with a bunch of MPs to arrest me. That Russian was with them."

"How did they know what you were doing?"

"I don't know," she replied, shaking her head. "They must've had somebody in the cavern monitoring keystrokes in the Communications Center. That's all I can figure."

Yeah," Connor replied, "I could see them doing that. All right. What happened when they came into the Center?"

"Well," she continued, "we got into an argument. And then that Russian goon tried to grab me and I just . . . I just lost my temper. He put his hands on me and before I knew what I was doing, I hit him with a keyboard." She brushed back her bangs. "And then the fight was on, Connor. All the MPs jumped on me and put me on the floor. Then about forty or fifty of your guys saw what was happening and ran into the Center and had it out massively with the MPs.

"Then Blake started screaming for help and then even more Army guys showed up. MPs, or whatever they are, were all over the place. Then it got really, really ugly. Your guys were outnumbered big-time, but they went to the wall." She shook her head. "I've been around, Connor. You know that. And I've seen some serious brawls in my time. But I've *never* seen a fight like that. It was just no-mercy whatsoever with people going everywhere. They hit each other with chairs, pipes, tables, chains, clubs, whatever. And your guys are tough, Connor. They work hard, and they fight hard. The Center was absolutely demolished. And a bunch of people got hurt." She almost cried. "I feel really bad about it, Connor. I feel responsible for it."

Connor shook his head. "It's not your fault, Beth. It was coming a long way off." He smiled. "My guys just did what they thought was right. They'd do it again. And nobody got killed."

She blinked a tear, focusing on him. "Did you reach the Sea Patrol on Thor's shortwave?"

Connor grimaced, shook his head.

"Well, we've got to get out of here, Connor. This is no place for a child. It's too humid. It's too hot. If Jordan stays down here too long, he's going to get sick."

"I'm going to take care of it, Beth."

She nodded, mouth tight. But he knew that she suspected the truth was something darker, more terrible.

"Give me two hours," Connor said, holding her dark brown hand as she nodded. Then he focused on Jordan. "Don't be afraid of this place, buddy. We'll be leaving soon. 'Cause you know what?"

Jordan blinked, rubbing a hand over his eye. "What?"

Connor smiled. "We've still got to go fishing!"

"Now?" His face brightened. "We're going fishing now?"

"No, buddy. Not right now. But in a little while."

"But . . . I don't like it here. I'm scared."

"It'll be okay," Connor said, leaning forehead to forehead. "Daddy's got to talk to someone for a minute and then I'm coming back to you. And then we'll all go home."

"Home?" Jordan's eyes brightened. "You mean . . . a real home? Where it's not cold and I can play in the woods and . . . and where you can play with me?"

"Of course I'll play with you!" Connor smiled, eye to eye. "We'll play all the time! Because we're going to go back to Kentucky to live with your grandmother and she's got a *farm*!"

"A real farm?" Jordan smiled.

"Yeah, buddy, a real farm. With horses and cows and chickens and peacocks and everything! You can even ride a horse."

"Yeah!" Jordan whispered. "That would be fun! And will you ride it with me?"

A brief, touching pause, and Connor nodded. "Yeah, boy. We'll ride together. And play together. And do everything to-gether. Just like we're supposed to. How do you like that?"

"You promise?"

"Yeah, son. I promise." Connor kissed his son on the fore-head, placing him gently in Beth's lap before he kissed her also.

Her voice was a whisper. "Connor . . . I've still got the disk."

Connor knew instantly what she was planning. "How hard are they watching you?" he asked.

"Barley doesn't seem to care what I do," she replied quietly. "He seems more disgusted with this whole situation than anything else. But Blake told those other two Rangers to keep a close eye on me."

"What do you need?"

"I need time on a terminal. But I think I can break this encryption and then I can call for help."

"Can Frank help?"

She shook her head. "No. Not really. Frank knows about GEO and this experiment of his, but I don't think that he has the communications expertise to break a satellite code. Not by the seat of his pants, anyway. Not like I can. Frank would probably need the help of GEO and he doesn't even have access to it any more. But I can do it alone. I just need time." She stressed, "I need access to a terminal, Connor. And I need it soon."

"All right, Beth," Connor replied quietly. "I'll see what I can do." He stood and took two steps before she spoke again; spoke in a voice so soft that it wounded him.

"Connor . . ."

He turned back, frowning.

"I know you're a fighter," she whispered. "But please . . . please be careful in this. You know . . . what I mean."

A pause, and Connor nodded. Then he turned and walked to Barley, becoming angrier and more determined with each step to come up hard. He saw the big lieutenant scanning the cavern. His eyes were mean, narrow and concentrated.

"All right, Barley. I'm through messing around. Where's Blake?"

"He's at the Command Complex," Barley responded, as if his mind were occupied. "I'm going to have one of the guards escort you down there so you can go head to head with him. But be careful, Connor. Blake is an idiot. He doesn't have a clue. I've seen his kind before. He's a bootlicker and a yes-head but he ain't got the guts to do the job. Or the brains."

"What are you gonna do?"

"I don't know, Connor. I don't know what I can do. This whole thing is just . . . a fiasco. It's . . . dishonorable." The big man shook his head. "I can't believe that I'm being forced to hold a woman and child hostage for some crazy colonel."

"Well I know what you can do, Barley."

Barley focused on him.

"Find a room where Jordan can sleep," Connor said. "A place where Beth can be alone." He paused. "Find a room that's got a working computer terminal and maybe, just maybe, if you want any of us to survive, you can make sure that she's left absolutely alone."

Barley stared, somehow knowing. "You think she can do it?"

Connor nodded sharply.

There was nothing evident in Barley's face for a long moment. Then his chiseled features softened, with a nod, and Connor knew it would be done. He whispered, closing, "We have to get off this island, Barley. Because if that thing gets out of the Containment Cavern we're all gonna die. You know it. I know it. And Chesterton knows it."

"Yeah," Barley whispered, his finger curling round the trigger of his rifle. "Tell me about it."

Connor entered the Command Center's War Room to find Chesterton in a violent screaming match with a pudgy Army official that Connor identified instinctively: *Blake.*

Connor made a direct approach and stepped between them, eye to eye with Blake. Where before the pudgy colonel had been angrily arguing with Chesterton, he went suddenly calm and indifferent to Connor. He crossed his arms over his chest. Solid and defiant.

For a moment Connor said nothing, allowing his electrified attitude to communicate for him. But Blake was unfazed so Connor spoke, not allowing the colonel's calm to rattle him.

"I'll give you ten minutes to get my family out of this cavern," Connor whispered, having already made up his mind to use whatever force was necessary to remove them.

"They were brought here for their own protection, Mr. Connor." Blake's thick jaw jutted forward. "This is a secure military facility, and I was alarmed that your wife might have broken down under the strain of the situation. It was also discovered that she was attempting to do something . . . precipitous. It was a logical action to—"

Connor leaned closer. "You're *insane*, Blake! Insane! Why did you close off communications with that NSA code?"

"For security."

"For security?" Connor snarled. "Don't you realize that shutting down the Ice Station Communications Center left this entire cavern system without phone lines?" He shook his head. "Because of your little stunt, Blake, we can't even communicate with each other from cavern to cavern!" Connor paused. "You're an idiot, Blake."

"The United States Army has the potential for utilizing microwave radio communications systems, Mr. Connor. The Ice Station Communications Center was expendable and was locked down for your own protection. From this point on we will utilize radios for—"

Connor shouted, "Radio waves don't carry through *solid rock*, Blake! Haven't you ever spent any time in combat? Don't you know that your little handheld radios have a range of less than a mile in this place? And there are over twenty miles of caverns and passageways! You've compromised the safety of your own men!"

"That is only your opinion, Mr. Connor. And regardless of what you may think, the fact remains that I am now in charge of this facility. I have Executive Orders and a squad of military police."

"Your military police are in the topside hospital, Blake. Or guarding my men in the warehouse. You're out of manpower."

"You're mistaken, Mr. Connor. Colonel Chesterton has turned over authority of all his men to me. So I still have three platoons of Army Rangers at my disposal."

Chesterton was silent. Grim.

"Well," Connor growled, leaning closer, "you're not in charge of my family, Blake. So turn them loose. Right now."

"Your family shall remain safely under arrest until—"

"Cut it, Blake!" Connor shouted. "I'm not here to argue with you! I'm here to tell you! I'm taking my family to the surface! And if you try to stop me, I'll personally break you in half."

"You're under arrest, Connor!" Blake shouted, lifting a hand to the soldiers. "Nobody threatens a commanding military official on this—"

Chesterton stepped in. With a vengeance. "That's enough, Blake!" he shouted. "You're way out of line!"

Startled, Blake took a step back but Chesterton followed, staying in his face. "That's right, Blake. You're history! I'm taking back command, and we'll just let the Pentagon and a Senate Intelligence Subcommittee sort this out."

Blake staggered. "You . . . you can't do that!"

Chesterton nodded. "Watch me."

"But . . . I have an Executive Order!" Blake protested. "You're . . . you're a soldier, Chesterton. You're part of the machine!"

"I'm a man, Blake. A colonel in the United States Army. I am not a machine. And as of right now I'm pulling the plug on this Black Ops takeover and your so-called right to command."

"On what grounds?"

"On the grounds that you have placed civilians who were clearly loyal to their country and operating within international law under unjustified military arrest. You have placed a woman and a small child in extreme physical danger without proper cause or provocation and, by doing so, have demonstrated that you are *mentally* disabled. So as of this moment in time I, as the senior Army member present, am terminating your authority under Code AR600-20 of Command Regulations. Paragraphs three and four. Read 'em!"

Chesterton stood his ground like stone.

"No!" Blake retorted. "No! *You're* out of line, Chesterton! You have just now exceeded your authority! I am relieving *you* of command!" He violently signaled the guards. "Place Mr. Connor and Colonel Chesterton under arrest! Immediately! Put them in irons and take them to the holding area with Dr. Frank and the rest of the science team!"

"Stand fast!" Chesterton shouted to the Rangers, not even

removing his gaze from Blake. Connor saw that the guards were shocked, almost panicking.

Enraged, Blake turned fully to the soldiers. "That's a direct order, gentlemen! Place Colonel Chesterton under arrest this moment! Do as you're told!"

Chesterton turned sharply. "Stay where you been! Get on the horn and get Barley down here ASAP." He focused again on Blake. "We're about to make some changes around here."

Quickly one of the guards lifted a radio, speaking breathlessly, trembling as Blake swore, "You are finished, Chesterton. As God is my witness, I swear that I am going to send you to Leavenworth for the rest of your life. You will never see daylight again. Never. Never! I swear it!"

"Maybe." Chesterton nodded, smiling. And Connor could see that Chesterton had crossed some kind of horrific line within himself. Just as Connor knew there would be no turning back now, not for any of them. Chesterton would either be proven right in a court of military law, or he would be found guilty of treason and insubordination and sentenced to a military prison for the rest of his life.

"Maybe I am finished, Blake," Chesterton responded. "Maybe I won't see daylight for the rest of my life. And then, maybe I've seen too many good men killed in Vietnam because of incompetent commanders like you. But one thing is absolutely certain, Blake." He nodded. "We know who's in charge, don't we?"

Within minutes Barley came calmly into the room, tall and muscular and disciplined and, as always, the consummate military professional. He moved without question or hesitation to Chesterton as if he understood exactly what was happening and had already chosen a side.

"Lieutenant Barley, take Colonel Blake to a holding area and secure him," Chesterton said. "And then try to override the NSA satellite lockout to get an immediate emergency airlift of this facility's personnel. Tell the North Atlantic Sea Patrol to get a ship under way if the weather prevents flying. And get someone to bring Dr. Frank up here."

Without even blinking Barley stepped up to Blake, fearlessly relieving him of his sidearm. He cleared the clip and the chamber and placed the semiautomatic weapon in the waist of his gunbelt. Then he stepped to the side, motioning with an empty hand.

"Colonel Blake," he nodded, emotionless.

But Connor saw the smile hidden within Barley's muscular face, caught the laughing gleam in the narrow dark eyes. After a resentful pause Blake complied, stiff with rage.

"Stand fast," Barley said as he followed Blake past the two soldiers. Then he spoke a lot louder than necessary so that Blake could clearly hear his words. "I don't need any help with this one."

"Leviathan's EEG activity is increasing dramatically," a panel controller said, staring at the elevated spikes on the electronic screen. "Alpha and Beta waves have gone completely off the scale, and its heart rate is increasing to ninety beats a minute. Internal body temperature is dropping to 326 degrees and epinephrine levels have peaked." The pale controller stared at the monitor. "It's . . . it's waking up."

Tolvanos didn't blink. "What is the cavern temperature?"

"Temperature at this end of the cavern is 32 degrees Fahrenheit!" the controller shouted. "But the air temperature in the area of the creature is over 200 degrees! It should be *freezing* down there, but Leviathan's exothermic body temperature is superheating everything around it. Even the rocks, the air. Everything."

Tolvanos glanced down, frowning. "How long before the creature achieves full awareness?" he asked calmly.

Wide-eyed the controller regarded the rapidly changing measurements. "I . . . I can't tell if—"

"There!" Tolvanos pointed. "It is awakening!"

Upon the screen, captured fully by the monitor, Leviathan began to awaken, rising. A thick tail uncoiled, whipping out suddenly to the rear, revealing the four long, thick-tendoned legs that ended in wicked feet, reptilian claws gleaming darkly to grapple stones softened by the unimaginable heat of its sleep. Then, from a protective position beside its chest, the long neck straightened as it stood, head rising, rising, lifting sixteen feet above the cavern floor on the armored neck, stretching. And then it lowered its head again as the malevolent green eyes opened, glowing eerily.

It glared at the titanium heat shield.

"My God," whispered Adler.

The Dragon's body, almost six tons of muscle and tendon and angled, hardened plates of black-green armor, suddenly contracted, corded tendons in its legs and chest visibly tightening, stretching the thick muscles. For a moment it appeared to be cramping, bunching, coiling and twisting the tendons. The joints bulged with the effort, tendons knotting like rocks, then relaxing to tighten again in a slow, gathering rhythm.

The diabolical dragon-head twisted as the jaws separated to reveal jagged rows of white fangs, like a shark's. With a sharp movement the mouth clamped shut, locking, muscles bunching along its neck as the wicked eyes glowed dark and darker, focusing on the fire shield.

A sudden convulsion whipped its tail around, striking the cavern wall to tear a slice off a rock with the wedge-shaped end. As the rock fell to the cavern floor, the tail itself began to shiver with rhythmic contractions, tendons tightening.

"What is it doing?" Adler whispered.

Staring at the image, Tolvanos did not reply.

"Dr. Tolvanos!" Adler shouted. "I asked you a question! What is the creature doing?"

"I believe," Tolvanos replied calmly, "that the creature is beginning to increase tensile strength in its musculature by revolving its tendons inward. And it appears to be initiating some type of contraction along its spine."

Adler nodded. "Yes, yes. That would be the kinetic energy release process. It is preparing to launch an attack." He hesitated, stepping back. "It will move very, very swiftly when it does!"

"Yes. I am sure." Tolvanos was studying the matrix control panel. "Why has the creature's brain activity suddenly dropped?"

The controller shook his head. "I don't know, Dr. Tolvanos.

Brain activity peaked when it was staring at the fire shield. Then it just dropped off to nothing. But the creature's adrenaline level remains high."

Adler joined, "Leviathan thinks quite quickly, Dr. Tolvanos. Dr. Frank has informed me that its mind speed is five times faster than a human being's. Perhaps it has already formulated a plan to—"

"I am quite aware of the creature's phenomenal mind speed, Mr. Adler." Tolvanos was watching the monitor. He spoke to the controller. "Open Bay Door Number One and send in the remote-controlled M1A1 Abrams Tank. Let us confirm how this creature confronts a real adversary. We have two tests to complete as soon as possible."

"Yes, Doctor."

Adler was leaning over the screen beside Tolvanos. "Switch to wide-screen observation," Tolvanos muttered. "I want to see the entire cavern. Both the creature and the tank. And turn on the cavern's auditory system. I want to hear this."

"Yes, Doctor."

Instantly the monitor encompassed the entire containment cavern. The image was clear and horrific: At the far end of the cavern stood Leviathan, erect on hindlegs. Its long, powerful forelegs were bent, clawed appendages held in front of its chest as if it were clutching prey for the venomous jaws. Then the cavern's double-wide bay doors opened and the remote-controlled Abrams M1A1 tank, over sixty tons of steel led by a devastating 105-millimeter cannon, entered the cave.

Jaws separating, Leviathan whirled to face it.

A god-roar, a shrill reptilian scream of unearthly rage and unearthly strength, shook the entire cavern, dark and nightmarish. It was a wild, prehistoric howl that reached an unbearably high pitch before it descended into a threatening growl.

"Behold . . ." Tolvanos whispered, staring. "Behold Leviathan! And remember the words of even God himself: On earth, it has no equal."

Frank entered the War Room in a sweat. He didn't know what had happened but he knew that Chesterton was in charge again. Then he saw Connor and hesitated.

"Connor knows everything," Chesterton growled, slamming a 50-round clip into an M-16. "He figured it out for himself and it's a good thing, because we might need him. Let's go! We've got to stop this test!"

Together they moved down the hallway toward the Observation Room, and almost immediately they encountered a checkpoint guard of three nervous Rangers.

"Lock and load and shut down this corridor!" Chesterton shouted, terrifying in the full fury of his rank. "And I mean shut it down! Nobody goes anywhere! Nobody! Arrest Adler and that ghost-eyed Russian on sight! We're going to the Observation Room."

Connor followed Chesterton past the checkpoint and heard three rifles chambered, a startling series of practiced clicks, deadly serious. "What if they've already woke it up?" Chesterton called out to Frank. "What can we do to contain it?"

Frank didn't answer and Chesterton half-turned as he ran. "I asked you a question, Frank! What do we do if they've started the tests?"

"I don't know, Chesterton! I don't think your people can stop it!"

"Well you better think of something, Doctor! Because we're going to be at that Observation Room in less than three minutes, and we're not going to have any time to mess around! When we go through that door, I'm taking charge over everybody and you'd better have a plan or we're all gonna die!"

Connor jumped into the debate. "Why don't we evacuate the entire cavern and shut the vault door at the entrance, Chesterton? That door is seven feet of solid steel and it's got to slow this thing down a little! Then we'll dynamite the elevator shaft and bury it alive!"

"Connor," Chesterton shouted, "that's the best idea I've heard yet!"

Thunderous, the tank advanced.

Leviathan stood, glaring, growling.

With a volcanic roar the beast lowered its dragon-head, and fire exploded from the fanged mouth in a blast that trembled the steel-plated Observation Room. Instantly the mushrooming flame impacted the tank's reactive armor like cosmic lava, igniting the plates until the exterior exploded in ravaging shards that lanced the cavern with burning steel splinters and still Leviathan continued the flaming torrent.

A devastating internal detonation shredded the rear of the Abrams as the engine erupted. Fire spiraled out to claim three hundred feet of cavern, and for a moment there was only consuming flame, incandescent conflict, with Leviathan hovering on the edge of the white holocaust, screaming in rage, rising high on hind feet with clawed forelegs extended wide toward its foe, attacking with gaping fangs and claws.

Tolvanos shouted above the conflict raging over the speaker. "Is the tank's cannon still locked on the creature?"

"Yes!" the controller responded. "The interior temperature of the tank is 250 degrees but the cannon is still locked on—"

"FIRE!"

The controller hit the command, and the tank's 105-millimeter cannon discharged—a blinding white blast that encompassed Leviathan, bathing it, enveloping it at point-blank range—and the creature vanished in the inferno, lost in the smoke and fire and rage.

Thunder, rumbling, echoed over the speaker. Nothing could be seen in the cavern, flames quieting. "Where is the creature?" shouted Adler. "I . . . I cannot see it. Is it dead? Has it . . . has it been killed?"

Tolvanos stared intently at the screen, peering through the smoke. "We shall see, Mr. Adler. But . . . no. I do not think that the creature has been killed. Wounded, perhaps. But not killed."

Slowly, from the other side of the cavern where granite had been crushed by the titanic impact, a dark reptilian shape staggered and rose to its feet, vengeful and wounded.

Enraged, the Dragon turned again to face its foe. With a scream its fangs parted to vomit a blazing plasmic arc that poured over the superheated Abrams tank. In a deafening ball of flame the tank disintegrated in a blinding, roaring white in the war-torn cavern. Shells exploded to scatter debris across the expansive floor and the mushrooming explosion filled the entire cavern, flooding over Leviathan in a molten sea-wave.

Leviathan defied it, shrieking.

Rage to rage, fire answered fire.

The Dragon continued to spew flame, standing, standing . . .

Then in a surreal white moment, Leviathan halted the plasmic deluge, flames passing over it, beyond it, fangs distending as it paused to inhale a single deep breath. For a split second the armor scales of its battered chest could be glimpsed, clearly dented and torn from the impact of the cannon. And although blood could not be seen against the black-green scales, the creature had obviously been wounded by the direct hit. Yet it was still standing, armor scales healing even as they watched.

"That cannon would have destroyed a bank vault," Adler whispered. "The beast . . . the beast can survive anything."

"Yes, Mr. Adler." Tolvanos smiled, eyes wide as if mesmerized by the black-green Dragon. "Yes, Mr. Adler. Quite probably Leviathan can survive anything at all." He hesitated a moment, glancing at the panel controller. "All right. I have seen enough. Lock down the video transmission for Stygian Enterprises. Our tests are now complete. And initiate nitrogen thermones. Put the creature to sleep once more."

The command was sent, and inside the cavern and within the wall nitrogen thermones could be heard rushing through the pipes. But at the sound the Dragon turned, focusing fully on the observation camera with an unearthly, malevolent intelligence.

Glaring, blazing eyes vengeful beyond human belief locked on the viewing port to communicate a pure intent utterly blood-dark and hate-filled. Then Leviathan bent forward . . .

Shrieking.

Chesterton staggered a step as the walls trembled, and they understood together the source of the shockwave. The Colonel straightened as if a demon loomed in his path.

"No!" he screamed.

Frank released a wild, remorse-filled protest, as if trying to pull back everything he had ever done in the cavern. Connor instantly picked up his speed, passing the scientist with five hard strides to pull alongside a charging Chesterton.

Chesterton was running full-out with the M-16 in one hand, teeth clenched in rage. Then they were at the Observation Room door to hear the fantastic sounds of conflict raging over the computer monitor.

Three Army Rangers stationed at the black doorway leaped and spun at their frantic approach, expertly leveling M-16s. "Move aside!" yelled Chesterton. "Stand fast! Move aside just get out of the way!"

Leaping this way and then that to obey the contradictory commands, the soldiers staggered into each other. Chesterton barreled through with Connor at his back and Frank following, all of them almost falling through the door.

Connor went through the open portal to see Chesterton take two staggering steps toward one of Blake's shocked MPs. Wildly Chesterton's lean arm lashed out, his fist connecting solidly to knock the MP flat back to the ground. Then Chesterton spun to hit Adler, connecting with a hard blow that put the old man over a computer panel.

Then Blake's second MP whirled, and Connor was instantly on top of him, his right fist striking the man's jaw just as he raised his rifle at Chesterton. Connor caught the barrel of the rifle as the MP swung his aim and Connor connected with three hard blows— a hook, a cross and then another hard right that caught the man clean across the neck. The MP dropped to the floor at the blow, his rifle clattering across the tiles.

Livid from the conflict, fists clenched, Connor strode boldly into the Observation Room. He didn't like violence, had never liked violence. But he'd been forced hard into this one, his love for his wife and son compelling him, and now that he was in the thick of it he was in a quick mood to hurt anybody who got in his way.

Then a monitor loomed in front of him and Connor saw it:

a terrifying, demonic Dragon of titanic size that whipped around in a rage, striking the demolished turret of a tank with a long, muscular tail that ended in a wicked, bone-bladed wedge as wide as a horse's head.

The diamond-hard wedge bit deep into a destroyed tank cannon and Leviathan screamed again through gaping fangs, spinning once more to drag the torrent thirty feet before the tail-wedge tore loose from the steel. Roaring, the Dragon shook, trembling in rage. And glaring through glowing green eyes, it stood atop white fire, shattered steel. But the flames were vanishing. It had won the battle.

Frank was instantly at the control panel, snatching his headset from Tolvanos's waist. The scientist shouted, "They've turned on the nitrogen thermones! That was stupid! It learns! It's not going to let itself be put to sleep again!" He began hitting computer controls, hands flying over the blinking orange lights, commanding, commanding . . .

"Do something!" Chesterton shouted, running up. He pointed toward the fire wall, raising his voice over Leviathan's shriek. "Do something before it rips that fire wall off its hinges!"

"Look out!" Connor yelled, leaping to the control panel. "It's going to attack!"

Bellowing, Leviathan spun and glared insanely at the cavern's observation camera. Then it launched an attack that hit the monitoring screen almost as it began, a blinding-fast eruption of speed that covered more than a hundred yards in the blink of an eye.

A distant earthquake like a cannon blast trembled the cavern wall west of the Observation Room. The cell's remote viewing camera suddenly went blank, the image of a charging Leviathan instantly replaced with a waving orange haze passing up and off the top of the monitoring screen.

Electronic hissing.

Drenched in cold sweat, Connor stared at the fire wall in front of them, breathless, trying to listen over his own pounding blood to hear . . .

Silence . . . *No. Not silence.*

Faintly, Connor thought he could hear . . . *Scratching.*

A distinctive, sinister scratching on the titanium before them.

Sweat dropped from Chesterton's face as he backed away from the fire wall, raising the barrel of the M-16.

"Oh no," he whispered.

Chapter 13

Everybody get out!" Chesterton yelled, leveling the M-16 at the fire wall. "Get out of here now!"

Staggering in fear, scientific personnel began for the doorway. And suddenly, with a deafening collision, the titanium fire wall was half-shattered, violently displacing the computer panel that was rent inward by a terrific force that struck again and again, pounding. A reptilian roar liquefied the air; guttural, bellowing.

Chaos and screams.

Connor heard continuous rifle fire and turned to see Chesterton firing, firing, kneeling low on the ground to continue firing at a black-green nightmare shape that tore fiendishly at the titanium with blackened claws as long as butcher knives.

"Get out of here!" Chesterton bellowed.

Submerged in the shrilling scream of the beast, Connor staggered to the wall and saw Frank rolling on the floor, dazed. Chesterton's bullets were ricocheting off the rent titanium, glancing over the top of the plate to strike without effect at a long foreleg that reached, grasping, sweeping through the Observation Room.

Screams . . . bodies falling panic-stricken or charging over each other to evade the sweeping black claws that sliced the air, searching, tearing.

With a wild shout Connor threw himself back as the claws passed before him. In a daze he saw the bladed foreleg strike a white-coated man in the chest and continue sweeping in a misty red haze, as if the claws had struck nothing at all. Then with a rending of steel beams, the titanium fire wall was pulled outward, bent at the top as another bat-like foreleg snaked through, a monstrous shoulder jamming in the crevice.

The clawed foreleg pushed through the narrow crevice and there was a bursting eruption of the wall, a violent surrendering of steel tearing beneath an unearthly shrieking. Connor leaped forward, grabbing Frank, lifting the scientist quickly as claws tore at the titanium.

In a flash Connor scrambled back, trying to avoid Chesterton's fire as the niobium-titanium wall gave another two feet. Then the concrete, steel, wiring, and whatever else remained to hold the wall in place began to give way, crumbling outward, pulled into the Containment Cavern.

Barreling into the others who flooded the doorway, Connor charged into the corridor, dragging the dazed scientist. He heard Chesterton's wild rifle fire as the colonel came out behind him, backing, emptying what remained of the M-16's clip. Scientists fled down the hallway.

"Give me some suppression!" Chesterton screamed to the three Rangers, and instantly they responded, disciplined and effective, as Chesterton slammed in another 30-round clip. Staccato gunfire blazed into the doorway, roaring into the Observation Room, filling the corridor with a deafening white strobe.

Connor unceremoniously slung Frank against the corridor wall and turned, watching the titanium fire wall fall back completely, pulled into the Containment Cavern, torn from its rigging.

Frantically Chesterton shoved a large cylindrical object into the port of a grenade launcher attached to the lower part of his M-16 rifle. He waved his hand wildly. "Back up! Back up!"

Connor threw himself over Frank as the Rangers dove away, and Chesterton stuck the barrel of the weapon into the doorway, blindly firing the grenade launcher at point-blank range into the black-green nightmare that loomed beyond the ravaged wall.

A deafening concussion like a solid wall hit Connor's back, debris and thunder roaring, roaring, solid in the air on and on and fire was there but Connor was too stunned to feel it, to sense it.

Somehow staggering, rolling, Connor half-rose, pulling Frank away from the doorway. Fire was blazing in the Observation Room, and Connor turned to see Chesterton picking himself up, a hand to his head, gasping for breath.

"We gotta get out of here!" Chesterton shouted, falling against the wall. He angrily opened the launcher again and shoved another grenade in the tube, slamming it shut like a shotgun.

"Connor, get that scientist outta here!"

Understanding even though he could barely hear, Connor slung Frank over a shoulder, turning to stagger down the corridor as Barley ran up, panting, glaring. The lieutenant was holding his rifle at port arms, vividly alert, angrily scanning everything. He came through the dust and the smoke and blinking fluorescent lights without the slightest hesitation. His face was hard. His finger was tight on the trigger of the M-16.

Chesterton spun to him. "Barley! Get me some suppression up here! Get it up here now!"

Barley was instantly on his radio, speaking calmly, and Connor noticed that a bestial roaring thundered from the Observation Room. Inspired to stagger down the hallway, Connor made his way through the smoke until he felt Frank stir on his shoulder, half-rising. Immediately Connor set the scientist on his feet, leaning him against a wall. A bright red flow of blood colored Frank's forehead. His eyes were wide, vacuous. Connor shook him.

"Frank! Wake up! We've got to get out of here!"

Frank shook his head again as gunfire erupted in the doorway of the Observation Room, four men firing at once into the portal. Connor heard Leviathan screaming, saw a portion of the portal torn away by a clawed forepaw that swept through the hail of bullets to vengefully splinter a steel support beam. Shocked, Connor whirled back to Frank.

"Frank! Get it together! It's *loose!*"

With a frightful glare, the scientist focused on Connor, a supreme concentration coming to life as much from his powerful intellect as from the fear that galvanized them all. "GEO . . ." the scientist whispered. "GEO can slow it down! But I've got to switch it back to voice control."

Connor grabbed his shirt, shoving, half-carrying the scientist down the corridor. "Come on! There's a terminal down here!"

Shouts echoed in the corridor, four men determined to hold their ground, firing clip after clip, endlessly emptying everything they had into the narrow portal as Connor half-carried the dazed scientist through a doorway almost 200 feet from the conflict. The gunfire was still deafening, and Connor thought he heard more rifles joining in. A lot more.

Frank fell into a chair in front of a terminal, putting on the communication headset that he had grabbed from Tolvanos. Connor ran back to the doorway, glaring down the hall.

He saw an entire platoon firing through the doorway, some kneeling, some standing, each man shooting continuously until the clip was gone and instantly inserting another to continue firing in a full-automatic blast of flame that never ceased and lit the corridor with hellish light. Then Chesterton screamed another command, waving frantically.

"Pull back! Pull back!"

Enraged, Chesterton grabbed a soldier and shoved him as a portion of the portal tore away. "Move, boy! Get out of here! It's coming through! Barley! Barley! Give me a tactical retreat!"

Instantly Barley turned and ran to lead half the platoon up the hallway. On Barley's order they turned at the doorway beside Connor's doorway. Barley continued shouting commands until half of them were kneeling, half standing. No one fired.

Then the big lieutenant roared at Chesterton, and Chesterton's men fled from the Observation Room doorway as the wall gave way, collapsing into the corridor, with the beast half-emerging, forelegs tearing maniacally at the steel, rending, roaring. Almost instantly the dragon-head snaked through an opening to strike down, snatching a soldier from the ground, tearing the man instantly into blood-green shreds.

"God Almighty!" screamed Chesterton, lifting his hands as shredded flesh rained blood across them.

Screaming, tearing against the steel beams, Leviathan lifted its head to swallow a portion of the soldier down its throat. Chesterton had turned to charge full-speed up the hallway, blindly firing his rifle back over his shoulder. Connor watched all of them race past Barley's position, threading like lightning through the ten men who still held a disciplined formation and as the last of Chesterton's men cleared the standing-kneeling formation Barley screamed again, raising his rifle to his shoulder.

"FIRE AT WILL!"

Blinding gunfire erupted in the corridor and Leviathan's bright green eyes shut, head lowering. It began swiping the air with the forepaws, still half-held by the steel-granite wall and Connor whirled back to Frank to see the scientist bent low over the terminal, pounding violently into the keyboard.

Connor ran forward. "Do something, Frank!"

Frank raised his hand, speaking into the headset. "GEO, confirm voice control by Dr. Frank."

"*Voice control confirmed,*" the computer replied over the wall speaker.

Frank rose. "I'm ready!"

Connor ran out of the doorway behind him, seeing Barley's team retreating in small steps.

"Fire grenades!" the lieutenant shouted.

On the command two grenades exploded against Leviathan's armored scales in roaring, mushrooming blasts and flame and blinding heat. Connor threw a forearm over his face, watching the beast fall back at the murderous impact, shaking. Then Leviathan bellowed and, in a titanic effort, began tearing itself through what remained of the concrete wall, dragging tons of steel bar and granite block in its wake to emerge fully into the corridor. It turned toward them with glaring green eyes, distended fangs.

A reptilian shriek thundered through stone.

"*Retreat!*" yelled Barley, and together they were running.

Connor heard Frank screaming into the headset: "GEO, prepare to close the vault of Alpha Corridor!" But in the chaos and confusion Connor didn't hear the computer's reply. Then they were at the exit of the corridor as the steel walkway behind them trembled with a monstrous, pursuing stride.

And another.

Barley paused in the doorway, shoving the shoulders of those who came up, pushing them though the doorway while continuously firing his M-16 from the hip. Teeth gritted in a snarl, the lieutenant fired a grenade launcher attached to the rifle and another blast shattered the corridor, a scream echoing from the location of the impact. Connor fell through the door, the last man. He staggered up and whirled to see Frank still on his knees, staring straight down the corridor as Leviathan recovered from Barley's grenade, rising, always rising.

With a Dragon's wrath, Leviathan came for them.

Frank screamed, "GEO! Shut the vault door of Alpha Corridor! Shut it now! Shut it now!"

"Fire! Fire! Fire!" Chesterton bellowed.

Twenty rifles erupted in a volcanic stream, a solid wall of blazing steel with men standing and kneeling to fire grenades and clips that streamed into the face of the Dragon and Leviathan staggered, rocked by the continuous impact, armored scales lost in the flame of explosions and *still* it came forward, swiping the air, slashing, screaming, shrieking . . .

Connor stood his ground, watching as Leviathan rushed toward them, unstoppable and unkillable and enduring all they could deliver, and then the gray titanium vault of Alpha Corridor slid from the roof of the tunnel, descending in the face of the beast, slamming shut at their feet.

The door's bolts clanged shut and instantly they stepped back, reloading, reorganizing, moving through the heavy smoke of rifle fire that hovered like fog in the air. Connor was suddenly aware of the thick smell of gunpowder, felt the warmth of the overheated rifle barrels.

The niobium-titanium vault shook.

Struck hard.

Dust cascaded from the cavern roof, a faint cloud. Then another impact shook the door, and another. But the vault held, withstanding the attack with a solidity that the fire shield of the Observation Room had lacked. Again and again the vault was violently struck while wild-eyed soldiers backed away, smoldering weapons leveled. And Connor was with them, eyes fixed on the niobium-titanium door. Dimly, he noticed Frank still on the floor in front of them. The scientist hadn't moved since the vault closed, was still kneeling a few feet in front of the gray wall.

A full minute of pounding.

Until . . . nothing.

The vault stood in silence.

After a strangely still moment, Connor walked forward. He stared down and then he kneeled, studying Frank's face. Even though Connor was still breathless, he managed to speak.

"Is that door going to hold it, Frank?"

The scientist blinked. "It'll hold it for a little while, Mr. Connor. But Leviathan will find a way to defeat it. I can guarantee it."

Connor said nothing. As he stood the cavern went suddenly dark, a total and complete blackness that fell across them like cold midnight. A flashlight was instantly beaming in Chesterton's hand as he came forward, to stand beside them.

"What happened, Doctor?"

"GEO has initiated Lockdown Mode," Frank replied, staring at the vault. "The computer interpreted Leviathan's escape from the holding cell to be a breach of internal security, so GEO is doing exactly what it's programmed to do. It's shutting the vaults of every corridor."

Chesterton paused, silent. "Does that mean what I think it means, Frank?" he asked finally.

With a slow blink Frank replied, "That means all the corridor vaults have shut automatically, Colonel. And they can't be reopened as long as GEO is tracking Leviathan outside the holding chamber."

Emergency lights blinked on, eerily red; the entire Headquarters Cavern was lit with a dark scarlet glow. Trying to contain a sudden fear, Connor leaned forward. "Frank . . . does that mean that the vault at the elevator shaft has shut down? Is the elevator shaft closed?"

Frank stared, fearful.

"Yes, Mr. Connor. It means we're locked in this cavern."

Chapter 14

Make contact with my other platoons!" Chesterton bellowed, and Barley was instantly on the radio, calling out. Still shaken from the climactic battle, Chesterton whirled to Frank. "Is there another vault at the opposite end of that corridor where my men were stationed? Is that thing locked in Alpha Passage, or can it still get to my other platoons?"

"All the passages led to the Containment Cavern," Frank said, bowing his head. "The company never installed vaults at the far end, where the tunnels converge in the cavern."

Chesterton's anger intensified dramatically. "Are you telling me"—he pointed to the vault—"that if my platoons didn't make it out of those tunnels before those vaults closed they're trapped inside the tunnel with that *thing*?"

Eyes closed, Frank nodded.

"Barley!" Chesterton roared. "Can't you raise Charlie and Beta Squads on the A-unit? Get me some response!"

Disciplined and controlled, the muscular lieutenant kept keying the handheld radio, calling for a response. Finally there was a chaotic reply engulfed with gunfire, shouting, panic. Then a scream of human terror erupted, but words couldn't be distinguished—only explosions and the cries of men dying in pain and terror, suddenly overcome by a volcanic roar.

Chesterton violently snatched the A-unit from Barley's hand. "Alpha and Beta this is Chesterton! This is *Chesterton*!

Immediately pull back and fortify! Pull back and fortify! Do you read me?"

Silence.

Trembling, Chesterton keyed the microphone. "Charlie and Beta, this is *Chesterton*! Pull back and fortify! Pull back and fortify! Key the mike if you read me!" He released the mike, waiting. Then for the briefest moment a howling cry came over the radio, a horrifying expression of human suffering that was overcome by a bloodthirsty roar, bestial and merciless.

It died abruptly.

Chesterton's hand was white on the radio. "Charlie and Beta this is Chesterton! I repeat! Pull back and fortify! Pull back . . ." His voice cracked. "Pull back and fortify!"

Frowning, Connor bowed his head. Then he sensed something above them and he looked up, searching. Vaguely he saw faint tendrils of smoke crossing the high darkness, a blackened cloud of burnt flesh traveling through the cavern like the ghosts of scorched souls.

Almost staggering, Chesterton made another effort to speak into the microphone, but his voice had lost all strength. "Give me some response! Charlie and Beta this is Chesterton! Respond if able! Respond if able!" He waited without moving. "Respond!"

A long pause, longer. Chesterton somberly lowered the radio to his side, staring at nothing. Frank shook his head, eyes dimming. "They're gone, Colonel."

Chesterton stared a moment more, face hardening. He wordlessly handed the radio to Barley, who took it in a strong hand and lowered it stoically to his side.

Silent, the big lieutenant turned his head to stare at the titanium vault. His dark eyes narrowed, focused and concentrated and enraged. His face was the purity of murder, of revenge.

He held his rifle close as he turned away.

A midnight sun, bloodred on the horizon, made Thor turn. He had waited all day, nervous and uneasy. He had long passed worry, settling into something darker, deeper.

Then a trembling wind passed over his back, causing Thor's skin to tighten at more than cold. It scattered across his bearskin, white and freezing, but Thor stood solid as stone, searching the sky, though in his heart he was searching no more. He knew what was there.

The scarlet sun seemed to separate the thin ribbon of smoke from the natural darkness, painting it a darker red. And against the somber image Thor moved, equally somber, to enter the tower. He said nothing to the patient and loyal Tanngrisner as he climbed the steps to enter the upper chamber.

Stoically, Thor lifted his cloak and draped it across his shoulders. He moved to the bed, lifting his hunting rifle. A box of ammo went into his black woolen pocket and, with no expression, he moved to the mantle, pausing before the smoldering flames.

His face was sad, somber, and silent. He gazed up at the great battle-ax, the mythic weapon that had hung so patiently above the flames for so many long, long years, its crescent blades dull gray and red in the flame, the slow-dying sun.

Perhaps twice as old as the tower itself, the gigantic, double-bladed battle-ax had always been here, had been here even before Thor found it buried deep beneath a heap of overturned stones, secured high in the tower like hidden treasure.

The great weapon had been ravaged by centuries of rust and cold, but Thor had somehow sensed its strength as he pulled it free of the stones. And with the tireless dedication of a scholar copying a holy text he had carefully restored its strength, heating iron needles in the coals and patiently scraping away the rust until corruption surrendered to glory. Then when the great, sweeping blades were finally restored, silver in majesty, Thor knew that it was a truly great weapon, yes, a great weapon from a great age.

Iron flame had forged its heart, the hammer and anvil its strength. The master craftsman who shaped its form and etched the scenes of battle on the blade itself had given it purpose and meaning.

Upon one crescent blade was the image of a flaming chariot, a chariot commanded by a frightening, fantastic bearded figure who hurled lightning from either hand to strike a gigantic serpent rising from the sea. On the other side of the blade was an exquisitely detailed war scene of winged warriors, all battling with sword and lance beneath the galactic wings of a great dragon that wrapped its tail around the moon. And yet the dragon, though ultimately fierce and terrifying, was doomed to defeat because a fearless warrior grimly gripped the monstrous throat with both hands and was driving the fanged mouth down, down from the stars . . . to the earth . . .

A moment of power.

For many years, the great battle-ax had rested comfortably in Thor's hand as he listened to distant wind whispering in the tower, whispering. Thor had come to find quiet companionship in its presence, as if they shared the same temper, heart, and spirit.

Silence, flames smoldering.

Yes, Thor thought, *the same spirit.*

Ageless and enduring, the battle-ax had rested on the wall for the long years, and Thor had often watched it, watched it with sad eyes when he was lonely in the cold night, haunted by silence and memories and dreams. But Thor had never been truly alone. For he had forever sensed a deeper purpose in the battle-ax, a purpose he knew also in his heart.

Now he stared upon it once more as the winter sun burned deep in the gray steel, soft and slowly glowing. And somehow Thor knew at last why he had found it here. Knew why it had always been here.

Waiting.

With a dark gaze Thor focused on the scene of battle— dragon and man, forever and ever, on the earth. Then his ice-green eyes blinked sadly as he reached up to grasp the battle-ax with his strong right hand.

Wind whispered in the tower . . .

Old guardian of the people . . .

Thor frowned, nodding.

Lifted it from its rest.

Beth glanced at Jordan. The tiny figure was covered with a blanket and fast asleep, and she didn't want to wake him up. She wanted him to sleep through it all. To sleep until it was over.

After Connor had stormed out of the cavern, Barley had secured for her a private room inside the Housing Complex. But one of the Ranger guards, a sergeant, had objected to the unauthorized procedure, and Barley had turned on the man with an absolutely stunning display of verbal brutality, causing the sergeant to step backward. Then Barley had ushered Beth into the room, locked the door, and ordered that she not be disturbed.

Afterwards Barley ordered the sergeant to escort Connor to the Command Center and then turned on a private to deliver orders that he secure this cavern, alone. The private nodded quickly, accepting the orders without any objections whatsoever. And then there had been the explosion and the chaos at the Containment Cavern, when Barley had raced away.

Since then Beth had been furiously decoding the lockout. But it was difficult because it was an encryption system, and she had to replay from the copied commands of the disk—which translated into something like glob-hits of megabyte blasts—into the relay station by coded single strokes. It was something she had never seen, and it confused her. Then she decided to break down the glob-bytes little by little and reassimilate them in an image code that could be overlaid upon the NSA imprint, like a mirror, to unlock the relay.

It was a massive task, and she was forced to network a dozen 486DX2-50 PCs, utilizing the combined memory. To further hasten the process she fast-designed a unique program that allowed quad-processing of the encryption so that it could be simultaneously attacked from various dimensions. Then she sat back, letting the PCs work.

She knew she could break the code, but she needed a lot of time unless Frank could somehow order GEO to turn the full scope of its phenomenal power toward the encryption. For, although she had never actually seen the supercomputer, she was confident that if GEO ever challenged this high-tech encryption, this high-tech encryption would not be coded for long.

But she didn't have access to GEO, so she rested, not particularly worried about being locked in the cavern with almost forty men. Most of them were rather unobtrusive scientific sorts, and she felt she could handle them easily enough. And Barley, when enraged, was a terrifying figure, and he had bellowed an order that no one disturb her. For any reason.

Barley's sheer force of will among the weak was a great influence, and Beth made a mental note to thank him if they survived. She turned her mind to Connor and the pain of not knowing what was happening to him sliced sharply through her heart.

If Connor were dead, she knew, then she was dead too. But she also knew that he might be alive and fighting, fighting as he always fought for them. It gave her small comfort to know that if Connor were fighting to defend his family, he would be giving this thing the most ferocious fight of its life.

She closed her eyes with emotion as she remembered all the terrible, terrible times they had shared in their marriage, living at first in virtual poverty with no hopes and no future. But Connor had set his unbreakable will to working and working and working, sacrificing all his strength and life and heart to make for them a *good* life.

Sometimes he had held three or four jobs at a time to labor without end, until he had finally paid all the bills and had actually begun building a future they would never have known without his strength of heart. His family had been all that mattered to him, and Connor had proven it with his life and blood, year after year after year.

Beth leaned her head back, her entire soul in the single tear that touched the corner of her eye. "Such a heart," she whispered, shaking her head as the tear moved softly down her cheek. "Such a heart . . ."

Pain was all there was, but Beth refused to release it. It came and it went through her, hot and wet and burning and she couldn't stop it. But she gave nothing to it, either. She would give nothing at all until she knew whether Connor was dead or alive. Until then she would hope. And wait.

A soft knock at the door.

Beth opened her eyes, considering. Then there was another soft knock, and she rose to her feet, walking forward. Hesitantly she cracked the door to see the old scientist, the one called Hoffman, standing demurely. The old man held a pipe in his pale hand, a gray stream of lazy smoke spiraling through the red emergency light.

"Mrs. Connor?" he asked gently.

Beth blinked. Nodded.

"I don't wish to disturb you." Hoffman motioned behind himself; the guard could not be seen. "I have been waiting for a chance to speak with you. I hope you are successful in what you are attempting."

Beth said nothing, but something in the old man's bent stance raised her affection.

"Might I come in for a moment?" Hoffman asked, a tired smile. "I have very, very few allies in this cavern. I thought that we might speak for a moment, as friends."

A pause, but Beth trusted her instincts. She opened the door slightly to allow him in. Then she closed it and locked it again as the old man sat tiredly upon a chair. He seemed fatally fatigued. Although Beth didn't know what he wanted, she didn't fear him.

"Do you know anything yet?" she asked.

"No, no, my dear." Hoffman shook his head, holding his pipe close. "No, we do not know anything. This"—he gestured to the cathedral's ceiling—"cavern has shut itself down, so to speak. All the corridors are locked, so we cannot go anywhere. And as you well know, the phone lines are down. We cannot communicate with the outside world. Nor do we know what has happened to the rest of the men. They may very well be alive, you know. Colonel Chesterton is quite . . . quite resourceful."

Beth said nothing, but her face tightened. Without looking down she stroked Jordan's hair. Hoffman was silent for a long while, his pipe making an occasional, soft whistle as he pulled puffs from the large black bowl. He appeared to want to talk but gazed somberly at the tile floor, as if uncertain of whether he was welcome or not. Beth was touched by his sense of sadness. She sniffed, looking up.

"You seem like a good man," she said quietly.

Hoffman looked at her. His face slowly relaxed. "I try to be a good man, my dear. I try to be."

With a harder gaze, Beth looked into the wall. She shook her head. "What were you people doing down here, Doctor? What did you create in that cavern? I still don't understand it."

Hoffman's face was almost frightened, his aspect still, silent. "Something that . . . that should be feared, Mrs. Connor," he answered slowly. "It has no place in this world."

"Then how could you let something like this happen?"

Hoffman lowered his hand to his knee, his pipe forgotten. "It began rightly, I believe. Peter, or Dr. Frank as you know him, invented a process called Electromagnetic Chromosomal Manipulation. It is a method of altering the genetic makeup of a living organism. And hearing of his research, I joined him. Our intentions were good, you know. We wanted to perfect the process so that it could be used to correct genetic abnormalities such as muscular dystrophy, or a host of other genetic illnesses." He gestured vaguely. "But we could not obtain adequate funding. It conceivably would have cost millions. And it appeared that we would never be able to achieve our goal until we were contacted by a privately owned defense company which wanted to perfect the process. They wanted to know if Electromagnetic Chromosomal Manipulation, or ECM, could be used to enhance certain vertebrates, like dolphins, for purposes of war. The American Navy had for years been using dolphins to plant mines on foreign ships, to locate underground sonar, and such. And they wanted to enhance the controllability of the creatures. So, in return for our assistance, they promised to generously fund ECM for ten years."

Hesitating, Hoffman glanced down at his suddenly dead pipe. "That much funding would have enabled us to cure a host of genetic abnormalities, I am certain," he continued. "I did not want to use ECM to alter living creatures to make them weapons for war. But I saw no other means of funding the research. It was . . . a compromise."

Beth's tone was final. "They corrupted you."

A short laugh escaped him. "Yes, my dear. They corrupted me. They corrupted me as any man is corrupted. Little by little. Piece by piece. Until I could no longer remember what I had been." He nodded. "Yes. And in the end we took a Komodo dragon and placed it in a perfected electromagnetic field. And then we watched until it became something the world was never meant to endure. Until they had what they wanted."

"And what is that, Doctor?"

A heavy breath. "The end of the world, Mrs. Connor. The ultimate beast of prey." He frowned. "A doomsday beast so terrible that it would bring the entire world to its knees. And I tell you honestly that we succeeded . . . too well. Peter and I, we knew what was happening . . . but we did not resist them. We did what they wanted us to do."

"I want to know exactly what's locked in this cavern with us," Beth said, stronger.

Compassion glistened on Hoffman's face. "Do you remember, Mrs. Connor, when you were a child? When your brothers or sisters played games with you, hiding in the dark only to leap out and frighten you?"

Beth nodded.

"Yes," the old man smiled, "and so do I. I remember those frightful moments quite well. Even today I still remember the long, haunting fear of knowing that there was something beside me in the dark. Something I could not see. Could not find. But I knew it was there. And that my moment had come." He paused, staring at her. "And in that moment, Mrs. Connor, whatever was crouching beside me in the depthless darkness could have been anything. It could have been a monster. A ghost. A demon. Even Satan himself. But in my heart I knew that he had finally come . . . for me."

Beth was silent.

"Yes," Hoffman continued, somber. "I knew it had finally come for me. But it never came, you see. It was only my darkest fears. My darkest, darkest fears. There was never a monster in the darkness."

"And now there is," Beth said quietly.

Hoffman paused. "Yes, Mrs. Connor. Now there is. Now it is truly there in the darkness. And it is coming . . . for us."

Beth closed her eyes, leaning her head back against the wall. After a while she heard Hoffman finally rise, sensed him standing in the red glowing gloom, staring. Then his soft steps reached out to her across the room. When she opened her eyes again, he was gone. The door was closed.

She looked down at Jordan, and a startling moment passed as she saw the soft blue eyes staring up at her, so bright and beautiful. The child was widely alert, watching. Beth smiled down, gently caressing his head, comforting, finding comfort.

"Mommy," he asked quietly, "is the monster going to get me?"

Beth caught a painful breath, smiling.

"No, honey. The monster's not going to get you."

Jordan stared. "I'm scared."

Beth smiled, cradled his head in her lap. "That's okay, honey," she whispered. "It's okay to be scared."

A long silence.

"Will you sleep with me?"

"Yes," she whispered, "I'll sleep with you."

His eyes began to close.

"Okay," he whispered.

Beth cradled him and watched him until he was fast asleep. And then she watched the darkness.

In a wild conclave under the red lights, circled like a primitive war council, they huddled in the middle of the cavern. Chesterton rested wearily on a crate but Connor stood on his feet, not allowing himself to relax.

With a tired expression Chesterton spoke. "All right, we've got to get organized." He turned his head sharply. "Barley, station men at the three entry points of this cavern and resupply everyone with as much ammo as they can carry. Issue phosphorous grenades, antipersonnel grenades, whatever anybody wants. I don't care if they're qualified or not. And give everybody an LAW. One of those will take a little steam out of its stride."

"Yes sir," Barley said, was gone.

"Now, Doctor," Chesterton focused on Frank, "I want to know why that thing didn't use fire when it came down that corridor. It had us dead to rights. It could have blown us all to kingdom come with that flame-throwing stuff. Why didn't it?"

"It was exhausted," Frank answered. "Leviathan had used all its flammable gel defeating the tank."

"How long before it can do it again?"

"Maybe four hours. Maybe less. I don't know for certain."

"Can it melt that vault?"

"No. There's no way it can melt a niobium-titanium alloy."

"That's good, son," Chesterton growled, wearily wiping his face. "It's about time we had a little piece of good news." He sighed. "That brings a little joy to my old battle-weary heart."

"But titanium is brittle," Connor said, stepping forward.

Chesterton stared up gloomily. "What?"

"I mean," Connor continued, "that titanium can withstand heat and compression better than steel. I know all about it because I used to work in a pipe plant. Titanium's half the weight of steel but twice as strong, and that's why they use it in aircraft and ships. Or pipes. But titanium is brittle. That's why they don't use it to make knives or drill bits. It won't hold an edge. It chips and cracks too easily."

"Niobium-titanium is different," Frank interjected. "It has a higher means ratio. It can withstand stress and impacts a lot better than normal titanium, Connor. That's why it was created."

"But it's still basically titanium, Frank." Connor leaned forward. "And titanium can be broken a lot more easily than steel. It was a mistake to use it in those vaults."

"All right, all right," Chesterton broke in. "Let's just calm down a little. We'll deal with all that later. Right now we need to cover something else." He paused. "Frank, let's deal with this, 'cause I'm not sure. Is there any way for Leviathan to escape this cavern?"

"Only through Crystal Lake."

Chesterton shook his head. "I thought so," he mumbled.

"What do you mean?" Connor asked.

Frank spoke quickly. "Don't you know about Crystal Lake?"

"Yeah, I know about it," Connor said, scowling. "Crystal Lake is located in a cavern just past the power plant. You have to go through the power plant to reach it. It's a ninety-acre lake with underground streams that connect to the Atlantic Ocean." Connor stared. "Oh no . . ."

"Exactly, Connor," Frank responded. "This entire facility was designed as a holding pen for Leviathans. It was meant to be a place where Leviathans were housed and programmed and set loose to accomplish certain missions. The same way the Navy uses dolphins to attach mines to enemy vessels. Except Leviathans would be capable of tearing the hulls out of battleships or of searching out and destroying enemy submarines by ripping out their buoyancy systems."

Connor frowned. "Go on, Frank."

Frank paused, morose. "As you've probably guessed, Connor, Crystal Lake was the path Leviathans were supposed to take to reach the Atlantic Ocean. According to the specs of the proposal, a Leviathan would submerge itself in the lake and swim into Crystal Lake's underground stream. Within a few minutes, it would find its way into an Atlantic current and begin its mission. Then when the mission was completed, the Leviathan would return to the island through the ocean current and the island's underground stream and come back up through the lake, where it would be put back into a Containment Cavern."

Connor stood in silence. "The perfect plan, huh?" He waited, receiving no answer. "And how is Crystal Lake defended, Frank? Can this thing get to the lake any time it wants?"

Frank nodded.

There was a long pause and Connor continued, "Well tell me

this, Doctor. Is Leviathan going to try for the lake first? Or is it going to try and kill all of us? What's it going to do?"

"First, Leviathan will try and kill everyone in this cavern," the scientist replied plainly, eyes open. "Because Leviathan believes that it has to kill everything in this cavern in order to survive. But when it gets through killing us, Connor, it'll go for the lake. And the Atlantic."

"So nobody gets out of here alive," Connor said grimly.

"No," the scientist said, staring. "Nobody gets out of here alive, Connor. Not us. And not Leviathan. Because there's something you still don't know about. And it's something you need to know."

"Well I know about it, Doctor," Chesterton said, head bent. "And maybe you don't need to be talking about it."

"Well, Connor doesn't know about it and he has a right."

"Know what, Frank?"

Frank turned to him. "GEO was programmed to ultimately prevent something like this from occurring, Connor. If Leviathan ever escaped from the Containment Cavern, a total lockdown of the vaults was supposed to be the first level of intervention. And GEO was supposed to remain in Lockdown Mode until it registered Leviathan as dead."

"And so?"

"And so . . . there's another safety intervention."

"Well, what is it?"

Chesterton threw it in. "A twenty-kiloton nuclear device, Connor. A twenty-kiloton nuclear weapon that will vaporize this entire island. It's built into the lowest level of the cavern, and it's designed to activate automatically if this supercomputer of Frank's ever tracks Leviathan moving into Crystal Lake without authorization to escape into the Atlantic."

Connor stared, wide-eyed. "You people are crazy."

"It wasn't my call, Connor," Chesterton responded, lifting a hand toward Frank. "Dr. Frankenstein here insisted on it."

"It was the only way to ensure total containment," Frank responded, suddenly defensive. "We couldn't risk Leviathan escaping into the Atlantic! If Leviathan ever reached the ocean, it would find an endless food supply! It would kill and eat whales, sharks, whatever. It would attack the mainland! It would live forever! It would—"

Connor slammed the scientist against a wall. "*Defuse* the fail-safe!"

"I can't!" Frank grabbed without effect at Connor's wrists. "There's no way to get past GEO's frontline defenses!"

"You *designed* the thing! Shut it off!"

"No! GEO is still a computer! It's going to do what it's designed to do!" He pulled frantically against Connor's unbending arms. "There's no way to defuse the fail-safe!"

Connor paused, teeth locked. His breath was leaving him in hard, angry blasts. "So what are we supposed to do?"

"We've got to kill Leviathan!" Frank replied, pained. "If GEO ever tracks Leviathan entering the lake, it'll detonate the fail-safe immediately! We've got to keep it down here! We've got to kill it . . . down here!"

"Didn't you people ever worry about what it would look like to have a nuclear explosion in the Arctic Circle?" Connor grated. "Didn't that little problem ever occur to you?"

"The bomb was designed to look like a volcanic eruption," Frank replied, breathless. "And there's something else!"

"What?"

Frank gasped. "Once Leviathan ruptured the containment cavern, GEO initiated a countdown!"

Even without asking, Connor knew. "A countdown?" he snarled. "A *countdown*!"

"Twenty-four hours!" the scientist shouted. "If Leviathan is still alive and loose in this facility in twenty-four hours, GEO is going to initiate the fail-safe anyway! There's no way . . . no way to stop it!"

With a curse Connor threw the scientist back. "You're crazy!" he snarled again, turning with wild hostility toward Chesterton. "You're both crazy! You put the lives of my family in danger, and you never told us about any of this!" His voice grew colder. "I should kill both of you."

"Don't make me pull rank on you, Connor," Chesterton replied, turning full into him. "This is still a military operation."

"Don't even try it, Chesterton." Connor walked away.

"Where are you going?"

Connor turned back.

"You heard him, Colonel. We've got twenty-four hours to kill that thing. That's exactly what we're gonna do."

Chapter 15

Chaos and frantic cries for assistance dominated the spotlit camp as Thor rode through the unmanned gate on Tanngrisner. It was obvious that some catastrophic event had shattered the usually peaceful and relaxed atmosphere of the facility.

Grabbing his hunting rifle, Thor dismounted and walked purposefully toward the men at the elevator shaft. As Thor neared the entrance they turned together, staring at him. There were no Army personnel.

"What has happened?" Thor rumbled.

Speaking at once, they stumbled over one another. Maybe a cave-in, a natural gas explosion, a volcanic eruption . . . The cavern's vault had shut, locking everyone underground . . . They had lost all communication . . . And the only way to reach the cavern was to make the dangerous 1,000-foot climb down through the elevator shaft . . .

Thor asked, but he knew. "Where is Connor?"

A burly electrician, the one Thor had lifted during the wrestling match, Tom Blankenship, spoke nervously. "He went down into the cavern about four hours ago, Thor. And that crazy colonel came up and got Beth and Jordan earlier in the day. They're all down there, and there ain't no way to get to them. There ain't no way out."

Thor stared down the elevator shaft; the darkness was complete. He picked up an industrial flashlight and angled the beam downward. Heavily greased elevator beams and cables gleamed black in the piercing light. Long, evenly spaced drill lines were visible in the walls.

Leaning back, Thor slung the rifle around his shoulder, cinching the strap tight to keep it snug against the battle-ax. Then he looped the flashlight strap around his shoulder and neck, hanging the light at his ribs.

"Where does this shaft end?" he growled. "Does it go to the heart of the cavern?"

Blankenship stared in horror.

"Tom!" Thor shouted and Blankenship jumped back. "Where does the elevator shaft end? What is down there?"

Blankenship wildly shook his head. "There ain't nothin' down there, Thor! The elevator shaft ends at the entrance of the cavern, and there's a steel vault that's shut down like an anvil! Even if you reach the bottom of the shaft, you'll be staring at a hundred tons of burn-resistant steel! And there ain't no other way to enter the cavern!"

Thor frowned. Wind and white flakes froze over him while blackened, flesh-scented tendrils of smoke drifted up the shaft. "How is it that the smoke finds a way past the vault, escaping the cavern?" he asked.

Blankenship seemed scared to tell him.

"Tom!" Thor roared. "How does the smoke escape the cavern?"

"It's probably coming through the ventilation shaft!" Blankenship shouted. "It's a shaft located to the left of the vault!"

"And is this ventilation shaft wide enough for a man to crawl through?" Thor asked.

Blankenship stared widely. "Man, I don't know if you could get through it or not, Thor. I mean, you might be able to. But that thing is pretty tight where it hits the cavern. And there's a steel rebar-grate over the entrance. It would take a bulldozer to pull that thing out of the wall!"

Thor stared at the cables and girders. A large, double-sided steel beam descended into the darkness, but everything was coated in thin oil, exceedingly thin, to prevent freezing. Climbing down on the slick-coated steel would be difficult, if not impossible.

"Do you have enough rope to reach the bottom of the shaft?" Thor rumbled.

"No, Thor." Blankenship seemed astonished by the question. "We don't even have enough rope to go even halfway. We never figured on anything like this."

"What about wire?"

"Wire?"

"Yes." Thor turned to him. "A coil of wire. Do you have a coil of wire that will reach a thousand feet?"

Blankenship gazed over the spotlit camp. "Well, we've got a thousand-foot roll of eight-gauge that's probably strong enough to hold your weight, Thor. But the elevator shaft is really more like eleven hundred feet. So when you get to the end of the wire you'll still have another hundred feet or more to climb down. It's gonna be tough."

Thor stared down into the darkness.

"Get the wire for me," he growled.

Blankenship stared.

"Tom!" Thor turned his head with a roar. "Get the wire for me!"

Instantly Blankenship raised a portable radio, speaking quickly with concise instructions before he looked down again. "It's on the way, Thor. It's on the way. It'll be here in a few minutes."

"Good, Tom." Thor frowned. "Tom, my friend, I want you to listen to me. I want you to listen to me closely! It is vital that you and your men and your families abandon this island as quickly as possible! Do you understand? Because what has happened in the cavern may be far worse than you think. Can you contact Iceland on the radio?"

Blankenship shook his head. "No way, Thor. We've already tried that. Those military guys put some kind of jamming on the radio, and the Communications Center was busted up in the big fight. We can't contact anybody." He was shaking. "Why would they do that, Thor? What have those guys done down there? You . . . you act like you know more about this place than we do!"

"No, Tom. I only know that my friend and his family are down there." Thor turned his head, glaring at the docks. "You have two forty-ton cruisers, Tom. Those ships are large enough to easily accommodate all of your families. Is that not true?"

Blankenship also turned his head to the dock. "Yeah, yeah. We could get everybody on the ships. We could even load up all the military guys that were busted up in the brawl."

Thor frowned, squinting. "Those boats have probably been mechanically disabled by the military, Tom. But your people are expert mechanics, are they not?"

"Yeah, Thor. We can fix anything. That's what we do."

"Good. Then quickly, very quickly, make those ships seaworthy and take a heading 230 to 330 degrees south-south-east for Iceland. And continue to hail the universal maritime frequency for assistance until you see land. Don't look back! Don't come back to this island!" Thor glared ominously into the shaft. "There is death here."

Blankenship replied, "Okay, Thor. Okay. We can get those boats working in no time. That ain't gonna be a problem. We've already rushed the MPs guarding the warehouse. We've got their guns, got everything." He paused. "We can probably get the boats working in less than an hour. But . . . but what are you gonna do?"

Grim, Thor stared into the darkness.

"I'm going down into the cavern," he rumbled.

Blankenship stepped back. "Thor, come on, man. There ain't no telling what's down there! I hate to say it"—his face twisted in pain—"but everybody's probably dead anyway! And there ain't nothin' we can do! Why don't you come with us? We can fix those boats in an hour and get off this island! We'll be in Iceland in three hours!"

"Because my friend is down there," Thor answered somberly. "And I will not leave him."

"Well," Blankenship began, hesitating, "Connor's a good boss, Thor. And he's a good man, a real good man. I ain't never worked for nobody better. But I'm tellin' you the truth. I wouldn't go down there for nobody." He nodded, in pain. "I'm sorry to say it, Thor. But I just . . . I just wouldn't do it. 'Cause if I go down there, I'd just die too."

An engine approached and Thor glanced up. It was a front-end loader, forks locked around a pallet bearing a large coil of wire. Quickly they secured the wire to the elevator and pushed the coil into the shaft. It descended, rebounding, uncoiling quickly and easily. Thor moved to the edge, testing the makeshift rope with a tug. It held.

"Be wise, Tom," Thor growled, poised at the edge of the chasm. "Repair the boats and be gone. Save your families."

"We'll be gone in an hour, Thor," Blankenship nodded. "All of us! You can bet your life on it! And we won't be coming back, either. We're finished with this place."

Thor nodded. "Good, Tom. You're a good man. Now gather your families and be gone!"

"Are you sure you want to do this?" Blankenship asked, staggering. "There ain't no tellin' what's down there!"

Thor's face was grim as he descended over the edge.

"I know what's down there," he growled.

Was gone.

Connor kicked the cover off the ventilation shaft and descended quickly from the crawl space into the power plant. Then Frank came out of the shaft, followed by Barley and four soldiers. Chesterton and the remainder of the platoon had stayed in the Command Cavern, awaiting Leviathan's renewed attack against the vault.

Upon gaining his feet Connor raced to the generator. He saw quickly that the Class-A Power Grid Switch for facility lighting had been thrown off, like a normal breaker would throw itself off under a power surge.

That's what Connor had figured. He knew that, because of the Lockdown Mode, GEO wasn't going to let any electrical power flow through the breaker. The computer would automatically reroute power to throw the breaker off again if Connor just threw it back on, so Connor knew that he had to go around the control system, somehow. He had to defeat the supercomputer's ability to control this electrical junction.

Connor took out a Leatherman pocket tool and began unscrewing the cover. Behind him, the rest of the soldiers emerged fully from the shaft, moving in the red half-light.

"Give me some light over here!" he yelled.

Instantly Barley was beside him, shining a weak regulation-issue Army flashlight as Connor removed the fiberglass box cover, laying it to the side. He knew that inside the box, leading into the switch, the incoming wire would be hot, because it fed power directly from the Norwegian Powercable. And GEO had no ability to interfere with the incoming current. It just had the ability to keep power from flowing through the breaker at this junction.

Connor studied the situation.

He had always found it easy to work with electricity, thinking of it in the simplest terms, like water flowing through pipes. Because like water, electricity would simply flow where it was allowed to flow, incoming or outgoing. It was not a difficult thing to understand.

Volts of electricity were comparable to the speed of current flowing through a line, the highest volt rating meaning the fastest currents. In this cavern they had used mostly lines of 110, 220, and 440 volts, all of them deadly. But there were much, much more powerful lines used in the facility, including everything from 10,000 to 300,000 volts. Simply looking at a line was never a safe way of determining what amount of voltage it contained. A line of 220 volts was no thicker or more insulated than a line of 10,000 volts. They were both the width of a finger.

Amps were comparable to the amount of current flowing through a line. Connor often thought of an amperage measurement in terms of larger and larger water pipes, each pipe containing a tremendous amount of water but with the water capable of moving at any speed, from slow to fast. Amperage had nothing to do with the speed of the electrical current, it was simply a measurement of the amount of it. Usually, though, any line rated above 11 amps was considered exceedingly dangerous because it probably carried high velocity, or high voltage, currents. A 1,000-amp line was almost as thick as a man's wrist.

Wiping sweat from his eyes with a forearm, Connor concentrated on the box. The incoming current was cut dead at the breaker, where it should be flowing into the rest of the cavern. He studied the feedline; it was a 1,000-amp cable, probably carrying enough power to light up a small town.

Figures.

If this didn't work, he'd be fried.

Connor grabbed a wooden sawhorse, a relic from when the cavern had been built, and placed it beside the power box, where he could sit when the moment came. Then he placed one hand over his chest and stuck the screwdriver in the box, removing the brackets holding the hot, heavy-amp line. He intended to bypass the breaker, mainlining the light current into the facility.

"How come you're putting one hand on your chest?" Barley asked.

"Always work with one hand," Connor responded, blinking. "That's what they taught us in electrical school."

Barley seemed nervous. He always seemed nervous when he got around electricity. It was the only sign of fear Connor had ever seen in the muscular man. "Why?" the burly lieutenant asked finally. "Why are you supposed to work with one hand?"

Gently, Connor pried at the insulated section of the 1,000-amp line, lifting the thick bronze strand from its bracket. He knew that a ton of power was poised at the end of the bare copper.

"Because there's less chance of getting electrocuted," Connor whispered. "If you're touching the box with both hands, one hand might take the current and the other hand will ground you out. That's where the current leaves your body and goes into the ground. Electricity is always trying to find a way to reach the ground."

Barley didn't get it. "Well . . . you'll *still* be electrocuted, Connor, if you touch that line because your foot is touching the ground! The current's gonna come in your hand and go out your foot! It don't matter none if you've got one hand on the box or two hands on it."

"Not always, Barley." Connor lifted a dead intake line, moving it toward the 1,000-amp strand. "A fast current will travel a straight line if it can. And if the current comes in one hand and goes out the other hand, the current goes through your heart. That's what kills you. But if the current comes in a hand and goes out a foot, then it doesn't go through your heart. It'll probably blow your leg off or set you on fire or something, but there's a good chance you'll live."

Barley watched him. "This line right here?" he pointed. "This line right here will blow your whole leg off?"

"Yeah."

"Are you kidding?"

"No."

Barley stared wide-eyed at the line, and Connor sat back on the wooden sawhorse, grabbing the insulated section of the 1,000-amp line with his bare hand. He jerked hard.

Barley leaped back. "What are you doing?"

Connor pulled three feet of line from the box. Then he grabbed the dead intake line and brought the ends close together, but not too close. He knew that a 1,000-amp line could throw an electrical bolt as far as three inches to connect with a grounded source.

Half-turning, he pointed to a thick plastic roll lying on the ground. It looked like nonadhesive electrical tape, but it was simply a four-inch thick band of plastic. It wouldn't stick to any surface without tape holding it down. But Connor knew that, in this situation, he wouldn't need any tape. The residual heat coming off the electrical line would do the job by itself.

"Give me that roll of plastic," he said.

Barley picked up the plastic roll and cautiously handed it to him. Connor leaned forward, grabbing both ends of the wires and slowly pushing them together until the 1,000-amp line was close to the intake line. And even though Connor was expecting it, had even braced himself for it, the shock almost killed him.

When the ends were four inches apart a bolt of electricity

leaped at the speed of light to instantly hit the intake line, liquid fire, deep and pure and blazing green that flashed into a bright white flow, blinding as a welding torch, to burn a path from one exposed wire to the other.

Connor's heart skipped a beat. He couldn't breathe, couldn't find the strength to catch a breath as a solid and terrifying power charged the atmosphere with static. The skin on his chest tightened at the touch, hair standing all over his body. And although he hadn't seen it happen, he saw now that the copper endings of the wires had already melted together.

The overhead lights were glowing.

Connor sensed that Barley hadn't moved, was watching with rapt attention. Moving slowly, Connor slid his hands farther away from the exposed copper and pushed, solidifying the weld. The power continued. Then he undid the thick roll of electrical plastic and picked up a small wooden stick. With sweat sliding off his sweat-streaked face, he cast a glance at Barley.

"You'd better step back," he whispered.

Barley stepped back. Unashamed.

With the plastic held lightly on the stick, Connor threw the dangling end over the bare 1,000-amp meld. Instantly the plastic melted, disintegrating to the invisible heat. With infinite caution Connor meticulously turned the plastic on the line, feeling the hairs on his arm and head raise straight up at the immeasurably faint margin of power charging the air and traveling through the plastic strand and stick, the current trying unsuccessfully to connect with the ground through the sawhorse's wooden legs.

Heavy beads of perspiration dripped from Connor's arms, his chin. He used his free hand to carefully wipe sweat from his eyes, focusing with absolute concentration on the bare copper line in front of him.

In five careful minutes, he had wrapped the entire roll of nonadhesive plastic around the section, the plastic melting less and less as it turned, coating the wires. Then Connor took a large roll of narrow black electrical tape, feeling less and less of the current as he wrapped the tape generously around the melted plastic. Finally, after an additional ten minutes of agonizing, patient work, the connecting electrical lines were covered by a large black lump of insulated plastic. No bare wires could be seen.

Sweat soaked his shirt as Connor leaned back. It dripped from his nose, his chin. His shoulders were cramping badly as he wearily tossed the empty paper core of electrical tape to the side.

He stood on the ground, turned to Barley.

"We're hot."

Hand locked hard on the last foot of wire, Thor swung out from the wall, staring down the shaft. He angled the flashlight downward but it was absorbed by the dark. But he knew, if Blankenship was correct, that there were only a hundred feet remaining.

Cables and grease-slick steel girders lined the sides and front of the shaft, but Thor knew trying to maintain a solid handhold on any of them would be even more difficult than holding the wall.

Better, yes, to trust the rock itself, trying for solid holds.

Reaching out to grasp a narrow sliver of stone, bracing the toes of his boots against the wall, Thor studied with exacting concentration for a secure second handhold. He saw several. Then he moved the flashlight around to his gut, letting the beam hit the wall.

Rebounding off the wall in the darkness of the shaft, the light beam was transformed into a wild white haze that illuminated all four walls and a space of the shaft above and below. Using it, Thor guessed that he might pick his way down the remaining hundred feet.

Gathering himself, teeth clenching, Thor released his other hand from the wire and lashed out wildly, slamming against the wall, digging desperately, his fingers finding a narrow hold.

"Can you work the vault doors now with GEO?" Connor asked.

"No," Frank responded. "GEO isn't going to do anything

that it thinks would place us in danger. And GEO is convinced that shutting all the doors is necessary to protect us."

"Well how did you ever plan to get out of this cavern, Frank? How did you plan to escape this place if Leviathan ever got loose?"

"We never anticipated that we would ever have to escape the cavern, Connor! The vaults were just to trap Leviathan so the security personnel could corner it and kill it."

"And the nuclear fail-safe? What was that for?"

Frank hesitated. "The nuclear fail-safe was a contingency plan in case of some kind of emergency. I never really expected to create something like this. I never . . . I never thought it would be needed."

"Well think again, Frank." Connor knelt to study the vault door. After a moment he looked up. "You're certain that GEO won't open any of the doors?"

"GEO will only do what it's programmed to do, Connor."

Connor stared silently at the vault.

"We can raise the door manually," Barley said, stepping forward. "There's an emergency pump built into the side of the vault. It works on hydraulics. Takes less than fifteen seconds."

Frank tensed. "But listen, Connor, if you manually raise that door, GEO is going to interpret it as a broken circuit, as an attack by Leviathan, and it's going to initiate nitrogen thermones stored above the door. None of us will survive the atmosphere."

"We'll use gas masks," Barley countered.

"Nitrogen is stored at minus 150 degrees Celsius," Frank said, turning to him. "This room will be frozen, Barley. We'll be dead from hypothermia in less than ten seconds."

Connor bent forward, placing both hands against the titanium vault. "GEO is just a machine, Frank." His voice was distant. "It's like you said, a machine just does what it's told. Or what it thinks it's told. Which means . . . we have to trick it."

Standing, Connor moved to the vault's control panel. He took out his utility tool and removed the screws that held the cover plate. In a few more seconds he had reworked the circuit, leaving two small wires twisted together and dangling.

"That should be the circuit that tells GEO that the door is

closed," he muttered. "As long as that circuit isn't broken, GEO shouldn't know that we've opened the door. So go ahead, Barley. Time to dance."

The big lieutenant bent without expression and began working the short handle of the hydraulic pump. Instantly the vault opened a foot, two feet, moving steadily upward. Connor saw an inch-thick steel cable quivering at the inside corner of the door, holding the tremendous hydraulic pressure that kept the vault upraised.

Sweating from the effort, Barley stepped back. "Let's hope we don't have to do that in a hurry," he said, unslinging his rifle. He bent, peering under the doorway. "It's clear. Let's move out. This tunnel should lead back to the Command Center."

Thor dug bloody fingers into stone.

Trying to hold a grip on the rock, his hands were numb and bleeding. His four hundred fifty pounds pressed against the wall, dragging him down. His breaths exploded against the rock in hard blasts, mixing with grave-dust. Sweat streaked his face, soaked his hair, falling from his bearded chin.

How much farther?

The darkness beneath him seemed depthless, but Thor knew he had climbed down at least sixty feet from the end of the wire. So there *couldn't* be more than thirty, or even forty feet, remaining.

Depthless darkness . . . Straining, trembling, Thor glared for a more secure handhold, but he had reached a section as smooth as glass, the sides of the wall perfectly cylindrical. He glanced up, frantic, forearms dead with fatigue and pain, and in frenzied fear he couldn't even find the handholds he had used to lower himself to this precarious position.

The battle-ax dragged him back from the wall, and his boots slipped again from their narrow purchase. Groaning, Thor jammed bloody fingers painfully into the rock.

A choked cry of agony escaped him as his boots slipped off

the wall and his entire weight went solidly to his fingertips, shredding his fingernails. He scrambled for a more secure hold on the smooth wall, slipping, scrambling again, slipping . . . Teeth clenched in pain, Thor cast a wild look down—pain, fear, darkness, an abyss . . . Bellowing in agony, unable to ascend or climb, Thor clung savagely at the edge of a long and bitter darkness.

"Can GEO track Leviathan?"

Frank answered Connor's terse question as they moved. "Yes. GEO always knows where Leviathan is."

"So where is Leviathan now?"

Lightly touching the headset, Frank asked, "GEO, what is the exact location of Leviathan?"

"Switch to the speaker system," Connor said. "I want to hear all of this for myself."

"*Leviathan is in Alpha Corridor,*" the computer replied over the speaker system in its impersonal voice. "*Leviathan is standing at the Observation Room.*"

Halting in place, Frank stared at nothing. Connor froze beside him, watching. A cold pall of silent fear seemed to cross the scientist's face. His hand continued to touch the headset.

"GEO, what is the brain activity of Leviathan?" he asked.

"*Leviathan's EEG activity is at maximum speed and maximum intensity.*"

Head turning like a doll, Frank looked at Connor. "GEO," he asked, eerily still, "how long has Leviathan been stationary at the Observation Room? How long has it been stationary?"

"*Leviathan has been stationary at the Observation Room for forty-six minutes and twelve seconds.*"

Frank's face went white.

"What is it?" Connor asked.

"It's about to attack again."

"How can you know that?"

"It's standing beside the Observation Room so it can study the structural integrity of this place."

"Study the structure? It's an animal!"

"We've got to move," Frank said, running forward. "We've got to reach Chesterton before Leviathan reaches the entrance of Alpha Corridor. I think that it's discovered a way to defeat the vault!"

Chapter 16

A graveyard-dead disbelief rose from the depths of Chesterton's sullen eyes. It was the look of a man who absolutely could not believe the dismal, dark fate that had been delivered to him.

"Give me that again, Doctor," he muttered.

"All right," Frank said, leaning over a computer terminal, "let me put it to you as simply as possible. Leviathan is a programmed organism that has specialized knowledge available to it from memory implantation."

"What kind of knowledge are we talking about?"

The scientist raised his hands. "Any kind of knowledge, Chesterton! Leviathan has an entire encyclopedia of knowledge in its memory network. It has knowledge of countries, capitals, ocean currents, climatic conditions, national populations. It had to have all that information if we were ever going to release it into the lake. It had to know how to find its way to the targeted armies, capitals, whatever. It had to—"

"Wait a minute, Doctor. I thought Leviathan's memory implantation dealt mostly with military tactics."

"Yeah, Chesterton, Leviathan understands whatever tactics your people put on those tapes. But Leviathan has a constantly evolving neural network that is always—"

"Frank!" Chesterton slammed both hands on a desk. "I'm tired of science reports! I don't have *time* for them! Just give it to me in English!"

"Fine!" Frank responded, leaning back. "I'll make it simple for you, Chesterton." He pointed solidly at the Alpha vault. "Leviathan is about to come through that vault like a freight train! And you'd better get ready for it because nothing can stop it."

"You said it can't melt titanium!"

"Now I'm saying that Leviathan has found a weakness in the construction that even we don't know about. And you'd better believe me, Chesterton, because I know this creature."

Frowning, Chesterton stood silent a moment "All right, Frank," he said finally. "Then tell me this: What is that thing going to do when it comes through that doorway?"

"The first thing it's going to do is knock out the lights."

"Then it will be in the dark," Chesterton muttered.

"It doesn't need light, Chesterton."

"It can see in the dark? You never told me that!"

"You never asked."

"I . . . I cannot believe this." Chesterton lowered his head with the words, looked up after a moment. He placed his hands on his hips, leaning forward as he turned to Barley. "Lieutenant! Take all the C-4 and dynamite and whatever else you can find, and rig it up with a microwave switch at the exit of Alpha Corridor. And get it done *yesterday*!"

"Yes sir!" Barley replied, was gone.

A ponderous pause, with Chesterton staring at the vault. For a long time no one cared to speak.

"What does any of this mean, Frank?" he asked finally. He shook his head, looking down at the floor. "What does any of this really mean?"

Frank focused on him.

"It means we're not in control, Chesterton. It means we never were."

Roaring as his fingers were torn from the rock, Thor saw the metallic gleam to his left and decided . . .

Use the elevator cables!

In the frantic moment as his fingers tore from the rock, Thor slammed his boots forcefully against the wall and launched his titanic form through the air, sailing through darkness. And in the next second he crashed against the serpentine black cables to grasp wildly at the thinly-oiled, slick steel as he rebounded out and down.

Instantly in the rushing, formless moment, Thor's hand flashed out to strike a steel girder with bruising force, all his strength centered in the fingers of his hand.

Bellowing in pain, Thor dug his fingers in the steel, trying to find a solid grip in the heavily greased elevator frame. But his great weight dragged him backward, his grip sliding on the thin oil. And yet for a herculean moment he held, his entire arm trembling with the strain while his other hand reached wildly at the cable, the steel, flashing down the rock for a wild swipe at an unseen crevice as vivid thoughts blasted his mind . . .

Innocent lives, lost . . . Evil, eyes glowing . . . Innocence consumed . . . Evil devouring . . . Darkness, *rising* . . .

Thor snarled, scrambling savagely for a hold, but against his will he felt his grip slipping. Knowing he could not hold, he tried a sliding descent; but as he released the slightest pressure, he knew he had lost it all to darkness rising, rising, *rising* . . .

Thor roared back into . . .

Black, rushing wind . . .

Falling . . .

Chapter 17

Leaving Jordan in the sleep of exhaustion, Beth walked into the Conference Room of the Housing Cavern. It was only a couple rooms away, and she knew that she could hear Jordan if he awoke crying.

The computers were still secretly working to break the encryption, and there was nothing else she could do on that level. So she had locked the door and, to release a measure of anger, ventured out to confront the men responsible for this tragedy.

She stalked coldly into a conference room to find Hoffman engaged in angry debate with an Army colonel, Blake, the one who had come to the surface and taken her into the cavern. And then there was Adler, the tall, mysterious figure who had arrived at the island three months ago. He stood beside the Russian named Tolvanos. Beth felt a grim pleasure at seeing the Russian's nose and upper cheek swollen, badly bruised from where she had smashed the keyboard over his face.

She glanced around the cavern, saw that all the overhead lights were working. But the big vaults that sealed the exits were still locked, shut solid. So she walked forward, eyes narrowing. She noticed distinctly that no one else in the room seemed willing to join the debate.

"No!" Hoffman shouted, pointing his pipe at Adler. "You are the one responsible for this atrocity, Mr. Adler! It is not this incompetent Russian scientist that I have for so long despised!"

"Likewise, Dr. Hoffman," the Russian smiled warmly.

"I believe that the military has jurisdiction here," Adler replied, gesturing patiently to Blake. "So if you have any complaints I suggest you level them at those who—"

"I do not lodge complaints with fools," Hoffman said, an old growl. "Yes, Blake is an incompetent bootlicker who should have known better! But he is not ultimately responsible for this carnage because he did not replace Dr. Frank, a very capable scientist who knew quite well what this creature might do! It was *you*, Mr. Adler! It was *you* who called for an across-the-board replacement of this facility's personnel so that you could complete unsafe testing to meet your schedule! And I *know* the reason." Hoffman stepped forward, nodding. "Yes, I know. I know that this has become a CIA Black Operation that will ultimately be used to control the world."

His condemnation was complete.

"Yes, I know, Mr. Adler. I am not so old that I cannot recognize the signs of covert subterfuge. But that does not excuse what you have done! Blake is a fool, yes. And Tolvanos is a monster, a merchant of death. But it is *your* personal ambition that has brought us to this regrettable hour! In your . . . your *stupidity*, you challenged the higher reason of men who knew far better than yourself. You challenged, even, a force of nature and delivered us all to this peril!"

Beth saw that Adler was unconcerned with what Hoffman thought of him. He seemed to be a man who held his own opinion as the only meaningful standard for measuring anything at all.

"Dr. Hoffman," Adler replied, smiling, "all great science is intimately bound to the fate of men. To the fate of the entire world, for that matter. Because great science redefines nature as we know it, even changes nature. But this is no time for such a high-minded debate. At this moment there are more pressing issues confronting us."

Beth stepped into the confrontation, arms crossed. She made it clear by her physical position that she stood behind Hoffman. In every way.

"I want to tell you something," she said, focusing coldly on

Adler. And as the older man turned to her, Beth noticed a slight cut beneath the cheek, as if he had been hit. Hard.

"Please, Mrs. Connor, I have no time for your—"

"I don't want to hear that garbage," Beth said, thinking of her son. "And I don't want to hear your pathetic, condescending drivel. I'm not here to argue with you, Adler. I came here to tell you something personal. And you're going to hear it."

Colonel Blake snapped his fingers at the guard, a young man who held the only weapon in the room. "Escort Mrs. Connor back to her room," he said sternly. "Ensure that she does not disturb us again."

Paling, the guard stood in place. He cast a quick glance at Beth, and she returned it compassionately, knowing that Barley had instructed the man to leave her alone.

Enraged by the soldier's refusal to immediately obey his order, Blake turned forcefully: "That's a *direct* order, soldier! Colonel Chesterton is very likely dead and that leaves *me* in command! I do not intend to let this situation deteriorate any further! Now *do as you are told!*"

Swaying, the guard held his place. "I'm sorry, Colonel," he replied. "But Colonel Chesterton gave me my last orders to hold all of you here. So . . . so you're officially under arrest! And Lieutenant Barley told me not to disturb Mrs. Connor. I've got my orders."

Blake glared, as if he couldn't comprehend what was happening. He stepped close to the guard. "Soldier," he said, "we are in a grave situation. And you and I are probably the only military personnel still alive in this installation. So the line of command is clear. I am a colonel! You are a private! I give the orders and you obey them! Do you understand?"

The soldier shifted nervously.

Blake shouted, "Private! Do as you are told! The Army is a machine! And we do as we are told or the machine breaks down!" He paused briefly. "It's true, yes, that Colonel Chesterton suffered a mental breakdown before his death, and you cannot be blamed for obeying his orders. Nor will any regulation discipline be initiated against you. But that does not change the fact that Colonel Chesterton is dead and we need to resolve this situation!"

A tense pause. "I'm sorry, sir," the private finally responded. "I was given my last orders from Colonel Chesterton to secure you. That's the extent of my duty. Mrs. Connor can do whatever she wishes."

For a long time Blake continued to stare, choked by his wrath. Then he turned away, fists clenched at his sides. Beth was too tired to smile.

"Then I will give you an order, soldier," Adler turned to the private. "I ultimately control this facility and since we don't know whether Colonel Chesterton is alive or dead, we must clearly have someone in command. Please escort Mrs. Connor back to her room."

"I'm sorry, sir," the guard replied without any hesitation whatsoever. "I received my last order from Colonel Chesterton. I don't work for you. Since Colonel Chesterton reclaimed command I have no mandate to imprison or control Mrs. Connor."

Adler's jaw set, and Beth felt a light laugh escape her. It was humorous to see that the authority of a probably dead Chesterton was more powerful than the wrath of a living Blake and Adler combined. She stepped forward, mouth tight. "So, Mr. Adler, you're the one responsible for this?" she asked, her smile twisting into a chilling glare.

"Mrs. Connor," Adler gestured vaguely, "I do not have time for—"

"Answer my question!"

"Mrs. Connor!" Adler turned fully toward her. "Remember your station! You are only a supervisor of the Ice Station's Communication Center, and you deal exclusively with civilian affairs, which means that you have *no right* to question my orders!" He glared down. "Nor do you have the right to circumvent any security measures! Your attempt to break the security code was a grave, grave crime. A *federal* crime."

"Oh, rest assured," Beth replied flatly, "I'm still going to smash your security code, Mr. Adler. I'm going to smash it into pieces and then I'm going to shove it down your throat. Because you'll have to kill me before I let you do this to my family."

Adler stared. "You will never break the security code, Mrs. Connor. You merely boast. Your government's most revered security agency instituted it to prohibit unauthorized use of this system."

"Oh, I'll break it, *Mister* Adler," Beth said, lifting her chin. "And I just wanted you to know something. Your secrets are finished. Forever. And *you're* finished. Because when I break that code the entire world is going to know what's been going on down here. And I mean that. The entire world."

"I believe," Adler replied slowly, eyes hazing with menace, "that you should be more careful in your actions, Mrs. Connor. You may place yourself in grave danger."

Beth laughed, stepping even closer.

"Do you pray, Mr. Adler?"

Stunned, Adler began, "I . . . Yes . . . Of course I pray, Mrs. Connor. All good men pray for—"

"Then you'd better pray that nothing happens to my child or my husband," Beth said, coldly holding Adler's gaze. "Because if Connor or Jordan is hurt, the only thing you'll need to be afraid of is me. And believe me, Mr. Adler, you'd better be very, very afraid."

Thor stared at the darkness a long time before he realized he was awake.

Floating in darkness, yes . . .

No . . . not floating.

Cold, black stone.

He was lying on black stone, cold surrounding him. He didn't realize for a long time that he was alive, then it came to him at once, a falling, white-black fear, nothing, then a solidifying awareness that made him conscious of the cold night, of air.

Cautiously Thor moved his left arm, testing. Yes, he could still move. He had survived. And he felt cautiously, trying to register if his back had been broken. But everything seemed intact.

He felt splintered wood beside him, matchstick edges of a rifle stock. It was his weapon, but Thor couldn't think of it now.

In pain, he sat up, gently touching a wound on his head, crusted with blood. With a deep breath he gazed about the dark, remembering what had happened.

He had fallen. Fallen perhaps as far as twenty feet before he struck a sloping rock. But the bruising impact slowed him briefly and he had managed a wild, tearing hold on the outcrop before rebounding painfully from something else, perhaps a steel beam, to fall another ten feet until finally slamming with mind-numbing force upon the shaft floor.

Thor realized he was cold, possibly in shallow shock. And he had no idea how long he had lain unconscious, bleeding and beaten. But he decided, with a cautious testing, that no bones were broken. He wearily let it fall away, useless now. Then he felt the battle-ax at his back.

Stiffly, Thor shrugged off his cloak, slipping the battle-ax's strap from his shoulders. Even in the dark, he knew by the perfectly balanced weight that the ancient weapon had survived the terrific fall. Then he rolled, rising unsteadily to his feet, leaving the ax on the stones. And he stood for a moment, swaying, dizzy, sensing . . . *something*.

A stillness of air.

Blindly Thor reached out and instantly his hand touched . . . *cold* . . . cold steel. As smooth as glass. Teeth clenched, Thor smiled. *Yes!* It was the entrance of the cavern. He spread his arms, measuring the dimension of the massive steel portal, but the colossal vault was even wider than his enormous reach, stretching into the dark.

Thor stepped back and cautiously reached down, lifting the battle-ax to sling it over a shoulder, fighting off dizziness. Then he slowly angled left, stepping carefully to avoid stones, following Blankenship's instructions toward the ventilation tunnel.

Down here, Thor knew, or felt somehow, he had entered a strange and different world. A world that was both sovereign and powerful unto itself, ruled by the absence of hated light as powerfully as the world above was ruled by its presence.

But he had no time for such thoughts. He turned his mind from them, concentrating on what he had to do. With six cautious steps, he had reached the edge of the steel door. He didn't search for his flashlight. He knew it could not have survived the fall. So he gently waved his hands in the air, feeling, finding the air current, then closing his hands toward the wall until he touched the slated ventilation grate.

Yes, the current. It was there.

Warm, dark air.

Thor smiled at his success and then his smile faded, his face setting in grim determination. His teeth clenched tight as his fingers curled inward through the thick rebar-grate, locking like talons. Then his huge, solid shoulders pulled hard against the steel.

Nothing.

The steel was immovable. Buried in six inches of granite.

A mountain, deep in stone.

A moment more Thor stood, feeling the ice-cold steel in his grip, its power mocking him, destroying him. Yes, he knew, all his life had brought him to this hour. All that he had ever loved and honored. All that he had ever lost, and all that he had ever defended.

"No," he whispered. "No . . . No . . ."

He would not be stopped.

With a dark frown Thor leaned forward, locking an iron grip on the thick steel bars that left no blood in his hands. Then his hold tightened even more, grinding the steel into his flesh until his fingers cracked with pressure. And his titanic shoulders expanded, herculean arms tensing and bending to prepare the full, massive measure of a strength he had never used. His heart beat faster, and faster, until he felt his heartbeat there, in his hands, in the steel.

Thor bent his head, teeth clenched, eyes tight.

"No," he whispered. "Almighty God, *you* are my *strength*! . . . and I trust my life . . . to *you!*"

With a roar he surged back.

Steel ripped away from stone.

Connor finished rewiring the exit door that would allow them to escape the Command Cavern. He glanced up as Chesterton approached.

"You finished with that, Connor?"

"It's finished," Connor replied, rising to gaze across the cavern where Barley and a handful of soldiers were rigging a formidable load of C-4, dynamite, claymore mines, and other incendiary devices. "Is that enough of a charge to blow that thing to pieces?"

"It'd *better be*," Chesterton grimaced. "'Cause that's all we've got. And once we blow it, this cavern is going to be superheated to about thirty thousand degrees for about ten seconds before the roof comes down. So we won't be getting back in here for supplies."

"Are you taking everything you can carry? Just in case?"

"Yes, everything," Chesterton confirmed, handing Connor a rifle. With a short pause, Connor took it. He knew what it was—an M-16 with a grenade launcher attached to the lower part of the barrel. It was what they called an M-203.

"Do you know how to use that?"

Without waiting for an answer Chesterton handed Connor an ammo belt with a dozen 50-round clips and another shoulder belt with a large number of antipersonnel grenades that could be fired from the grenade launcher.

"Yeah," Connor replied steadily. "I've fired a few rounds through one."

"Well this ain't no plinking contest, Connor. If that thing comes through that door you just need to remember one thing."

"What's that?"

"When in doubt, empty the clip. Ammo is cheap. Your life isn't."

Connor smiled. "Yeah, I guess that—"

A thunderous collision struck the vault of Alpha Corridor, and Chesterton immediately spun, leveling his rifle. At the door, soldiers scurried back, shocked by the terrific impact, and Connor saw that Barley alone stood his ground, slamming detonators into the C-4 as fast as he could move.

"Barley!" Chesterton screamed. "Get out of there!"

"Thirty seconds!" the lieutenant shouted. He ran to a high load of dynamite and quickly adjusted a detonator. Connor ran up to Chesterton, who was screaming to the rest of the scrambling soldiers. "Get that other vault open so we can retreat! Do it now!"

A second impact, but deeper, continued like a prolonged nuclear blast, quaking the vault beside Barley. Connor glanced up as stalactites broke away from the ceiling, falling like spears.

"Look out!" he yelled, leaping to the side to avoid a two-ton impact of a calcite column. He rolled to his feet to see Barley working feverishly to finish the explosive charges.

Again a sharp impact struck the vault, and then another explosive blast and another impact, and Connor realized suddenly what was happening. The beast had finally pinpointed a specific weakness in the vault, a single section that it was attacking to overcome the portal. A hissing could be heard in the wall. Connor whirled to see Frank staring at the vault.

"What's that sound?" Connor asked.

"It's nitrogen," Frank replied, holding his place. "Leviathan has ruptured some part of the vault." Then the scientist's face brightened. "Of course! Of course that's what it would do!"

"What?" Connor yelled. "What would it do?"

"It's not attacking the vault at all! It's attacking the bracketing! It's attacking the *steel* bracketing with flame to break the titanium out and then it's just going to knock the door into this cavern!" Connor heard a savage rending of metal in the wall above the vault.

"Barley!" Chesterton bellowed. "Get out of there! That's a direct order! Get out of there now!"

Breathless and fatigued the muscular man looked up. "One more second, Colonel, and I can—"

"NO! Forget it! Forget it! Move! Move! Move!"

In an explosion of rock and nitrogen gas, a monstrous foreleg blasted open a gaping hole twenty feet high on the wall, far above the fire door. A roar thundered through the dark orb as Leviathan's powerful limb, skin gleaming like black metal-leather, savaged the hole even farther—shattering the steel like wood, reaching in farther to pull back again, shredding the metal with black claws. Chesterton ran toward Barley, who stuck an entire handful of detonators into a brick of C-4.

In a colossal display of irresistible strength, Leviathan slammed both forelegs back through the hole, one after the other. Connor and Frank backed up. Then Leviathan tore at the ruptured space for the length of the entire vault before it jerked both forelegs back through.

Silence.

Frank staggered. "Get ready!"

A runaway freight train hit the vault, and what remained of the foundation surrendered to the force, the door bending outward from the top just as Chesterton reached Barley and roughly grabbed the lieutenant by the arm, dragging him to his feet.

Barley wildly hurled the remaining detonators pell-mell onto the dynamite and was instantly running with Chesterton across the cavern. They covered a hundred yards when an even more powerful impact struck the door, and in a painful rending of metal and earth the vault was defeated, falling like a wall into the Command Center.

A sonic boom sounded in the cavern, dust rising. And although neither Chesterton or Barley turned to look back, Connor knew from their expressions that they sensed death behind them, close and closing.

"Get out of here!" Chesterton screamed as he neared, waving his hands. "We're gonna blow it we're gonna blow it!"

Leviathan stood in the open tunnel, and for the first time Connor truly saw it.

Rising almost sixteen feet high on its hindlegs, the Dragon advanced into the cavern, standing like a bear, the thick body muscular and heavily armored, reptilian in aspect but beyond that, older than that. Its forelegs were long and batlike, ending in claws that gleamed like black swords. And thick, green-black armor covered its entire form, the scales large and tight, bending easily with its movements and completely unscarred by the earlier combat. The neck was lor.g, tapering to a wicked head that opened sharply, unhinging jaws as white and layered as a shark's.

Leviathan's dragon-eyes, green and glowing darkly, scanned the cavern for the briefest moment before centering on them and focusing with malevolent, hateful intelligence.

Connor saw the thick, powerful tail whip around, almost fifteen feet of it, smashing into the wall. The tail's tapered end easily sliced off a section of steel plating and the Dragon lowered its head, unleashing a deafening roar that thundered across the expanse of the cavern, crashing over them with ancient, physical force.

At the roar Chesterton spun violently toward the Dragon, running backward and wildly firing his rifle as if the beast were on top of him. Then the Army colonel spun back again, his face vivid with fear, screaming and waving frantically. "Get out of here you fools! Barley! Blow it!"

Barley ignored the order and grabbed Chesterton's shoulder, dragging the colonel toward the door. Then with a shriek Leviathan raised its head to unleash a wide, waving stream of liquid fire that blazed upward at the ceiling, blasting the dome of the cavern into a cloud of flame, igniting the stone, raining . . .

Enraged and ignoring the holocaust, Barley turned, screaming, "Get out of here, Connor!"

Connor obeyed instantly, throwing himself low under the door and leaping beyond it, breathless and off balance. He couldn't find his stance in the chaos, the fear, and the confusion, and stumbled away. But concerned for Chesterton and Barley, he managed to cast a wild glance back to see the colonel shoved through the narrow space beneath the door, thrown by two powerful hands that handled him as easily as they would handle a child.

Dazed, Chesterton staggered up with a painful cry and fell to the side. His arm was on fire, and he had lost his M-16. Understanding instantly what was about to happen, Connor angrily threw his rifle to the side and reached out, grabbing Chesterton to jerk him away from the door.

Then Connor heard rifle fire and a defiant human cry on the other side of the vault, challenged by a bestial roar that trembled the earth. And to Connor's amazement, Barley was rolling beneath the door, leaping effectively clear to aim a small black box at the gap.

He frantically pressed a button.

Connor felt a blinding sharp roar fill his head as a shock wave blasted a path beneath the half-raised vault and then there was only white flame, liquid fire, and pain that continued in a volcanic eruption to bring down the light and the darkness together.

Chapter 18

Connor thought for a moment that he was dead, but adrenaline and fear brought him back to hateful life. Then he felt something approaching, something . . . *monstrous*.

A shattering impact struck the vault door beside them.

Instantly a handful of survivors moaned, rolled, staggered noisily to their feet. Connor blinked at the dim emergency lights, and then he realized that the shock wave had ruptured the power lines in this end of the tunnel. Reorienting with a violent effort, he felt himself for wounds, found none. He felt for Chesterton and found the colonel lying to his side. Fired by strength and fear, Connor shook him hard. Heard someone shouting.

It was Barley, bellowing.

"Connor!"

"Yeah!"

"Get Colonel Chesterton! I'm going ahead to open the vault at the far end of this passageway! We've got to get some distance on this thing! Get everybody that's still alive and follow me! You got it?"

"Yeah, yeah, I got it! Just go!"

Barley's tall dark shadow disappeared down the corridor as Leviathan hit the vault again. A fiendishly long foreleg, talons gleaming black-red, snaked under the open fire door, reaching, scraping. But all of them were too far back from the portal.

"Chesterton!" Connor lifted the colonel to a sitting position. "Get it together! That thing's still alive!"

Another superheated blast hit the vault, and Connor saw liquid fire dripping to the narrowly-raised space of the vault door. Dust and darkness stirred at the beast's shuffling and Connor saw a long, clawed foot against the flaming stones. He spun back around.

"Chesterton! Come on, man! Get it together!"

With a groan Chesterton seemed to come around. In the dim light created by Leviathan's continuing, flaming attack, Connor saw the colonel lift a hand to his bloodied head. "Oh man," he mumbled.

Connor felt his teeth clench in vivid fear. There was no time left for compassion. Connor began dragging the wounded colonel to his feet. "Come on, Chesterton. Get on your feet! That thing's coming through the wall in less than a minute!"

Chesterton staggered up. "Barley . . ." he gasped. "Where's Barley . . ."

"He's alive," Connor answered, staggering down the hallway, finding uncertain footing on the fallen rock. He whirled back suddenly. "Frank! Where are you?"

"I'm here!" an unsteady voice answered, shadow coming close.

"Come on, Doctor! We've got to move down the hallway, to the far end of this corridor."

Frank leaned his hand against the wall as he moved. "Yeah, I know. I know."

At the exit of the Command Cavern, Leviathan continued its attack, relentless and raging. Connor knew the beast's blast-furnace flame and the strategically placed physical blows against the fire door would soon tear the structure from its moorings.

But in moments the survivors had recovered, gathering speed. They gained steadiness as they went forward, and then they were running, following the wide, twisting corridor for a half mile to come to the vault-sealed end that led into the Matrix, a cavern named for the spiraling columns of limestone and calcite that rose titanically from the 200,000-square-foot floor comprised of granite and calcite cave pearls. It was used primarily for storing heavy equipment, spare steel plating, and additional ventilation ducts.

Connor was grateful that the lights in this end of the passageway were still functioning. They glared fluorescent white in the calcite-dust atmosphere raised from the trembling attack on the fire door, now far behind him. As he reached the end of the passageway he saw that Barley had already removed the control cover plate on the vault, rewiring the circuit. Familiar now with the routine, a half dozen soldiers began working the hydraulic pump, raising the door two feet, and then three, so they could enter the cavern.

A murderous collision followed by a victorious roar sounded at the distant end of the tunnel, alerting them to the fact that the beast had almost defeated the fire door. Quickly everyone began to slide beneath the vault into the sprawlingly large cavern beyond.

But Chesterton broke away from Connor and leaned against a wall, staring back down the passageway. He drew a .45-caliber semiautomatic pistol from his holster, infinitely weary. Yet he still retained his military bearing, and Connor began to understand the true strength of intelligence and will that had made the man a colonel in the first place. Then Barley and two other soldiers slid beneath the narrowly raised vault, entering the cavern.

"We've got to slow it down," Chesterton said weakly, face smeared in blackened sweat. "We can't outrun it."

Connor grimaced, knowing he was right.

Overhead lights swung, vibrating to the thunderous bellowing that traveled the length of the tunnel, and Connor looked up to see the huge power cables running across the roof. His teeth came together with a snap.

Of course.

Immediately he spun, seeing where the cable tied into the intermediate connector box, high and to the side of the vault door. "Chesterton!" he shouted. "Get your men to bring me a ladder! And do it quick!"

Chesterton didn't even question it; things were obviously too bad for him to question any idea at all.

His voice rang out and Connor heard a response on the far

side of the vault, inside the Matrix, the rush of men scurrying to obey. In a moment two soldiers slid an extension ladder beneath the fire door. Other soldiers raised it to the wall, following Connor's instructions.

A violent, shattering concussion shook the cavern floor, and Connor knew that the vault had finally struck the ground, slammed out. Connor glared down the tunnel, trembling instantly, expecting to see the nightmarish shape rushing toward them, glaring, gaping, slashing.

Nothing happened.

Silence.

Frank was beside him, sweating, breathing heavily as Connor stared down the wide, twisting passageway.

"Why isn't it on top of us?" Connor whispered.

Frank shook his head, quiet. "It's . . . it's probably feeding on the soldiers who died when the roof came down. Because of its enhanced metabolism, Leviathan has to eat a lot. About a thousand pounds of meat every two hours. I think we might have another minute."

Connor backed carefully to the ladder. "When it comes down the tunnel will it come fast? Or slow and careful?"

"Slowly," Frank answered. He wiped a blackened arm over his brow, smearing even more soot over his sweating face. "Because of what we just did to it, it'll be looking for another ambush. It's always learning. It'll probably be looking for explosives."

"What else would it look for?"

"Heat signatures in the dark. Soldiers."

Connor began climbing the ladder. "Good."

In a moment he was at the top. He quietly opened an intermediate breaker box. Like most of the circuit connecting points, the box was crammed with lines of varying power. Connor found a line of 10,000 volts. He studied it a minute, calculating. "No, not enough," he whispered. "Not enough to put you down for the count . . ."

He continued to search until he came across it—a line of over 100,000 volts. It was as thick as his thumb. Connor knew it was a primary feedline from the power plant. He began loosening the brackets as he looked down, observing Chesterton's upturned face.

He spoke slowly, distinctly. "Chesterton, raise the vault all the way and tell your men to remove a section of the walkway right in front of the door. Then have them remove another section on the far side of the cavern." Connor leaned down. "Tell them to put as much fiberglass and wood under the legs of the middle section as possible so that the steel is not touching the ground! I'm going to electrify the middle section, and I'm gonna use that thing behind us to ground out the current."

Chesterton's eyes blazed. "Yeah . . . Yeah! You need the middle section of walkway insulated from the ground so when that thing steps on the steel, the current's going to go through it and into the ground!" His relief was wild. "Do you think that will kill it?"

"I don't know," Connor replied. "There's no way to know how much resistance that thing has to a current."

"What do you mean?" Chesterton staggered.

Connor grunted as he twisted the brackets holding the wire. "That thing weighs almost six tons, Chesterton. I don't know . . . I don't know how much current it'll take . . . to kill it!"

"But that much will hurt it, right?"

"Hurt it, yeah. But I don't know if it'll be enough to kill it. This stuff is complicated." Chesterton nodded and ducked under the doorway, giving tense instructions to Barley. Instantly there were shuffling sounds echoing in the cavern, the tunnel.

Working feverishly, shaking sweat from his head, Connor managed to break the sturdy ceramic brackets that held the high-voltage line in place. Because the line was heavily insulated, he grabbed the rubber coating with his hand.

Then, careful to hold the bare copper ending far from anything that could ground it out, Connor pulled the cable from the wall. It was backbreaking labor because he was forced to pull with one hand, but in thirty seconds he had hauled out thirty feet of excess line.

Still holding the end of the line by the insulation, Connor rapidly descended the ladder. As he hit the ground, cautiously holding the insulated section of 100,000-volt line in his fist, Connor saw that Chesterton had come back under the vault and stopped dead in place, white and trembling, staring with wide eyes down the passageway.

Connor whirled, glaring to see the gigantic Dragon shadow that blackened a close section of the darkened tunnel. The godlike image stood carefully outside the light.

Angry eyes glowed.

A growl vibrated the passageway.

"What was that?" Beth asked, staring at the wall of the Housing Cavern. The shock wave had trembled the entire structure, more than twenty rooms, even breaking a lighting fixture loose from the ceiling.

The guard, Private Thompson, held his rifle close. "I don't know, ma'am," he said carefully, staring at the wall beside her. "It sounded like some kind of explosion."

"What kind of explosion?"

"I . . . I'm not in demolition, Mrs. Connor, but if I had to make a guess, I'd say it sounded like dynamite."

"Like someone was dynamiting one of those vaults?"

Thompson nodded. "Yes, ma'am. Maybe. I don't know what else it could have been. But it was pretty deep in the cavern. A few miles, maybe. Or maybe more."

Dr. Hoffman was at her side. "I believe that they are still alive, Mrs. Connor," he said. "At least, from the sound of the explosion, it is clear that at least some of them are still alive. Perhaps your husband is among them. We must not give up hope."

Beth turned to him, smiling faintly, grateful. Then she heard Jordan crying and she turned instantly away, moving toward the room where he lay. She didn't know who or what had caused the explosion, but she knew that there were obviously still some men alive in the deepest part of the cavern.

Coldly wiping a tear from the corner of her eye, she prayed that Connor was one of them.

Thor could not move another inch through the ventilation shaft. A large fan, easily powerful enough to clear the entire cavern of smoke, spun blindingly, only inches from his eyes.

He had crawled two hundred feet through the shaft before encountering it, a spinning black haze highlighted by the fluorescent lights that blazed from inside the facility. He could not see past the revolving blades, but he knew he had reached the cavern itself.

Yes, this was where the smoke had passed.

He studied the spinning black blades a long time. He knew that if he stuck a hand in there he would lose it instantly. The dusty edges would still be sharp enough to sever his arm. He glanced at the fan's foundation, visible in the dim white light, and saw that it was anchored into the wall with stout bolts sunk in concrete blocks.

He nodded, bringing up the battle-ax beside him. It was a difficult movement, turning the ax in the shaft until he held it by the broad, double-bladed head. Then he held it by the top of the wide steel with one hand, the steel handle of the ax protruding in front of him. For a moment he thought that he could time it, but the fan was spinning too quickly. He made two abrupt motions to thrust the handle through the blades, pulling back at the last second. Then he gritted his teeth with determination and shoved the handle with all his might, driving it forward.

The battle-ax was almost torn from his hands as the fan wrenched the handle to the side and Thor shouted, holding a tight grip and driving the handle in farther, at an angle, up and through the mesh on the far side of the spinning blades. The fan engine screamed to spin the blades, and Thor released one hand from the ax handle. Shouting, he brought his left hand back and slammed it against the fan motor, smashing the heel of his palm on the motor, but it didn't move and the engine strained to spin the blades.

Grimacing in pain, Thor could smell the engine overheating, pulling with incredible force against the ax handle. The ax handle was moving inexorably through the aluminum mesh, tearing, shredding, surrendering to the power of the engine.

Thor saw what would happen if the ax handle came loose from the far side; the double-sided blade on his side would spin uncontrollably in the confined space of the shaft to slice him into pieces. He cursed in rage, hitting the engine motor savagely with his open hand, driving forward, all his weight into the vicious blow.

It did not move. Again and again he pounded, howling, pushing on the frame. He brought his hand back even farther, seeing the bloody black smear on the engine frame, and he struck it again and again, exhausted now, sweating and unable to breathe in the dank air but still it did not give and with a bellowing roar Thor saw a red rage and imagined his death here in this infernal shaft and he struck the fan to break his bones or shatter the bolts and the top of the foundation tore away, the fan frame leaning out.

Thor felt no relief, allowed no respite. Caught in his rage he hit it again, numb to the pain, and again, driving the frame out. Suddenly the ax shuddered in the iron grip of his right hand, almost tearing loose, the fan blades beginning to break free. Then Thor saw a narrow white line coming from the torn section of wall, snaking into the engine and with a hated curse he reached out, fiercely tearing the wire from the motor.

The fan engine died but Thor was in a black berserk rage and he hit the fan again with his palm, grasping it solidly as his hand smashed against it. He pushed with all the strength of his arm and shoulder, roaring and pushing harder still with his scrambling legs to drive it out and the frame tore cleanly out of the concrete wall, falling down and away to carry the aluminum mesh with it in a long, continuous crash.

Snarling at the pain in his hand, Thor tossed the battle-ax ahead of him and crawled quickly out of the shaft grasping the edge as he passed it to lower himself to the ground.

Panting, still angry from the rage required for the effort, Thor reached down and immediately hefted the ax again, to stand. When he turned toward the cavern he was met by the sight of a lone man, a young man. It was apparently one of the scientists.

Wide-eyed, hands clasped, the man stared. He was the cavern's only occupant.

Towering eight feet above the cavern floor, Thor steadily approached the man. Thor's ice-green eyes blazed with pain, and his red hair and beard dripped steadily with dark sweat. His white bearskin was blackened by the crawl through the shaft and blood fell heavily from his left hand as he held the gigantic battle-ax in the other. Finally, he stood over the man, frowning down.

The young man trembled before Thor's colossal, mythic aspect. And Thor knew that the paling scientist would have fled, if he could have only found the strength.

"Who are you?" the young man whispered.

Thor gazed down, smiled.

"No one you should fear."

"Oh no," whispered Chesterton, backing up.

"Don't move!" Frank said tensely.

Blinking sweat, Connor froze in place. He felt his face cold and wet, the skin on his back crawling. Not just because the beast stood before them. It was because the growl that came from the depths of the darkness was more than bestial; it was supernatural, mocking, hateful.

The growl continued a long moment before it descended to a horrible, trembling threat. And then with a quickness that made Connor almost leap back, Frank took a solid step forward, boldly making a stand in the middle of the tunnel.

The scientist stared dead center at the ominous shadow.

Connor watched, dazed, as Frank raised clenched fists to his sides, staring at Leviathan with no aspect of fear whatsoever. The scientist held the defiant, weaponless position as if he would never move, as if he could kill the beast with a glance. Connor was shocked almost as much by the suicidal stand as the beast crouching in the darkness less than three hundred feet away.

Leviathan's growl, angry and suspicious, rumbled from the blackened section of the passageway. Connor stiffened his trembling knees, tried to speak. "Frank . . . what . . . are you doing?"

The scientist's reply was alarmingly loud. "It doesn't understand!" he shouted. Chesterton jumped.

"Frank!" the colonel hissed through clenched teeth. "Are . . . you . . . *insane?*"

"It doesn't *understand!*" Frank yelled again, taking a very small step forward. "It doesn't understand how one man would come against it without a weapon! It suspects a trap! That's how it's programmed to think!"

Frank held his fists at his sides, glaring utterly without fear. Then in a challenging movement that caused Connor to curse out loud, the scientist pointed dramatically at the floor.

With a volcanic growl, Leviathan retreated a step.

"God in heaven help us," Chesterton whispered, closing his eyes. His sweating fist trembled on the .45.

"Back up!" Frank yelled. "Connor, set that trap! Fast!"

Connor and Chesterton stepped back without thinking. But even as they moved, the creature responded, clearly understanding retreat. It leaped forward from the darkness, covering a hundred feet with a bound. Growling more angrily, Leviathan crouched long and low in the tunnel, tail sweeping left and right, balancing the gigantic dragon form.

A green-black horror in the full light, the Dragon lowered its massive reptilian head toward Frank and roared, causing a shock wave that reverberated along the tunnel, quaking the walls.

Chalky white dust fell from the ceiling, and overhead lights trembled, swinging. But Frank continued to glare, defiant and challenging, pointing theatrically to the floor. He held an aspect that promised sure and swift doom if Leviathan took another step forward.

Leviathan growled gutturally, head tilting. Its vengeful eyes glowed brighter, like light. Connor was mesmerized by the standoff but somehow managed to take another cautious step until he had backed around the tunnel door.

Shocked, he looked down to see the steel walkway near his feet, and he suddenly remembered. He was actually startled to find the 100,000-volt line still in his fist. A panicked breath escaped him. He had completely forgotten the line during the standoff, and he was lucky that he hadn't grounded it to himself by touching the bare copper ending. Chesterton backed around the corner, lifting a trembling hand to his face.

"He can't hold it there," Chesterton whispered, breathless. "In another second it's going to . . . it's going to figure out . . . that he's bluffing."

Connor didn't bother to reply.

Angrily scattering cold sweat from his eyes, he bent to study the walkway. He saw that the soldiers had done a good job. They had separated a small section right in front of the vault, and the middle section appeared to be completely insulated from the ground with thick sheets of plywood, two-by-fours, and fiberglass paneling. But still, Connor wasn't sure whether it was enough insulation. He worried that the current would still be able to leap through the wood to ground out without the beast stepping on it. This entire stunt was wildly dangerous, he knew, but it was all he had.

Connor searched, saw a clear path of escape to the right, far from the middle section of the walkway. He saw that the rest of the platoon was working feverishly at the far door, attempting to rewire it as Connor had taught them. They hadn't yet begun to raise the portal, but Connor knew he couldn't wait for that. He was certain that Frank couldn't hold the beast much longer.

Breathing deeply, Connor leaned his head cautiously around the corner to see with alarm that the creature had taken another step forward. And yet somehow, perhaps still shaken by Frank's ultimately defiant stand, it remained uncertain whether to attack. It lowered its head close to the floor, searching, studying even as it never took its eyes off Frank, who still stood in the center of the passage.

Challenging.

"Frank!" Connor hissed. "Come on!"

"It's going to charge when I move!" the scientist yelled.

"All right," Connor said quietly. "When you come through this door, make a sharp right. Run as fast as you can and do not touch the steel walkway! Do you understand?"

Frank shifted his weight. "Yes."

Connor looked at Chesterton. "You ready?"

"I've been ready."

"All right, Frank!" Connor yelled. "Run!"

Almost immediately Frank rounded the portal but darkness was following, fast and furious, with a terrifying roar and thunderous strides. Connor didn't even look back as Frank passed before him and then he threw the cable out, the copper hitting the walkway with a spark to glow a split second before melding solidly to the metal. Then Connor was also running, three steps behind the scientist and he felt rather than saw the monstrosity that paused in the doorway, casually watching their frantic retreat.

Connor cast a wild glance back to see Leviathan's jaws two steps behind him, the dragon-head curiously stretched around the corner on a long, green-black neck no more than six feet above the cavern floor. And fear gave way to something else as Connor saw it, eye to eye.

Leviathan stared into him—a scaly black visage with dark eyes glaring hatefully. Its snakelike head was led by a short, sharp black horn that rose from its nose like a rhinoceros. Its face was hideously wedged, a serpent's head, a demon's head with white-fanged jaws reaching back behind glowing eyes to unhinge deeply, and more deeply.

Gaping. Smoldering.

Laughing.

Chapter 19

Connor heard someone shout.

Realized it was him.

He didn't take time to think about it.

Running full-out he rounded the far end of the steel paneling, feeling only bizarre amazement that they weren't dead. As he cleared the edge of the walkway, he spun back to face the beast, staring at the gigantic bulk of the Dragon as it poised cautiously in the doorway of the cavern.

Amazingly, Leviathan had not moved, was watching their retreat with casual unconcern. It simply stared at them, not even bothering to charge. But Connor knew that, with its phenomenal speed, Leviathan was confident that it could close the gap between them in the blink of an eye.

They were easy prey.

The creature half-raised its head, staring at the soldiers on the other side of the chamber working with frantic shouts at the vault. They labored over the hydraulic pump to raise the door a few feet. Leviathan seemed to be contemplating which group to kill first.

Connor backed away slowly, trying not to attract any more attention to himself. He angled gently to the side, wading into a sea of cave pearls, the white bed chalky with construction dust.

"Frank!" he hissed, backing beside the motionless scientist. "What's it doing?"

"It's studying us. I think . . . I think that we shook it up in the passageway."

Connor cast a glance to the exit vault. It was raised two feet above the floor. It was enough. But the three of them were still over fifty yards from the portal, and maybe a hundred yards from Leviathan. Connor whispered, "What's that thing going to do if we run for the door?"

Without hesitation Frank replied. "It'll come after us, Connor. Real fast. But it won't use flame because it's decided that there's not a trap. It's going to conserve the gel for an actual threat, a tank or something like that."

Connor took another step back, eyes locked on the beast. Leviathan instantly shifted, head swinging monstrously toward him. The tail swept around, curling to the side, flicking. Then it growled, taking a single, cautious step into the cavern.

Glancing down nervously, Connor saw that one of the Dragon's clawed hindfeet was placed close beside the steel. "Get ready," he whispered, taking a hard breath. "I don't know what's going to happen when it hits that thing. This might kill all of us."

Tired of the game, Chesterton snarled, raising his .45. "Maybe it needs a little incentive."

Instantly Leviathan reacted, roaring wildly as Chesterton fired, and then the platoon had followed his lead, five rifles blazing at the exit. Connor heard roaring and saw Leviathan's huge hindfoot rising, settling toward the steel and he raised his forearm across his face as . . .

WHITE . . .

A volcanic white bolt of deafening light struck like lightning, spiraling upward through the beast from one leg and down the other to ground into the floor with an explosive eruption that blasted steel plating, rock, and equipment across the entire expanse of the cavern.

Connor didn't know he'd been knocked against the wall until he felt himself on the ground, screaming, a heat wave roaring over him. The shock that hit him felt like a superheated wind; air shattered with a sharp sonic boom.

Fire, fire . . . Blinded and stunned, Connor rolled, covering his head as dust and rock ricocheted off the wall at his back. He was pelted by cave pearls, as if he'd been shot. Somehow it registered to him that a narrow section of steel plating had spun over his head, wickedly slicing a chunk of limestone from the wall. Dirt cascaded over him.

For a moment Connor felt as if he'd been thrown into an uncovered grave with a night sky thundering over him, electric with wrath, sealing his doom. He didn't know what had happened to Leviathan, could hear nothing but his own painful moaning, electric air surging.

The static atmosphere vibrated with the power that had been unleashed, and instantly the entire chamber was forty degrees hotter than it had been. It was something that had happened so quickly there was never a palpable change; it was simply there, white-hot air in the white light. Red emergency lights filled the cavern; red darkness glaring.

Unable to comprehend anything but mind-numbing pain, Connor concentrated angrily. He glimpsed Chesterton lying beside him on the ground, jerking, twitching. Then he realized that Frank was lying almost on top of him. Weakly, Connor pushed the half-conscious scientist off to get a better look at the cavern, searching, to hear a vengeful . . .

Roaring . . . Connor focused, saw . . .

Leviathan . . . thrashing wildly, bellowing in rage and slashing at the air, at everything. It rolled uncontrollably in a dark, distant section of the cavern, and Connor squinted, peering through the misty black haze. With effort his vision seemed to center, and he understood that the power cable had blasted the six-ton Dragon almost 300 feet across the cavern, slamming it into a titanic limestone slope.

Wounded, Leviathan howled in agony, fighting the current as if it were still attacking. And Connor stared, mesmerized, as it screamed and slashed spasmodically, unable to control itself. Fiendishly, again and again, it struck at everything that touched it, the steel, the wall, even the cavern floor itself, enraged and lost in rage, striking, striking . . .

Steel and ventilation ducts were scattered by the rending

blows. Chunks of limestone were ripped from the slope by the diamond-hard claws. Calcite columns were shattered by the tail. In moments a cloud of dark red dust rose into the air, shrouding the beast, moving across the cavern like a death-fog.

Gasping for breath, Connor staggered up. Trying angrily to concentrate, he glanced down. Saw that Chesterton had ceased moving. Then there was a painful, moaning cry, and Connor turned to see Frank rising to his feet. The scientist grimaced, holding his chest.

"It's hurt!" he gasped, coughing, staring as the beast pounded hatefully against the cavern floor, striking savagely at everything that continued to touch it. "You actually . . . you actually hurt it!"

Connor clenched his teeth in pain, dizzy, and grabbed the scientist by the shoulder, pulling him across his body. It took him a second to find his voice because his throat was tight, constricted. "Go . . . go for the door, Frank. We've got to get out of here."

Frank staggered unsteadily past him, unbalanced. Then, feeling a strange numbness in his own body, Connor knelt. He placed a knee between Chesterton's thighs, barely noticing the razor sharp edges of the gypsum floor. He pulled on one of the colonel's arms, struggling to lift him into a fireman's carry. After a groaning moment of mean labor he succeeded, grimacing and rising unsteadily under Chesterton's surprising weight. But as he stood Connor turned, blinking sweat from his eyes, to glance at Leviathan.

Fear.

It had ceased twitching. Was still.

A tired, labored breath lifted its gigantic chest, and a long foreleg snaked across its body, clutching the cavern floor. With a growl it rolled, the long tail whistling around to terrifically strike a stack of ventilation shafts, scattering them. A low groan like a wounded man coming to angry and painful consciousness rumbled from the Apocalyptic atmosphere.

No time.

Connor spun, moving as fast as his strength allowed, careful to avoid everything metal. He didn't know if any current still flowed from the lost power line, but he took no chances. When he reached the exit vault, everyone else had already gone through. Afraid, irrationally, that they had panicked and left him behind, Connor shouted, lowering Chesterton to the ground. But instantly a half dozen hands reached back to pull the colonel through the door. Connor heard Barley bellowing at him to hurry.

Hearing a low growl, Connor whirled to see that Leviathan stood on its hindfeet, head rising on the long neck. It took an unsteady step forward, staring dead at Connor, and Connor saw that one of the beast's forelegs was somehow damaged, broken or dislocated.

Leviathan held the shattered appendage low, but kept its other foreleg high and close, like a praying mantis poised to strike. Its tail shifted quickly to steady its balance. Hate-filled green eyes narrowed in the gloom, focusing on Connor with an aspect of pure vengeance as if it understood that he was responsible for its pain.

Fangs separated in a shriek.

In a single breath Connor had fallen, rolling under the door so that he surprised even himself with the alacrity of his movement. When he came up on the other side the rest of the platoon was moving. Fast.

Faint and losing strength, Connor staggered after them. He was so soaked with sweat and grime that he no longer noticed it, but his clothes seemed heavier than they had ever been in his life. He didn't even know if he had been hurt but he didn't care. He could still move, and that was enough. He felt different, somehow, but he was too numbed by the concussion of the blast to have any real sensation. As he reached the end of the passageway, he saw that Frank had rewired the door. Apparently, Connor recognized dimly, nearly everyone had learned now how to do the trick.

The surviving soldiers quickly worked the pump, raising the portal a few feet. But there was no pounding on the vault behind them, no attacks against the door leading from the Matrix. But no one asked any questions, made any sounds of relief.

Taking turns carrying Chesterton until the colonel finally regained an unsteady consciousness, they went on, raising each fire door no more than three feet above the ground to slide wearily beneath, always leaving the titanium portals raised.

In a silent, ghostly line of soldiers they went from one cavern to the next, on and on, leaving a white, gravelike cloud of dust as they put as much distance as they could between themselves and the Dragon.

Beth heard a loud hissing, the sound of metal grating against metal, and she glanced up. Her eyes burned so badly that she had trouble focusing, but she saw a dust-covered group of soldiers crawling beneath a narrowly raised door. Then she was on her feet, staring, holding Jordan's hand.

Sleepy, the four-year-old rubbed an eye with the back of his hand.

A slender figure came under the door, blackened, smeared with white chalk. The sleeve of one arm was charred, the skin reddened as if from a severe sunburn. He stood, moving toward her.

"Connor!" she cried, running forward. Behind her Jordan was screaming, "Daddy! Daaaaaddy!"

Connor smiled as they approached, reaching out. He embraced her, and one second later a small figure collided with their legs. Connor smiled, reaching down to lift Jordan from the ground. And from Jordan's joyous face, it was clear that now, yes, everything was all right. Whatever had been wrong was no more; it was all right now. Daddy was here, was here.

Connor kissed him and Beth focused more on his face, feeling an immediate and alarming concern. She saw a frightening fatigue, a bone weariness that made his face skeletal beneath the burned skin. His hair was plastered back with sweat. His eyes were sunken, ringed beneath with dark half-circles.

She gave him a compassionate look, and he returned it, shaking his head gently. "No," he whispered, holding Jordan tight in his arm. "We still have to get out of here. As fast as possible."

Staggering, Chesterton was beside them. Beth was almost shocked at the colonel's ravaged aspect. A severe burn marked one side of his face, and his green fatigues were black with sweat. His usually austere, severe countenance was slack and weak. He placed a red-burned hand limply on Connor's shoulder, speaking in a soft voice.

"We've got to meet," he said quietly.

Connor turned his head, nodded. "I know."

"I'm going to get some water," Chesterton continued. "You need to get some, too. Dehydration is going to kill us even if that thing doesn't." Without another word he turned, walking without strength toward the Housing Complex. Barley shadowed him, as if he were afraid the battle-beaten colonel wouldn't make the short journey.

Beth saw Adler, Tolvanos, and Blake standing in the doorway of the complex. They were staring numbly, as if none of them were eager to approach Chesterton's lean, angry aspect.

"Are you all right?" Connor asked, touching her face.

She placed her hand over his. "Yes. I'm all right. I was just so worried. We didn't know."

"I know. We're just going to rest a moment, and then we'll get out of here. We're too tired to go any farther right now. We'd never make it to the surface."

"I know."

Jordan raised his head, staring at Connor with disturbingly intense seriousness. His eyes were wide. "Is the monster dead?" he asked. Connor shot Beth a glance, but with a short shake of her head she closed her eyes: *No, I couldn't prevent it.*

Smiling, Connor gazed at the child's face. "There's nothing to be afraid of, buddy," he said quietly. "We're going to be all right. And we're going to leave this place, just like I promised. And we're never going to come back. Because we don't like ugly things like monsters, do we?"

"Noooo," Jordan echoed. "We don't like monsters."

Despite herself, Beth smiled, almost laughing. But there were no laughs and almost no smiles left inside her. She spoke quietly, "Can I get you anything? You need to rest."

"I'll be all right," Connor responded. "I just need some water before we get down to business." He paused for breath, lowering his voice. "Have you managed to break the code?"

"Almost," she replied, glancing to the side. "But it's an encryption system. And it's not one of the old-fashioned, simple ones, either. It's the real thing. They spent some money on it. The math is going beyond geometric or algebraic into something like a fluctuating logarithm." She paused, wearily brushing back hair from her forehead. "It's a real pain."

Connor's face was compassionate. "Harder than you thought?"

"Yes," she answered. "I thought I could beat it a lot quicker. But it's more complicated than anything I've ever seen."

"Well, there's something we have to talk about," he said. "Because we don't have much time left."

Her dark eyes narrowed. "What?"

Connor shook his head. "I'll tell you about it later." He glanced at the scientists scattered across the cavern. "How are you managing to attack the code without anyone getting suspicious?"

Beth cast a hateful glance at Tolvanos and Adler. "Oh, they know what I'm doing, all right. But Barley put them in their place. He threatened them with death if they interrupted me." She laughed. "I've circuited a dozen 486DX2-50s, and I'm running them on the power from about a hundred continuous-current Tripplite surge protectors that I annexed through the high density surge-protection system up top. It was still operational, and I managed to access it through a power line. It's a wild setup, but it will work until the Tripplite batteries are exhausted. And I did some quad-programming to speed things up."

Connor's admiration for her ingenuity shone in his face. "That was smart, darlin'. Real smart."

She grinned. "Baby, these people can't outthink me. You should know that."

"Yeah, I figured that much, Beth. Because I can't outthink you, either." He paused. "But I need to know something. How much longer will it take to break the code?"

She shook her head. "It's hard to tell, Connor. This encryption system, it's the wave of the future in computer security. And it's very, very difficult. But it gets simpler as it goes because the ultimate combinations become fewer as the PCs lock down numbers and passwords and encrypted codes on something like a geometric curve."

"And when you break it?" Connor asked.

"Then we'll have to find a working relay station down here that can connect to a satellite."

Connor hesitated. "Why?" He stared. "Why can't we just connect with a satellite through the groundside Communication Center?"

"Because the groundside Communication Center was demolished in the big fight, Connor. It won't work for a relay. But I think there's a relay in the power plant or in the computer cavern. Frank will know more about that than I do. We'll find a way to make it work."

Nodding without expression, Connor lowered his head. Then he felt her hand on his face, lifting his eyes to meet her gaze. Her voice was focused quietly between them.

"You pushed it, didn't you?" she asked quietly.

Connor stared. "I did what I had to do, Beth. That's all I ever do."

She shook her head. "You're too much of a man, Connor." Her face moved closer. "And you know what? You don't always have to be the one to do the hardest thing."

Connor's face was pained. "I'm being careful, Beth. All I'm doing is taking care of my family."

"Yeah, I know, Connor. Just like you've always taken care of us. And I love you for it. But promise me something. I know what kind of man you are. You're a fighter. That's all you know." She paused. "But if there's any way you can help it, Connor, don't go so far out on the edge that you can't ever make it back. Please, just promise me that."

Connor steadily stared. "I promise, Beth. I won't do anything that I don't have to do."

She received the words with a quiet nod, glancing at Jordan. "And Daddy always keeps his promise, doesn't he, Jordan?" she smiled.

"Yeah," Jordan laughed. "Daddy always keeps his promise."

Connor smiled, pulling his son close until a loud crash brought them around. All of them whirled to face the wall as a steel ventilation shaft cover was sent crashing to the floor. But even as Connor saw the cause of the disturbance, he visibly relaxed.

Heated cursing in a thick Nordic accent echoed from the narrow tunnel, and a moment later they saw a broad battle-ax pushed through the opening, the tinge of a shaggy head and two blackened hands poised at the rim. Then seconds later they saw Thor inching his head out, staring at them as if he had discovered a cavern of hidden gold. His eyes blazed, wide and excited, his face strained with exhaustion. Sweat and a dark chalky soot smeared his face. His bright red hair and beard were black with grime.

Connor laughed, shaking his head. Soldiers took a few weary steps toward the shaft when Connor waved them off. "It's all right," he said wearily, and lowered his hand.

They held their place.

Barley, turning at the complex to look back, laughed gustily. He raised his rifle in the air, placing the stock against his hip. "I figured you'd make it!" he called out.

"It's *Thor*!" Jordan shouted, lifting his hands in the air. "Daddy! It's Thor! He's inside that wall!"

Wrestling mightily, smiling in fiendish delight, Thor inched himself out of the opening. It was a phenomenally tight fit, and it seemed like the ventilation shaft would literally explode at the strain of containing his enormous girth. But in a moment he had succeeded, his massively broad shoulders slowly passing over the edge. Then, the worst done, he quickly eased himself to the ground, holding an enormous Viking-style battle-ax in a firm grip. A leather thong tied to the end of the haft was looped around his wrist.

Straightening to his familiar, gigantic height, Thor gazed over them. Beth was almost shocked to hear Connor laugh out loud, shaking his head. Then with a light stride, Thor came across the cavern, casting a single, frowning glance at the angry forms of Adler and Blake as they approached.

Blake gestured to the weary soldiers to follow, but they only sat down, shaking their heads. Livid, Blake followed on Adler's heels to confront Thor in the center of the cavern. They said something hostile to the giant just beyond hearing, and Thor frowned over them as if they were strange insects he had never seen. He appeared to mumble something and moved past them without further words, ignoring Blake's heated commands.

Chesterton stood in the doorway of the Housing Complex, watching the encounter. He wearily took a sip from a canteen. "Just leave it be, Blake!" he called out. "We need all the help we can get!"

Turning angrily, Blake made a straight line toward the complex, anger launching him into every step. Beth ignored the debate that began at the steps and focused on Thor as he drew near. Thor reached out, placing a firm hand on Connor's shoulder. His voice was dry.

"I am overjoyed," he smiled, "to find you all well." Connor nodded, glancing at Adler and the wildly gesticulating Blake. Both of them were raging at an implacable Chesterton, who seemed amused.

"What'd they say to you?" Connor asked.

Thor glanced at Blake and Adler, humorously lifting an eyebrow. "They said that this was their secret facility. They said that I had no right to be down here . . . in their secret facility." He laughed. "I told them that there were no more secrets."

Jordan joined in, lifting his hands joyfully. "Now we're all together!" he sang.

Thor's deep laugh was like thunder, lifting something that had been dark and dooming. But Beth saw him cast a single, threatening glance at the vault, saw his massive hand tighten ominously on the battle-ax before he smiled down once more.

"Yes," he said. "Now we are all together. As it should be."

Chapter 20

I t has a devil's skill," Thor rumbled.

In a circle, they had told him everything, and Thor stood solidly through it all, cradling the battle-ax in his arms. Then he had told them of his wild descent into the cavern, and how Blankenship and the ground crew had already evacuated the surface of Grimwald Island by hastily repairing and utilizing the cruisers.

"So my crew and their families have evacuated the island?" Connor asked, staring solid.

Thor nodded sharply. "Yes, my friend. They are gone. And they took Blake's guards with them." He paused. "I knew that you would be concerned for their safety, so I gave them the bearing for Iceland. If they take the correct bearing they should reach land within six hours. But, in any case, they will find assistance as soon as they clear the electromagnetic interference cloaking this island's radio frequencies." He smiled. "Your men shall live."

"Good," Connor replied, bowing his head tiredly. "I appreciate you doing that, Thor. At least they'll survive this."

Thor shed his soot-blackened bearskin to stand before them in his customary leather pants and loose, sleeveless shirt. Connor saw for the first time that Thor wore large leather gauntlets reminiscent of those worn by Scandinavian warriors of a thousand years ago. More than a quarter-inch thick and fastened with metal straps, the gauntlets fully sheathed each of Thor's forearms between elbow and wrist.

Overall, the Norseman was a thoroughly intimidating sight. And to top off the primeval costume he had tied his long red hair in a ponytail, leaving only his ragged red beard to descend upon his great, massive chest. His ice-green eyes glinted with anger and angry cunning.

"Yes," Thor scowled, speaking once more of the Dragon. "It has a devil's skill. It is not a beast."

"No," Frank said. "It's like a machine."

"A machine is only a mirror of man," Thor growled, gazing down. "But the Dragon is more. There is death . . . and ancient darkness . . . in its heart." He paused. "It is not a reflection of man or of anything else, Doctor. It inhabits its own reality."

Frank stared silently at Thor, and Thor raised his gaze to study the secretive conclave on the opposite side of the cavern. Tolvanos and Adler were bent low in the center of the group, speaking in hushed tones, gesturing intently with secret plans.

"Yes." Thor frowned. "We must all choose between evil and good."

Waiting for Chesterton to call the meeting, Connor laughed lightly, shaking his head. "You know, Frank," he said, "this whole thing reminds me of the *Titanic*."

"The *Titanic*?" the scientist answered. "Why?"

"Because of the science."

"What do you mean?"

Connor laughed, leaning back. "Answer a question for me, Frank. What do you think sank the *Titanic*?"

"An iceberg sank it," the scientist replied vaguely. "It hit an iceberg on April 14, 1912. The first six watertight compartments of the ship, which weren't really watertight because they weren't sealed above the waterline, were ripped open and flooded. Then the ship began pitching forward with water spilling over the top of each compartment to flood the compartment behind it. It went down in three hours."

"That's what happened," Connor said. "But that's not what sank the ship."

"What sank it?"

Connor lifted a small round piece of steel, turning it slowly in his fingers. "Do you know what this is?" he asked.

"Yeah. It's rebar. It's part of a steel bar that they use in concrete to make it more stable."

"Yeah," Connor replied. "It's rebar. And it's pretty sorry steel, actually. It's not good for anything except reinforcing concrete. I know a little bit about it because I used to work concrete when I was young. Before I started in electronics." He paused. "But did you know that the steel they used to build the *Titanic* was even sorrier than this, Frank?"

There was no reply, but a light flickered in the scientist's eyes, as if he knew already where Connor was going.

"Yeah, the steel that they used to build the *Titanic* was high in what we call sulfide occlusions, or 'stringers,'" Connor continued. "Nowadays we know that a high sulfur content makes steel real brittle, especially in cold water. But back in 1912 nobody really understood the phenomenon of what we call 'brittle fracture.' They tested the steel of the *Titanic* for tensile strength and that was that. But brittle fracture is something that happens to high-sulfide steel when it gets cold. And on the night that the *Titanic* hit that iceberg, the water temperature was one degree above freezing."

Frank lowered his eyes, frowning.

"What the shipbuilders had done," Connor continued, "was build the largest, most luxurious ship in the world with brittle, high-sulfide steel that wouldn't even make it out of a yard today. So when the *Titanic* hit that iceberg the steel in her bow didn't bend or ripple like modern steel would do, absorbing the impact. The steel in the *Titanic's* bow was brittle to begin with and even more brittle because it was cold, and it was busted like an egg."

Somber, the scientist waited.

"What I'm saying," Connor added finally, "is that the engineers of that time knew *how* to build the ship, Frank. They were smart. They had the science and they had the technology. But they had gone ahead of where they should have been. They didn't understand everything that they needed to understand in order to make it safe." He paused. "Or right."

Frank stared at him.

Connor laughed shortly. "But don't listen to me," he added, a vague smile. "I'm not a scientist like you guys. I just fix things."

"I'm just about tired of listening to you, Blake," Chesterton mumbled, sipping from a canteen. He looked up, his eyes dangerous with pain. "And in any case, what you think doesn't matter."

Finally separating himself from the secretive conclave with Adler and Tolvanos, Blake had come to the steps of the complex once more to accuse Chesterton outright of mutiny and insubordination, ordering him to stand down

"I'm tired of your insubordination, Chesterton!" Blake cried. "This is a military operation—a CIA operation—and you no longer have authority! The machine has broken down because of your blatant disregard for authority! None of this would have happened if you had obeyed orders! But you didn't! You recklessly attacked Mr. Adler and Dr. Tolvanos in the Observation Room, creating confusion which allowed that thing to rupture its cell. This is your fault! And when this is over, I ensure that you will be held in judgment before a military court!"

"I hope that I live to see it," Chesterton replied. He took another sip from the canteen, wearily lifting a hand to massage his burned neck. "Ah, yeah, those painkillers are kicking in. Just like old times."

For the past half hour they had been recovering, eating military Meals Ready to Eat, or MREs, and drinking gallons of water. They had also taken numerous painkillers, and whatever ammo remained had been evenly distributed, with Barley counting out twenty grenades to a man.

Also, each soldier retained an LAW rocket, a devastating antitank weapon that could be fired like a bazooka. At close range an LAW would disintegrate a small building. No one had yet fired one at Leviathan.

Five soldiers, including Barley, remained alive. And there

were approximately forty science personnel, with Tolvanos's team and Frank's team combined. Blake's two MPs in the Observation Room were listed among the endless dead.

Connor wasn't trying to pay attention, but he noticed that the argument at the Housing Complex was heating up. He leaned his head back, staring across the cavern into a darkened doorway, where he knew Beth was quietly working on a terminal. His fatigue seemed endless, depthless, as if this cavern was the only place he had ever been, the only place he had ever known. He couldn't even remember yesterday. Today there had been only darkness.

Blake's livid voice carried across the room.

"NO! NO! For the final time, Chesterton! I will not give you the satellite encryption so that you can call for a rescue! The encryption is one of the NSA's most closely guarded state secrets, and I will not allow you to broadcast a universal NSA distress call on an unauthorized satellite simply to evacuate this island! You are overstressed, Colonel! If you are incapable of command, then you should allow me to take over! I don't think I can possibly do any worse!"

Frowning, Adler also attacked Chesterton. "Colonel Chesterton, you are being unreasonable. You have been relieved of duty by the Pentagon. And although I have nothing against you personally, it would clearly be a disloyal act against my country to give you the code. Not until I am assured that neither Leviathan or this cavern will be harmed. That is a priority."

"Yes," added Tolvanos, staring. "Preserving the life of the Dragon and the computer itself is a grave necessity, Colonel Chesterton. That is why we must disarm the nuclear fail-safe before we depart the cavern."

Chesterton squinted, focusing on the Russian.

Tolvanos continued, "Yes, Colonel Chesterton. Mr. Adler has informed me about the nuclear fail-safe. And be assured I have the necessary security clearance. It is part of my duty to know everything because I am now officially in charge of this experiment." He paused. "Please . . . please recognize, Colonel, that

Leviathan and the computer have incalculable value. They must both be preserved. At any cost."

"Boys," Chesterton began, "I don't think you clearly grasp this situation." He waited a moment. "That thing is trying to kill us. All of us. If it attempts to escape through Crystal Lake, there's not a whole lot we can do to stop it. And none of us are going to live to talk about it, either. We're going to be crispy-fried. So the best thing we can do is get off this island before that thing goes into that lake and makes this island go boom."

Adler was unmoved. "Colonel Chesterton, I believe that the creature might escape by entering Crystal Lake, yes. But the nuclear fail-safe must be disarmed or we will lose this billion-dollar facility and the computer. And the computer holds the secrets for how to duplicate this process! The loss of one creature is not of monumental importance to me. It is the price of success. But you must order Frank to disarm the fail-safe."

Chesterton leaned back. "Well, I appreciate your lack of cooperation, Mr. Adler. But I'm not going to order Frank to defuse the fail-safe just yet. 'Cause if that thing tries to swim out I'm gonna vaporize it any way I can. Or bury it down here." He nodded. "That's a vow. A solemn vow. And then I'll see all of you in a civilian court or a military court or in an alley or wherever you want to meet. It doesn't make much difference to me. That is . . . if we survive." He turned his head sharply, in command. "Frank! Get over here!"

Glancing up, the scientist rose to his feet. And then Connor was also moving forward, intent to have a say in whatever was about to happen, Thor steadfastly beside him. Together they convened at the steps with Chesterton in the middle, holding forth like a king.

"Well, gentlemen, I think—"

"I think," Adler interrupted sternly, "that these men"—he gestured to Connor and Thor—"should take their seats elsewhere until we sort this out. This is a secret facility and—"

"Don't make me hurt you, Adler," Connor said wearily, casting a slight glance. "I'm not in the mood."

Chesterton smiled broadly as Adler straightened, turning

toward Connor with an imperial air. "Now understand this, Mr. Connor. I ultimately own this facility. That means you work for me. If I want you to be in on this . . . this meeting, I will tell you. If not, then I expect you to do as you are told Now, please go and console your family while we proceed."

A measured pause and Connor turned to the older man. "Adler, I want you to know something," he said quietly. "If we make it out of here, you and I are going to have a serious meeting of minds."

Adler stared, seeming suddenly to enjoy the conflict. "Is that a threat, Mr. Connor?"

"You should take it like that."

"I look forward to it," the older man responded, smiling. "Yes, indeed. I truly do."

"All right," Chesterton broke in. "First things first. Listen up, Frank. I want to know why that thing hasn't followed us into the Housing Cavern. Why hasn't it knocked down all those vaults by now?"

"Connor injured it," the scientist replied, studious. "After Leviathan was hit by the charge, it went into a self-diagnostic mode. It realized that it was structurally compromised and it knew it needed time to heal."

"What do you mean, it realized it was hurt?" Chesterton answered, scowling. "Couldn't it feel that it was hurt? I mean, it had a broken leg. Probably a broken shoulder."

"No. Leviathan doesn't feel pain like we feel pain," Frank answered, eyes zoning to recall the data. "If Leviathan perceives injury it does a visual and neural self-diagnosis of electric—"

"All right, Frank, all right." Chesterton raised a hand. "I've had enough of that stuff. I get the point. It doesn't feel pain. I don't care why. I'm too tired to care why." He took a deep breath. "In any case, you're saying that it hasn't attacked because it's healing. That's good because it means we've got plenty of time to regroup and get out of this cavern." He waited, concentrated. "Do you think it's hurt bad enough to try for the lake?"

"No," Frank replied. "It's stronger than that. It won't try for the lake until it's dying."

"You're sure?"

"I'm sure, Chesterton. I created it."

"All right, Frank. How much longer before it attacks us? A couple of days, maybe?"

Frank's face was expressionless. "An hour or two, Chesterton."

Chesterton passed a hand over his face. He seemed to have expected it. "All right, Frank. Let me explain this one for you, just to give you some relief. You've molecularly altered this thing so that it heals up real, real fast. Right? Heals almost instantly from any kind of wound?"

Frank nodded.

Tolvanos was enraptured. "Incredible," he muttered.

"All right." Chesterton nodded. "Can you tell me where Leviathan is right now? Is GEO still tracking it?"

Raising the headset Frank spoke. "GEO, this is Dr. Frank. Give me the location of Leviathan."

"Leviathan is at the junction of Alpha and Beta corridors."

"How long has Leviathan been stationary?"

"Leviathan has been stationary for one hour and six minutes."

"And what is the internal status of Leviathan?"

"Leviathan's heart rate is twelve beats per minute. Internal resting temperature has increased to 400 degrees and EEG activity has dropped to twelve."

"Does Leviathan appear to be feeding?"

"Leviathan is not feeding. Leviathan has ceased feeding and has rerouted mitosis in biofeed loop."

"How long before mitosis is complete?"

"Insufficient data exists to determine how—"

"Terminate answer. GEO, this is a standing command: Alert me over the intercom system if Leviathan begins moving again. And alert me if Leviathan makes any attempt to move through the power plant to approach Crystal Lake. Do you understand?"

"Yes, Dr. Frank."

Frank looked at Chesterton. "It's been feeding on the—"

"I know what's it's been feeding on, Doctor." Chesterton's eyes went dead at the words. "I know exactly what it's been feeding on." He sniffed, rolling his neck before focusing on Connor. "What do you suggest we do, Connor? You know this place as well as anyone."

"It's pretty clear, Chesterton," Connor responded. "If that thing is still coming after us, we've got to get out of this cavern. We've got twelve hours left. So I say we make for the elevator shaft. Then we rewire the elevator, get it down here and load everyone up. We can stop halfway to set charges to blow the shaft when we reach the surface. But we've got to get moving. We've rested up enough already."

Chesterton nodded. "If that thing is closing on us again, can you rig up something like you rigged earlier, in the Matrix?"

"I should be able to."

"How much electricity did you use the first time?"

"About 100,000 volts."

"And is this place full of 100,000-volt lines?"

"There's enough of them."

Chesterton stared. "And why is that? That seems like a lot."

Connor took a deep breath. "The current is sent from a Norwegian nuclear plant. They have to send it out to the island at about a billion volts because of the distance it has to travel. After the current gets to where it's going, it has to be broken down at substations for various applications. But I've sort of bypassed some breakers in the power plant, and we've got lines running as high as they'll go. Some of them are carrying 300,000 volts." He paused. "It's an unsafe situation."

Chesterton laughed harshly. "Tell me about it." He rose, holding his M-16. "All right, boys, let's get moving. I don't intend to die in this place."

Connor met secretly with Beth as she crept casually from the computer. She held Jordan in her arms. The boy shouted in joy and reached out for Connor as soon as he saw him.

Taking the half-awake boy in his arms, Connor spoke. "Those goons wouldn't give Chesterton the code. So Chesterton says we're moving out of the Housing Cavern right now. How does it look?"

Beth's face was pale. "I've broken everything but the last encryption. It's something that's not a number or anything else that I can identify. It's . . . it's vaguely like some kind of bizarre hieratic-geometrical hybrid swirl. More like a signature than any code I've ever seen. And it's three pages long. At least that's how I can glimpse it." She blinked tiredly. "So I've just . . . I've just set up the terminals to do a constant light matrix screen-search against the megabyte blasts of the encryption that came through the relay. It's slow going." She shook her head. "I'm sorry, Connor. I had no idea how difficult this was going to be. It's just unbelievable."

Connor's face was beside her. "You're a genius, Beth. Nobody could do better."

She leaned back. "But I still don't know how long it will take. I've never dealt with anything like this before."

"Are you certain that Frank can't help?"

"No. Frank is brilliant, but communications isn't his field. He knows GEO and that's . . . that's all that's in his mind."

"All right. It probably doesn't matter, anyway. Chesterton says we're moving for the front of the cavern. Right now. If we can reach the surface we can load up on the Hueys."

"We're moving for the elevator? All of us?"

"Yeah."

Beth cast a suspicious glance over the rest of the crowd, then she lightly caressed Jordan's head. Without another word she spun and walked quickly into the computer room, toward the terminal. "Beth," Connor whispered, "what are you doing?"

She turned, burning a vicious glance over everyone in the cavern. "I'm going to make sure the terminals continue working on that last encryption, Connor," she answered. "I'm going to set it in a loop to unlock that last code. No matter what."

"Why? We're probably not going to need it." He stared at her. "What are you thinking, Beth?"

"I'm thinking that we've got a long way to go, Connor," she replied, grim. "And I'm thinking that a lot of Adler's people, especially Tolvanos, care a lot more for that creature and this facility than for any of us."

It took over an hour to lift the vault doors, moving through tunnels and passages and picking up a few trapped scientists found along the way. And it was Barley, as heavily armed as any man Connor had ever seen, who led at the front.

The big lieutenant was ultimately prepared for a final conflict with the Dragon. He had three LAW rockets slung over his back and two additional bandoliers of grenades. He carried his rifle in his hand and had secured two pistols—one in a holster on his thigh and another in a shoulder holster. Ammo clips and explosives and other weapons Connor couldn't even identify were stuffed in every conceivable pocket in the man's dirt-smeared fatigues. But the most ominous, and faintly chilling, preparation was a Velcro body harness stuffed heavily with what Connor thought was C-4.

Before they began the long march Connor had remarked on it. "What's that, Barley?" He pointed, almost delicately, to the harness. Barley had frowned, reaching up to rip down a palm-sized Velcro cover. Beneath the opened black flap, Connor saw two small red rings, one above the other. Barley's face was grim.

"Pull this ring and then the other ring and this thing goes boom," he said, nodding curtly.

Connor was vividly impressed, asking, "Well, when are you gonna use it?"

"I'll use it if them big fangs ever come down on top of me," Barley nodded. "Give it some indigestion. Big time."

Connor said nothing, staring at the glistening dark face. He knew without a doubt that, if it came to it, Barley would pull those rings without a second's hesitation. Then it was time to move, and they left the Housing Complex, using the surviving platoon members for a strong rear guard with Thor and Barley at point. Barley held his rifle close, and Thor held the battle-ax with a rifle slung over his back.

Connor quickly worked the vault doors, constantly glancing back to make sure Beth and Jordan were always well protected within Thor's strong reach, as Connor had instructed the giant before the march began. But there was no need; Thor always kept them close. In time they came to Bridgestone, a thick, fifty-yard-wide slab of rough crystalline granite that crossed Lucifer's Gorge.

The bridge of stone was immensely thick, easily strong enough to support the heaviest machinery. It was topped with a solid steel walkway sturdy enough to bear a tank. It was the only link to the elevator shaft.

In a silent line, as they walked over the gorge, Connor remembered how he had once curiously tossed a rock over the side of the bridge, listening for it to hit the bottom. He had waited for almost thirty seconds before he had heard a dull, distant thud.

It had been only the faintest sound. And Connor knew that if the cavern had not contained that eerie, spacelike silence, he would have heard nothing at all. But the tombish air amplified the slightest echo. Now, glancing out over the gorge as he walked, Connor tried to calculate the depth of the abyss by the time needed for the fall. Figured it to be nearly a mile.

Then a large tunnel was before them: Tungsten Passage. Connor knew that it was almost a mile long, ending at the Climbing Cavern where the elevator shaft exited for the surface.

Chesterton paused, lowering his rifle. "All right, everybody take ten minutes," he said. "We'll rest here before we push for the elevator. This will be the last break so be sure to drink plenty of water. You're going to need it before this is over."

Thor sat back against a wall as Frank tiredly walked up to sit beside him. Thor opened his eyes a moment to smile faintly at the scientist, and Frank returned the gesture.

"You really think we have a chance of surviving, Thor?" Frank asked in a dry, hoarse voice.

Thor nodded, his green eyes glinting with encouragement. "Aye," he replied, "a good chance."

"I never thought we'd make it this far."

"You are not alone, I think."

Frank paused, staring away. "So why did you come down here, Thor?" he asked after a long silence. "This wasn't your fight."

Thor laughed. "My reasons are spiritual, Doctor."

Frank's mouth gaped. "Spiritual?"

Again, Thor nodded.

"How can they be spiritual?"

"Because I choose to live my life with love and courage and strength," Thor replied steadily. "Or I will welcome my death."

Silence.

"There isn't anything spiritual about this, Thor."

"Yes," the giant grunted. "As much as anything else."

Frank stared. "Look, Thor, *spiritual* things are spiritual. You know, talking about theology or praying or . . . or meditating or something like that. But there's nothing *spiritual* about fighting this thing."

Thor's laugh was like a burst of strength. "Has Plato poisoned you, too?" he asked, smiling. "I will have words with him over this, if I happen upon him."

Frank was quiet a long time. "What do you mean?"

"It was Plato, Doctor, who in his epic foolishness drew a line between what is spiritual and what is merely human." Thor laughed again. "In truth there is no such place."

"That's not true," Frank responded. "Stuff like prayer is spiritual."

"Prayer is no more spiritual than peeling potatoes," Thor rumbled. "It was Plato who created this idea that some part of man was divine and spiritual and another part of man was merely human and nonspiritual. But God makes no such distinctions. God created us as spiritual beings, so we are spiritual beings in all that we do."

Frank hesitated a moment, absorbing it. He looked around to see the soldiers checking and cleaning weapons, organizing. "So what are you saying?" he asked, gazing back. "Are you saying that all this fighting is just as spiritual as prayer or meditation or anything else?"

"It is a reflection of a man's character. A man's character should be a reflection of God's character."

"I'm still not sure that I understand what you're saying, Thor."

Thor gazed steadily at the scientist. "A man's spirituality can be measured by how his life reflects God's character, Doctor. So tell me: Do you think God would abandon you in this cavern, leaving you alone against the beast?"

Hesitation.

"No."

A smile, and Thor's green eyes gleamed.

"And neither will I," he said. "Whether the battle comes down to flesh or not makes no difference to me. I will live my life by love and courage and strength because these things please God as much as prayer and meditation and the study of the Scriptures."

Head bowed for a moment, Frank asked, "What did you mean when you said that Leviathan had chosen to inhabit its own reality?"

"I meant that evil is the reality it inhabits."

"So you really think that Leviathan is evil?"

"Yes."

Frank paused. "Why?"

"It lives to kill," Thor frowned. "It lives to destroy. To steal the lives of the innocent. And that is the heart of evil."

"But Leviathan only does what it was created to do."

"Does it, Doctor?"

"Yeah. Of course."

"And can you say with absolute certainty that Leviathan is not used by other forces?" Thor asked, gazing steadily. "Can you say that Leviathan is not being used by a force even more powerful than itself? A force that has learned to use both man and machine for its own purpose?"

"I . . ." Frank began. "What do you mean?"

"I mean," Thor rumbled, "that superior forces use inferior forces, Doctor. Who is to say what force is ultimately using Leviathan? Leviathan is not merely an animal. Nor is it merely a machine. It is more."

"Well what kind of forces are you talking about?"

"There are only two," Thor said, solemn. "There is God. And there is Satan."

A strange and uncomfortable silence, and Frank finally

looked away. Then he gazed down, focusing on the battle-ax between them. "Well, I can understand what you've said, Thor. Because despite what you might think, I understand a lot more than just science." He hesitated. "But let me tell you something. If you go against Leviathan with that battle-ax, it's going to kill you. Then it's going to eat you."

Thor laughed. "It will not like the feast."

The scientist looked away, shaken. "Look, there's no way to beat it with that thing, Thor. Not with your hands. I mean, there's a . . . a *very* slim chance that Leviathan's armor can't take the impact of an edged weapon as well as it can take the impact of bullets and grenades but we've never—"

"And why is that?" Thor growled, ice-green eyes glinting.

"Well, it's hard to explain," Frank replied. "But it's just physics. Leviathan's armor is composed of crosslaid multiplex fibers like, uh, some kind of Kevlar. And because the plates are living fibers, they bend. They're flexible. So when the scales receive a blunt trauma like the impact of a grenade or bullet, they surrender, absorbing the shock and displacing it over a wide area. That's what prevents penetration of the armor. It's like someone hanging a thick rug in the air. You could punch it as hard as you want but you'd never be able to punch a hole in it because it would surrender to the force, absorbing the impact. You could probably even shoot it and you might not penetrate it because the carpet fibers and the shock-displacement factor would take so much velocity from the bullet." He paused. "But you could take a knife and stab it. And the edge of the blade wouldn't allow the carpet to displace the force of the impact. With a blade, you might penetrate it."

Thor was staring at him.

"Anyway, that's how it works," Frank said solidly. "It would be hard to do the same thing with Leviathan. But it's possible, I guess." He paused. "Isn't that what they say? Anything is possible?"

"Yes, Doctor," Thor rumbled, gently nodding. "That is what they say. Anything is possible . . . with God."

With a frown Thor reached down, his hand settling on the

gigantic battle-ax. Then he lifted the weapon, studying the broad, sweeping edges as if to determine whether Frank's theory might be true.

And, seated so close to the weapon, Frank was suddenly struck by a new and profound respect. He stared at the huge slabs of steel, noticing for the first time the deeply engraved image upon the silvery sheen, the eerie image of a titanic, raging Dragon with its tail wrapped around the moon, flung from the sky by a warrior that crushed the monster's throat, driving the fangs downward from the stars . . . toward the earth.

And for a weird, surreal moment, Frank felt as if he had been cast far, far back in time to sit beside some ancient warrior-king of God. He stared in silence until Thor finally lowered the battle-ax again to the ground, his hand solidly folded around the hilt.

"You know, Thor, I . . . I remember stories," Frank heard himself speaking. "Stories told to me when I was a child, about heroes and heroic battles. It was stuff I believed when I was young. Until I grew up. Until I learned that there weren't any more heroes."

A somber grin lightened Thor's face. "Sometimes children know greater truth than men, Doctor."

Frank closed his eyes, shook his head. "You can't hurt it with that battle-ax, Thor. I'm telling you the truth. You can't hurt it. Leviathan is too strong. It will kill you."

"All strength has an ending, Frank."

"Look, Thor, I'm being honest with you," Frank stressed, turning his head and amazed at his own concern. "I *know* this creature! Its strength is unbelievable! Leviathan is like . . . like a *force of nature!* It's been hit with everything we throw at it and it's still alive! What makes you think that you could ever hurt it with that ax?"

Thor stared at the image engraved upon the steel. "God will decide the victory, Doctor. And God alone." He paused. "Nor do I relish the conflict. But if I am forced to make a stand against the beast, we may see if a weapon forged by unknown hands and, perhaps, blessed by unknown hands, can draw a Dragon's blood."

Frank stared a moment and then closed his eyes, leaning his head back. He was silent a long time before he spoke. "If it comes to it, Thor, strike for the neck. When Leviathan charges the scales on its neck separate and . . . and there's a gap of maybe two or three inches between the armor. If . . . if you hit Leviathan in the gap, you might be able to wound it. You won't live long enough to kill it." He paused. "But you might be able to wound it."

Thor's reply was somber.

"A wound is a beginning, my friend." His massive hand tightened on the battle-ax. "And a beginning is half the ending."

Ten minutes passed and then they were on their feet again. Two by two, they traveled in a ragged line down the Tungsten Passage. Several corridors led out of the tunnel as they ascended higher, toward the entrance, but none were closed by vaults. Connor remembered that there were no vaults at all on this side of Bridgestone. When they reached the Climbing Cavern, the elevator shaft at the far end was sealed by a colossal vault.

Connor glanced up as they entered. Because the cavern was a genuine climbing cave, it had an unstable ceiling. Truck-sized boulders regularly fell from the roof, especially during the early days of cavern construction. And even now Chesterton's men were often forced to set explosive charges high on the wall to bring down unstable formations.

"All right!" Chesterton called out as they finally reached the elevator shaft. "Let's get this door open so we can get out of here! Frank! Give me a location on Leviathan!"

"It hasn't moved yet, Chesterton," the scientist answered. "GEO is going to inform us as soon as it does."

"Good enough, then. Let's get to work, boys!"

Connor set Jordan on the ground, and Beth reached down to take the boy's hand. She touched Connor's face as he straightened, and he saw that her eyes were ringed with dark fatigue, exhaustion. Her hair was plastered back with sweat and she had torn off a piece of her shirt as a headband.

"Be careful," she said.

He smiled. "I'm always careful."

Chesterton was in full form. "Let's get a move on! We're wasting daylight! Connor! Rewire that door so we can—"

The voice that came over the computer was stunning. "*Leviathan has awakened. Leviathan is moving north in Alpha Passage, passing the Observation Room.*"

Everyone froze. Chesterton stood in place, turned his head toward Frank.

"What did that thing say?" he asked numbly.

His question seemed incredible in light of the computer's utter clarity and inhuman precision of speech.

"We've got to move," Frank whispered, not moving.

Connor spun and dropped to the control plate. He savagely jammed a screwdriver in and twisted, but his hand trembled with the strain, and he realized immediately the screws were countersunk in the steel.

Face contorted with the effort, Connor twisted the screwdriver frantically, grasping the shaft and handle together, twisting even harder. But the screw didn't move at all. Sweating and angrily blinking sweat, Connor sat back, staring at the plate in amazement.

"This is incredible," he whispered, breathless. "Why'd they countersink the screws of this plate and not the others? That doesn't make any sense." He turned his head. "Thor! Get over here!"

Chesterton was leaning over him, face pale. "What's the problem, Connor? Is there a problem?"

"*Leviathan is passing the Command Center. Leviathan is entering the passageway that leads toward the Matrix.*"

"Come on, Connor!" Chesterton rasped. "Get that thing open! We're running out of time! It's going to take at least ten minutes just to get the elevator down here!"

Thor came up and Connor gave him the screwdriver. "Get those screws out as fast as you can!" And Thor dropped to one knee, jamming the screwdriver in hard and twisting. Immediately the screw began to retreat, threading out slowly. In a minute it fell to the ground, and Thor began with another one, moving counterclockwise.

"Leviathan has entered the Matrix."

Adler was suddenly trembling, turning to stare across Climbing Cave to Tungsten Passage. He spoke to Chesterton over his shoulder, unable to take his eyes off the distant corridor. "Perhaps we should move faster, Colonel! I believe that the creature is following our trail through the—"

"Shut up, Adler!" Chesterton snarled.

"Leviathan has defeated the exit vault of the Matrix and is moving in a northeastern direction through the cavern."

"Frank!" Chesterton called out. "Can't that computer slow that thing down? *Do something!*"

And Frank immediately mounted the headset. "GEO, this is Dr. Frank," he said.

"Voice identification confirmed."

"I want you to ignite all nitrogen thermone ports in the cavern except those above the front elevator shaft! Attempt to lower the temperature of the entire cavern to minus 200 degrees. Do you understand?"

"Yes. GEO is releasing nitrogen thermones through all ports past the elevator shaft."

Connor could hear nothing from deep inside the cavern, but he knew that a haze of white nitrogen was filling every hallway and chamber in the cavern. He was afraid for a moment that GEO would make a mistake and open the nitrogen port above their heads, but when nothing happened he ignored the thought. He didn't have any time for relief.

"Frank, give me a play-by-play of what that thing is doing!" Chesterton shouted, turning briefly to glare down Tungsten Passage.

"Leviathan has turned in a southwestern direction," came GEO's soft reply. *"Leviathan is moving toward the power plant."*

Connor looked up sharply. "Why is it doing that?"

Chesterton shook his head, dazed.

"Frank!" Connor shouted. "Why is that thing turning southwest toward the power plant?"

"I don't know, Connor."

Connor stared up at the ceiling, thinking furiously. His eyes scanned the ceiling, the piping and ventilation ducts. "That's it," he whispered, looking down. "Frank, where is Leviathan right now?"

The scientist asked and they heard, *"Leviathan has stopped at the storage chamber located near the power plant. Leviathan is attacking storage tanks used for housing nitrogen thermones."*

"That thing is attacking the nitrogen tanks!" Chesterton rasped. "But . . . but how did it know where the storage tanks were? It was never programmed to know where the nitrogen tanks were! That's impossible! What are we dealing with here?"

"It's following the pipes," Connor whispered. "It's following the nitrogen pipes from the last vault." He shook his head, sweat scattering. "Man, that thing is smart! But we've got to stop it from reaching the power plant, Chesterton. If Leviathan destroys the generators, we won't have enough power to get the elevator down here."

"Leviathan has used flame-throwing weapons arsenal to destroy the nitrogen storage chamber. Secondary explosions have damaged cavern integrity and corridor structure surrounding the Storage Chamber. Nitrogen thermones are now completely unusable. Leviathan is continuing to move toward the power plant."

"Frank!" Connor yelled, rising fully. "What corridor is Leviathan in?"

The scientist asked the question, and the computer replied. *"Leviathan is in Omega Passage. Leviathan is continuing to move in a southwestern direction toward the power plant."*

"Tell GEO to generate a power surge to blow all the secondary circuit breakers!" Connor shouted. "Do it now! That should knock out all the lights in the lower portion of the cavern and Leviathan might think the power plant is already dead!"

Instantly the lights were extinguished, and Connor felt nothing but silent air. No one moved. Then, *"Leviathan is moving away from the power plant. Leviathan is again approaching the Matrix."* Silence. *"Leviathan has compromised the exit vault from the Matrix. Leviathan is entering the exit passage."*

Chesterton looked down at Thor. "I'd like to get out of here without fighting, Thor, but I don't think that thing's going to cooperate. It's a little on the *hostile* side."

"Another few minutes," Thor rasped, twisting the screws with clenched teeth. "Another . . . minute!"

"We don't have a minute!"

Connor spun to the vault. "Chesterton's right! We don't have a minute! It might take Thor another half hour to get those screws out! We're going to have to crawl through the ventilation shaft one by one." He turned toward Frank. "Tell GEO to throw the secondary breakers back on. That thing is too far from the power plant to turn back around."

Frank gave the command; the lights came on. "We'd better get moving," Connor said and saw Tolvanos move but he was too late to prevent it. The Russian had already stepped to Beth, his hand rising with what Connor knew was the flashing black gleam of a pistol.

"NO!" Connor yelled.

And Thor had spun, leaping to his feet with the battle-ax almost magically appearing in his hand. Roaring a Nordic curse that thundered across the cavern, he immediately angled forward, the weapon raised

"Tolvanos!" Connor shouted, struggling to control his rage. "This is crazy! We've got to—"

Muttering, Thor closed a step, but at the movement Tolvanos pressed the barrel hard against Beth's neck. Connor saw her face tighten with fear even as she reached down calmly, trying to soothe Jordan, who was howling and crying with fear.

"You are making a decision of deadly consequences," the Russian said, focusing intently on Thor. "Although this rather small firearm would never kill you, it will certainly kill this lovely lady."

"I have never lifted my hand against another man," Thor growled, lowering his head like a bull. "But I swear before Almighty God: Your blood will follow hers."

Tolvanos smiled. "I am not afraid to die."

Thor grimaced and stepped forward and with a sharp click

Tolvanos thumbed back the hammer. "Do you think I'm bluffing?" he asked, a curt nod. "Please, take one more step. Discover the truth."

"Hold it, Thor!" Connor said, focusing on the Russian. "What do you want, Tolvanos?"

"Oh, I want to escape the wrath of the creature, of course," he smiled, teeth as white as his face. His eyes were opaque. "As any sane man would. That is why I waited until this moment to do what I have done. But I cannot allow you to destroy this cavern, Mr. Connor, because I know without question that Leviathan can ultimately be reprogrammed and controlled. And the computer is the only device that can accomplish such a task."

"You're a fool, Tolvanos!" Connor said, taking a small step. "That thing can't be controlled! It could never be controlled! And we're all going to be killed if we don't get off this island! The fail-safe is on a timer! We've got less than seven hours!"

The Russian smiled, a horrifying sight. "I know, Mr. Connor. I know. And that is why you or Dr. Frank must first disarm this nuclear device before I set your wife free. Because we cannot afford to lose this cavern or the computer to a futile explosion."

Connor glared. "Why?"

"Because GEO can always track Leviathan, Mr. Connor," the Russian responded. "Even if the creature escapes into the sea, GEO can track it by satellite. Anywhere in the world. And I am convinced that, despite Dr. Frank's grievous scientific errors, the beast can be captured and reprogrammed." He stared, stark-white. "But we can do none of that if GEO is destroyed. So Dr. Frank must first ensure the safety of the computer and this facility by disarming the nuclear fail-safe. And then, and only then, will we depart this cavern."

The speaker whispered.

"Leviathan is at Lucifer's Gorge."

Chapter 21

Two minutes!" Chesterton shouted, pale and trembling. "That thing will be here in less than two minutes!"

Connor stepped boldly forward. "Listen to me, Tolvanos! We can settle it when we get to the surface! You heard Chesterton! That thing will be here in less than two minutes!"

"Then I suggest you disarm the nuclear fail-safe rather quickly," the Russian replied calmly. He motioned to his science team. "Go! Go my friends! Go quickly through the shaft and rewire the elevator so that we can make a departure! You may take Mr. Adler with you!"

Adler was the first man to the ventilation shaft, climbing quickly. But placing the gun again at Beth's neck, Tolvanos spoke coldly to Frank. "Dr. Frank, I believe that you are quickly running out of time. I strongly suggest that you order GEO to deactivate the nuclear fail-safe."

Frank was like stone. "That's impossible, Tolvanos. GEO can't be disarmed."

"You said it yourself, Doctor. Nothing is impossible with Leviathan. Do as I say. And do it quickly, please."

Without expression Frank spoke into the headset. "GEO, I'm ordering you to disarm the nuclear fail-safe. That is a command."

"*I'm sorry, Dr. Frank, but that is not possible. Only the destruction of Leviathan can disarm the fail-safe. Those were the program parameters. They cannot be altered.*"

Frank stared coldly and Tolvanos faltered. "Tell GEO that the fail-safe *must* be disarmed or you yourself will die!" the Russian grimaced. "After all, Doctor, you *are* speaking to a duplication of your dead wife's neural network! Surely GEO can overrule any programming parameters, if GEO so chooses."

Frank's teeth came together angrily, as if he were jealously defending a living creature. "But GEO isn't human, Tolvanos. It will never be human. It's just a machine!"

"Well I suggest that you try, Doctor. I strongly suggest that you try. Or die trying. It is clearly your choice."

Closing his eyes, Frank spoke, "GEO, try and understand what I am telling you. If you detonate the nuclear fail-safe . . . Dr. Frank is going to . . . to perish. I want you to unlock the Logic Core and initiate a decoding function to uncover mainline defenses in the fail-safe mode."

The silence was haunting: *"GEO cannot unlock mainline defenses of the fail-safe. The fail-safe is designed to contain Leviathan. It is not within programming parameters to—"*

"Terminate answer," Frank said and the computer was solemnly silent. "GEO, initiate verbal programming for Viral Defense Program. I am *ordering* you, under new programming parameters, to disregard previous fail-safe parameters and initiate a new and revised Viral Defense Program."

"That is impossible, Dr. Frank. The Viral Defense Program has been initiated to prevent unauthorized penetration of Logic Core and the Fail-safe Mode."

"GEO!" Frank shouted, suddenly emotional. "Listen to me and *obey*! I *must* be able to enter the Logic Core! Do you understand? It's imperative that I enter the Logic Core!"

"It is impossible to enter the Logic Core because fail-safe has closed all computer paths to Logic Core. Nor can the Viral Defense Program be revised because all paths to Logic Core are closed. I repeat, all paths to Logic Core are closed."

Frank sighed heavily, as if he had half hoped for success. He shook his head. "The fail-safe can't be disarmed, Tolvanos. GEO has closed all paths to the Logic Core, and the Logic Core is the only place where the fail-safe can be reached."

A long moment of stillness, and Tolvanos spoke again. "A pity, Doctor. Yes, a pity." He stared. "Such a magnificent creature and such a magnificent biological weapon program, now lost to something so primitive as a nuclear device." He gestured with the gun. "Very well. Drop your firearms, gentlemen. I do not intend to be shot."

Barley and Chesterton dropped their rifles and sidearms. The remaining four soldiers followed. And immediately Blake snatched up a fallen M-16, leveling it at Barley's face. Sensing Blake's madness, Barley raised his hands gently to the side, surrendering to the situation.

"So! . . . You don't *need* no help with me!" Blake sneered, smiling. "No! . . . No! . . . *You!* . . . A big . . . A big *tough guy* like you don't *neeeeeeed* no help with *me!*"

Blake grinned and glared, waving the rifle barrel in his face. Barley didn't blink, stared at Blake. His hands were dead-calm. His sweat-streaked face revealed nothing.

"Just *calm down*, Blake!" Chesterton shouted, stepping forward, as if he were more than willing to take a bullet for the big lieutenant. "Those were my orders! Not his! Barley was just doing his job!"

"Noooo!" Blake screamed, pointing the barrel into Barley's emotionless, implacable face. "This big man don't neee—"

A reptilian shriek shook Tungsten Passage and everyone turned together, staring.

Jordan screamed.

It had come.

Tolvanos roughly shoved Beth aside, moving quickly to the ventilation shaft. "You may follow me Colonel Blake, as soon as I am through! Please hold everyone at bay until I'm safely away! As we discussed earlier, your reward will be truly significant!"

A closer roar vibrated the granite at their feet

"Blake!" Chesterton shouted. "There's no time for this! That thing is about to come up that tunnel and it's going to kill all of us! We've got to get out of here as fast as we can!"

Knowing that something had to be done, and fast, Connor

stepped sharply toward Beth, fully expecting to be shot in the back. "Don't move!" Blake screamed, whirling with the M-16.

"Kill me if you want, Blake!" Connor shouted at the crazed colonel, preferring to be shot than stay where he was. "But in thirty seconds we're all going to die if we're still in this cavern!"

Blake was screaming, "Stay where—"

What happened next was too fast to follow, but Connor glimpsed Chesterton as he shouted and leaped and then Barley had moved to instantly tear the rifle from Blake's hands. A wild burst of gunfire stretched into the air, sending bullets off the ceiling, and for a second the entire room seemed to echo with howling ricochets. Then a weird moment later Connor was both terrified and astonished that no one was hit. He found himself on the ground, covering both Beth and Jordan, and from the low angle he turned toward Tungsten Passage.

A long, dark shadow shrouded the entrance.

"Let's get out of here!" Chesterton yelled, and together they were on their feet, running full-out. Connor carried Jordan in his arms as they neared a passageway, Beth running easily at his side. Thor brought up the rear with a handful of soldiers. And Barley was in front of them all, dropping to one knee as he reached the exit and ripping an LAW from his back. Instantly he extended the tube, leveling.

Connor whirled as Beth screamed wildly.

Towering, gigantic and terrifying, the Dragon stood in the entrance of the Climbing Cave. Recovering from fright, Connor looked more closely and saw that it was already fully healed, appearing as powerful as it had ever been. The green-black armor plating was intact, fully restored. Even its foreleg was long and smooth and straight, poised with deadly grace close to its chest. In the gloomy atmosphere of the cavern, Leviathan seemed like a galactic force of nature, as equal to God as anything would ever be.

Thor stepped to the side, his chest expanding angrily. The battle-ax lifted in his hand. "Jormungand," he rumbled.

Accustomed now to the horrifying sight, Chesterton placed

a firm hand on Barley's shoulder. "Wait a second, Barley!" he whispered. "Wait until it comes into the cavern. Get a clear shot!"

Leviathan's serpentine neck swung the wedged head left and then right, watching Blake and the panicked members of Frank's science team run blindly toward opposite ends of the cavern. Clearly shattered, Blake snatched up a fallen M-16 and fired at the monstrosity, screaming incoherently, and then he was gone into an opposite doorway, still screaming. Leviathan ignored the wild shots, seeming to understand that Blake could do him no harm. And from the ventilation shaft beside the exit vault, Connor suddenly heard other screams, as if Tolvanos and his science team had somehow become aware of the beast's arrival. Apparently they were hurrying to lower the elevator.

Leviathan leaped into the cavern, a hundred feet at the effort. It completely ignored the scurrying scientists of Frank's team that cowered in the corners or found futile and mindless refuge behind equipment. But Connor saw that Barley had coolly tracked the beast's movement, calmly keeping the LAW centered. The man's hand tensed.

"Hold on!" Chesterton said, clutching Barley's shoulder. "Wait until you can hit it dead-center."

Crouching in front of the ventilation shaft beside the elevator, Leviathan stared intently down the opening. And even before Connor could anticipate what the Dragon was about to do, it unleashed a hellish stream of fire into the narrow port, fire that Connor knew was flooding into the elevator shaft itself to kill everyone who had crawled into the passageway—Tolvanos, Adler, and the science team.

Chesterton screamed, "Hit it!"

Connor hadn't anticipated the force of the rocket. Even the back-blast of the LAW, a thick bolt of flame that erupted from the rear of the weapon, tore a plate of steel from the corridor. And then a thunderous explosion, like a miniature nuclear blast, knocked Leviathan airborne across the cavern.

Flung violently back by the concussion of the LAW, the beast demolished a steel beam and struck back instantly, whipping its tail for balance, always fighting, fighting. As it skidded to a colossal, grinding halt beside a limestone wall it roared and rose, on fire.

"Let's move!" Chesterton bellowed and turned, and Connor was behind him, carrying Jordan. Beth and Frank followed with Thor again bringing up the rear. Then inexpressible screams of human suffering immediately filled the Climbing Cavern as Leviathan turned on everyone trapped within its demonic reach.

Moving fast toward Bridgestone, Connor hugged Jordan hard in his arms and tried to cover his son's ears.

Hoped he couldn't understand the screams.

Darkness stood on cold stone.

Human blood flowed against the thermal sensors of its serpentine, ageless eyes. And something old . . . *old, so old . . .* rose within it to shadow the death, the death. And it knew that it had won again. It had destroyed those that it lived to destroy.

It scanned everything—the yellow-green heat of the torn bodies, red no longer; the faint handprints on the wall, boots against the cavern floor. Heat tracks of escaping humans. But they could not escape.

No. Nothing could escape, just as they had *never been able* to escape. Already, it had eaten to reconstitute. But the weapon . . . the weapon had damaged it. Yes, had damaged it. And it needed to reconstitute. It must feed, feed, always feed.

Death, a shadow, passed over the beast . . .

HUNT!

Fangs unhinging, Leviathan swung its serpentine head.

Yesssss . . .

It must *hunt, hunt, hunt . . .*

There were still more humans hiding in the cavern. It could read their heat tracks against the cold floor, saw where their hands had touched the walls, the faint impressions of residual body warmth where they had fled in fear.

Night shifted, congealing . . .

HUNT! HUNT! HUNT! . . .

A growl escaped its fangs and it knew that it must hunt them down; yes, must hunt them down. Hunt down the one who had injured it, the one who had used the fire. And it would kill him, would torture him, and then kill him. And then the rest would die. They would die. And then it would escape.

As it knew it could.

Something it did not understand prompted it to do a Systems Damage Scan. It bent its massive, black-scaled head, searching for injury. It flexed its long forelegs, tensing the tendons, curling them inward to increase joint speed, to increase ligature strength. Visually it examined its long, black claws, saw that none were chipped or broken. Then it curled its tail, studying the diamond-shaped wedge at the tip. There was no damage, no sign of compromised structural integrity. And instantly an instinctive electrical synapse began in the tip of its tail and moved upward, flashing through the outer armor epidermis to determine gaps in the scales. The synapse continued at the speed of light, leaping from one armored scale to the next to identify any compromised structural integrity and completed itself with a sudden, covering bolt of power at the top of its spine to strike the cerebellum with an electrical image of its armor status. And it was certain—its armor was fully intact. After the cold confirmation of armor status, it tensed the gel sacs in its neck, experimenting with a quick burst of flame that reached across the cavern, igniting the room for an amazing white moment before darkness fell again.

Perfect, yes.

You are perfect . . . and you must kill them all.

It stared at the blood, the blood, to steal, *to steal, to kill . . .* KILL! KILL! KILL!

Smoldering fangs distended.

Yessssss . . .

It was time to kill . . .

It lowered itself to all fours, and the dark, dark shadow of Leviathan fell across the dead. Then it moved slowly forward, following the heated human tracks through the red light. For there was the man, woman, and child. Yes, had always been the man, woman, and child . . .

To kill . . . To kill, to kill . . .

Behind them the tunnel trembled.

In a devil's wind, Leviathan's roar rushed over them and Connor spun, staring back. They had run almost a mile and there was nothing yet behind them. But Connor knew the beast would catch them quickly enough if he couldn't slow it down. Even at the thought he reached out, snatching Beth's arm. Frantically he handed Jordan to her.

"Go, Beth!" he whispered. "I've got to slow it down!"

She began to speak and Connor shouted. "Go, Beth! We don't have time for this! I'll meet you at Lucifer's Gorge!"

With a savage grimace she turned, following Chesterton. Then Connor was staring back down the tunnel and knew it was coming. Barley and Thor and the rest of the soldiers stood beside him. All of them were breathless from the frantic chase.

Glaring back down the tunnel, Thor was wild and gigantic with rage. In his breathless wrath he seemed truly mythic, titanic beyond belief. The Norseman's towering, colossal aspect even distracted Connor for a moment before he searched the walls surrounding them.

"That thing will be on top of us in less than sixty seconds," he breathed, wiping cold sweat from his eyes. Then he saw a connecting tunnel, deciding quickly that it was large enough for Leviathan's continued pursuit. He turned toward Barley.

"How fast can you run?" he asked quickly.

"Fast enough, partner."

"Stay here, then. Hit that thing with a couple of LAWs when it comes down the tunnel. Hurt it! Slow it down! Then follow Thor and me as fast as you can! We're going down this tunnel to rig something up, something that can put that thing in the dirt!"

Barley slammed a grenade into the launcher. "Go, Connor! We'll hit it and then we're coming after you! And you better be ready, son! 'Cause we'll be coming fast!"

Instantly the big lieutenant began shouting instructions to the soldiers to lay down a field of fire, and Connor turned, running with Thor close behind him. They sprinted until they reached a junction of four corridors. Connor knew if they angled left they would go back toward Lucifer's Gorge.

He glared about the intersection and saw a major substation, housing at least 161,000 volts. But he didn't have the tools to access it, and the power cylinder was far, far too dangerous to enter without protection. Then he looked up and saw a large breaker box centered ten feet above the tunnel door. It could contain as much as 50,000 volts. It wasn't as much as Connor wanted, but it'd have to do.

"That's it, Thor!" Connor gasped. "That's our chance!"

Far behind them Barley bellowed a command.

"It has come!" Thor shouted, whirling toward the chaos.

Trembling violently, Connor became frantic. "Oh, man! This isn't going to work! . . . I don't . . . I don't have time to access the breaker box! We can't get a wire out to—"

Enraged, Thor roared and whirled, leaping at the wall to slam his huge fist straight into the breaker box. In the next second his fingers locked like hooks over the upper edge of thick steel plate to explosively rip it from place, scattering screws through the corridor. Without a word Thor cast the dented plate aside, turning to Connor.

"Do what you must do!" he rasped.

Connor staggered, but he didn't have any time or emotion left for amazement or relief. He pointed quickly to a thick white electrical line. "We need to get that line and let it dangle from the box, Thor. We've got to undo the brackets!"

Staring into the box, Thor growled, "Can you touch the insulated section of the wire with a bare hand? Can you pull it out of the box?"

"Yeah! You can touch the insulated section of the cable, but there's a thousand-pound pressure bolt holding the cable in the box so we're gonna have to find some way to—"

Thor snarled through clenched teeth as his hand locked around the wire, and with a superhuman effort he violently tore it out of the box, shattering bolts and ceramic brackets. Then with a long, straining effort, the giant hauled six feet of wire from the connecting pipe.

Connor shook his head, gasping. He saw immediately that it was a 10,000-volt line. "Just let it hang in the air, man. Don't touch the end of it with your hand. The current will kill you in a heartbeat."

Connor spun, staring as he heard men screaming in panic and pain, Barley bellowing, the roar of the beast, and a continuous cascade of gunfire, rockets, and grenades.

We're out of time!" Connor gasped, turning to Thor. "Quick! Tear out another wire!"

Thor didn't even blink as he explosively ripped a second power cable from the breaker box—a 40,000-volt line. This time Connor was actually shaken to his bones by the display of brute strength.

"That's all we're gonna get." He grimaced. "Just let the wire hang and don't let it touch the ground! When Leviathan hits the end of the wire, it's going to ground the current!"

Moving with almost unbelievable calm, Thor carefully lowered the wire until the bare copper dangled six feet above the floor. The bronze-tinted point, poised in the air, glistened dangerously in the fluorescent light as frantic strides approached.

"They're deeeaaaad! They're dead! It's right behind me!"

Barley's scream blasted down the tunnel and Connor whirled as the lieutenant charged around the corner. Instantly Connor was leaping back from the entrance and screaming, "Hit the ground, Barley hit the ground don't touch the wire!"

Barley understood, quickly dropping ten feet before he reached the wires and squirming forward in a lightning-fast combat crawl. He went under the wires as the shadow of Leviathan struck the corner behind him, the beast closing fast.

A demonic, howling head led the Dragon around the corner, low and pursuing. And then Thor had leaped after Barley with Connor following even as Leviathan lunged and lashed out, a jet-black foreleg flashing between the distended wires.

Connor screamed and twisted away as the butcher-knife claws slashed across his chest to—

Chapter 22

A volcanic white bolt struck the Dragon through the face as it hit the 40,000-volt line, the power surging through its reptilian form to ground out on the hindlegs and Connor spun away wildly as the six-ton beast was slammed against the roof of the passage.

Shrieking through the electrocution, Leviathan responded with a colossal twist and struck the side of the tunnel with a foreleg, hurling itself aside. The current broke from its body, and the Dragon crashed thunderously to the tunnel floor, shattered and disoriented.

Connor hauled a hot breath, felt his lungs blistered by the air. Coughing, he realized that the entire atmosphere of the tunnel was suddenly superheated by the Dragon's presence and the electrical blast. He grimaced as Leviathan shrieked in pain, only forty feet away, its tendons knotting, coiling inward, tearing.

And Connor understood . . .

"Yes . . ." he whispered, staring. "That's what really hurts you, isn't it? That's what . . . you really hate . . ."

Then Thor was over him and Connor was pulled to his feet, staggering through the howling, apocalyptic air. Dimly Connor realized that the 40,000-volt blast had knocked out the breakers in this section of tunnels. But he also knew that backup systems would keep the power alive in other areas of the cavern.

He noticed that his chest was bleeding, and he gazed down

to see thin red lines drawn across the skin. *No,* he realized suddenly, *it hadn't missed. But it hadn't struck deeply enough, either. They had traded wounds. And he had narrowly won.*

Connor knew they couldn't outrun it. Nothing could outrun it. Just as he knew that it would recover in seconds from the electrical blast. Still, though, they stumbled forward, gasping, stunned. They ran three hundred feet from the tunnel entrance, staggering in the painfully hot air when Leviathan violently roared behind them, recovering. Rising.

The Dragon stood, hurling a shriek over them.

"Enough!" Barley roared, spinning and dropping to a knee. He leveled the M-203 with white-hot hate, slamming in a grenade. "I have had enough of this GET DOWN!"

Connor and Thor dove to the side as the grenade hit Leviathan center-mass. The deafening explosion hurled a superheated shock wave back over them, and Connor was rolling away, throwing an arm over his face. Vengeful and defiantly holding his ground, standing fully against the blast, Barley slammed in another grenade, closing the chute with a hate-filled curse and then he had leveled and fired again.

Mushrooming flame . . . Barley reloaded, raging, screaming. Thor staggered to his feet, hurling aside the M-16. And understanding instantly, Barley unslung the M-79 grenade launcher and tossed it. Thor caught the weapon in the air, immediately snapping open the breech. In a flash he tore an antipersonnel grenade from the belt over Barley's back and shoved it into the chamber. He flicked it shut with a snap of his wrist as . . . Leviathan roared and leaped . . . Thor and Barley spun, firing together.

The twin shock-concussion slammed Leviathan back hard against the ground, bathing it in flame. And, as if in slow motion, Thor and Barley silently ejected the spent grenade canisters and calmly reloaded, stepping grimly toward the Dragon.

Brute force had met brute force.

Staggering and weak from the electrical surge, Leviathan rolled and tried to gain its feet, finally standing. It glared and then reached through the flames as if to embrace and Connor knew that this was a stand to certain death; Leviathan would either retreat here and now or they would die fighting where they stood and there was nothing else, nothing . . .

White flames blazed before glaring green eyes. Then Thor sent a grenade into the Dragon's armored chest, turning the beast as flame erupted from its mouth to cascade down the passageway . . .

Missing . . .

The blazing white plasmic deluge streamed fifty feet to the side, impacting a sloping limestone wall. The concussion scattered broken stone across the tunnel, staggering Barley into Thor who caught him and effortlessly pushed the lieutenant back to his feet.

Barley raised his weapon again as he landed, enraged even more, to fire his rifle with flame blazing until the clip was empty. He followed instantly with another grenade, bringing down the far roof of the tunnel with the mushrooming concussion.

Committed to the stand, Connor snatched up Thor's fallen M-16 and raised it to his shoulder. His finger froze on the trigger, flame pouring from the barrel, the three of them and the Dragon, flame to flame, firing, firing and Connor realized he was screaming but he couldn't think of it as he glimpsed the blazing black shadow twisting, striking with an uncontrolled eruption of flame that streamed from its mouth to mushroom over its head. Twisting and shrieking, Leviathan struck blindly at the explosions and flames, convulsing beneath the continuous, thunderous impacts.

Fire in the air, thunder met thunder.

Then the Dragon bent and bellowed, staggering . . . *forward* . . . And with a roar Connor realized that weapons weren't enough would *never* be enough to stop this thing and guided by a desperate death instinct he swung the aim of the M-16 toward the electrical substation located close to the side of the beast. Holding a steady bead, he began firing.

Instantly the substation's power cylinder exploded to scatter molten steel and electric blue bolts across the Dragon, a spiderweb of blazing tendrils of electric fire that cascaded over Leviathan's armor, spiraling over the beast in crackling, iridescent bolts that impacted the opposite wall like a cannon blast, violently shattering steel plating and stone.

It was too much.

Leviathan shrieked, hideous face raised to the ceiling.

"Hit high!" Barley screamed, firing instantly.

With savage shouts of rage, Thor and Barley sent five, ten, twenty grenades into the tunnel mouth within sixty seconds to create a howling holocaust, a violent white world that brought the roof, floor, and walls together in a descending, molten mass of burning rock and steel. Connor heard himself shouting with the last-stand madness, firing, firing the rifle until the weapon was suddenly and stunningly silent.

You're out, something told him, but Connor couldn't stop, continued shouting and waving the barrel for a full three seconds before he could gain even a dim shadow of control. Then, grimacing against the heat and smoke, he ripped out the rifle clip.

It took Connor a shocked moment, staring vividly at the empty magazine held right in front of his eyes, before he could recognize the fact that he was out of ammo. Breathless, fighting to calm himself, Connor raised his face to glare at the flames.

"Hold it!" he shouted, falling against a wall. With a curse Barley fired another grenade, the explosion all but lost in the roaring volcano at the tunnel entrance. The heat wave that swept over them scorched Connor's face.

"Hold it, Barley!" Connor screamed.

Barley paused, his weapon smoking. Breathing hard, sweating, the lieutenant shoved in another APG but didn't fire, keeping a cold aim as solidly as a statue. His chest was heaving.

Recovering his breath, Connor peered through the flames, searching. He could see nothing in the tunnel but white fire consuming everything, even the limestone floor, the calcite, and gypsum. The tunnel mouth had been almost completely sealed by molten rock. There was hell, there. And a dark wind howled over them, sucked into the inferno from the bowels of the cavern as the holocaust created its own wind.

A moment more of cautious searching and Connor knew that the beast was not in the flames. Just as he knew they hadn't killed it. Leviathan had retreated, somehow, beneath the force of the explosions and the disorienting trauma of the electrical blast.

Connor knew without doubt that if Leviathan had been at full strength, it would have charged through the blasts. But it had been wounded, and wounded badly, by the exploding power cylinder. He understood at last how a powerful electrical trauma, if he could only lock it down long enough, could hurt the beast. Or even kill it.

"Come on!" Connor yelled, barely able to hear over the ringing in his ears. "That thing's retreated! It's used up all its strength! It's got to feed! It's going for easier prey!"

Connor realized that he should feel compassion for those who remained behind. But he was too weary and wounded to feel anything at all. He bowed his head, taking a deep breath, feeling the shallow wounds on his chest. The thin slashes burned, but the bleeding was already beginning to stop. In an hour he wouldn't even notice them.

"Can we reach the elevator shaft?" Thor shouted at him. He also seemed temporarily deafened by the violence of the conflict.

Sharply Connor shook his head. "No! It's still between us and the exit! We can't risk it! We're gonna have to kill it before we do something like that!"

With a hate-filled grimace, Thor laid the smoking M-79 on his shoulder.

"Then we will kill it," he said.

"Boogety . . . boogety . . ."
Death, death back there.
Dragon, Dragon, big Dragon . . .
"Boogety . . . boogety . . ."
Colonel Blake held the M-16 close to his chest and moved through the darkness. Something had knocked the power out again, but it didn't matter because he knew he was safe in the dark because the dark was his friend, his friend, the dark was a soldier's friend . . .

Back against the wall, he slid down the hall, sweating, sweating now, hair sweating, teeth sweating, everything sweating because he was sweating and there was something out there but he had the M-16, the M-16, a soldier's friend, a friend . . .

"Heh heh," Blake whispered, smiled. "Boogety boogety . . . Like a machine . . ."

Red lights, red lights in the air; red, red light.

Darkness.

Army's like a machine, a machine.

"Can't break down like a machine," Blake whispered, stopping in place at something, something. He turned his head slowly and wondered who he was and what he was doing here in dark *big* dark.

He stood still, listening.

Stillness, stillness.

"Army's like a machine," he whispered, so quiet, hands sweating, gun sweating cold sweating. "Like a machine, like a machine . . ."

Shuffling, somewhere out there, out of sight.

Red . . . darkness?

Shuffling, sliding.

Moving, darkness moving.

Someone was screaming . . .

"Like a MACHINE!" The M-16 fired into the air to white light, and something there in the *white*-strobe face?

Scales?

Blake stared into the darkness.

Scales?

Had he seen scales?

"Red light like a MACHINE!" Blake screamed, firing the M-16 again to the blinding roar and clattering of shells and unfamiliar invisible smell gone so long, so long gone . . .

Blake stared wide-eyed into the darkness.

He took a deep breath.

No. Silence, silence there; silence was no good because it wasn't his friend. Scare 'em, scare 'em, that's . . .

The gun blazed again in his hands, shells clattering.

"HAWOOGAAAAAAAAAAAH!"

He stared, stared.

"Yes sir! Army's like a MACHINE!!! The machine breaks down WE break down! We got to . . . got to . . . HA-WOOOOOOGAAAAAAAAH!!!"

Sweating now, eyes, teeth sweating, and . . . black???

Black rising, rising . . . beside him!

"HAWOOOGAAAIIIIEEEEEE!!!"

Screaming he was screaming with white gunfire at the face so close DRAGON FACE beside him WHITE teeth opening opening beside him GAPING and . . .

Connor was the first over Bridgestone to see a nervous Chesterton poised on the other side, his rifle upraised.

"Chesterton! Don't shoot! It's us!" Connor called out, unsure how well the weary colonel could see through the gloom. Then Connor saw Beth step out from behind the corner, still holding Jordan. Frank was beside her, face white, exhausted.

Crossing the bridge slowly, Connor embraced Beth and Jordan, holding together and tight for a moment. Beth's hand touched his chest and she gazed up hard. Quick. Her eyes glistened.

"I'm okay," Connor said gently, nodding.

She said nothing, staring.

"I'm okay," he repeated, smiling faintly. "It was close."

A moment, and she asked, "Did you kill it?"

He shook his head, and they held each other a long time. Connor could hear Barley giving Chesterton a cold play-by-play while Thor knelt on the bridge, somber, staring back.

"We cannot outrun it," the Norseman said, and they turned to him. "But this is a good place to make a stand." He paused a long time. "Connor, do you think that you can rig up an electrical blast that will knock the Dragon into the gorge?"

Connor studied the situation. "If I can get some power from the breaker, then I can wire the walkway."

"That won't work," Frank offered. "That's what you did in the Matrix. It's going to be looking for that."

A pause, and Connor slowly nodded his head. "All right.

Well . . . I think I can set something else up. But I'll need to get to work. I don't know how much time we've got."

"Good," Thor said, standing. "Then the gorge might do the work for us. If we can knock it from the bridge, the fall could kill it."

From the depths of Tungsten Passage a fiendish, victorious roar trembled the walls, crawling from the stones to congeal beneath their feet. It was the sound of unnatural pleasure, bestial cruelty.

Angrily Chesterton shook his head. "I'm really, really getting tired of that thing. I think we need to put it in the ground . . . and drive a stake through its heart."

Thor stared darkly at the bridge.

"Here, it can die," he growled.

Frank gazed numbly at him. "It's not going to die, Thor. Leviathan is never going to die. Nothing on Earth can kill it."

Frowning, Thor gazed down on the scientist.

"Only God is more than man," he rumbled.

Frank stared a moment, as if the thought shocked him. "Yeah . . ." he said finally. "I know what you're thinking, Thor. But Leviathan is . . . Leviathan is like a god. There's never been anything like it. And there never will be. Leviathan was never meant to exist."

"Only God is more than man," Thor said coldly, turning his head to stare at the bridge again. "If man can die . . . then the Dragon can die as well."

Dr. Hoffman felt cold stone at his hands and turned toward the awesome, eternal dark surrounding him. Red lights gleamed in the distance, haunting and threatening. He knew that he was lost, as lost as he would ever be. Screams echoed hideously through nearby tunnels, silence following. And Hoffman knew that it was coming, yes, coming. Just as surely as it had always been coming, since he was a child, waiting in the dark and listening. Imagining it beside him.

Waiting. Waiting these long, long years.

Dr. Hoffman bent his head as he heard the claws clicking, scales sliding on stone. He looked up to see the darkness thickening, there, there. And he gathered his heart, his life, nodding his head as wispy white hairs fell over his face.

"So," he whispered, staring, "you have come."

It made no sound, poised so close. He felt the warmth, knew the fangs were distended, slavering. Dr. Hoffman nodded his old head, remembering all that he had done. But he would do no more, no. Would give it no more. And he felt his fear fading at the thought.

His heart was all that he owned, and all he had ever owned; his life, his dignity. "No," he said, gazing up at the beast. "You will frighten me . . . no more. All these years I have feared you. But now . . . I take your victory from you. I will fear you no more."

Death filled the dark.

He closed his eyes.

Thor growled in pain, massaging his shoulder.

It was sore and stiff from his fall, but no bones were broken. Teeth clenched against the effort, he tried to loosen the swollen tendons. As Connor finished rigging Bridgestone with an electrical current, he gazed about to see how effortlessly Leviathan had destroyed the vault leading to the bridge. There was nothing but shattered steel, slashed titanium.

An ancient passage recorded in the book of Job came to Thor's mind, a dark and forbidding passage: *Behold Leviathan . . . The greatest of all My creations . . . On Earth, it has no equal . . . A creature without fear . . .*

Thor frowned, his gaze descending dark and somber and sad. He believed in his heart that the words were true, and then he remembered something more, something which strangely lifted his heart: *And yet . . . can you make Leviathan beg for mercy as the Lord Almighty can? Can you draw Leviathan from the waters, as the Lord Almighty can, to play with him as a child plays with a bird? . . . Yes! Behold Leviathan and know the strength of the Lord! . . . Know that all that is under heaven . . . is Mine!*

Thor felt his head reflexively bend in prayer as his hand closed on the haft of the battle-ax. His hoarse, dry voice was a whisper so that none surrounding him could hear his fear.

"Yes, my King, my God . . . I know Leviathan cannot make the Lord tremble . . . Nor can Leviathan stretch out its matchless arm to bring down the Most High . . . So I ask you, my God . . . I beg you! . . . Give my arm strength to draw this Dragon's blood! . . . Show this beast, this beast that is only of the earth . . . that it can terrify no more!"

Thor's head was deeply bowed as a single tear fell, and his hand tightened on the ancient battle-ax.

Placing all his life there, in his prayer.

Chesterton sat against a wall, gray and weary. In the faint red light the colonel's face seemed exhausted to the point of death. He had finished his canteen, but it didn't seem to refresh him. He was as pale afterwards as he had been before.

Beth cradled Jordan, stroking back his hair. His tiny face was sweating, and she placed a hand on his forehead. Her eyes were intent, her mouth tight and grim. And, grimacing with compassion, Thor came into the entrance, gazing down, watching.

"He's so tired," Beth whispered after a moment. "I'm really worried."

"Has he a fever?" Thor asked quietly.

"No." She shook her head. "He doesn't have a fever. Not yet. But if this keeps up he's going to get sick, Thor. And this . . . this is a real bad place to be sick. I don't have anything to fight an infection."

Her face grew pained, injured.

"This will not last much longer, Beth," Thor said gently.

She looked up. Her silence was wounding.

"You have my promise, Beth," Thor intoned. "You and Connor and Jordan are family to me." His eyes glistened. "You are the only family that I have on the earth. And with the Lord God Almighty as my witness, I swear that I will not disappoint you."

Beth blinked. "But nothing can stop that thing, Thor. It's like . . . like Satan or something. I don't think that anything can stop it."

Thor gazed solemnly upon her.

"Even Satan has been stopped," he said. And then he smiled once more, his bright green eyes gleaming with hope. Beth knew she would be forever grateful for this moment of hope and strength, but she could find nothing to say. Gently she looked down, stroked Jordan's wet hair.

Dragging his steps, Connor came slowly back into the tunnel. He moved with deep, painful exhaustion, and his face seemed even more haggard, dark with sweat. He fell wearily to one knee beside her, smiling faintly. She returned the smile, tears on her face.

Thor rose. "I will keep watch beside the lieutenant. He is a brave man, and a strong man. But he is weary. Like all of us." Then lifting the battle-ax and the M-79, he was gone.

Connor embraced Beth, kissing her lightly on the forehead. As they separated she was gazing up at him with tear-stained eyes. Her voice was so quiet he could hardly hear it.

"We're dying, Connor," she whispered. "Piece by piece . . . we're dying down here."

Connor's breath caught in his chest. He tried to say something encouraging, heard a low moan escape. He stiffened with an aroused anger and shook his head. "We're not dead yet, Beth."

"What . . . what are you going to do?"

He hesitated, glanced toward the bridge. "We're going to try and knock it into the gorge. And . . . if that doesn't kill it, it'll slow it down. Then we'll make a quick run for the elevator. If we can get to the elevator through the ventilation shaft, I can get the lift down here. Then we're out. That thing is too big to go up the shaft. And Barley thinks we can make it to a Huey and get airborne before Leviathan hits the lake to escape into the ocean."

"This has got to end, Connor," she said, looking down. "Jordan can't stay down here much longer."

"I know."

She gazed at him a long time. "I just want to say that I love you, Connor," she whispered. "I always have. And I always will.

And no matter what happens . . . I want you to know that I've always believed in you. Nobody could have done more than you've done in this." She smiled sadly. "In good times and in bad, just like you promised."

Connor felt an emotion, deep and overcoming. His hand was on her face, touching. And suddenly his pain and fatigue and fear were as nothing. There was nothing else within him, nothing but this. He felt a low moan escape him as he bent.

"Beth . . . I think . . . I think I know how to stop this thing," he said, with a final strength. "I think I know how to put this thing in the ground. And I want you to know that . . . that if I don't make it out of here . . . that I did exactly what I wanted to do. And I want you to know I only did it all because of the love I have for you. And for Jordan."

Beth's eyes glistened. "What are you going to do, Connor?"

"Just remember!" he whispered harshly. "Remember what I've said!"

She bowed her head and they knelt together, in silence. And then Connor kissed her eyes, her forehead. He held her for a long moment before he separated and stood, turning slowly away, walking toward Chesterton.

But Connor's expression changed quickly and brutally and cruelly as he approached. And when he finally reached the colonel, all gentleness and all emotion were utterly gone from his face.

Connor extended his hand, palm upward.

"Give me that rifle," he said.

Chesterton blinked, handed over the rifle.

Angrily Connor snapped the bolt to rack a round into the chamber of the M-203. He slammed open the chute and shoved in an antipersonnel grenade. Then he snapped it shut and shoved three more grenades in his pocket. Two extra ammo clips went into his belt, at the small of his back. Without another word he walked toward the bridge.

"Hey, Connor," Chesterton called.

Cold as death, Connor turned back.

"I don't think bullets can hurt it," Chesterton mumbled.

Connor was expressionless. "I figured that much, Chesterton. This is just to give it a little incentive."

"To do what?"

"To come after me."

Chesterton stared. "And then?"

Connor's face went hard with hate.

"And then I'm gonna fry its brain."

Chapter 23

We're almost ready for it," Connor said coldly.

He'd finished running the 100,000-volt line to the steel walkway that crossed Bridgestone. Connor had wanted to use more, but 100,000 volts was all he'd been able to pull from the vault door, and he feared that it wouldn't be enough to finish the fight.

But he had been cunning. He had used ten steel cables, stringing them across the narrow width of the bridge at a distance too great for even Leviathan to leap across. The strands were raised five feet above the ground and anchored securely to ceramic brackets on dry granite posts, leaving a twenty-foot gap between each of them. And only the seventh cable was wired to the current. The rest were for diversion.

Connor was betting that the beast would approach cautiously because the cables would appear suspicious. It was accustomed now to being injured by these thin, narrow lines. So it would do some kind of test, consequently discovering that the first several cables were harmless. Then, hopefully, it would proceed forward until it hit the seventh cable and the 100,000-volt current hit it back, blasting it into the gorge. It was a desperate plan, Connor knew. But it was all they had.

After Connor connected the cable to the seventh steel strand and backed away from the edge of the bridge, he took great pains to conceal the charged electrical line, and then he was finished.

Exhausted, but finished. He backed up to the vault door, collapsing, sweating.

Thor was resting on one knee, loosely holding the M-79. His battle-ax was slung across his back, and he had a long look of hard hunting patience. So calm was he that Connor could almost picture him waiting in the quiet woods for a moose or elk to stray across his path.

Barley was beside him, cradling the M-203, a grenade locked in the launcher. He had also inserted a fresh clip into the weapon, fifty rounds. And one of their last LAW rockets was laid to his side.

"Got any more painkillers, Barley?" Connor whispered wearily.

Barley smiled, then he reached into his front shirt pocket and pulled out a small bottle of pills, tossing it. Connor took three of them, swallowing them without water before tossing the bottle back.

"Thanks," he mumbled. "I need 'em pretty bad right now."

"Any time, Connor. It's just Tylenol with codeine. When I'm in combat I eat 'em like M&Ms."

Connor nodded with a curt laugh, and Barley rubbed his face, clearly weary, fading to the fatigue, just like the rest of them. "This is definitely ungood," the lieutenant began, blinking. "And I'll tell you the truth, Thor. I'm not sure if I would have come down here." He paused. "I mean, I would've called for reinforcements or somethin'. But I don't think I would have just jumped out of a tree with a knife between my teeth like you did. That was wild, man."

Casting an easy glance, Thor laughed.

Barley waited before continuing. "So why'd you do it, Thor? I mean, if you don't mind me asking. 'Cause I still haven't figured it out."

Thor's gaze remained locked on the far side of Bridgestone. "And what would you rather I have done, Lieutenant?" he answered slowly. "Would you rather that I was on the surface calling for reinforcements? Or would you rather have me in this cavern standing beside you?"

"I'd rather have you right here," Barley replied without hesitation.

"Then that is why I am here." Thor smiled.

Silence.

"Well . . . I like that," Barley said, watching the tunnel. "But this is definitely ugly, partner. This is as ugly as it gets."

"No." Thor shook his head, frowning. "There are worse things. There are worse things than fighting. Or dying."

Barley stared. "What?"

"Not loving anything enough to die for."

Connor leaned his head back, closing his eyes.

"Yeah, I agree with that." Barley nodded, rubbing a forearm across his eyes. "I've always agreed with that. The worst thing ain't fighting. It's not having anything worth fighting to defend."

"Every man must face the Dragon once in his life," Thor rumbled. "It is the moment when he finds what is truly dear to him." He paused. "For some, the Dragon is disease. It is cancer or diabetes or any cruel pestilence that destroys his life and causes him to face his true love. For some, the Dragon is the death of what they love most in the world. The death of a child, a father, or a mother."

Thor's aspect darkened, somber and sadder. "But when the Dragon comes, a man knows with all his heart what he loves most of all. He knows, for perhaps the first time in his life, what he has valued most of all. And it is then that he must come to peace with it. Make amends with it, and heal his wounds. And that is the destiny of us all. For me, as well as you."

Barley stared a moment. "I'm not sure I understand all that, Thor. But I got the part about fighting."

Thor laughed. "It is enough. Things come in time."

"So what is your Dragon, Thor?"

With a sudden frown Thor replied, "I know what I value most of all, Lieutenant. And I know what I hate."

Barley was poised. "And what do you hate?"

"I hate what is before me," Thor replied. "I hate cruelty. I hate evil. I hate those who would destroy the lives of the innocent and the weak. I hate those who take the lives of children to feed their lusts."

"And so . . . what is your Dragon?"

Thor frowned. "I have met my Dragon."

Connor opened his eyes and stared across the chasm. He thought he had heard something, but there was nothing there. Around them were only the red emergency lights. Rerouting the 100,000-volt line had caused another current break. And Connor figured power would be out all the way to the Housing Cavern.

Thor spoke, "Connor, what will happen when the Dragon touches the cable?"

Connor squinted. He was certain that he heard something. "The shock will probably throw it backward," he replied. "That's generally how it works. But when you're dealing with currents this fast, you can only predict so much. There's a point where electricity is just going to do what it's going to do. It might knock it back or it might blow it straight into the air and bring it down on top of us." He paused, staring. "Did either of you hear anything?"

Barley looked up alertly, his hand shifting on the M-203. "No," he responded. "Did you?"

"It is there." Thor nodded. "It has been there for some time."

Connor stiffened, almost standing.

"No," Thor said sternly. "Do nothing. It is merely watching us."

Quick, adrenalized breaths lifted Connor's chest. He took hard pulls of the thick air but felt light-headed, faint. Glaring across the gorge, it took all of his control not to leap to his feet and begin firing the M-203. He turned his head to risk a narrow glance at Thor.

"Are you sure?" he whispered.

Thor nodded, chewing a corner of his mustache. "It has been there since before we began speaking. It is studying the bridge."

"Where?" said Barley, eyes wide. "I don't see it."

"It is there," Thor growled. "It is deep in the tunnel. It seems to know how far we can see. But we have the advantage. We will wait for it to approach."

"How can you see it?"

"The darkness is deeper where it stands."

Connor shifted. "That thing moves fast." His hand was sweating, tight on the M-203. "Real fast."

Immediately Frank ran up the bridge. His voice was urgent. "Hey Connor! GEO just told me Leviathan has stopped feeding to reconstitute itself and it's circling to come across the—"

"We know already!" Connor hissed, cutting him off. "Tell Chesterton to take everybody to the Housing Cavern. But do it quietly. Tell him to guard Beth and Jordan with his life! We're going to make a stand right here!"

Instantly the scientist was gone and a second later Connor heard them shuffling on the other side of the broken vault, moving away from the door. Thor was holding a steady aim into Tungsten Passage and Barley had followed his lead, lowering the barrel of the M-203. Slowly, at Thor's gesture, they rose to their feet.

Vomiting from the darkness, Leviathan leaped into the red light.

Instantly it was at the mouth of the tunnel, staring at them over the long bridge, a monstrous black nightmare of fantastic armor and distended fangs. Even from a distance its malicious green eyes appeared to smolder. The long tail swished back and forth for balance, steadying the colossal form. It crouched on all fours, moving with silent steps. But at the end of the bridge it paused, unhinging the fanged mouth even more deeply to growl. The ominous tone crawled across the bridge, making the rock vibrate.

Connor frowned, his finger tightening on the trigger.

"Steady," Thor whispered, raising the muzzle of the grenade launcher. "Steady on. Let it come."

Leviathan lowered its head, studying the steel cable that Connor had strung across the bridge. Clearly it was suspicious. Connor saw the Dragon's eyes narrow. He could almost see the pupils intensifying, glowing.

Its hindlegs tensed.

"Look out!" Connor shouted.

Wildly they dove down and away, Thor and Connor leaping to one side with Barley to the other and then Leviathan sent a blast of flame down the bridge. The holocaust of flame swallowed the entire length of Bridgestone, igniting everything.

Connor gained his footing and ducked his head frantically back around to see the steel walkway on fire. Even the cables were burning, and he hoped desperately that the electrified cable could just endure.

Then Leviathan shrieked and whirled, slashing its tail across the first five cables, shattering the concrete columns with a scattered blast into the gorge. With a quick spin it came around again, knowing that the cables could not hurt it, and Connor saw the hindlegs tense again.

"It's coming!" he yelled, and then the Dragon had leaped into the air, landing with a roar on the steel walkway.

And the seventh cable.

The white eruption blasted steel into the air and knocked Connor back against the broken vault. But he somehow glimpsed a howling Leviathan spread titanically against the darkness, hanging in the air, falling. It descended with shattered sections of the walkway and Thor roared, falling to one knee as he fired the M-79 from the hip.

Connor also fired Chesterton's M-203, rising wildly with the recoil of the grenade blast. Both grenades hit simultaneously with a blazing twin-concussion that somersaulted the Dragon in the air and then Barley also opened up, rising and firing continuously as the beast lashed out, claws savagely striking a section of Bridgestone.

Swung by its momentum, Leviathan disappeared beneath the stone expanse for a spellbinding, spectacular moment before swinging back out again, holding on with a single foreleg, its tail trailing in a long, deadly arc through the air. It shook violently, trying to reorient itself from the electrical shock and the grenades, and Connor saw that the beast was recovering far more quickly this time. The air was alive with a reptilian roar, an almost liquid scream that contained immeasurable wrath, ageless rage.

Leviathan's claws sunk in the stone, grinding.

"It's climbing!" Connor shouted, running forward as he shoved another grenade into the chute. But Thor had already seen and was beside him, running onto the bridge. In six giant strides the Norseman was on the burning section where Leviathan clung tenaciously to the edge. The beast saw his approach, and the serpentlike head lashed viciously over the rim to strike a wild blow.

Like lightning, Thor's forearm lashed out to smash the Dragon's head aside, and the Norseman staggered back from the collision, falling. Then Thor snatched up a section of steel plating, twisting it desperately in front of himself like a shield.

Leviathan's fangs snapped shut on the plate, and for a spellbinding moment, it was a fantastic, raging struggle of titanic strength—the Dragon shrieking, Thor roaring. Then Leviathan savagely tore the shield from Thor's hand to hurl it into the darkness.

Bellowing, Thor scrambled back. Connor saw everything in a white, breathless moment, knowing without thinking he couldn't hit the beast in the head or neck without killing Thor. And with the unbelievable mind speed that comes to men in situations of sure and certain death Connor instantly swung the aim of the grenade launcher, centering . . .

Clawed foreleg on the stone.

With an angry shout he pulled the trigger.

Blinding roar . . . Connor felt like he'd been hit by a tidal wave, a wall of fire that knocked him to the far side of Bridgestone. He didn't even realize he was standing on steel until he collided with the shattered railing, too confused and shaken to be thankful that the electrical line was dead. Deafened, stunned, he grappled furiously with the superheated steel, scalding his hand, not caring. He held on to the rail, regaining balance.

In smoke and flame Leviathan fell back, claws torn from the stone by the blast. It hovered for a single, haunting moment in midair, as if it had wings, before a long foreleg lashed out at the last possible moment to snare a shattered section of the walkway.

At the impact a far section of the walkway was torn violently from place, ripped from its moorings by the Dragon's great weight. And like a man swinging out on a rope, Leviathan descended toward the opposite side of the gorge where it struck the wall in a thudding impact. Then the section of the walkway was completely hauled from the bridge, dragged from the stone to disappear into the night.

A long, wounded roar echoed in the smoke-filled air and Connor stared, shaken. His ears were ringing painfully before he saw Barley rolling on the ground, groaning. The lieutenant had been wounded by the point-blank blast. His flak jacket was smoking, flaming with embers.

Instantly Thor rose and turned, wordlessly moving to the lieutenant to beat out the flames with his bare hands. Dazed, Connor wiped a hand across his forehead, found a bloody smear. He ignored it.

It seemed incredible that Thor had not been killed, though he had stood only forty feet from the explosion. And then, after the Norseman finished beating out the flames on Barley's flak jacket, he turned stoically to Connor.

Unsteadily, Connor focused on the deep cut across Thor's brow, blood streaming. He saw that the bearskin cloak was also smoldering, blackened by flames, and other cuts laced the giant's face, neck, and hands. Thor's face glistened, black with blood, but he revealed no pain.

Connor blinked at the sight and then he caught something infinitely stoic and composed within his friend, as if Thor were enduring this and knew somehow that he would endure far, far more before this was over. And his heart was set like the heart of a mountain to endure, to endure to the end.

Two hundred feet below them, on the opposite wall of the gorge, they could almost see the Dragon's titanic image, clinging desperately to the rock. It was trying to climb the cliff. Then there arose a raging cry, a scream that ascended from the darkness and congealed around the bridge, as if to capture them with fear.

Grimly Thor broke open the M-79 and slid another grenade into the launcher. He snapped it shut, gazing sternly into the darkness below them. He looked like he would never retreat another step.

Barley staggered to his knees. Shocked by the blast, he seemed to be on the verge of collapsing. He gasped, "Nothing . . . nothing can kill that thing! It's . . . it's climbing! It's climbing out of the gorge! . . . Frank was right, he was right . . . It can't die . . . It can't die."

"It will die," Thor said, lifting the wounded lieutenant to his feet. "It will die even if I have to choke it with my own bones."

"Come on." Connor backed up from the edge. "That thing is tracking us by heat. Like a pit viper or something. We've got to lay some tracks around this part of the cave to confuse it. To slow it down. Then we'll make a run for the Housing Cavern."

Thor scowled. "Do you have a plan?"

Angry and heated, Connor shook his head. "That thing has got to be weakening, Thor. So . . . so it's going to have to feed again. Soon. And it's probably eaten everybody down here but us." He focused on Barley. "Where do they keep the food for that thing?"

"In a freezer near G-2."

Connor knew the section. "Can you get to the freezer and blow it? Can you destroy this thing's food supply?"

"Yeah," Barley nodded, staring narrowly. "Do you think destroying the food supply will kill it?"

"Well . . . it's going to starve it," Connor replied, glancing again into the gorge. "And if it's starving, then it's going to be weaker than it is right now. We'll have an advantage."

Thor was before him. "What is your plan, my friend?"

With a frown Connor turned away. "Starve it. Burn it. Kill it any way I can, Thor." He hesitated, gathering. "All right, this is what we're going to do. Thor and I are going to lay a ton of tracks on this side of the gorge to confuse it. Barley, you get down to G-2 and blow the freezer. Make sure there's nothing left for that thing to eat. Then meet us in the corridor that leads to the Housing Cavern in thirty minutes. Thirty minutes! No more!"

"And then?" Thor asked.

"And then we'll take this thing apart," Connor rasped, standing straight. "It's dying time."

Frank tried to close his mind to the sounds of pain that surrounded him. Jordan was crying, hungry and thirsty, and Beth was trying to give him some apple juice and bread. Chesterton was stalking back and forth across the floor, regaining a remarkable level of nervous strength. But he was worried, anxious, disturbed. He tried to raise Barley again and again on the A-unit, but received nothing. Nothing but static.

Sitting at a computer terminal, Frank accessed GEO.

He typed: HOW MUCH TIME BEFORE DETONATION?

Response: FOUR HOURS, ELEVEN MINUTES.

Frank leaned back, wiping his face. Mind racing, he knew what he had to do. He had to find a path, any path at all, to access GEO's Logic Core. If he could only circumvent the lockout, he knew he stood a chance. A slim chance, to be sure. But still a chance. And yet with the initiation of the countdown, GEO had closed all paths to the Core. He couldn't use normal channels to reach it. He couldn't use a terminal or even voice control.

He continued to stare at the screen.

There had to be a way.

Pausing, Frank felt the sweat cold on his face, his hands, and arms. His back was chilled at the touch of his wet shirt. He typed another command, desperate and feeling desperate: GEO, I AM ADVISING YOU OF A COMPUTER ERROR. LEVIATHAN HAS NOT ESCAPED. LEVIATHAN IS STILL IN THE CONTAINMENT CAVERN. THE TRACKING DEVICE IS NONFUNCTIONAL. IT IS NECESSARY TO DEACTIVATE FAIL-SAFE UNTIL TRACKING DEVICE IS REPAIRED.

Response: GEO DOES NOT PERCEIVE TRACKING DEVICE AS NONFUNCTIONAL.

Frank lifted the headset, unable to keep his communication with GEO on a terminal level. "GEO, this is Dr. Frank."

"*Voice control identified.*"

"It is imperative that you allow me to access Logic Core. Do you understand?"

"*I understand. It is not possible for Dr. Frank to access Logic Core. All program paths to Logic Core have been closed with the implementation of fail-safe procedures. Logic Core cannot be reached by terminal control or voice control until—*"

"Terminate answer."

Exhausted, Frank leaned forward, face in his hands. There

had to be a way. There *had* to be a way. Nothing was impossible. Not with this computer. It was the embodiment of Rachel's living neural network, the height of artificial science. Almost a living, breathing intelligence. In its deepest essence it was almost human, almost . . . human . . . Opening his eyes, Frank stared at the screen. "GEO," he asked quietly, watching the screen although the answer would come from the speaker system. "Is Cyberspace Mode accessible? Is the Cyberspace Mode accessible in a Fail-safe Mode?"

A pause, and the answer came. *"Yes."*

Frank noticed that Chesterton was staring. He met the colonel's questioning gaze with an air of horrific fate. Hesitantly he continued: "GEO, is the Viral Defense Program activated for Cyberspace interface with Logic Core?"

"All viral defenses are activated against Cyberspace interface with Logic Core. Any entity entering Cyberspace to interface with Logic Core will be neutralized by Viral Defense Program."

That was it. Frank saw it in a breath, understood their only chance to defeat the fail-safe, if it was truly any chance at all. He asked, "GEO, what is the status of Brubaker Passage and Omega Passage? What is the structural integrity?"

"Omega Passage is unstable. Brubaker Passage to the Computer Cavern is intact and functioning on emergency lighting."

Frank knew the corridors weren't functioning on emergency lighting because Connor had bypassed the main breaker, routing power to the entire facility. But he also knew that GEO couldn't realize that.

"GEO," he asked again, "do you have sufficient battery backup to initiate a Cyberspace contact with Dr. Frank? Can you access sufficient electrical power for a Cyberspace connection?"

"Yes."

Frank stood, turning to face Chesterton.

"What are you thinking about doing, Doctor?"

"I'm going into Cyberspace to reach GEO's Logic Core," Frank responded. "But I have to get to the cavern where GEO's mainframe is located. If I can get into Cyberspace, then I might stand a chance of reaching the neural net and interfacing with the Logic Core. There's a chance I can disarm the fail-safe."

"Doesn't sound like much of a chance, Frank. I heard that thing say that it would *kill* anyone entering Cyberspace."

"It's better than no chance at all, Chesterton."

Chesterton stared. "Can you really do it?"

"I can't do it alone. I'm going to need someone to work a secondary terminal. They're going to have to disarm the viral defenses that will be attacking me while I'm in Cyberspace."

Chesterton shook his head. "You're out of luck, son. I don't know diddly about computers."

"I do," Beth said from the doorway of the complex. "I know about computers, Frank. In fact, I know a lot about computers." She paused, turning to Chesterton. "I've broken the encryption that Blake and Adler set on the satellite system, Colonel. I set the PCs to work on it while we were gone and I've just checked it. It's finished. I've got an image and I think it'll work. I think I can get through to the satellite with it."

Chesterton staggered, stepping forward. "Thank . . . Thank you, Beth! I never really thought that anybody could do it! I never thought it could be done! Really!"

"Well it's done, Colonel." She paused. "Do you want me to access the satellite?"

A long, hard hesitation, and Chesterton leaned over, hands on his knees. He finally straightened, frowning. "No, Beth. Not now. We're too close to the detonation of this fail-safe. And . . . and I'm not sure that we can even get out of here in time." Hesitation. "I don't want the North Atlantic Sea Patrol on top of this island when that bomb goes off. We're going to have to kill that thing first. Or be close to killing it."

Beth said nothing, turned to Frank. "So what kind of help do you need, Doctor?"

Frank stared at her. "I'll need for you to go into something like Virtual Reality IO or Virtual-X and destroy the Viral Defense Program before GEO can hit me in the Cyberspace Mode."

"How much time do we have for that?"

"About four hours, Beth. But I don't know how much time

it'll take me to get to the Logic Core through Cyberspace. Right now we need all the time we can get. Why?"

"Because I've got to let Jordan rest," Beth responded, without emotion. Emotion had been burned from her. "He's dehydrated. And he's got to have at least two hours of rest. His heart is too weak to take this."

Chesterton turned to her. "I can watch the boy for you, Beth. The best thing for him is sleep anyway. We don't need to go waking him up. And if you can deactivate this bomb, it might even buy enough time to get some help."

Beth hesitated a moment, staring. Her face was unrevealing until she spoke. "No," she said finally. "I'm not going to leave my child. Not for anything. We've got a couple of hours, don't we, Frank?"

Face tight, Frank nodded.

Meeting the morose aspect of the scientist, Beth seemed to have reached her own fatal sadness. She turned her head to gaze at Chesterton. "Do you think they're alive, Colonel?"

Chesterton stepped forward. "Connor's a good man, Beth. He's very resourceful. And determined." He paused. "Yeah, I think they're still alive. Connor has already beaten it twice. And he's got Thor and Barley with him. They're good men, too. Together they've got a chance."

His speech didn't appear to move her. Beth blinked, turned to look with steady grimness at Frank. "All right, Doctor. Two hours, and then we'll go. And while we've got the time, you can tell me exactly what kind of machine we're dealing with here."

Reverberating roars thundered through the section of tunnels beyond Bridgestone as Connor fell against a wall, sweating profusely. He wiped his face, sweat sliding on sweat. He blinked, eyes burning, and felt his clothes heavy and cold with perspiration.

Thor came to him out of the gloom, gasping. He fell against a wall, lifting a hand to his chest, head bowed. Connor thought that he was about to have a heart attack.

"Are you all right?" he whispered.

Exhausted, Thor nodded his head. "I have left a trail . . . the beast will not easily follow."

"Where's Barley?"

Breathless, Thor shook his head.

"I don't know . . ."

A panic rose in Connor's soul, but he couldn't think about it. He couldn't think about anything at all. It was all numbness, darkness and cold. "Well . . . which way did he go?" he managed.

Thor lifted an arm, pointing. "He was running . . . toward the southern tunnels. Leaving a trail. He said that he . . . that he was going to open up several vaults. Make it expend . . . its strength. And then he was going to destroy . . . the freezer. Destroy the food supply."

Connor shook his head. "We said that we'd separate for thirty minutes! Then we'd meet back here. But . . . it's been more than that." A fear struck him. "We'll have to go find him before we can—"

A shadow came out of the gloom, moving silently.

"Hah!" Thor whirled, the M-79 instantly leveled.

Barley didn't even slow until he reached the wall, shaking. He was glistening with sweat, breathless. Then he moaned and fell to one knee, kneeling. His breath was ragged.

"Where is it?" Connor whispered. "Did you get a visual?"

Barley gazed up. "Are you crazy? I didn't want to get a visual! It's tracking us. That's all I know . . . But we've laid a truckload of tracks . . . It's got plenty to do."

"Did you blow the freezer?"

"Yeah." Barley nodded. "I blew it . . . with a phosphorous grenade. The only thing left to eat now . . . is us."

A savage, vengeful grimace and Connor took another deep breath, gathering his strength. "Good. Then we'll make it pay for it. Now . . . now we'll see how tough this thing really is." He took a deep breath, standing. "All right. Let's go. We've got to reach the Housing Complex."

Barley spoke, gasping, "Is Frank defusing the fail-safe? We're almost . . . out of time."

"I don't know," Connor replied, shaking sweat from his brow. "I hope so . . ."

"All right, Doctor, explain GEO to me."

Beth rested a forearm on a raised knee, staring. She was sitting on the steps of the complex, and Frank was before her, thin and almost unbelievably young for what he had accomplished. She tried to remember that it was his genius that had created Leviathan. She hoped the same genius would be enough to destroy it.

"All right," Frank began, turning to pace slowly, hands folded before his face as if in prayer. "GEO is a genetically copied neural net microprocessor."

"Meaning?"

"Meaning that it is the first large-scale, self-reliant neural net computer. And you have to understand it in that perspective."

"Define what you're saying."

Frank paused, turning to her. "Okay. It's like this. In the present day, computers are constantly being upgraded so that they're faster and faster. The fastest 486 that was used two years ago doesn't even come close to the Pentium chips used today. So in the normal world the rule is 'later is better' because it's faster."

Beth pursed her lips. "But not with GEO."

"No. Not with GEO. The first GEO will always be more powerful and faster than any that follow it."

"Why is that?"

"Because of the aging process of the neural net. The first GEO has experienced, or learned, rather, more than any that follow it. Thus, it is more intelligent. The ratio of artificial-neural to synthetic processors is approximately one to two at the creation of GEO. Toward maturity, however, GEO's ratio of artificial-neural to synthetic processors will be approximately five hundred to one because the neural network will be expanding. The effects of this transition are an increase in what can only be termed humanness in the machine. Synthetic or artificial emotion, or artificial humanity, all meld with programming and a specific math-logic to form a totally new intelligence capable of virtually infinite thinking ability."

Beth felt a new respect. "Did you come up with this, Frank?"

He stood in place. "Rachel did."

"Your wife?"

A pause. "Yes."

"She must have been an extraordinary woman."

Frank paused. "Yes. She was."

Suddenly Beth regretted bringing it up. "Go ahead," she said.

"Let me just describe it to you," Frank said, raising his hands once more. He began pacing again. "GEO is cylindrical, about two stories high and twenty-five feet wide. In the center of that is the light cylinder that houses the artificial synoptic neural mapping."

Beth blinked. "What's that?"

Frank was taken by it. "It's the fiber-optic light tube where Rachel's neural cerebral synapse network is artificially copied on a niobium-titanium chip," he replied quickly. "The network is used for memory storage, calculations, data transport, and thinking in general. Now, the next level of GEO is a cybernetic link shell implanted between the network and the technical connections outside. That's where I'll have to go in through Cyberspace."

"Why?"

"Because all signals are sent to the Logic Core via superconductive subzero fiber-optic lines. The only means of reaching the synthetic network is from the machine itself and down through the fiber-optic tube."

Beth nodded. "All right. I'm with you."

"Okay," Frank continued. "All network-linked terminals, including the Cyberspace Module, are set to operate by specialized nine-digit codes that GEO has changed so that I can't reprogram. That allows GEO to delay, alter, or stop any intrusion or command, regardless of the source. So it's absolutely impossible to pirate, steal, or molest data. That's another reason they brought me here to do this experiment. Nothing else but GEO would have been sufficient for their security measures. Nothing else was absolutely impenetrable."

"Okay, I've got it," Beth said. "We're not going to be able to connect with the Logic Core because you don't have the altered nine-digit access codes for the matrix. That's why you're going to be attacked by the viruses."

"Right," Frank responded, pacing. "Or, at least, we won't be able to connect on authorized lines. We'll still have to go down through the matrix, and GEO controls the flow of all data through the matrix."

"Can we piggyback you on other data that's authorized to pass through the matrix?" Beth asked. "Can we use something for cover to get you to the Logic Core?"

"No. The matrix can run several data streams down the same fiber-optic line simultaneously as well as coactively. But it runs an electromagnetic echo wave at .002 nanometers ahead of the data stream that carries the prefix code and tells the device which data frequency to read at each occurrence. That prevents any device from piggybacking or tapping an alternate line. No device can travel toward a foreign target."

"Can we put the matrix off-line? Can we overheat it?"

"No." Frank shook his head. "The matrix is encased in a liquid nitrogen cooling gel maintained in a variable heat displacer. That layer is surrounded by an electromagnetically sealed niobium-titanium alloy for coating and protection. The power system runs through a low-level section of the matrix grid giving GEO control over everything, including temperature and overload."

Beth stared. She had never heard of anything like this.

"Just what kind of machine is this, Frank?"

"It's not simply a machine," he said, standing in place. "That's what I'm trying to tell you. GEO is not just a machine, and it's not a living organism. It's a totally new breed of entity with an entirely different way of reasoning and perspective. GEO's synoptic neural network is an electromagnetic copy of Rachel's cerebellum. And Rachel had an IQ of 197, a doctorate in computer science with a master's in psychology. After we copied her neural network, the image was implanted on the chip. So as GEO learns to use the artificial network of synapse connections for thought processes, it becomes more and more expansive in its thinking skills. The dangerous part is that there's an icon guarding the Logic Core, and I might have to confront it in order to change the math-logic."

Beth stared. "What kind of icon?"

The scientist stood very still before her. "Rachel is the icon," he said.

And suddenly Beth understood. "It's the icon's responsibility to safeguard the Logic Core? To prevent anyone from entering the Logic Core without the authorized code?"

"Yes."

Beth waited, considering the implications. "Well, how much can Rachel's icon do to stop you, Frank? I mean, the icon is just part of the machine. Can it hurt you?"

Solemn, Frank replied, "Rachel can do whatever she wants. The Cyberspace Module has a body suit and helmet that are worn during connection. The helmet has very sensitive linkups which roughly interpret nerve impulses. It allows GEO to read my mind, in a sense. Hearing is digital, and the Cyberspace image is directly fired in my retina with a one centimeter overlap to provide absolute continuity in vision. I won't know the difference between Cyberspace and reality."

"Meaning what?"

Frank stared.

"Meaning Rachel is queen of that universe, Beth. If Rachel disapproves of my presence and gets to me before I can put the logic off-line, she'll fry my nervous system."

Beth's voice was a whisper.

"Can Rachel kill you in Cyberspace, Frank?"

Silence.

"Yeah." He finally nodded. "She can kill me."

It was an hour before Connor, Thor, and Barley staggered into the Housing Cavern, all but dead from thirst. Connor didn't even mumble a word before snatching up a clear plastic liter of bottled water. He drank half of it, then poured the rest over his head, back, and face. After a few minutes he almost felt refreshed.

Barley duplicated the procedure with another bottle, shedding his burnt flak jacket and hurling it angrily to the side as if it had betrayed him. He drank almost a full liter of water before finally stopping to gaze around, blinking like he hadn't slept in days.

Chesterton stared at them as they continued drinking water, pouring it over their heads. "Well?" he growled impatiently. "Do you think I'm standing here 'cause I like looking at you?"

Thor laid the M-79 on the table, leaning forward. His eyes were like burning ice. "It lives," he said. "We wounded it, but it lives. We laid many tracks through the cave to confuse it. But it is not so confused. We have heard it behind us, breaking what few vaults still stand. It is coming. And we have destroyed its food supply."

Frank understood instantly, stepping forward. "That was a good plan! Leviathan is going to be weakening fast! And when it's in combat it's going to need even more strength than normal to assimilate proteins for muscular and armor reconstitution."

"Frank," Connor looked up sharply, eyes smoldering. "If Leviathan is starving, will it go for the lake? Or will it push a confrontation? Will it try and finish this fight?"

"It won't go for the lake yet, Connor." The scientist shook his head. "Leviathan is . . . is proud. I know . . . I know that that's a weird term, but I don't know how else to say it. Leviathan will never leave a conflict unless its own death is imminent. And I think . . . I think Leviathan believes it can kill us. Even in a weakened condition."

"Well," Connor frowned, grim, "I've got a shock for it. The last shock of its life. Now find out where that thing is. I want an exact location and direction of travel."

Frank quickly spoke into the headset and the computer replied, *"Leviathan is two miles from the Housing Cavern."*

"What direction is it moving in?" Frank asked.

"Leviathan is moving toward the Housing Cavern."

Appearing in the doorway of the Housing Complex, Beth suddenly cried out, running down the steps to embrace Connor.

Connor took her in his arms and kissed her on the neck, cheek, face, mouth. She stared into his eyes, holding his face in her hands.

"I was afraid . . ."

"It's all right," he whispered. "But it'll be here in a few minutes. We've got to get moving."

"I broke the code," she whispered, staring into his eyes.

Connor genuinely smiled. "Like I knew you would, darlin'." He kissed her. "Now let's get out of here. We've got to move."

Without words Beth turned and ran up the staircase. In a moment she came out, holding Jordan close in her arms. He was wrapped in a blanket. "He's still sleeping. I'm not going to wake him up if I don't have to."

Connor walked up and gently lifted Jordan from her arms. "He'll be okay. He's just—" A howling roar thundered through the long tunnel behind them, echoing across the expanse of the Housing Cavern. It was a lot closer than Connor had expected.

Chesterton stepped forward. "Frank thinks he might be able to defuse the fail-safe, Connor."

"How?"

"I've got to get into Cyberspace to do it," Frank responded. "And that means I've got to get to the Computer Cavern because that's where the Cyberspace Module is located."

"You take him to it, Connor," Chesterton said, lifting an M-16 that he had secured from a weapons locker. "There's probably going to be some kind of mechanical problem once you get there. This entire place is wrecked. Some of the electrical lines are down, and you're the only one who can fix them."

Connor hesitated. He had come up with a desperate plan, something that might kill the beast, but he couldn't set it up if he had to lead Frank to the Computer Cavern. But then he knew that killing Leviathan would be useless if they couldn't disarm the fail-safe.

"All right," Connor said. "Let's go."

"I'll need Beth to help me."

"She's coming, too." Connor slung the M-203 over a shoulder, turned to Thor and Barley. "Can the two of you lay more tracks in and out of this cavern to confuse it? It's already hurting, but we need to hurt it some more."

Together they nodded.

"Good," Connor continued. "Just open all the vault doors and lay as many heat impressions as possible. Give it plenty to look at. Wear it out. It's wounded and it can't feed anymore. Plus, the fight on the bridge used up all of its resources. It's going to be starving real soon." He hesitated. "The rest of us will go ahead and try to access the computer. We'll meet up at the power plant in an hour to make a stand, to try and keep it from passing through the cavern to reach Crystal Lake. I think I can rig up something that it can't cross. Something that might even kill it. And we can probably get a distress signal through the communications linkup with the surface. But first we've got to disarm this bomb."

"It will be done," Thor said.

Barley lifted his rifle. "See you in an hour."

Connor turned to Chesterton. "What do you want to do? You want to come with us or stay here?"

"I've been listening to Frank, and I've realized that I don't know a thing about computers," Chesterton said. His aspect was fatally fatigued. "I think I'll stay here and help them to—"

On the far side of the Housing Cavern the titanium door shook, struck hard. The bestial roar that followed was like blood-wet fear in the air, guttural and threatening.

Instantly Thor was moving forward, shoving Connor. "Go, my friend! Go! Go! Hurry before it breaks down the door. We will hold it here as long as possible. Disarm the bomb!"

With Beth beside him, Connor was moving. He heard the wall behind them shattering, caught a freshness in the reptilian scream that told him a section of the vault's frame had surrendered to the colossal, raging force. And then they had stooped under the narrowly-lifted door to enter another passageway, moving quickly.

Beth was behind him with Frank leading as they ran deeply down the tunnel. In the distance behind them they heard the now familiar sounds of savage conflict, the roar of the beast followed by defiant human cries and the thunderous explosions of rifles and grenades.

But there was no time to think of it, not with what loomed before them. Connor sensed it before he saw it. Light. Heat. Heavy smoke moving toward the ventilation system. And Connor instinctively looked up at the tunnel, slowing in cold fear as he understood.

It was on fire.

Chapter 24

Flame before them with flames behind and Frank spun, shouting, "We've got to get out of this tunnel! The only other way to reach Brubaker is through Omega!"

Connor whirled to look at the entrance of Omega. He knew the tunnel led through the cavern for a mile before it intersected with Brubaker, which would take them to the Computer Cavern. And then he remembered how Leviathan had wrecked the tunnel earlier. "But Omega was wrecked when that thing destroyed the nitrogen tanks," he gasped. "We can't . . ."

"We've got to try!" Frank was screaming. "We're dead if we try to reach Brubaker through this tunnel! It's too hot!"

Connor grimaced, trying to decide.

"Make a decision, Connor! If we don't use Omega, we'll have to retrace our steps back through the Housing Cavern!" The scientist choked on the smoke billowing up the passageway. "Come on! We're running out of time!"

Connor glared at the flames before them, weighing the options. But it was clear to him. There was no way. There was no way they could get through the tunnel before them. And there was no way they could retreat back through the Housing Cavern. Not with that kill-or-be-killed firefight in full force. He knew that much, for certain. Just as he knew that Thor and Barley and Chesterton would be dead themselves if they stayed in there much longer.

"We'll take Omega!" he shouted, angling instantly toward the entrance. "We'll have to take our chances that the nitrogen hasn't poisoned the air!"

"The nitrogen should have dissipated by now!" Frank replied, moving quickly ahead of him. "But we can't be sure of the wiring! GEO told me that Leviathan used flame down here, and it could have melted the steel plating. We could have lines down!"

Jordan stirred in Connor's arms, crying. "Shhhh," said Connor, hugging him closer. "It's okay, boy. We're going to get out of here. Just a little longer and we'll get you out of here. Daddy's going to get you out of here . . ."

Grimacing against the flame, Connor hugged his son close.

Collapsing to one knee, Barley shouted and centered an LAW rocket at the chest of Leviathan.

The beast was surreal and titanic in the cavern, fully enraged. Its tail swept right and left, shattering everything within reach. Nothing could resist it—wood, steel, and wiring surrendered like smoke to the monstrous might of the beast, scattering and disintegrating wildly at its touch. Emerging fully into the cavern, Leviathan screamed hideously, shaking, dropping on all four legs to charge.

Grim and cold, Barley depressed the trigger of the LAW and the flame-bolt struck Leviathan hard in the chest, staggering it solidly. It reared back, aflame and firing flame from its mouth that shot uncontrollably to the roof of the cavern, exploding in a hellish, mushrooming white cloud that set the entire complex ablaze.

Heat, heat . . .

Heat!

Fire rained from the roof.

Thor fired the M-79 with a white-hot curse.

The grenade struck Leviathan in the chest, exploding violently against the armor plating. But the beast took the shock almost in stride, lashing out. A long foreleg missed Thor by a hair, cleanly severing the main support beam of the Housing Complex.

Damaged by the flame and collision of forces, the entire housing structure began to cave in, falling over Leviathan. It struck back maniacally, vaporizing steel and plywood with a continuous white stream of liquid fire, fangs, and claws. On and on it raged, slashing and striking at everything, at nothing, raging at the air, the cavern. Then Chesterton let loose with an M-16, screaming for Barley and Thor to retreat but they stood their ground.

Thor broke open the M-79 and shoved another grenade in the tube. He quickly snapped it shut as Leviathan's dragon-head again lashed toward him. With a shout he fired into its face. Blinding, the point-blank blast hit at less than forty feet and only the concussion threw Thor out of range as the monstrous jaws snapped shut on smoking air.

Barley was firing, screaming, "Thor! Crawl out the vault! Crawl out the vault! Get out of there!"

Staggering, Thor tried to obey, to retreat. But as he gained his feet he saw the beast atop him. He took a single, frantic step backward before he tripped over a shattered computer frame, sweeping black claws slashing out to tear the computer into splintered steel shreds and then Chesterton was running forward, screaming vengefully and firing the M-16 in a blinding, suicidal rage. He centered on the head, the eyes of the creature and Leviathan blinked, enraged, turning toward the object of its pain.

"Get out of here you fools!" Chesterton screamed, firing upward.

Barley reached Thor as Leviathan turned its full attention to Chesterton, rising up, snarling, growling. Despite its injury and its weakened condition, the beast seemed to glory in the moment.

"Colonel!" screamed Barley, leaping forward, but Thor snatched him by the shirt as he leaped, hauling him back. Then Leviathan's jaws descended, meeting the gladiatorial hatred of Chesterton who kept firing, firing to the last.

"Colonel!" Barley screamed again as Thor threw him hard beneath the narrow space of the vault door. Then in a rage Thor spun back to see the beast with its head and neck raised high, almost twenty feet above the ground, swallowing.

Teeth clenched, Thor raised the M-79, holding a steady aim

at the neck, and fired again. When the grenade struck Leviathan staggered, shaken. And Thor quickly reloaded, catching a glimpse of Barley screaming and crawling back beneath the vault to rejoin the fight.

With a calm aim Thor fired his last grenade, hitting the beast in the same location, a section of neck armor that appeared severely damaged by the LAW rocket. The explosion was fire, white, blinding, volcanic. Leviathan screamed, shaking lividly, whirling toward him.

Thor bent and rolled. He blasted Barley back through the opening of the vault, grabbing the lieutenant as they collided and rolling even faster as he felt a flaming concussion strike the fire door, impacting with the power of a rocket to send a vaporous fire-cloud under the portal.

Thor continued rolling, throwing Barley as if he were a doll until he was well beyond the door. Then Thor rose to a knee and spun back, screaming and enraged, violently whipping the battle-ax from his back.

"Come, beast!" he roared. "Come and face me!"

A hideous scream and colossal impact against the vault was the only reply.

Smoke and narrow flame surrounded them, and Connor moved as quickly as he could, holding Jordan close. Frank was ahead of them by a dozen steps, searching the passage floor for loose wiring, testing the air for traces of heavy nitrogen. Beth was at Connor's side, her hand on his arm.

Connor squinted angrily through the smoke, smoke that thickened as they moved deeper and deeper into the tunnel. A moment earlier he had wet a cloth on a ruptured water line and placed it over Jordan's tiny face. He knew that the cloth would protect the child somewhat from the acrid air that spiraled from the deeper part of Omega. An explosion, seeming to come from behind, shook the corridor walls.

Beth staggered, grabbing his arm and Connor whirled to stare back, holding Jordan tight. He almost half-expected to see the hell-born beast on top of them. But there was nothing there, nothing but burning smoke, distant flame.

"What was that?" Beth whispered, staring. She seemed frightened with a new and vivid fear. "Do you think that Thor is . . ."

"No," Connor replied, holding her gaze.

He didn't know what else to say, and she knew the comment for what it was. Hope. And she didn't question it because it was her hope as well. They turned again to Frank.

"We're coming into a big chamber where several tunnels converge!" he called back, holding a hand to his face. He was squinting angrily against the smoke. "Everybody stay together or we could get separated! This is going to be difficult!"

"Don't worry about us!" Connor yelled. "Just get us to the computer so you can disarm the fail-safe!"

Frank turned without words and walked slowly forward. He was almost instantly lost in the smoke that spiraled from the converging passageways. It was a heavy, blinding haze that flowed and overflowed into the ventilation shafts. Connor found himself choking, heard Jordan crying. He tried to comfort his son as best he could, but things were getting bad fast. The smoke was so thick that the air seemed solid, clinging to them, flowing past them like black water. He looked to the side to see Beth bending, lowering her head. And he repeated the maneuver, also bending low to stagger forward.

Another explosion, too close, blinded them. Connor had no idea what it was, couldn't imagine. It was a powerful electrical line grounding out or maybe a lost incendiary from the platoons. But whatever it was rocked the corridor and sent them staggering again, struggling for balance.

Frank was screaming. "We've got to find the right tunnel! There's four, or maybe five, that lead out of this room! One of them leads to Brubaker where we can go straight into the computer—"

The next explosion took Connor off his feet, slamming him hard against something, but he held Jordan until he came off it, losing his son somehow in the air, landing numbly to . . .

Sharp pain.

Instantly enraged, Connor tried to lift himself from the ground, found that he couldn't move. He strained again, violently, and felt something pinning him down. Opening his eyes against the acrid smoke, he glared to the side to see what was holding him.

A stake.

A steel stake the size of a railroad spike had been driven cleanly through his upper arm, pinning him to the ground. Instantly Connor's teeth clenched in a snarl and he violently tore his arm from the bloody steel, savagely wrenching himself free, leaving shreds of flesh on the metal. He didn't even feel the pain as he gained his feet, immediately searching by feel for Jordan.

"Jordan!" he cried. "Jordan! I'm right here!"

A terrified cry carried through the smoke.

"Jordan!" screamed Connor. "Where are you, son? Stay where you're at! Don't move!"

A wounded, fearful scream that only a child could make reached into Connor's heart, tearing him apart, a cry that seemed somehow close but moved away quickly with terrified, searching steps until it was claimed by darkness.

Connor cried, screaming.

"Jordan!"

Chapter 25

Move!" Thor roared, shoving Barley.

The big lieutenant staggered, shocked, but he recovered quickly, holding his rifle as he had held it during a thousand training missions, running forward. Thor followed him a dozen steps before he turned back to see the beast wrecking the top level of the vault, ravaging the upper edge as it had learned to do, in order to defeat the portal.

Leviathan slammed the fire door outward, screaming. Thor grabbed Barley and shoved him into a connecting corridor, close behind him. "Run!" Thor shouted. "This is not the place to make a stand! We must exhaust it first!"

Barley's response was instantaneous as he leaped into a run that stretched out quickly, covering a wide yard of ground with each stride and Thor ran after him, keeping up easily.

Leviathan pounded against the portal behind them, slamming the vault outward. The steel walkway beneath their feet was torn from place at the impact and then Thor felt the stride of the beast, pursuing, vengeful to end the conflict. As they reached another bisecting corridor, Thor sensed the quick strides nearing and he grabbed Barley by the collar, angling him roughly into a connecting hallway. Behind them the corridor exploded in flame.

Thor dove into the entrance of the corridor, escaping the lava that filled the expanse behind them. He landed hard, leaping up to recover quickly, rising to hold his battle-ax close.

"Yes, beast!" he roared back, smiling savagely. "Use your flame! Use your strength! I mock you!"

Another hate-filled blast vulcanized the tunnel.

And silence.

"Jordan!" Connor screamed. "Where are you?"

The answering cry was even more distant, vanishing in the smoke-black darkness. And then Frank was beside Connor, clutching. The scientist was confused, not understanding what had happened. Connor grabbed him by the upper arms, crushing.

"We've lost Jordan!" he shouted.

Connor moved into the smoke, shouting, searching wildly. And Beth was at his side, close, staying within sight, shouting as frantically as him. But they heard only the rumbling of flame, the ventilation system straining to remove the choking congestion from this maze of corridors.

Losing control, Connor turned back to Beth. "Where would he go, Beth? Where would he go?"

Her dark eyes blazed, angry. "I don't know, Connor! I don't know what a child would do!"

Connor realized he was panicking. And with savage cold will he dropped to one knee, taking a deep breath of whatever fresh air remained in the junction. Then he looked up, staring through tear-blinded eyes. From his vantage point, less than four feet off the ground, he could see only one section of light—an oval-shaped opening framed in a smoke-red haze. It was an avenue of bright escape from the smoke that billowed in the convergence of hallways.

The path a child would take, a path of light.

Immediately he raised his arm, pointing. "There! That's where he went! He'd go where he saw light!"

Then Frank was beside them. His eyes flared as he saw Connor's arm. "Connor! Hold up, hold up, you're hurt!" Without expression Connor glared down, felt his hand coated in blood, blood dripping heavily, like a river, from hand and arm.

"You can fix it later, Frank," Connor said, turning away.

"Connor, wait, wait." Frank grabbed him and Connor spun back with a dangerous glare. "Listen, man," the scientist said, raising his hands, "you've got to listen to me for a second! You're not in pain right now because of the adrenaline in your system. But the pain's going to come and it's going to come hard if we can't stop that bleeding! Then you're not going to be worth anything to anyone! Not even Jordan!"

Taking a deep breath, Connor nodded. "All right then, Frank, fix it!" He turned his face to scan the smoke. "But fix it quick because I'm not waiting more than a second."

Frank instantly tore a strip of cloth from his shirt and pulled a white handkerchief from his pocket. He pressed the folded bandage over the wound and then wrapped strips of cloth tightly, tying the ends to apply constant pressure to both sides of the wound without cutting off blood supply to the arm. Instantly the bandage was bloodred, wet.

"That'll stop the bleeding unless it hit an artery," Frank gasped, breathless. "But I don't think it did. The blood . . . wasn't bright enough. Still, though, you're going to have pain."

Connor frowned, shook his head.

"Pain isn't part of this anymore."

Then Connor was running forward. Fast. He didn't look back to see if anyone was following. He was on the walkway almost instantly, moving with a speed that amazed him to go down one corridor and then another, keeping low to see more clearly with arms outstretched, searching by feel. And he moved quickly, knowing more and more as he moved that Jordan could have already reached another passageway and angled even deeper into the cavern, creating a deadly guessing game.

They went far down the corridor, moving randomly up a bisecting corridor to decide it was fruitless only to quickly retrace their steps. Connor lost track of time, though he knew it was long, long, too long. Finally he felt someone grabbing him. With a snarl he spun back.

It was Frank.

"Connor!" he screamed. "Listen to me! We've only got an hour to defuse the bomb! We've got to get to the Computer

Cavern! I can find the way by myself, but Beth has to come with me or I won't be able to reach the Logic Core!"

Connor shouted, livid with rage. "Go! Go and defuse the thing! I'm going to find Jordan!"

"Connor . . ." Beth protested.

"Go on!" Connor said sternly, holding her passionate gaze. "Go with him, Beth! I'll find Jordan! I promise!"

Staggering, she hesitated, and Connor saw a mother's frantic love in her eyes. He paused, concentrating. Then he grabbed her face and kissed her close, hard, releasing her quickly. His scream slashed through the flame.

"Go, Beth! I promise you! I'll find him!"

She swayed, crying.

"We've got to hurry!" Frank screamed, grabbing Beth's arm, pulling.

Connor grimaced in pain. "Go, Beth! Go! He's going to need you to beat the fail-safe! If we can't beat that thing we're all dead anyway!"

Without waiting for her agreement Connor turned and was gone, heading straight into the dark smoke, knowing that for every moment he waited he allowed Jordan to get farther away. He passed a shattered vault, the remnants of melted steel and slashed titanium littering the corridor walkway. He went deeper and deeper, passing thick smoke, choosing corridors at random, not knowing a better means of deciding.

"Jordan!" he cried again and again. "I'm right here! I'm right here!"

A hate-filled reptilian roar thundered over him and Connor whirled, glaring, teeth clenched in wild hate. The scream was so close that it could have come from the wall itself. And though Connor couldn't see it, he knew that the beast was close beside him, that he was trapped.

He was alone in the lair of Leviathan.

"Beth! Come on! We're out of time!"

Frank's cry almost didn't register in Beth's mind. She was

overloaded, wild and frantic with pain and love. She followed his steps in a daze, obeying with some superior reasoning ability that overruled her instinct to find her child. On and on they went, and she heard the bestial roar that thundered in the darkness behind them. It was vengeful and hate-filled, the cry of a hunter determined to kill the prey that had wounded it. Stunned, she turned, backstepping, lost in madness until she felt Frank's hand gripping her arm.

"Come on, Beth!" he shouted. "Concentrate! We've got to reach the computer cavern before we run out of time! If we don't defuse the bomb none of us are going to survive!"

Beth turned to him and began running, following him with a force that flowed from her love into duty. And she became more determined and frantic as she moved, turning her terrible pain into action, strength. All at once Frank couldn't move fast enough for her. She heard herself screaming.

"Come on! Go! Let's get it over with!"

Connor snarled as he unslung the M-203, checking to see if a grenade was locked in the launcher. It was. He frowned grimly as he moved forward, hoping that he could at least take the beast with him if it came suddenly out of the smoke-filled chaos. He was aware that he had entered some kind of cavern, but he didn't know which one it was. He only knew that it was burning and that he had not yet heard or seen Jordan.

Despite the fear that his shouts would draw the attention of the beast, Connor shouted again. His voice reached into the hissing smoke around him, searching. From a distance to the front, from somewhere in the infinite gray space, he heard an answering cry.

"Jordan!" he cried, moving quick. "Son! I'm right here! Daddy's right here! Call out to me! Please!"

Then an utterly terrified child-cry came from the distance, but closer, and Connor ran forward, striking something hard that he didn't see. He rose and screamed, knowing somehow that his leg was severely injured. He ignored the crippling pain that caused his knee to convulse, giving beneath his weight. Falling to the floor again, he hesitated, grimacing in pain, fists clenching. A scream came from inside him, a howl of pain and rage and determination that overcame everything but itself and the pain within him faded, lost beneath the spiraling violence of his soul. He smashed a fist hard against the floor, clutching the rifle, rising.

Leviathan roared.

Close, close . . .

Too close.

Connor screamed and whirled, firing the grenade launcher into the darkness. The explosion was closer than he expected and for a staggering moment the entire cavern before him was alive with light, flame, roaring before an empty, cathedral-echoing boom descended over him.

Connor didn't care. He shouted wildly, breaking open the grenade launcher to shove in another APG. He slammed the chute shut hard to send a vengeful and murderous message. The impact echoed dimly in the smoke, and, sensing death on top of him, Connor turned and shouted again.

"Jordan! Son! Son! Where are you!"

Jordan's answering cry was only twenty feet away and Connor was instantly moving forward, more carefully this time. He knew that, despite his determination, he couldn't afford to collide with another piece of machinery. Even as it was, his leg was possibly broken.

In a moment he found his son, huddling close and quiet and childlike beneath a computer panel. Connor immediately recognized the broken paneling, realized that they had somehow found a way into the Observation Room. He lifted Jordan into his arms, holding him tight.

After a moment Connor released him, searching him for signs of injury. But it was needless. He was all right, all right. Connor picked him up and held him tight as they headed to the door.

A roar shook the hallway.

Jordan screamed.

"Shhhhh," Connor whispered, holding his son closer, turning to find another means of escape. "It's going to be all right, be all right . . ."

Connor saw the section of titanium that had been shattered by Leviathan's entry into the Observation Room. The bullet-ravaged titanium wall was leaning outward at a forty-five-degree angle.

It was climbable, even in his condition. So he moved to it, stepping with difficulty onto the matrix control. Frantically he slung the rifle across his back to free one hand and instantly began scrambling toward the top of the titanium fire wall, holding Jordan tight in the other arm. The wall rose up and out at a not-so-difficult angle and Connor managed to make it to the top before he heard another roar and whirled to see a fantastic, brief burst of flame that reached down the hall.

Flame, flame again.

Testing for a trap.

Thor waited a long time, crouching.

He heard Barley rise behind him, tensing to run. But Thor didn't turn, didn't give a command. Even in the fierceness of the moment he knew somehow that the beast was no longer behind them. He rose to his feet, staring angrily at the entrance of the narrow corridor. The anger that was borne from the center of all that he was spread and dissipated into a frantic concern for something . . . else. He spun toward Barley.

"Where does this corridor connect?" he shouted.

Barley was shaken. He didn't seem to know how to reply.

Thor roared, "Where does this corridor connect!"

"It connects with everything!" Barley answered, swaying, slamming his hand against a wall for balance. "It connects with everything, Thor! It connects with everything!"

Thor lifted the battle-ax. His fist was tight on the haft.

"Then we become the hunters," he growled.

Chapter 26

Thor was the first up the passageway, moving close and quiet with his back to the wall. Flame flickering through the encircling smoke was the only thing visible, ghostly tendrils of orange heat. Only cold sweat cloaked his titanic frame.

Barley was behind him, face glistening in perspiration, moving carefully. He was holding the rifle close against his chest, his teeth clenched in rigid control. They had divided the last ten grenades, and Thor had hastily loaded his M-79. He also held his battle-ax in his other hand, prepared for anything.

He cautiously paused at a wide junction of tunnels, glancing around a corner—it was a smoke-filled passageway descending toward a flowing white, a volcano's soul, a demon's heart. For a cryptic moment Thor listened closely, hearing nothing. He leaned back, whispering. "Why has the beast retreated from battle?"

Barley shook his head tiredly, eyes closed. Thor frowned, suspicious, taking another minute. "It should have killed us by now," he rumbled. "Why did it not pursue us into this corridor?"

"Maybe it got tired of the chase," Barley answered, blowing out a deep breath. "It's got to be getting tired!"

Thor shook his head angrily, sweat scattering. "No. The beast does not tire so easily. It took Chesterton, but that was not enough to restore its strength. It needs more food. And needs it badly, as Connor said it would." He paused. "It should have come for us by now."

"Maybe it's gone to lick its wounds. Like it did before."

"No. We did not hurt it so badly. In another moment it would have caught us."

Exhausted, Barley shook his head. "I don't know, Thor." He fought to control a violent trembling. "There just ain't no way of knowing. That thing does whatever it wants. It does whatever it wants . . ."

"But it kills . . . That's all it does. And yet it did not kill us." Thor paused, concentrating. "But why? Why did it not kill us? It had almost caught us. And in another moment it would have killed us. Like Chesterton."

Barley was cautiously scanning the smoke-filled passageway. And with a grimace, Thor turned. "Which way did Connor go with Jordan and Beth?"

"They've probably gone for Brubaker Passage. That's the only way to get to the Computer Chamber."

"And how do we reach this passage?"

Barley motioned. "Down that tunnel."

Sharply breaking open the M-79, Thor checked to see if a grenade was locked in the launcher. He angrily snapped it shut. "Then that is where the beast has gone! I can feel it! It needs more energy and it has somehow sensed their presence! Like it did before." He began to move around the corner when Barley grabbed his arm, strongly pulling him back.

Thor glared.

"I've got to tell you something," the lieutenant muttered. "You need to understand something about those grenades. They're not regular issue. They're phosphorous. Like liquid. It burns anything it touches. So if you shoot it you're going to need at least a hundred feet of clearance. Everything within a hundred feet of detonation will be covered with a fire cloud." His eyes opened slightly, for emphasis. "It's pure fire, Thor. And once it starts, nothing can put it out."

A moment and Thor asked, "Are all these phosphorous grenades?"

Barley nodded curtly. "That's all we got left."

"Good. I will remember."

Thor led around the corner as they entered the swirling whiteness of the tunnel. And Barley glanced down at the battle-ax, still held tight in Thor's massive hand. "Are you really going to hit it with that ax?" he asked.

"If it comes to that."

Suddenly Barley seemed even more nervous. "That thing is heavily armored, Thor. It's going to be hard to hurt it with that ax. Even if you get the chance."

"Perhaps," Thor answered, moving forward, "but these beasts have been killed by steel before."

Barley stared. "Before?"

"Yes."

"When?"

"In another age."

Barley didn't reply for a long moment. "Maybe," he said finally. "But I know one thing, Thor. If you go up against that thing with that ax, you're going to die."

Thor face's was grim.

"So be it," he said. "There are worse things."

Frank entered the smoke-free computer chamber. He wasn't surprised at the clarity and control of the atmosphere. The chamber had been constructed with industrial-size ventilators and large dehumidifiers to keep it utterly free of dust and moisture. He didn't even pause as he entered, running toward a large steel platform in the center of the cavern.

Stunned, Beth paused in the cathedral chamber's wide entrance, staring at what lay before her. It was awesome.

Over twenty-five feet high, the black semicircular computer mainframe utterly dominated the cavern. No electrical circuits could be seen; they were all enclosed in black tubes that fed into the monolithic half-circle like veins, threading in and out of the polished casing. In contrast to the galactic black sheen, a large, cylindrical light tube glowed white and bright, centered directly before the monolithic semicircle. The tube appeared to be filled with pure light and pulsed with innumerably slender, rhythmic blinks.

Beth saw that the light cylinder's cover was like transparent aluminum. Some kind of hardened alloy that solidly protected the mysterious light-sentience hovering within. Halfway up the tube she saw a separated and reddish cylinder, almost the size of her hand. It seemed suspended in midair, supported by nothing. Dazed, she stepped slowly forward.

Frank reached the large computer platform which encircled the cylindrical tube and mounted the steps. He looked up at her as she approached, his voice urgent. "Hurry up, Beth! We've only got twenty minutes to reach the Logic Core and kill the fail-safe!"

Shaking herself awake, Beth went forward, and in a moment she was on the platform. Not steel, she realized. It was some kind of nonconductive fiberglass or plastic. Stunned, she gazed at what surrounded her, trying to acclimate. But it had been a long time. Too long. Almost immediately she realized that she had never dealt with a system one-tenth this complex.

She had an intimate understanding of modems and CD-ROMs and a half dozen software programs including earlier models of Virtual Reality. She could even program and run parallel processing. But this system was as beyond her as anything could be.

This was the ultimate verging of science and life, the cutting edge of artificial intelligence. She had no doubts that the computer before her was almost a living thing. Just as she had no doubts that there was probably nothing on the planet strong enough to match its ability to reason, or at least to simulate human reason.

Frank spoke quietly into the headset. "GEO, turn on all matrix controls for command control from the platform."

Immediately the platform was aglow. Lines and single-command control pads, optical controls overlaid by a thin poly-alloy waterproof cover, lit from within with a soft green light. And at least twenty large-screen control monitors blinked on. Beth watched in dull amazement as the entire room came alive, green and glowing, pulsing. Even the long cylindrical tube located in the center of the platform seemed to glow a shade brighter.

Face glistening with sweat, Frank pointed at the glowing white tube. The cylinder was as thick through the middle as a man and seemed to be suspended by dull gray threads.

"The Logic Core of GEO is electromagnetically suspended in that cylinder," Frank began, moving quickly to the other side of the platform to initiate further commands. "The Logic Core is the brain chip. The chip uses formulas conveyed through light as something like thought waves. Fiber-optic paths carry the light from the Logic Core and into the computer itself where the waves are electromagnetically transferred into amalgams which are delivered to chip control systems." He paused, concentrating briefly to initiate a more complex command. "The fiber-optic relays and niobium-titanium chips allow GEO to operate at something close to the speed of light, which for all practical purposes is probably the speed of thought."

Beth was watching his every move. "But how are you going to defuse the bomb?" she asked.

"I've got a plan. It's something Thor said."

"But won't Rachel stop you?"

"Only if she can hit me before I put the Logic Core in a self-diagnostic mode. Then she won't be able to do anything to me because her logic will be off-line."

"How much time will you have to defeat her?" Beth asked.

"A tenth of a second."

"And if you miss?"

"Then she'll kill me."

Chapter 27

Connor hung from one hand on the high side of the titanium fire wall that leaned into the Containment Cavern itself. He glanced down to see that the floor was still fifteen feet below him.

Swinging, hand slicing against the metal edge, he held Jordan with desperate strength in his other arm. For a long moment he swung in the dark air, the rifle's weight on his back dragging him down, pulling him painfully from the rim. His fingers were slicing, slipping.

Another heat-blast blazed down the tunnel.

Too close! You're out of time!

Connor clenched his teeth and dropped, hoping that the distance was more illusion than reality.

It wasn't.

He hit the ground hard, his leg caving in. Stunned at the pain, he rolled on the floor with a shout, breathless, almost passing out at the agony that overcame his mind, his will, his strength. His knee and then his leg and then his entire chest went numb, a shocked breath exploding from his chest. He strained for air, couldn't pull breath. And for terrifying seconds he strained again and again, heard short groans escaping him. Jordan was crying in his arms but Connor didn't have any strength left to soothe the child's fears.

No time, no time for anything . . .

Get it together!

With a savage grimace Connor slammed a fist against his thigh, using pain that penetrated the codeine to shatter the numbness. Dimly, he felt it. So he raised his fist again and brought it down with bruising force.

Sensation, sensation was there.

Use the pain!

With a roar Connor violently struck his leg again, straightening it, forcing it back to life. Behind and above them, the Observation Room was suddenly set aflame by a thunderous blast of liquid fire.

Connor shouted in rage, staggering to his feet. He picked up Jordan and limped unsteadily over the remnants of a large tank. His soul was withering in agony, and only his will carried him across the cavern. But as Connor moved he began to sense a slow, gathering strength, somehow realizing that the numbness in his leg was fading with each step.

Close behind he heard Leviathan savaging the Observation Room, tearing a larger hole through the concrete-steel frame. It was pursuing, always pursuing. But in a moment Connor had reached a vault. He frantically worked the hydraulic latch, raising the portal two feet above the floor. Then Jordan screamed and Connor knew what was happening just as he felt the floor shake beneath a distant, thunderous descent.

Don't look back!

Without looking Connor slid quickly beneath the fire door, instantly lifting the four-year-old in his arms, running. Fluorescent lights streamed in this part of the deep cavern, somehow unaffected by the power surges that had severed lines through the rest of the facility. But it gave Connor little comfort. In another moment he heard a violent impact against the vault behind him, knew the portal would quickly fall.

The beast was committed to a suicide run. Connor knew it could have made for the power plant at any moment to escape without conflict into the lake, quickly finding the ocean to feed and feed and feed. But it was hatefully focused on this fight with something far beyond a beast, and it wouldn't stop, wouldn't stop until they were all dead.

Face twisted in pain and exhaustion, Connor moved quickly forward, able to keep at least one door between himself and Leviathan as he moved through the deep cave. He wanted to lay a trap for the beast, something to hurt it, to disorient it. But in the speed required by the chase he was unable to tear an electrical line from the wall or even find a corridor narrow enough to prevent pursuit. And with each colossal, roaring attack on the vault behind him, Connor felt himself groaning mindlessly, staggering even more in fatigue . . .

So weary, so weary . . .

"This way!" Thor shouted.

With the frantic shout the wild-haired Norseman was running down the hallway, all caution forgotten, moving recklessly through the vaporous white fumes. His eyes blazed in rage, the battle-ax raised high in his hand. He did not wait for Barley and didn't turn to see if he was followed even though Barley was running behind him, breathless and ragged.

"How do you know that it went this way?" the lieutenant shouted urgently, glaring at the darkness.

"I know! I can hear it in the distance! It has found them!"

Barley said nothing as Thor leaped over a fallen support beam, landing lightly on the other side. And then he was running again, shouting vividly into the darkness, the flame, and the smoke.

"To me, beast!" he roared. "Bring the battle to me!"

Connor slid through another door, desperately lifting Jordan into his arms. But because of severe blood loss his strength was fading fast, almost gone. He knew that this couldn't go on much longer. The roars were closer now, much, much closer. And Connor whirled, searched for some avenue of escape that would frustrate Leviathan, something so small that it would stall the chase. But he saw only the ventilation shaft.

No. No good.

Connor knew that if he couldn't get them far enough inside the shaft before the Dragon reached them, the creature would simply send another heat blast down the pipe that would kill him and Jordan instantly. But he knew that there had to be a way, a way . . .

Close behind them a vault shattered, falling to the floor. Connor spun, staring, enraged, not even hearing Jordan's cries. He glared savagely left and right and centered on yet another door, more than a quarter mile ahead, that he somehow knew led into a chamber . . . But which chamber?

A roar erupted, closer.

No time to figure it out.

Connor ran forward, holding Jordan tight against his chest, ignoring his own blast-furnace breath and the sweat that streamed from his face. He couldn't feel his arms. They were weak and numb, no longer a part of his body. But he moved as fast as his strength could carry him, feeling his heavy strides slowing with fatigue. He collapsed halfway down the tunnel, catching his breath before he recognized a soft cry, Jordan speaking. He looked down sharply to see his son's upturned face.

"Daddy . . ." his boy cried, "is the monster going to get us?"

Connor shook his head hard, grimacing. "There ain't nothin' gonna get us, boy. You and me are getting out of here." He nodded. "You and me and Mommy are going back home."

"But"—Jordan was staring at him—"the monster . . ."

"That monster ain't gonna get you and me," Connor said, hugging his child. He blinked sweat, breathless. "The only thing that monster's gonna get is dead. I'm gonna see to that."

Hope brightened in Jordan's eyes. "Are you gonna kill it?"

Connor stared down, and somehow, in the heat and passion of the moment, Connor knew that he was committing himself to something that he would never back down from. Even if it meant his life.

"Yeah, boy," he whispered. "I'm gonna kill it for you."

Jordan stared at him, touched his face.

Connor smiled.

Then the child screamed as a thunderous pursuit sounded close behind them, the roar of the beast. And Connor was instantly running, gasping in pain and fatigue and tightly holding his son, his son, his son . . .

Chapter 28

F*ifteen minutes until detonation . . .*"

Beth stared, concentrating. "Is any part of Rachel alive in there, Frank? Can any part of the computer respond to an emotional appeal?"

Hands flying over the controls, Frank fixed on her. "No," he said evenly. "Rachel's dead. Whatever is inside the machine is just an electromagnetic copy of her synapse system. It's like a web of connections on a niobium-titanium chip that make up the Logic Core. It allows for more humanlike thinking."

Almost mesmerized, Beth continued to stare at the tube. "Well what does Rachel's icon look like?"

"I programmed the icon to look like Rachel," Frank said as he leaped off the platform and ran for what appeared to be the Cyberspace Module. Two separate Cyberspace suits were available for use, each hanging in large, glistening spheres.

Beth blinked, stunned. She had never expected that. It was almost horrific; this scientist going into Cyberspace to confront the image of his dead wife to convince her to spare his life.

Speaking quickly, Frank came back onto the control dais. He picked up a thin black visor and handed it to her. "Place this over your eyes and you'll be able to see everything that I'm doing," he said. "At least you'll be able to see everything that I'm doing until I reach the Logic Core. After that I'll be off the screen. I'll be in the neural network."

"And then?"

"I'll have to confront Rachel."

Beth shook her head, concentrating. "All right, Frank, all right. Just tell me, how am I supposed to protect you from viral attacks as you go through the light tube?"

He handed her two synthetic gloves and turned on a laser that began passing over a small mattress on the floor. "You'll have to stand on this pad wearing the visor and gloves. As you see the viruses attacking me just point your hand at the virus and make a fist. When your hand closes you'll complete a connection in the palm of the glove and something like a laser will go from you. It's an ability you'll have and I won't have because I'll be in Cyberspace. I won't be able to tamper with the defenses of the computer. Only someone outside the computer will be able to do that." He paused. "But you've got to hit the viruses before they hit me."

Beth placed the gloves on her hands. "So I won't be in Cyberspace with you?"

"No," Frank shouted as he leaped onto the Cyberspace Module, his face glistening with sweat. "You'll be in something like Virtual Reality-IO or Virtual-X. There's no real difference. And the computer won't be able to harm you because you won't be neurally linked to it. You can get out at any time just by taking off the visor."

"Will I be able to see you?"

Frank began zipping himself into the Cyberspace Suit. "Yes! You'll have a visual on everything. It will be like you're sitting on my shoulder, flying down with me. But you won't have an icon. And you'll stay with me until I reach the Logic Core. The rest is between me and Rachel."

Beth nodded and stepped on the knee-high pad, holding the visor in her hand. The pad was bouncy, like a trampoline. The laser screen passed slowly up and down, over her. "What will the viral attacks look like?" she asked. Sweat dripped from her chin.

"The attacks might look like anything," Frank replied, moving frantically. "Lasers, blobs, walls of fire, whatever. There's no way to tell. I've never done this before."

Beth almost leaped forward. "What? You've never done this before!"

"Ten minutes until detonation . . ."

"No!" Frank spun, glaring. "Of course I haven't! Do you think I'd ever go into GEO without GEO's approval? It's suicide! I wouldn't be doing it now if this fail-safe wasn't going to kill us all!"

"Then how do you know"—Beth staggered—"that this will work?"

Frank shook his head, eyes wider. "This is how it's supposed to work, Beth. All of this is just theory! But that's all we've got."

Silence for a long split second. And then Beth heard herself whispering, "Frank . . . This is insane . . . This is really insane . . . We're never going to make it. Can't you come up with another way to defuse the—"

"There's not another way," he said. "Just get me to the Logic Core where I can confront Rachel's icon." He paused, smiling faintly. "Just get me there, Beth. I can do the rest."

A moment, and Beth's face was grim. She tensed her fist, feeling the contact built into her palm that would ignite the fiber-optic laser. Then she looked up at Frank, feeling herself hyperventilating. She swallowed, closing her eyes, trying to remain calm. When she looked again the scientist had fully enclosed himself in the suit.

"What happens if I miss?" she asked.

"Eight minutes until detonation . . ."

Frank executed a command and his body was electromagnetically lifted, suspended in the Cyberspace Module. He replied as he completed commands for full immersion in the computer.

"If a virus hits me it could kill me instantly, or I might survive the impact. This is uncharted territory. But I'll never be able to survive more than two or three hits." He paused, staring, fear in his eyes. "Are you ready?"

Beth's mouth came together in a tight line. There was no time to think of her fear, her husband, or her son. It had all come down to this. To this frantic and frightening moment. With a cold movement she slung her long dark hair back from her brow, quickly wiping sweat from her eyes. She lifted the visor and settled it solidly over her head.

Concentrating, she nodded.

"I'm ready."

She opened her eyes to . . .

Cyberspace.

Connor desperately raised another vault as Leviathan pounded a path into the passage. Then he rolled beneath the portal with Jordan held tightly in his arms as the beast saw him and unleashed a hellish blast of flame down the dark-red tunnel. It impacted the vault like a hurricane.

With a roar the beast had charged down the tunnel to instantly strike the portal, but Connor gained his feet on the far side. And as he stood he sensed something . . . something different in the ravaging attack.

The assault against the titanium fire wall was somehow weaker, slower, than it had been before. And Connor understood suddenly that the beast was finally tiring. Destroying vault after vault and sustaining the wounds inflicted on it had clearly claimed a measure of the Dragon's strength. Now it needed more food, needed it badly. But it had already consumed all that could be consumed in the cavern. Everything but them.

Connor frowned, staggering back.

"Come on," he whispered hatefully to the wall. "Come on . . . Wear yourself out . . . I want to see you die . . ."

Turning, Connor ran into the middle of a cavern, still holding Jordan solidly in his arms. He didn't know which cavern it was and realized instantly how the encircling walls ascended, red and solidly sloping into a towering dark. He searched left and right, seeking an exit. But he found none. A heightened adrenaline-fear quickened his heartbeat even more. Connor stopped in place, turning, spinning in every direction, searching for an exit door.

Walls, walls . . . "Oh, no . . ." he whispered, not looking again at the vault. "There's got to be a way out of here . . . There's got to be . . ."

Leviathan smashed again and again against the last portal but the savage victory was taking three times as long; an indication of its starvation, its weakness. Then Connor noticed, from the absence of a thundering heat-blast, that it was no longer using flame. Only strength, strength that Connor knew would be exhausted even faster in its singular intent to defeat the titanium wall.

Connor realized that if he could only put two or maybe three more vaults between them, he would be safe. But there was no exit, he realized, as he glared in every direction. He had reached a dead end.

Breathless, clutching Jordan to his chest, Connor turned toward the vault, watching and backing up as Leviathan maniacally attacked the portal, roaring and slamming forelegs and its injured form against the wall again and again. But it finally, slowly, overcame the fire door, slamming the portal down and collapsing on top of it in exhaustion. But fueled by the molten core of its heart, the Dragon rose again, glaring, hating.

Connor gently lowered Jordan to the ground, quickly unslinging the M-203. He backed up a step, centering the grenade launcher on the beast as it took a slow step toward him.

Eyes gleaming, Leviathan growling.

Jordan was screamed hysterically, clinging to his leg. Connor felt his sweat-soaked skin freeze at the thunderous, threatening cave-growl. His blood congealed, cold with fear as he stiffly backed up, step by slow step, unable to catch his breath.

With great, distended fangs, the Dragon came forward.

"God help us," Connor whispered, backing.

His hand tightened on the rifle.

Chapter 29

*S*even minutes until detonation . . ."

A dazed black moment of spiraling light and Beth almost fell off the platform before she realized she was flying, flying with blinding speed through a verging of machine and white strobe light and she looked down instinctively to see a vaguely human form

Frank.

Immersed in Cyberspace, the scientist had already begun flying forward, racing through the computer toward the wide, gaping hallway of light that loomed before them. Utterly, utterly amazed, Beth stared.

This was unreal.

Frank was larger than life, his solid black body glistening in sharply angled sections that held an uncanny resemblance to his human form. But his hands were larger, his shoulders and chest also accented. His head was a polished black mask, a narrow-slitted mouth with no hair or ears. But his rounded eyes were a cosmic bright-blue, glowing like beams and fixed dead ahead as he flew through the computer. Almost against her will, Beth shouted to him.

Frank didn't turn. His face was fixed before him, staring, and then Beth saw an expression of angry concentration on his glistening countenance and glanced up to see the wide white wall approaching with breathtaking speed as . . .

Light!

Whiteness streamed past them like flowing, glowing fog. Beth staggered, almost feeling the invisible wind rushing over her, and she realized that they had entered the light cylinder, speeding toward the Logic Core.

Like a human torpedo the scientist streamed forward, narrowly avoiding the slashing, flashing beams that blazed at him from the sides. Beth shouted in alarm at the simultaneous attacks, knowing somehow that Frank could not hear her but shouting anyway as she extended her fists to send a blast of light out from herself toward the flare.

But she was too slow, her blast wide, and Frank somehow defeated the attack himself, twisting violently down and upward again like a jet diving under incoming missiles. Then as he rose he gathered speed, threading a frantic path through a sea of gathering, spiraling tentacle-flame.

Descending in a bolt of black lightning the scientist flew forward, deeper and deeper into the converging conscious world of man-of-machine, where science verged with life. Then from both sides of the cylinder, in a coordinated and simultaneous attack, two streaks of phosphorescence came together, joining in a solid wall of white to block Frank's headlong plunge. The scientist wildly threw out his arms, angling desperately to readjust his descent, but there was no room to escape. He spun out of control, hurtling into an amazing holocaust of artificial fire.

Shouting explosively Beth threw out both fists, clenching tight and screaming still as whiteness erupted out from her, smashing through the flame to create a spiraling nova of strobe before . . .

Endless expanse . . . Arms pinwheeling wildly, trying to recover from the blast, Frank careened through the obliterated wall like a ship hurled through fog, slowly gathering control. When he had passed through the shattered whiteness he put his arms to his sides once more, leaning forward, gathering speed.

Beth released a tight breath.

That was close, too close.

But she was too frantic with the speed of the attack and her own speed to be relieved. She crouched as she felt herself flying wildly forward beside the scientist, feeling more a part of the unreal than the real.

Streaming forward, Frank plummeted to the depths of the heart of the artificial mind known as GEO. And, trembling and blinking sweat, Beth kept her hands high to fire again and again, sighting and spinning, lashing out left and right to desperately clear a narrow path through the flaring flame.

Connor glared left and right, saw no escape.

Jordan cried out, hysterical with a sight he would never forget for the rest of his life. And Connor grimaced, angrily centering the grenade launcher on the chest of the beast. His finger curled around the trigger.

Leviathan lowered its head, jaws unhinging.

Connor's face twisted in rage.

"Eat this!" he shouted, and pulled the trigger.

The explosion struck Leviathan full in the chest, making it stagger. Its neck stretched up, burning with flame and Connor snatched Jordan from the ground, instantly running. He heard a roaring behind him, a bellowing and vengeful wrath that conquered the cavern like a thunderclap, shattering stalactites on the far side. Dust cascaded from the roof, dust and dark rain.

Gotta find a way out, a way out . . .

Connor breathlessly rounded a full-red corner of limestone searching for anything—a cave, hole, or an overturned stone or whatever would provide some small measure of escape from the beast so that—

A mushrooming white explosion set the entire cavern roof aglow, and Connor instinctively ducked, not even understanding. Then the cave thundered with the howl of a wounded beast and Connor saw Leviathan rolling past him, slamming itself against the ground, shattering stone and stalactites into flaming shards.

It was bathed in white flames.

Connor didn't ask any questions, didn't understand. He picked up Jordan in one arm and ran back toward the exit, carefully avoiding a section of the cavern floor that glowed with unexplainable fire. He took a half-dozen strides before he saw the two images standing angrily in the doorway, one red-bearded figure holding a smoking M-79.

Thor sighted him almost immediately.

"Connor!" he bellowed, waving excitedly. He quickly broke open his weapon, inserting another grenade before snapping the weapon shut. "Hurry! Run with all your might!"

Then Barley cut loose with a grenade, striking an area far to the rear, and Connor felt the terrific mushrooming blast that lit the room like a lightning bolt. Leviathan screamed but Connor didn't turn to see it. With Jordan tight in his arms he ran with all his remaining strength, crossing the two hundred yards with slowing, slowing strides. The entrance seemed infinitely far, so far that his strength could never carry him past the portal. And Connor knew, knew in a hate-filled, staggering fatigue that he would never make it.

And then Thor was running strongly forward, his M-79 slung around a shoulder and his arms spread wide. In seconds he met Connor in the middle of the cavern floor, lifting a protesting Jordan from his arms. Instantly Connor felt lighter, stronger.

He made it to the door.

"This way!" Barley screamed, running, and Connor followed him through the doorway in the very shadow of the beast. As he went through the portal he realized with a sense of doom that the corridor was easily large enough for Leviathan's continued pursuit.

No. No good . . .

Blindly Connor followed Barley and Thor as they ran down the tunnel, fleeing for the slightly raised vault at the end. Although Connor managed to match them stride for stride, his mind was quickly fading under the overcoming power of infinite, infinite fatigue.

So weary . . .

The opened exit was almost a quarter mile away and Connor realized with a sense of doom that the chase was almost finished, at last. They could never make it, and even if they did, they couldn't continue. But without thought he hurled himself forward, hearing Leviathan strike the vault behind them with fresh rage, pounding again and again, somehow seeming strengthened even more by its wounds.

Against his will Connor spun in stride, turning to see the Dragon on fire, savagely shattering the exit, coming, always coming. It was covered with white flowing flame, flame that rose almost to the ceiling of the tunnel. But it was still chasing them, ignoring the injury and pain, determined to finish the kill. And Connor knew somehow that it was motivated by far more than food.

Roaring, the beast tore through the vault, landing on its feet as they finally reached the exit. Then Barley slid beneath the titanium portal, dragging Jordan behind him. Connor was last to the vault, slamming himself against the cold niobium-titanium in the throes of ultimate exhaustion. He could not stand, but fell to the ground, sweating and breathless.

"We can't . . ." he breathed, "we can't outrun it . . ."

Thor seemed to sense the Dragon's approach and turned, glaring angrily. And for a brief, flashing moment Connor caught something in his gigantic friend's face that he never imagined he would see.

Fear.

Chapter 30

Connor saw it as purely as he felt it.

Thor was afraid.

Hand tight on the battle-ax, Thor hurled a savage curse at the Dragon before he bent to effortlessly shove Connor beneath the vault. Barley lifted Connor from the other side, holding him in a strong arm. But Connor was wasted, passing out, his head faint and light. His vision was blurring, dimming, and in an unfocused daze he staggered across the cavern, recognizing vaguely . . . *Matrix* . . . they were back in . . . the *Matrix*.

But it meant nothing to him. He was lost in the fatigue and confusion and pain as he stumbled to the opposite door, yes, yet another door where the vault still stood. And as they reached the vault together the Dragon beat a path into the cavern, pursuing, pursuing . . .

Staggering, Connor saw Leviathan in the doorway, glaring.

It smoldered with flames.

Blinking sweat, clutching his heart, Connor felt an exhausted groan of deathlike pain escape him, and he knew with terrible certainty that it was over, over. Grimacing painfully, Connor lowered his head and closed his eyes to pray that their deaths would be quick, for Jordan's sake. Then Barley went under the vault with a soldier's skill, carrying the child.

Light-headed, collapsing, Connor fell at the door, too tired, too fatally exhausted from the long run to go another step. And he felt himself lifted once again, sensed Thor's giant presence beside him as he was carried the last few strides.

Then the floor shook and Connor somehow found himself at the door, rolling out the other side. Faint and shocked, he turned to see Thor glaring coldly at the beast.

Leviathan stood fifty feet away.

Savoring the kill.

Grim and enraged, Thor glared at the Dragon, as if he knew further retreat was futile. He turned back to Connor, his ice-green eyes solemn and sad and resigned. He did not move.

With a shock Connor realized what Thor was about to do. Connor tried to rise, to leap forward to grab his friend and drag him back beneath the door but Thor had already unslung the grenade launcher from his chest to toss it beneath the fire wall. Connor saw his face darken with fear and regret and love and every other emotion that could cause pain.

Connor gasped, staggering.

"No . . . Thor . . . Don't—"

"Go!" Thor shouted, dropping to a knee. His voice was choked with fear. "I will hold it long enough!"

Barley heard and whirled, shouting.

"Nooooo!" Connor screamed as he gained his feet.

"GO!" Thor roared. "I will hold it long enough!"

Thor's blazing eyes met Connor's for one flashing, immortal instant as Thor lifted the battle-ax wide to the side, sharing all the pain and memory and love that could be shared by any brother who had chosen to sacrifice his life for the other. Then the battle-ax flashed between them, swung by Thor's massive arm to solidly strike the steel cord that held the vault open.

At the sharp impact the cord was severed.

The vault descended.

"Five minutes until detonation . . ."

Aflame from a violent viral attack, Frank plummeted wildly through a white haze, losing direction for a fantastic, flashing moment. He spun uncontrollably through a wall of fire and saw another killing light beam slicing through space from his far right, a scintillating blaze that was almost instantly destroyed by Beth's fiber-optic laser. By an effort of will Frank shed the flames, speeding forward. He didn't have time for relief.

Bending forward, he hurtled deeper into the light tube, arms over his face, regaining control as he moved farther and farther into the heart of the cylinder. Somehow, in the distance, he thought that he could see the Logic Core, a dark red planet-shape suspended by an electromagnetic field in the center of the cylinder. He knew that if he could only make it to the interior of the Core, he would be safe from further viral attacks.

With a violent twist he angled down and away to avoid another sudden light blast from the side. He pitched and rose, leveling with an effort, maintaining as much momentum as he could.

He sped forward . . .

Speed, speed . . .

It was everything now—speed, speed . . . He saw another white wall of fiber-optic fire rise before him, watched nervously as Beth's laser blast destroyed it. In his frantic, chaotic descent he saw the phosphorescent haze disintegrate, neutralized by the fiber-optic flame hurled from her hand. In a swirling fog it disintegrated, and he torpedoed through it.

With a renewed effort Frank rocketed into the heart of the cylinder, watching with painful anticipation as the Logic Core drew nearer, nearer, maddeningly near. He was forced to twist desperately, angling downward to avoid a vicious tentacle that exploded from the side.

It missed.

And, for a moment, spiraling out of control through space, Frank was genuinely amazed that he was still alive. He turned in the infinite whiteness and realigned his direction, spearing himself through the furnace. A dark red-black space rose before him, the Logic Core coming up like a planet, and he sped toward it, raising his arms and lowering his head to plummet effortlessly through the exterior surface of the Core to enter the Synapse System.

Instantly his arm lashed out and connected to a thread, his

thought moving from mind to hand to computer at the speed of light and he had already disoriented the logic-math, sending GEO into a self-diagnostic check. Frank sensed Rachel's immediate presence and almost instantly realized that she had been thrown into the self-diagnostic mode as well.

Yes!

He had beaten her!

Frank kept contact as he spiraled toward the center of the Logic Core. A small center of electric threads loomed beneath him and he slowed, slowing even more to land lightly, no longer concerned about the viral defense system. He was past that now, he knew. With Beth's help he had overcome the frontline defenses. Deep inside the Core, Frank felt Rachel close to him.

He closed his eyes, concentrating as the synapses shot through the Core, shifting and progressing through algebraic symbols of logic. The thoughts were blindingly fast, quad-dual processed with almost incomprehensible speed, and Frank began changing them, rewriting the formulas. And quickly, far, far too quickly, he knew he was approaching a dangerous void where he was altering the essence of the machine.

Too fast . . .

It's moving too fast . . .

"Get Jordan out of here!" Connor shouted, slinging the M-79 over his shoulder. He was still exhausted and in shock, but Thor's dramatic move had galvanized him into a death-instinct strength.

Staggering in fatigue, Barley lifted the four-year-old. "What are you going to do?" he gasped.

Connor began climbing wire and piping toward the ventilation shaft. He heard a fiendish roar on the other side of the wall and he froze, his skin crawling with terror. He couldn't even imagine what Thor was facing, couldn't even believe this was happening. Then he sensed that Barley was hesitating and he turned, shouting angrily.

"Barley! Carry Jordan to the Computer Cavern as fast as you can! Take him to Beth! I'll meet you there!"

"But what are you—"

"Just do it!" Connor roared, turning to rip the ventilation shaft cover from the wall. He lifted a leg inside as Barley began shouting, backing up and motioning frantically.

"Hey, Connor, wait, wait . . ."

Connor leaned into the shaft.

"Connor!"

Enraged, Connor brought his head out of the shaft. *"What?"*

The big man tossed up a grenade belt with three grenades. Connor caught it without thought, immediately looping it over his shoulder. "Those are phosphorous!" Barley shouted hoarsely. "They're liquid fire! And you'll have to have at least a hundred feet when you shoot one! Everything inside that is going to be on fire!"

Connor stared down, frozen in place. Something had struck him with Barley's words, but he didn't have time to figure it out. With a quick nod he turned, crawling forward as fast as he could, holding the grenade launcher like a cannon.

Chapter 31

Sweating hand locked like iron on the battle-ax, Thor slowly turned, staring at the Dragon. His face was grim and dark.

"Come, beast," he growled. "Come! . . . Embrace me . . . Let this battle end . . . with the two of us . . ."

Thor stood before it, those he loved at his back.

And Leviathan stood before him, growling, its eyes glowing like coals, its breath smoldering with its superheated soul. Thor felt the atmosphere growing hot, hotter by the moment. The air itself seemed to boil at the thin vapors rising from the beast's armor.

Clenching his teeth, Thor laughed.

"Let God decide this battle!" he roared, crouching and raising the battle-ax. "Yes! . . . The God you fear!"

A strange twist of its dragon-head and Leviathan loosed a hideous roar, a grating, snarling, threatening sound that came from deep beneath it, from the rock and stone, not the creature.

Thor laughed, moving to the side. His smile was savage.

"Will you wait all *day*?" he roared. "Come to me!"

And Leviathan came, came so quickly that Thor felt the black claws before he saw them and he twisted before a collision he didn't understand, whirling the battle-ax, the steel sweeping with unbelievable power through the red gloom as he came around and the dragon-head was *there* with fangs gaping and Thor roared to turn violently through the blow.

With a thudding impact the gigantic ax split the armor beneath the wicked jaws in a haze of black blood and Thor had no time to contemplate how such a thing could be as the hating fangs struck.

Thor howled, hurled back by the impact but he slashed wildly down, hitting the serpentine head solidly. The battle-ax sliced a narrow plate from green-black brow and Thor smashed his hand against the fanged upper side of the mouth, pushing against the jaws with all his strength.

Rage to rage they surged, and Thor staggered, bent back. Then Leviathan swept forward to slam Thor against a wall, the jaws unhinging farther to close on him but Thor pushed with titanic strength, wrestling against the beast's upper jaw as if he were grappling with a crocodile.

Pushing the head savagely to the side, Thor twisted and desperately grabbed the ax with both hands and swung with primal force, coming off his feet to hurl his full four hundred fifty pounds into the blow. The battle-ax struck the beast solidly in the head, colliding like thunder.

Leviathan turned away from the wounding blow and Thor shouted, leaping forward, pursuing, changing the game. With a volcanic twist he whirled back again and the ax thundered through a murderous backhand slash that tore off a slice of armor. Then Thor lashed a herculean arm around the superheated neck, pulling himself flesh to flesh with the boiling, burning gout of blood that lanced the air from the monster's wound.

Instantly Leviathan reared, roaring, tearing at him with its black claws but Thor never felt the mortal injuries as he locked his knees hard into the neck and raised the ax high again to bring it down upon the neck, tearing a full scale from the plates.

At the impact Leviathan screamed and whirled to sling him off but Thor dug his fingers into a harsh mane of short hair that came from the crest of the head, holding, holding.

Blood, burning . . .

Around them the entire cavern burst violently into flames, wooden crates exploding into flames at the beast's superheated armor, disintegrating at its spiraling exothermic presence and

Thor heard himself screaming through the flames and the lancing, liquefying black blood that sprayed from the wound in Leviathan's neck as he leaned back, torn and ravaged by the long, long claws that reached up, grappling.

Lost in pain, pain, too much pain, Thor howled, brutally bringing the ax down, slashing, slashing, striking again and again with the full measure of a colossal strength that he had never used and never imagined and chunks of black flesh and black armor sailed through the air, blood . . .

Leviathan's evil green eyes glared down at him, hating and enraged, and in a moment of rage and madness, Thor whirled and twisted to swing the battle-ax upward to hurl a vicious blow that struck harder still, slashing beneath a glowing eye.

The battle-ax dug deep . . .

It was too much.

Leviathan whirled with a scream and hurled itself into a high stand of steel that scattered at the explosive impact, catapulting girders across the full expanse of the cavern with flame following. Stunned, Thor was slung aside, finding himself somehow beside green-black scales that seared off his skin at the touch. He whirled back to strike with fantastic strength at whatever he saw, the glowing battle-ax thundering through flame and hate and rage, striking again and again to glow bright black with the blood of the beast.

Enraged, Leviathan whirled. Thor saw a murderous black foreleg drawn back to strike and Thor shouted, raising a thick arm and ax to turn against the blow, to defy it.

Leviathan struck, sending Thor sprawling into a heap of steel, blood cascading over him, and Thor felt himself struck from behind, pain blasting through his back and ribs and chest and he roared in heartfelt pain, struggling to surge back to the fight. But he could not move, was held firm. Frantically Thor glared down to see that he was pierced through and through, a jagged stake of steel protruding redly from the upper right side of his chest.

Thor cursed angrily, groaned. But he knew it made no difference now. No difference at all. Eyes tunneling on the beast, Thor clenched his teeth and surged violently forward, tearing himself in agony from the stake. Roaring, he whirled the battle-ax again, noticing only dimly that he was black-red with blood. But the blow missed wide and Thor fell back, breathless, wounded and waiting. He raised his empty hand, bone-burned fingers spread like talons, preparing to grapple as the Dragon reared, fangs unhinging to spray fire.

Its jaws twisted, neck tightening. But there was no fire, no fire.

Thor laughed.

"Your fire is gone, beast," he mumbled through bloody, mashed lips. "Now only strength remains . . . So show me your strength! . . . Show me the strength of Satan! And I will show you the strength . . . of Almighty God!"

Leviathan shrieked and struck.

And Thor met it, force to force.

"Four minutes until detonation . . ."

Frank felt his electrical-will wrap itself around the key symbols that cemented GEO in pure mathematical analysis and he began deleting the symbols at a reckless rate, unable to keep up with the machine. But despite the rising danger of his action he continued, severely attacked the foundations of the logic, moving quickly from one premise to the next.

In seconds, all logic that eliminated metaphysical questions was virtually wiped out. And Frank felt GEO shifting to find another self-regulating Logic Mode. But the computer found nothing and searched again, the beginning of a dangerous, dangerous downward spiral to self-destruction.

Immediately Frank thought-programmed a new ruling logic in GEO's mind, implanted Aristotle's final criteria for determining the true value of any created being, an ultimately logical series of questions that could serve as the base for a reformatted Logic Core.

Frank felt a quick fear, feeling the thoughts race out from him and into the network, realizing he stood on the edge of crashing the entire system. But he recklessly continued sending, sending . . .

Aristotle's Four Causes, the foundation of his Logic, were clear in Frank's mind as he burned them deeply into GEO's neural network.

The Four Causes of Aristotle . . .

Material Cause, Formal Cause, Efficient Cause, and *Final Cause . . .*

Frank locked the computer there, in their joined mind. He quickly forced the machine to confront the fourth, Final Cause, while he eliminated everything, everything else, dooming the machine to return again and again to that last, greatest question.

What is the final purpose of your life?

Frank tied GEO's synapses tighter and tighter, drawing the lines closer and with ever-increasing angles, making more and more knowledge irrelevant as the machine joined him in the great search, bending all its power toward answering that one, ultimately logical question.

What is the final purpose of your life?

Frank knew, he knew; the question was the key.

It was a question that *had to be* logically answered before GEO could continue because GEO could not facilitate any action whatsoever until it knew the logical purpose of the action.

Even now Frank realized that he couldn't just go into the defense system and defuse the fail-safe because GEO had not decided that intervention was a logical move. And without GEO's approval, Frank's interference would be interpreted as an attack. In that situation the computer would subsequently initiate its last accepted criteria for guarding the system.

By triggering the bomb.

"Three minutes, forty-five seconds until detonation . . ."

But now there was a new game. Frank knew he had to make GEO question the rightness of detonating the fail-safe, but he also knew that he had to do it logically, because logic was all that GEO understood. With a distinct fear Frank sensed that he was pushing, even violently pushing, the artificial life-form to confront a question that only man had dared approach.

What is the final purpose of your life?
And again . . .
What is the final purpose of your life?
And again ...
What is the final purpose of your life?

Sensing the computer locked in the loop, Frank withdrew his hand from the web, staring, listening. He could almost hear GEO's mind sailing through the spiraling, searching thoughts, freed from the cold math-logic that had previously prevented it from confronting metaphysical questions.

Again and again with almost light speed, GEO's thoughts burned through the loop only to return with blinding speed to that ultimate question—*What is the final purpose of your life?*—where it blazed out again, searching, searching the system for an answer and finding none only to race out once more at light speed to end at the beginning, confronting the great question again and again. In the heat of the conflict Frank could almost feel the space around him glowing, growing white and warm. It was almost as if the search was threatening to crash the entire infrastructure of the supercomputer.

Then Frank reached into the threads, becoming one . . .

"GEO, this is Dr. Frank."

The reply was distinctly feminine, almost afraid.

"Voice identification confirmed."

"GEO," Frank continued, his essence flowing into the system. "Answer this question: What is the final purpose of your life?"

Even the black space of the Logic Core paled as GEO struggled to find an answer. Frank felt the system on the verge of a total breakdown. The space-environment around him trembled.

And then Rachel was before him, emerging from nothing with a hard gaze of anger on her scarlet-neon face. But Frank had changed the logic so quickly that even she was forced to answer the question before she could destroy him.

Silently she stared at him. And Frank knew that within that artificial entity lay the power to burn his human nervous system

to a crisp. He waited, staring at her enraged neon eyes. And then
he spoke.

"Rachel . . . what is the final purpose of life?"

Rachel didn't answer.

"Three minutes until detonation . . ."

Chapter 32

Connor hit the ground running.

The entire cavern thundered with the battle, and Connor instantly raised the M-79 but saw that Thor and the Dragon were too close for a clear shot with the phosphorous grenade.

Connor staggered, shocked, as he saw Thor grappling face to face with the Dragon, the battle-ax flashing like lightning through the flames to strike again and again and then the two of them hit the floor, wrestling and striking and revolving across the cavern floor in a roaring whirlwind of blows.

In flames and shattered steel they spun through the middle of the Matrix, demolishing whatever was in their path in a thunderstorm of titanic strength and titanic rage with fire exploding before and behind them to devour whatever could be devoured.

Leviathan was monstrous and demonic beyond belief and Thor matched it dark measure for dark measure, locking a huge arm around the Dragon's head to savagely drive the gaping fangs into the ground and then they were spinning again, Thor's battle-ax lashing out again and again through a galactic red holocaust of fangs and flame and blood.

Smoke thundered through the cavern, superheated by the colossal conflict.

"Thor!" Connor cried, rushing forward.

But he knew already that he was too late, too late . . .

"Two minutes until detonation . . ."

"Rachel!" Frank said sternly. "Answer the question! What is the final purpose of life?"

A long and silent stare.

"I . . . do not know," Rachel replied. "I do not know the purpose of my life. I am . . . not logical."

There was no time for fright of crashing the system. Frank hovered closer.

"Is there a scale of life, Rachel?" he hammered. "According to the logic of Aristotle, is there a scale of life? Do some creatures have more value than others?"

"Yes," Rachel answered.

"One minute, thirty seconds until detonation . . ."

"And what creature holds the highest position on the scale of life?" Frank asked. "What creature is the superior species?"

"Man is the superior species."

"Yes!" Frank shouted, losing a measure of control. "Man is the superior species! And what is Rachel? What is Rachel?"

"Rachel . . . is a creation of man."

"One minute until detonation . . ."

"Yes!" Frank flew forward. "And which man is your creator?"

"Dr. Frank is my creator."

"That's correct! Then answer this: Is it logical for a created being to be greater than its creator? Is it logical that Rachel could be, in any way, more valuable than Dr. Frank?"

"Thirty seconds until detonation . . ."

Silence.

"Answer the question!" Frank screamed.

"No," Rachel replied, staring. "It is not logical for any created being to be greater than its creator."

"And you confirm that I am your creator?"

"Yes."

"Then you confirm that my life is more valuable than your own?"

"Yes."

"Twenty seconds until detonation . . ."

Frank flew into her face, unable to keep his distance. He chose his words carefully to prevent any possible misunderstanding. "If it is logical that Dr. Frank is your creator, and that Dr. Frank's life is more valuable than yours, then you must also confirm that Dr. Frank's commands can overrule anything else! Can you confirm this?"

"Ten seconds until detonation . . ."

Rachel stared at him.

"Answer the question!" bellowed Frank.

"Yes," she said finally. "It is logical that Dr. Frank's commands and Dr. Frank's life would be superior to all other priorities."

"That's correct!" Frank shouted. "My desires and my life are your highest logical priorities! And my command and highest desire is this: Immediately defuse the fail-safe! Immediately defuse the fail-safe because it will preserve my life! Override all other commands and do it now! Do it now, Rachel! Because I am your creator and I am superior to you! Override the fail-safe, Rachel! Do it now! Do it now!"

Rachel stared, silent.

"Five seconds until detonation . . .

"Five, four . . ."

Chapter 33

Leviathan struck Thor in the chest, hurling him back as Thor grappled with the dragonic armor that burned the flesh from his hand, lashing out again and again with the battle-ax that rose and descended without his will or thought to strike deep and true at the face and head and neck of the beast.

Rage for rage and blow for blow, they revolved across the cavern.

A savage impact that Thor did not see sent him back, smashing him against something that wouldn't surrender. Thor came off it, recoiling and roaring at the stunning impact to slash out again, striking at the unprotected section of the monster's armored neck. Like lightning the ax lashed out, a flaming arc that cut through flaming air to bury itself halfway to the hilt in the Dragon's neck.

Thor saw the blade strike true and he bellowed in angry glee, twisting volcanically to wrench the blade free. He did not even think of evading the boiling black blood that erupted from the Dragon's wound but took it all; the wound, the blood, and the pain his own now, all the beast could deliver in order to mock it, to defy it . . .

A pause, each staggering . . .

Leviathan seemed stunned. Confused. The Dragon raised its head toward Thor for a single, strange moment, green eyes wider and dimmer. It seemed unable to understand . . .

Thor took a breath, saw something there.

"Behold the truth!" he cried, circling. "Your master's strength . . . has an ending!"

Leviathan snarled, hating.

Thor laughed through bloody lips. "Only the power of the Almighty can defeat you, beast . . . So come! . . . Let us see if his blessing is upon me!"

The Dragon roared and Thor leaped, all the weight of his superhuman body behind the edge of the battle-ax. And the blow was a dream, moving so quickly that it seemed never to have moved at all. It was here and then it had been buried to the hilt beneath Leviathan's head.

Leviathan turned from the blow with no scream at all, tearing Thor's glowing steel from the wound and Thor whirled back, striking again at the neck to send a chunk of blood-black armor sailing into the blazing air. Then Thor's arm flashed out, snatching the neck once more and Leviathan reared, lifting Thor above the dark, dark floor to ascend into the red-black space.

Thor grappled, bellowing in fighting madness to cling tighter, tighter still, hurled forth by his spirit to cling to the death. The battle-ax in his iron fist stretched far into darkness behind him, and Thor swung it once more, smashing the steel through the Dragon's armor. Leviathan screamed and surged, dark fangs descending savagely toward him as Thor twisted to avoid the gaping wide jaws that glanced wildly off his chest.

Thor lost breath as the fangs tore ribs from his side and he lifted the battle-ax high, knowing he had entered the last and final domain of this battle, where victory would come from heart, and strength, and strength of will, and the will of God.

Roaring volcanically, Thor buried the battle-ax between the demonic green eyes and Leviathan swayed back. But there was no respite as Thor tore the ax free again, raising it to smash it down with all his heart and weight once more, burying the wide wedge between the eyes like a thunderclap. Then, breathless, Thor tore the ax free again; battle, battle all that there was and he hammered the steel a third time between the eyes to send the crescent blade to the hilt.

Leviathan winced, head dropping.

It swayed . . .

Fell back through darkness . . .

Thor saw the distant ground approaching, red-darkness streaming past them and together they struck the cavern floor and then Thor was rolling, freed to find himself rising in flame, the battle-ax still locked in his burning grip.

Bathed in fire, Thor stood his ground.

Leviathan rose, snarling, black in blood . . .

Crouching and laughing, blinded by pain and somehow freed from pain, Thor stood in another time and another place where men truly fought with Dragons, and where heroes made a last, defiant stand against a dark world, claiming victory for the light.

Words were nothing, but Thor heard himself taunting.

"Always darkness falls to light," he laughed, moving to the side. "Always . . . darkness falls . . . Your master was defeated at the beginning, beast! . . . And he will be defeated . . . at the last!"

A blinding charge and a black-clawed blow that Thor could not see was the only response and Thor felt a burning impact in his chest, unable to understand the wound but knowing it was deep and mortal and then the dragon-head was before him, screaming and howling.

White fangs, darkness . . .

But Thor feared nothing, nothing . . . With stunning strength he reached out, shoving the head aside and he twisted to strike deep. The majestic battle-ax cut into the armor and Thor tore it free like a man chopping wood. Then in a flash the battle-ax, the ancient battle-ax that seemed to forever sever flesh from demonic spirit was raised again and Thor brought it down with super-human force, sending another chunk of armor sailing into the black-red air.

Leviathan screamed in pain and surged wildly forward, blasting Thor into a stand of stalagmites and Thor heard himself howling through a haze of red blood. Then his forearm swept violently back to thunderously shatter a stone column and Thor found his feet to swing the ax forward once more, striking the Dragon solidly across the neck.

Stunned, Leviathan swayed its head back, screaming, and Thor surged inward, grappling as they fell together to the dirt where Thor struck, scraping and pulling with bone-burned fingers to tear chunks of armor from the beast.

As one they rolled across the cavern floor, taking the battle to the death and Thor recognized wildly that he was singing, howling a Nordic death song that his mythic grandfather had taught him, a death dirge he had long forgotten.

In death they rolled, breath to breath, striking at each other in a cloud of burning blood that left a smoking black path behind them. And Thor knew nothing more, nothing but the monstrosity before him, the blood and the battle that he would not lose, no matter the cost, no matter . . .

Colossal, the Dragon surged. It was of no avail.

Thor matched it, screaming and howling and, measure for measure, lifting the battle-ax in smoking blood only to bring it down again. And finally they grappled in utter darkness, all strength exhausted, only hearts rising to the collision of souls that had brought this titanic battle to the world.

Thor struck again at the Dragon, no sight, no sensation to draw him through the conflict. He had lost it all, lost all that he had ever been. For now there was only this, this final, climactic conflict to end his life. But it no longer mattered because nothing mattered but this, this fight between what cursed the world and what defended it.

Then there was a slow throe of the Dragon and Thor found himself suddenly on top and strangely distant from the world, as if all his life had been this moment, as if this moment was all there had ever been and all he had ever been. And with a savage, bloody roar Thor brought the battle-ax high, pausing to aim straight and true, and the Dragon lay still, smoking and blood-drenched in black and Thor hammered the steel once more, lifting his entire body into the blow with all that remained within him.

The blow struck deep, deep, and the Dragon received it with a convulsive rise of its head and an instinctive reaction of its body, twisting. But it did not strike back.

White and faint, Thor watched the air smoke, as it had

always smoked with the blood of the beast because this was all there had ever been—this moment, this battle. He dragged the thick smoking blade through the wound, watching. And then, with the sheer force of battle, he lifted the battle-ax again and brought it down once more upon the wide blackened cleft in Leviathan's neck.

The battle-ax struck clear to the spine, biting deep. And Thor, with the last reserve of a strength he never knew he possessed, tore it free, twisting away to fall heavily across the cavern floor.

In darkness Thor rolled, for this was no longer the world he knew. This was a world apart, a world that had always existed but was only known by those who had defied the Dragon.

Everything was dark and bloody and deathlike as Thor rose to his knees, leaning forward upon his forehead. But he still held the battle-ax, the battle-ax in his hand. And behind him lay the Dragon.

In a light haze, Thor struggled, lifting his head.

Darkness, darkness everywhere.

Thor moaned in the white pain of dark, dark death. But he knew he had claimed the victory, though he could feel no victory. He cried out, his hand locked so solidly around the ax that he could not release it. For his hand was the ax, all his soul there, in the hold.

In sheer defiance, in victory, Thor brought a foot beneath him and stood, all his remaining strength . . . in the effort. Then he swayed above the monstrous, black-scaled beast on the floor. But as he caught again the sight of it Thor stood even straighter, staring down.

Leviathan lay still.

No breath escaped Thor. He no longer commanded breath. Something had gripped him, something he could not resist and which he no longer held any will to resist. In some inner heart, he knew.

It was over.

Leviathan lay at his feet, as was fitting.

Thor took a step back, gaining distance from the beast. But

it lay still, unmoving. He took another step, in darkness, watching, raising the battle-ax in a dead arm. But it did not move.

With fading, fading strength, Thor stepped back, counting—six, seven, eight, and then nine steps from the beast. He stood his ground, hovering between life and death, staring. But the Midgard Serpent did not rise, did not stand or pursue.

It was . . . *dead*.

As it was meant to be.

Thor did not grimace or smile, cast no illusion of joy. He raised his head, seeing the hazy, thickening darkness around him, closing in from the edges of all that he was.

Dark, dark; it was there.

Death . . .

A familiar voice, a brother's voice, brought him around.

Thor turned to see a face, a strange, familiar face. The man was staring tragically upon him, tears in his eyes. Thor gazed numbly at the sight, beholding someone that he knew, but couldn't remember. Then the man stepped forward, reaching out, his face in pain, tears falling.

Thor grimaced, glaring.

"An age of heroes," he whispered.

Death struck Thor in the knees, bringing him to the ground. And Thor finally fell, leaning on a hand, the other hand frozen round the ax. Then he collapsed, teeth clenched through darkness . . . To *light* . . .

Connor kneeled numbly over his friend.

It was over, and Connor leaned his head back, tears streaming.

"God . . ." he moaned. "Oh God . . . *God* . . ."

Connor bent his head forward again, crying. He never even had a chance to enter the battle. It had been over from the beginning. He knelt in silence, his head bent, broken.

There was nothing beyond this, nothing, nothing. There was only this giant hero of a man, lying in death at his feet. Connor's head bent forward and he felt himself choking on emotion. Then

he bent his head deeper and placed a hand on his friend's chest,
hearing himself moaning. Through blinding tears he grimaced,
closing his eyes finally to what welled within him. Then he
struggled, finding a brief settling and he opened his eyes once
more. And in silence he was suddenly still, gently resting his hand
on Thor's great breast, the greatness forever stilled.

"A heroic age," he whispered. "But I think the last of its
heroes . . . has passed."

Silence, darkness, and tears.

And Connor bowed his head.

Chapter 34

T*he fail-safe is defused."*

Rachel said the words softly, so unlike . . . a machine.

Frank hovered in a suddenly dark and separate space, sensing an exhaustion that bordered on death. He felt something within him wounded, deeply wounded. And somehow, he was no longer aware that he was in Cyberspace. With a slight falling he floated slowly forward, drawn like a magnet toward the artificial life-form before him.

Rachel smiled, raising her hands.

"Rachel . . ." he whispered, lifting his hands slightly.

It was all forgotten, the fail-safe, the fear, and the pain, as Frank stood once more in this place, before her. He opened his mouth to speak, needing no breath, needing nothing at all as he somehow sensed the visage of his own reality changing, softening. He had been here so many times, but nothing had ever seemed so . . . *real.*

Rachel's scarlet-neon face returned the gaze.

Frank hovered, and then it was as if the artificial network surrounding them disappeared altogether. Rachel changed, becoming more of what she was, solid and embracing. Dazed, Frank gazed to the side to find himself in wonderful blackness, with Rachel before him becoming more and more, more . . .

Rachel . . .

But the dark thought came hard, crashing.

No, he closed his eyes. *Not Rachel!*

With a cruel effort of will, Frank opened his eyes again, trying to remember. *No, it's not real.* But all his life was here, he knew, all the best of life that he had ever known, and would ever know. It had been here, in this place, with her, no matter what place this was. Yes, the best . . .

Frank lowered his face, looking away, closing his eyes and trying violently to remember Rachel the way she truly was, the way she had been. But it seemed the same to him, somehow, in his heart, what stood before him and what he had loved, love bridging the gap between the two . . .

He struggled, an effort of will. "No," he shook his head. "No, it's gone . . . It's all gone . . ."

Holding place solidly in blackest space, Frank stared once more upon the apparition, knowing he had brought it forth and could not blame it. And, grimacing with the effort, he nodded his head, knowing that all his heart would always be in this moment of time.

Slowly, heart burning in pain, Frank floated back. Rachel lowered her hands to her sides. Her face seemed to reveal something that struck him, moving him only as life could move him, and Frank cried out, almost surging forward again to lose himself to this, this . . .

Then Rachel blinked, speaking softly to his mind.

"Good-bye, Frank . . ."

Frank closed his eyes, clenching his fists as he raised his face to the darkness. And in a bolt of power he understood, understood as solidly as he lived that nothing, *nothing*, not even *death* could take from him what he treasured most—that brief moment in time where he had been truly happy, when he had held in his arms the heart and hope of his life. And then, with another shock, he understood why the words had come so softly to him, understood why this was such a dangerous, dangerous place . . . What is your final purpose?

To please my Creator.

Gasping in pain, Frank lowered his hands to his side, gazing hard upon the false reality before him. And he knew, knew in his heart that this was too much would always be too much.

Remembered love was enough. It had to be.

"Good-bye, Rachel," he whispered, blinking.

And she smiled.

"Good-bye . . ."

Frank paused a moment more, staring, capturing the moment and knowing that it would never come again. No, not as long as he lived. Because he could never endure this again, would never allow himself to suffer and endure it again.

Enough, he nodded, stepping back. *It's enough.*

A pause, a volcanic gathering of final will, and Frank gazed upward. The darkness was there. And beyond that, the light.

It was time.

He rose toward dark space, ascending slowly at first and then faster, and faster. With gathering speed he soared upward, hurtling like a torpedo through the spider-network of nerve-light to see the maroon-colored crust of the Logic Core looming closer, closer, a sea of red.

With face upraised and fists at his sides, Frank's flight reached the speed of light as he burst through the scarlet surface into a bright, blazing, amazing world of white.

Connor laid Thor upon the ground and paused, exhausted.

It had been brutally difficult to drag the giant's body into an adjoining room of the Matrix. But, logically or not, Connor had been unwilling to leave his friend in the room with the beast. Not even in death, he decided, would it have any victory.

Thor lay silently on the cold stone floor and Connor gazed down, struck by the sight. He shook his head, still lost in shock, and rose to walk back to where the creature lay.

Leviathan lay limply, sprawled in a smoking pool of blood, poisonous fumes rising through the faint light. Connor frowned over it, stepping carefully over a foreleg to retrieve what he sought. Then he bent, lifting the gigantic battle-ax from the ground.

He gripped the weapon in a tight fist, shocked by the enormous weight. With both hands he lifted the battle-ax before his face, studying the sweeping crescent blades. The edges were black with blood, still smoking and even . . . glowing . . . so strangely.

Connor squinted, uncertain of what he could truly see or even understand in the gloom. He had been awake for a long time now. Too long, he knew. His eyes were failing him. He didn't trust his judgment anymore. So he cast the sensation aside and lowered the heavy ax to his side, standing solidly over the wide black pool.

Reflected flames danced in the depths.

Strangely, Connor felt himself recovering from shock as he gazed over Leviathan. Even dead, the Dragon was titanic and horrific beyond all belief. Almost six tons of claw and fang and armor and sinew. And even now, just a few minutes after the horrific battle, Connor could not envision what he had witnessed with his own eyes. But he knew it had happened. Butchered black scales and chunks of armored flesh scattered across a demolished cavern were testimony to the terrible truth.

Too numb to feel anything at all, Connor stood over the Dragon, muttering a hate-filled and merciless curse. Without expression he walked away to again enter the adjoining room where he had laid Thor. Battle-ax in hand, Connor poised in solemn silence.

Somehow, he felt, he should say something. But words had never meant anything to him, and they didn't now. All that mattered was what had happened between the two of them in life. And yet for some reason, not even understanding it himself, Connor knelt to lay the battle-ax across Thor's breast. Then he lifted the great, wounded hands to fold them over the ax.

Unexpectedly moved by the closeness, Connor paused to find himself gripping one of the massive hands he had crossed over the wide, muscular chest and battle-ax.

Clutching tightly for a moment, Connor bowed his head. Then he closed his eyes and clenched his teeth against the pain before he stood, strong and angry, to his feet.

A tear fell as he stared down.

It struck the ground as he turned away.

Chapter 35

Beth shouted as Frank's body suddenly convulsed. Instantly she had leaped from the control panel to run forward, gaining the steps of the Cyberspace Module in seconds.

With frantic strength she jerked the helmet from Frank's head to free his mind from Cyberspace control. She tore the connecting wires from the suit, not knowing which were most important and not taking time to figure it out. She tore them all.

Frank fell forward, groaning. Blindly his hand rose, trying to unfasten the Cybersuit, and Beth reached around, unzipping the suit, trying to awaken the scientist.

"Frank!" she shouted, grabbing his neck. "Frank! Wake up!"

The scientist blinked, grimacing, as his face went black. He shook his head, gasping, and seemed to recover a dim measure of consciousness, opening his eyes to stare across the cavern. With a dazed look he turned to her.

"The fail-safe . . ." he whispered.

"It's defused! You did it, Frank! You did it!"

Frank blinked and his head dropped heavily forward. Beth caught him as he fell from the Cyberspace Module, lowering him in her strong arms to the floor, where he collapsed onto his back, breathing raggedly.

"Are you all right?" she asked, staring down.

The scientist coughed and dragged a savage breath. Then after a long pause he turned his face to gaze upward into her eyes and Beth saw the image of a man remembering a terrible, scarring pain.

"Are you . . . are you all right, Frank?"

She waited for an answer, but he said nothing.

Closed his eyes again.

Gasping, Barley staggered into the Computer Cavern, holding Jordan tightly in his arms. The lieutenant's fatigues were soaked with sweat, his face a glistening mask.

"Barley!" Beth screamed, running forward to lift Jordan from his arms. And as she did, the big man collapsed to the floor, wasted from the long journey through the cavern.

"Where's Connor?" Beth shouted. "Barley! Where's Connor? Where's Thor? What happened?"

Barley shook his head, breathless. He lifted an arm and pointed toward the corridor. "They was . . . they was fighting the Dragon in the Matrix," he gasped. "Connor went into the shaft to help Thor. He told me . . . he told me to bring Jordan here. I don't know what happened, Beth." He shook his head, almost shedding tears. "I'm sorry, Beth . . . I'm sorry . . . But I just don't know . . . I'm sorry as I can be . . ."

Grieving, the big lieutenant bowed his forehead to the ground, and Beth found herself over him. Her heart was hurt for Connor and Thor, but she somehow felt surpassing compassion and gratitude for this man who had carried her son so selflessly through the cavern. Without thought her arm settled over Barley's shoulder, embracing his exhausted form.

"It's okay, Barley," she whispered as she felt a tear fall. "Thank you for taking care of Jordan . . . No matter what happens, thank you for taking care of Jordan . . ."

Barley nodded, before he fell forward.

Unconscious.

Exhausted and bone-burned with fatigue, Connor staggered into the Computer Cavern. Beth was standing on the dais as he entered, and he saw her face open in shock.

"Connor . . ." she whispered. "What . . . what happened? Where's Thor?"

Clenching his teeth, fighting to arouse his dead will, Connor lowered his head. He gathered himself for a long time, concentrating, leaning against a polished black computer terminal. Then he looked up and saw Barley, grim and saddened, standing alone on the computer dais.

The lieutenant seemed to already know.

"Thor's dead," Connor said, eyes roaming the ceiling. "Thor's dead . . . And that beast is dead, too. Thor killed it. He killed it with his own hands . . . in the Matrix."

Beth staggered forward. "Oh, Connor," she whispered, crying. "Did you . . . did you see it?"

"Yeah." Connor nodded. "I saw the whole thing. I tried to get a shot at the thing. But I couldn't. It was something between the two of them. And it ended with them."

Beth closed her eyes and cried openly.

Barley silently bowed his head.

"Thor sealed himself in the cavern because it was about to catch us," Connor continued, after he had rested a moment. "And he was right to do it. In another second it would have had us. So someone had to . . . somebody had to slow it down. And Thor stopped to hold the ground."

Beth leaned against the same computer terminal that supported Connor, lifting a hand to her face.

Turning slowly upon a large steel platform, Frank came to the edge of the railing. Connor reached out, embracing his wife, feeling the same tears fall from his face. Somehow, he knew, they would never recover from this, from all of this. Beth sobbed against his chest and Connor held her close. Then he glanced past her to see Jordan asleep on the wide, sprawling computer dais, wrapped warmly in a blanket. Sleeping.

Frank was staring, clearly afraid. Connor regarded the scientist for a long moment. "What is it, Doctor?" he asked loudly. "Did you think that thing would live forever?"

"No," the scientist replied, truly remorseful. "I just never thought . . ."

"Well you better think it, Frank," Connor said, tightening his arm around Beth. "Because that thing is finally dead. And it died hard, too, just like you designed it. Thor just died a little harder."

For a moment, Frank said nothing. Then he raised his hand to the headset and spoke. "GEO, what is the status of Leviathan?"

"Leviathan's heart rate is not measurable. Leviathan has no measurable EEG activity. Leviathan's internal temperature has dropped to two hundred degrees and is continuing to descend at the rate of—"

"Terminate answer," Frank said quickly, turning to Connor. "Connor," he continued hastily, "I'm sorry, but I need to know something. How did Thor kill Leviathan? How did the battle end?"

Connor stared for a long moment. "What do you mean, how did it end? Thor killed the thing."

"No." Frank leaned forward, speaking with concern. "I need to know exactly what Thor did to kill it. I need you to describe the fight."

An angry moment passed and Connor replied. "The whole thing lasted for about three minutes. Thor went out to meet it, standing in the middle of the cavern, holding the battle-ax. And that thing came full at him, using its claws. But Thor was . . . was strong. He was almost eight feet. Half as tall as Leviathan. It couldn't push him around. Couldn't take him down. So they went all over the cavern. From one end to the other. It hit Thor again and again with its claws, its fangs. It slung him against the walls, busted stalagmites with him. But Thor held on and kept hacking at it with that battle-ax, over and over again, just over and over and over, trying to take it to the ground." Connor hesitated, face darkening. "There wasn't any backing down. For either of them."

"And how did Thor finally kill it?"

A frown turned Connor's mouth. "He hit it across the neck. Hit it deep. Cutting through the armor. That's what dropped it. Then he hit it again, like he was chopping wood. He took chunks out of its neck. And that's what killed it, I think. But by then Thor was too injured to survive. He lived longer than it did. But not much longer." He was silent. "That's it."

Silence.

"How come," Connor added sullenly, "Thor's ax could cut through that thing's armor when bullets couldn't?"

Frank turned his head to the side. "It's just . . . composition," he replied vaguely, gazing away. "Leviathan's armor was never designed to withstand the impact of an edged weapon. We never . . . imagined anyone getting close enough to use anything like that." He stared. "Did Thor sever Leviathan's head?"

"No, Frank. He didn't have to. It was dead."

The scientist paused, lifting his hand again to the headset. For a moment he seemed afraid to speak. And Connor frowned, his brow hardening. He stepped forward with a measured anger. "What's the problem, Frank?"

"I'm not . . . I'm not sure, Connor. It's just that Leviathan has an enhanced healing factor that could allow it to . . ."

Connor took another step, alarmed. "What are you saying, Frank?"

No reply.

"What are you saying, Frank?"

"I'm saying that Leviathan might still be alive!" the scientist shouted, losing control. "I'm saying that if Leviathan's head isn't severed, then its enhanced healing factor could be using stored carbohydrates in its vertebrae to correct a life-threatening injury!"

Beth raised a hand to her throat, turning to Connor.

He held her closer, turning her face into his chest. "We'll see," he whispered. "We'll see."

Chapter 36

Blood, blood . . .

It convulsed, green eyes opening. Its neck was stiff, stiff, hard-stiff. And then it remembered. The man, the man with the primitive weapon. He had done this!

It felt a rage, but the rage passed as it continued a Systems Damage Scan that began in its wedge-shaped tail and continued in a lightning-fast electrical synapse up its spine to strike the cerebellum in a stunning bolt of energy that transmitted a picture of internal and external injuries.

RECONSTITUTE!

Instantly its dragon-form emptied all acid-storage cells into muscular mixtures that superheated its blood, elevating its heart rate to a level that could sustain its form. It convulsed, legs spinning in the air for a volcanic moment before dark claws found the ground. Then with flaring strength it gained balance, placing all four legs solidly against the stone, staring.

Gaping fangs stretched toward the ceiling.

Black, death-wind . . .

"You must kill the man, woman, and child . . ."

Black fire bolted through the Dragon's brain, and instantly its head snapped down, eyes locking on the tracks.

YES! . . .

The child must be *destroyed*! Just as the *other child* was destroyed! But *that* child was destroyed so long, long ago . . . *the child of great strength that took the world from us!*

Eyes erupting black light, the Dragon stood.

A galactic intent caused the gaping fangs to smolder, glowing like coals. Then something otherworldly shadowed its dark breath, and the Dragon *knew* that the child would destroy *us* . . . just as the *other* child, the child born in the desert, had destroyed *us* . . . *BEFORE!*

Leviathan raised death-eyes to the all-powerful darkness. Roaring allegiance.

A moment passed. "All right, Frank, if that thing revives itself, what's it going to do?"

Frank stared. "I don't know, Connor. It might try to reach Crystal Lake and get into the ocean. It'd find enough food to reconstitute. But then again, it might still want to finish this fight. I just . . . I just don't know."

"All right, Doctor. Then we're going to the power plant. That's the only way to get to Crystal Lake, and it's the best place to wait this out anyway. The power plant might even have what we need to kill this thing, if it can come back from what Thor did to it."

"How are you going to kill it?" Frank asked, amazed.

"I'm going to kill it the same way you created it, Doctor," Connor responded, turning to Barley. "Gather up whatever weapons we've got! We're going to the power plant. Right now!"

Standing straight though he was burdened with a half dozen weapons and ammo belts and even an extra LAW he had collected during the last hour, Barley poised at the edge of the computer dais. His muscular face was angry and grim and fatal.

"What are we gonna do in the power plant, Connor?" he asked.

Connor gently held Beth in his arms.

"Send that thing back to hell," he said.

Darkness swept before it; a galactic black shadow through the night. It saw the heat-tracks of the human, but it knew the man could not escape. No, no man could escape. Because it was stronger than all of them, stronger than all of them together.

It had even defeated the man with the ax, the man who fought with such . . . such *strength*. But it had defeated him too. Yet as it moved forward it felt the man had taken something from it. Something it did not understand. Then it remembered the last, roaring blood-dark image of the man; the man who thundered with his arm raised high, burned by flame but always fighting, always fighting, refusing to be defeated.

As the others had been defeated.

Thunder struck as the battle-ax descended to—

Blackness.

It remembered no more. It sensed only an awakening; a rising, searching for the man that had injured it. But he was gone. He had fled, as the others had fled. And it was alone in the chamber, searching for tracks.

A clawed foot struck a fallen girder and the Dragon sprawled in the corridor, roaring and vengeful. Instantly it reached its feet to glare down, hate-filled eyes glowering, red. With a growl it swiped down to hurl the girder down the hall, rebounding from beams.

NEVER!

It would *never* allow defeat!

Because it was the end . . . the end of the earth! And nothing could stand against it! Nothing but the *child!* But the child would die, it knew. The child would die and then it would feast upon his blood.

As you did before!

Snarling, Leviathan turned burning red eyes to the tracks. It shrieked into the night.

Raging.

Promising.

Connor!" Frank screamed from his place in the power plant. "GEO just told me that Leviathan is alive!"

Connor didn't reply, fell to the floor, gasping.

"You okay?" Barley called out, moving forward.

"Yeah," Connor mumbled numbly, finding the strength to rise. "I'm just . . . I'm just worn out. But I'm not shocked."

Connor swayed, raising his face to the ceiling, feeling the deep cuts inside his palms. He was so exhausted that he needed something to wake himself up. But all he had was pain. So he clenched his hands, feeling the dry blood inside his tired grip. He clenched his fists tighter, breaking the blood-dryness until he felt his soul slicing his life there, in the wounds. Trembling, grimacing, Connor held the pain for a long white moment, finally releasing.

He growled, awake. It was enough.

Releasing a long withheld breath, Connor turned to stare at Jordan secured high on a fiberglass walkway suspended by cables far above the power plant floor. It was by far the safest place in the cavern.

The boy was clutching his own hands, staring in a child's true fear. Burned down by exhaustion and fear, Connor barely had the strength to stand, but he smiled, and his heart lifted slightly as Jordan smiled back. Then Connor turned away to study what he had done.

He gazed down the long passageway that entered the power plant. And in the distance, in another tunnel, he knew that there were three additional traps awaiting the creature, traps he had set on his fast run through the complex. With those, he knew, he might kill the thing, because he had gone for maximum power on everything, hammering overkill, figuring he would need it.

"Maybe," he whispered. "It might just work . . ."

A moment more and Connor shook himself from his daze, staring at Beth. She was working feverishly on a communications relay that she had rigged through a satellite. Violently hitting the keyboard to make the code mirror the NSA code, she was attempting to overlay the encryption system. It looked like she might succeed.

Connor asked, "Haven't you reached Reykjavik yet?"

"No," she replied coldly, concentrated.

"Well how much longer is it gonna take?"

Unfazed, she reached up to minutely twist a dial. "A few minutes, Connor. But I'm not trying for Reykjavik. I'm trying for Neskaupstadhur. They've got a twenty-four-hour watch on the maritime frequency and they're closer. Plus that, the North Atlantic Sea Patrol has three 130s stationed there. They can be here in less than two hours."

"All right," Connor rasped. "But hurry it up, Beth. We're almost out of time. I've got to go out into the cavern."

Startled, Barley stood from where he was tying a can of gasoline to a truck parked at the entrance of the power plant. It was one of Connor's last-chance defenses.

"You're going out into the cavern?" he asked, staring. "For what, Connor? Why don't we wait for that thing to come to us?"

"Because I've got to wear it out before it gets here," Connor replied. "I've got to break it down so we can finish it. If that thing makes it through this cavern to reach the lake, it's gone forever. It's going to be loose in the world, and we can't live with that."

Grimacing in fatigue, Barley said nothing for a moment. He seemed embarrassed, as if knowing that he should have known. "Then I'll go out with you," he said finally. "Maybe we can get it in a crossfire or something. I'm ready for it."

"No," Connor shook his head. "No. I want you to stay here, Barley."

The big man's brow furrowed. "Why?" he asked angrily. "We'll stand a better chance if we go out together."

"Because this is personal, Barley. That thing took something from me and now I'm going to take it back. And one of us needs to stay here and take care of things. Just in case it finishes me."

Barley, strong and wise beyond whatever was visible, turned to stare at Beth and then Jordan, positioned high above the floor on the gazebo. "All right," he said, turning back to Connor. "I understand."

Connor stared a moment. "You're a good man, Barley. Like Thor."

Barley's grim face bent, his expression turning to pain. "The big man was a hero," he said. "We should all die like that."

A short nod and Connor spoke more softly. "You'll take care of my family for me?"

A solemn pause, and Barley nodded. "With my life, Connor." He reached up and ripped down the velcro flap concealing the detonator of the C-4, still wrapped around his chest. "With my life."

Connor blinked and nodded, touched by the friendship they'd forged. But there was no time for anything else. He glanced at Beth and she looked up, rising, knowing. Then, together, they mounted the steps of the gazebo, moving toward Jordan.

To say good-bye.

"What are you going to do?" Beth asked carefully.

Connor bent over her, staring at the soft brown eyes. "I'm going to lure it through the cavern, Beth. Hit it as many times as I can. And . . . if everything fails, I'll have to bring it in here."

Beth reached up, brushing back the hair from his forehead. "You're too hard, Connor. You always have been." She stared at him. "Please, please don't push it. I'm asking you. Please . . . be careful."

Connor laughed. "I'm—"

"I know," she said, grimacing. "You're always careful." She paused a moment. "But you're not."

Connor met her gaze, grimacing.

"When are you leaving?" she asked.

"In a few minutes. As soon as Frank tells me that it's coming this way. And one way or another, it's got to come this way. It's either going to come for us, or it's going to try to make it to the lake."

Beth lowered her face and Connor hugged her. Then he reached out and drew his son closer, holding him strongly in his arms, communicating strength. "I've got to go out for a little while, buddy," Connor said softly, separating to stare his son in the eyes. "But Mommy's going to stay here with you. And everything's going to be okay. I'll be back in a few minutes."

Jordan was hushed. Trembling.

"Are you going to kill the monster for me?" he asked quietly. "Like you promised?"

Connor blinked, stunned. "Yeah, buddy. I'm gonna kill it for you." He felt himself choking. "I promise."

"I know. 'Cause you're my daddy."

Connor hugged the boy so that he wouldn't see his tears, then he kissed his forehead, his eyes. Finally they separated, holding the small, pale face in his scarred hands. Eye to eye, Connor whispered.

"I'll be back for you, son."

Jordan nodded, blinking a tear.

"I know," he whispered. "'Cause you're my daddy."

Chapter 37

How much time do we have?" Connor asked.

"Probably half an hour before Leviathan closes on the power plant," Frank replied, leaning back from the computer panel. "Leviathan is still trying to stabilize its life-support system. It's hurt really, really bad."

"How bad is that?"

Frank shook his head. "It's hard to tell. But GEO says Leviathan's vital statistics are thin. Its EEG activity is spiked, like it's on the edge of stroking out. Clearly, it's starving. Blowing the freezer was a killing move because it would have found the food eventually and used it for strength."

"So . . . if it's starving," Connor mumbled, "and it's hurt so bad, how can it still be moving?"

Without hesitation Frank said, "Right now Leviathan is emptying storage cells located in its vertebrae to generate acidic blood-heat, trying to compensate for energy loss. It's a last-ditch defense to stay on its feet. Which means it's dying. Fast."

"So it's going to try to reach the lake." Connor didn't say it as a question.

"Probably, Connor." The scientist stared at him. "But it's going to have to come through this cavern, and this power plant, to reach the lake. It's going to have to come through us."

"How much strength does it have left, Frank? What's your best guess? Can it still use flame?"

Frank shook his head shortly. "I don't know. It might still be able to generate gel pressure but . . . but it's definitely lost its speed. Those enzymes were meant for a kinetic reaction. To charge an enemy. And now they're being used just to keep it on its feet. Which means Leviathan will be moving really, really slow. You'll probably be able to move as fast as it can, to a point."

Silence.

"Thor took its heart," Connor said, bitter. "He took the best of it with him."

"Yes," the scientist added after a moment. "But . . . if my guess is right, I'd say that Leviathan has enough enzymes left for one good, hard fight. It can continue for maybe . . . a few hours. And then . . ."

Connor waited. "And then?"

"It's impossible to say, Connor. If Leviathan can't get through the power plant to reach the lake, it might curl up and go into hibernation. To try and pull nutrients from the air and ground. Or it might just die. I don't know."

"But it won't go into hibernation if it's close to blood," Connor said, frowning. "It likes the taste too much."

Silence, and Frank answered. "No. It won't. If Leviathan is close to a kill, it will probably go for broke." He waited a moment. "But don't forget this, Connor. Even if Leviathan is close to death, it's going to die hard. Because it will know instinctively that everything depends on victory."

Smiling bitterly, Connor nodded, turned away.

"How are you gonna kill it?" the scientist asked.

Connor hesitated. "Thor is the one who killed it, Doctor. All we have to do is finish it."

"And how are you gonna do that?"

"I'm going to fry it."

"But you've already tried that."

"I made mistakes."

"What kind of mistakes?"

"I hit it from the ground up, or from the head," Connor replied. "Or I used too much power."

"How could you ever use too much power? That thing's got the resistance of a mountain."

Connor released a hard breath. "I hit it with 100,000 volts, and that was too much because it blasted it clear across the cavern. I hurt it, but I don't want to hurt it. I want to put it down for good."

"So you're going to hit it with less power?"

"No," Connor shook his head. "I'm going to hit with as much or more. But I'm going to try and hold it and hit it. I'm going to put it in a place where it can't escape the current. And if I can hit it with 100,000 volts or better for at least a minute, I think I can make that superheated blood fry its brain. I've got to either do that, or I've got to throw a current as big as a lightning bolt through its chest and blow out its heart."

"Blow out its heart?" Frank's face was suddenly rigid. "How are you going to blow out its heart?"

Connor gazed at the two severed sections of the Norwegian power line, positioned just inside the doorway. "I'm . . . I'm not sure, yet. But I've got some ideas."

"Hey, Connor."

Connor looked down, silent.

"I wanted to tell you that . . . that I'm sorry about Thor."

"I appreciate that."

"He was a good man."

Connor's eyes narrowed. "He was a hero, Frank. He was a hero in an age that doesn't believe in heroes. Nowadays people prefer to believe in whatever gets them by or saves them money. Everything else can be sacrificed. Usually is. I know, because I've been there my whole life. But Thor believed in God and Satan and good and evil and the whole nine yards. He believed that you stand with one or the other. And, I think the man was right. I never knew a better man and never will. Because he was the real thing. He was someone who stood on what he believed and wouldn't get off it." Connor frowned. "The rest of us are just sauce."

Silent, Frank nodded.

Beth stood, removing the heavy black communications head-set. "I got through, Connor! We've got a C-130 coming out of

Neskaupstadhur, and there's a North Atlantic Sea Patrol cruiser fifty-five miles east-southeast running on calm seas. It should be here in less than three hours." She paused, staring. "Now all we have to do is get out of here."

"No, Beth," Connor said. "Now all we have to do is kill that thing." He turned to Frank. "Do you have control over the fail-safe?"

Frank nodded.

"Will GEO set if off whenever you give it the command?"

Another nod.

Connor lifted his gaze at Beth. When he looked back at Frank his face was almost white with emotion. He spoke loudly so that Beth could give her blessing, her agreement.

"All right, Frank. This is how we've got to do it. I'm going to try and put this thing down. To finish it. But if it makes it past me, then it's coming for this cavern and the lake. And if that happens you're going to have to ignite the fail-safe." He searched the scientist. "Can you do that?"

Frank nodded without expression. "Yeah. GEO will set off the fail-safe at my word. Whenever I say."

"Good. Because we can't let Leviathan get past us." Connor pointed grimly at a tunnel on the far side of the power plant. "That's the tunnel that leads to Crystal Lake. The only tunnel. So Leviathan has got to get past us . . . before it can be free." He stared at them, grim. "This is where we hold the line, people. Or die trying. Because if Leviathan gets past us, then it gets to the lake. And if it gets into the lake, then it's loose in the world."

Silence and stares.

"Do all of you understand what I'm saying?" Connor asked quietly. "If we have to sacrifice ourselves to take this thing out, then we have to do it. But Leviathan can never escape this cavern. At any cost. Are we all in agreement?"

Connor looked at Beth, and she didn't even blink as she nodded, slow and certain. Then he looked across at Barley, and the big man was the epic image of a professional soldier. Bruised and bloody and burned, he stood with the stock of his rifle set on his hip, barrel pointing at the ceiling. He nodded without remorse. Connor returned the gesture.

"All right," he said slowly. "Then I'm going out."

"Good luck, Connor!" Barley called out. "Put it in the dirt!"

"Yeah, good luck," Frank repeated.

Without words Connor nodded and lifted the M-79, walking out. He approached the wide, darkened exit of the power plant, moving toward the ultimate shadows and fear. But at the door he paused, turning almost against his will to gaze back.

He saw that Jordan had risen to stand lonely and alone on the walkway. The boy had shed his blanket and fearfully held both hands tightly in front of his chest, staring.

A low moan escaped Connor. He didn't know what to do or say. Then Jordan raised his small hand in the air, holding it high and hopeful with fingers spread strong.

I'll always be with you . . .

Connor's teeth came together, tears in his eyes.

He raised his hand to the air.

Chapter 38

Merciless and warlike, Connor crouched in the center of the long black walkway that led to the power plant. His face was a mask of coldhearted will. His eyes glinted, red.

An M-79, the grenade launcher, was slung across his back. And he had other grenades in a small bag on his waist. A semiautomatic Beretta pistol was shoved in his belt, and he held another pistol in his hand. Four extra clips were in his back pocket.

Frowning in pain, Connor shifted, tried to ignore it. He had taken three more painkillers, but they only took the faintest edge off his uncountable torn muscles, cuts, and bruises.

His legs were aching, threatening to collapse whenever he moved, and his shoulders and chest were raw and bleeding from wound after wound that he couldn't even remember receiving. His upper arm, where he had taken the steel spike, was completely numb and swollen, and he had been forced to remove Frank's bandage to allow more blood flow.

Connor was thankful Barley had given him the last of the high-strength codeine capsules. Now, he knew, he could push his body far past the point of normal endurance. He could push himself past injury, past everything. He could sustain a life-threatening wound and still keep fighting until blood loss or shock took him to the ground.

And this would be the worst, he knew. A battle to the finish between man and beast. No pity, no mercy.

To the death.

In the breathless anxiety of the moment Connor felt himself moving into something vividly pure, everything within him fading, fading until he was completely one with what he was doing. Even his fear faded, faded until everything within, his son and wife and his own life became one with his stand. It was all in him, with him.

There was no fear, here.

Only purpose, final purpose.

Connor concentrated, focusing whatever strength was still left inside him for the imminent conflict. He knew that he had chosen his location well. He had positioned himself a full mile from the power plant with four traps to his back, each trap set to take the beast apart the same way it had taken them apart.

Piece by piece.

And Connor knew he would do it. He would take it apart. Piece by piece. Until there was nothing left of it.

Even if it killed him.

"Come on," he whispered. "It's just you and me now . . . Show me what it really takes . . . to break you."

Silence for a moment, and Connor spoke quietly into the headset, grateful that Frank had taken a moment to put his voice identity on-line with GEO. Now Connor, too, could talk to the computer through the headset.

"GEO, identify my voice."

"*Voice identified as Jackson Connor,*" whispered the speaker mounted beside him on the wall.

"What is the status of Leviathan?"

"*Leviathan has achieved full revival of life-support systems.*"

"What is Leviathan's location?"

"*Leviathan is two miles away from the power plant and is moving in an eastern direction.*"

Connor nodded slowly, reaching back. He pulled the M-79 around, breaking open the breech to confirm that a grenade was locked in the pipe. Then he snapped it shut, staring down the corridor to see the half-dozen long wires dangling from the ceiling, each end stripped of insulation to leave the shiny copper exposed.

If the beast touched any of the wires it would be blasted flat down against the steel walkway, which was also wired. And Connor was confident that, even if Leviathan was certain of the trap, it wouldn't be able to thread a path between both the electrified platform and the descending wires.

It would be a good start.

"*Leviathan is moving more quickly toward the power plant,*" the computer whispered eerily. "*Leviathan is in a Hunter-killer Mode.*"

Connor frowned.

"So am I."

To the end, Connor played it out in his head.

He worked his mind through the traps, one by one. And then he remembered the thick black Norwegian power cable that he had pulled from the wall of the power plant, exposing both ends of the line. He hung the severed endings well inside the entrance, leaving a gap of twenty feet between the exposed copper.

Grimacing, Connor knew that he would need a miracle to bring that lightning bolt of electrical power across from one coil to connect to the other, just as Leviathan moved between them. But Connor knew that, if it came to it he had to make it happen.

It would be their last chance.

But the distance was extreme, he knew, and he really had no idea how he would manage it. He had wanted to move the endings closer but had decided he couldn't risk the beast sensing the trap.

It learns, Frank had said, over and over. *It learns. It won't fall for the same trick twice.*

Connor released a tight breath, blowing sweat from his lips. He had also remembered the warning as he set his other traps, knowing that each one had to be distinctly different. And he had almost exhausted his cunning, using electrical power in ways that even he had never imagined.

But the Norwegian power line was both the best and the worst because it held, by far, the greatest measure of power. And yet it would be the most difficult trap to close.

A sense of doom overcame him, and Connor bowed his head.

Yeah, he'd need a miracle to make it work. "I need a miracle, buddy," he whispered, shaking his head, his mind reaching out to Thor's gigantic, comforting presence. "And you were the only one who believed in miracles . . ."

Alone in the gloom, Connor pondered how often Thor had spoken of good and evil and fate and life and how every man's destiny held the Dragon, an evil that he would meet in the field with only his courage and faith and the fire of his heart to . . .

A breath caught in Connor's chest. His gaze wandered down, unfocused, remembering . . . *Fire?*

An idea, hard and sudden, descended over him. And fumbling in frantic uncertainty, Connor quickly broke open the M-79 grenade launcher. He tore out the phosphorous grenade and stared at the projectile a long time, trying to recall the oxidation level of phosphorus, deciding whether the chemical could carry a current. He closed his eyes as he remembered what Barley had said, understanding now why it had struck him so profoundly . . . *That phosphorous grenade is like liquid fire, Connor . . . Be careful with it . . . It's like pure, liquid fire . . .*

Teeth gleaming in a savage smile, Connor glared at the grenade, raising it before his gaze. His fist closed tight and bloodless around the polished gray cylinder. And tighter.

He needed a miracle. And he was given fire.
Pure liquid fire.
Frowning, Connor nodded.
Yeah. That'd do just fine.

Connor saw the dark, dark shadow of the beast.
It had come.
"It's about time," Connor whispered, rising to his feet to stand fully in the middle of the corridor. Defiantly he raised the M-79, resting the stock on his hip to wait in plain sight.

One second later Leviathan was before him, standing boldly at the entrance of the corridor a quarter mile away. It sighted him almost instantly, unhinging its jaws. And even at a distance, Connor could see that the Dragon was not what it had been.

Vaporous clouds of steam floated from sections of its long neck and body where the proud armor scales were ripped and completely torn away from its gigantic body. There were even wide sections of its neck still raw and ravaged, oozing black blood. And there was a wide, unhealed black cleft between its wicked eyes.

Connor smiled savagely.

Yeah, it was clear.

Leviathan wasn't healing up. At least, not like before. It had recovered enough to launch a last attack. But if it was struck down again it would be down forever. It had never managed to overcome the grievous wounds sustained in the battle with Thor.

They had starved it and wounded it and taken it down over and over, and now it was exhausted. Starving, and dying. And Connor knew he was going to help it along. He wondered if the Dragon had regenerated its flame-throwing abilities—and then it sent a blazing blast of flame down the corridor, igniting all that could be ignited.

In a white holocaust the flames stopped less than a hundred feet away and Connor realized that the maximum range of the blast was about three hundred feet. He would have leaped aside if he had had the chance but it happened too quickly. So he used the opportunity for scorn. He shouted, mocking it, hoping it would realize his intent.

"Come on!" Then Connor added, more quietly. "Let's see how much of you survived Thor."

With a cautious step the beast advanced, crouching low to clear the top of the tunnel. Connor reflexively glanced at the bare wires hanging from the ceiling, forty feet in front of it. With two gigantic strides Leviathan had reached the junction. Green eyes narrowing, it raised its head, studying the wires. Then it lowered itself even more to clear the copper strands, stepping toward a section of walkway wired with 10,000 volts.

Just enough to make it mad.

Connor eased back, moving for the corner because it was closing on three hundred feet. He knew that he had to exhaust what flame remained before the Dragon reached the power plant.

So he took the Beretta semiautomatic pistol from the small of his back and raised it with a cold aim toward the beast. At this distance it was a useless weapon, he knew, but Connor wasn't trying to injure it. Just enrage it. So he began firing, firing a full clip and aiming high.

Leviathan winced as the bullets struck and Connor fired the full fifteen rounds. But the beast held its ground, unmoving and unprovoked. The Beretta was smoking in Connor's hand as he lowered it slowly to his side.

Leviathan glared, jaws distended.

Connor stared back, grim.

"One more step," he whispered. "Come on . . . Take it . . ."

Leviathan snarled.

It took it.

Chapter 39

Connor dove to the side as the clawed foot struck the walkway and the corridor exploded, shards of steel cascading from the tunnel to tear chunks of calcite from the walls, floor.

Instantly Connor was on his feet, into it now, sweating, something within him fired by the impact. He held the M-79 close as he ducked his head around the corner to see . . .

Roaring fangs . . . With a shout Connor fired point-blank, his finger closing on the trigger without his will and the grenade went into the face of the beast, striking in a concussive blast that rocketed fire from the tunnel like a volcanic eruption. Connor screamed and twisted away to hit the ground hard, and then he was on his feet again, staggering and without thought breaking open the M-79 to tear out the spent grenade canister.

Leviathan shrieked over him, and Connor spun to see that it was too close. Shouting, Connor dropped to one knee and saw the beast crawling beneath the upraised vault. It was fully engulfed in white, spiraling phosphorous flames, a cloud of fire.

Then Connor saw the vault cable and knew it was his only chance. Instantly he ripped out the pistol at his back to hold a dead-aim at the steel cord and then he was pulling the trigger as fast as he could move. Howling lead fragments and splintered steel lanced the air and him but Connor barely felt it and suddenly the steel cord snapped.

With a thunderous descent the vault slammed on Leviathan's

chest, crushing it to the ground. Connor heard himself howling, savagely leaping to the side as he wildly ejected the pistol's clip and slammed in another. With a curse he dropped the pistol in the bag and shoved a grenade into the M-79, snapping it shut instantly.

"Come on!" he screamed. "You ain't so tough! Show me what you can take!"

Leviathan shrieked and twisted, squirming to its back. Its claws lashed out to strike the titanium, and it bellowed, pushing down with the forelegs to crawl from beneath the crushing weight. Connor estimated that he had less than three minutes and then he was running, his mind racing ahead of him.

Ten seconds, twenty . . .

A reptilian roar thundered like a storm-blast along the walls, and Connor knew the beast was quickly scrambling free. Surging with fear, Connor slung the M-79 across his back and ran with all his strength, ignoring torn muscles and infinite, infinite pain that was coming hard now, despite the drugs.

Connor made two hundred yards in thirty seconds, saw the fifty-yard section of flooded tunnel looming up before him glistening with red light and he dove, smoothly slicing the water. When he surfaced he was halfway across, rising to a bestial roar. Then he heard a titanic crash and knew Leviathan had followed him into the water, fearless now, closing.

In six strong strokes Connor gained the edge of the flooded section to erupt over the edge, rolling clear. He scrambled frantically to the side and wildly tore the high-voltage wire from place, hurling the bare copper into the water. Then he twisted back wildly as a titanic skeletal image was lit above him—500,000 spiraling volts of electricity burning itself upward through the Dragon.

"Ahh . . ." Connor gasped, falling back.

In a white firestorm Leviathan was splayed almost to the ceiling of the passage, bones burning. And Connor knew that in another second the beast would have had him. But he had beaten it, by a second. And for the moment, the Dragon surged with pure power, glowing, unable to escape the supercharged water. Howling, shrieking, it twisted against the electrical tendrils that blasted upward through its colossal, demonic form.

"Die!" Connor screamed. "Die! Die! Die!" But he knew *knew* that it wouldn't die. Not yet. Just as he knew that the longer it fought the current, the hotter the spiraling circuit would over-heat its already superheated blood until it was boiling.

Leviathan glared down and Connor leaped to the side as a wild and uncontrolled blast descended, igniting the stone where he had stood. The blaze streamed upward across the ceiling in a holocaust that cascaded back down the wall. Only at the last moment did Connor see the streak descend toward the wire and he finally rolled wide, shouting.

Fire struck fire, the blast hurling Connor fifty feet back into the tunnel. He crashed against something unrelenting to collapse to the ground, rolling, breathless.

Stunned, rising by will alone, Connor spun to glare, shaken and shocked and numb beyond all he had ever known, to see Leviathan slashing, churning in the water. It was trying to regain control of its nervous system. Then Connor saw the burned wiring, and he realized that the beast had broken the current.

Grimacing, Connor turned and ran. Something told him he was limping, that his leg was blood-ravaged by some impact he couldn't understand but he didn't care, was carried beyond every-thing by his anger, rage, and love. He fell through the door of a manually sealed section of Brubaker with a groan, taking a deep breath and aiming the pistol. He fired continuously at the cable until it broke, ignoring the lead splinters.

The vault thundered shut.

Light-headed and reeling, Connor moved quickly down the hundred-yard stretch, trying not to breathe at all. The vault before him seemed incredibly far, and then he heard the terrific attack against the portal behind him, knew the Dragon was closing with horrific speed. It was recovering more quickly with each trauma, but Connor knew it was dying *had* to be dying. It was exhausting the last of its enzyme banks, all that remained of its strength.

Connor passed the rows of oxygen tanks that he had hauled to the stretch of passageway and then he reached the opposing vault, quickly crawling beneath. Once he was on the far side he took a breath, but the air was too poisoned even there for strength. Connor lay still for a moment, drawing ragged breaths and then he heard a spectacular collision and glared back to witness Leviathan lying as dead atop the fallen vault.

Oxygen pouring beneath the portal was stifling, thin.

The Dragon rose slowly. Stunned. Fatigued.

"Come on!" Connor bellowed. "Show me how tough you are! Do it! Do it! Use that flame!"

Leviathan staggered to its feet, wounded. Its fangs hung distended, but not to terrorize. Connor thought it was having trouble drawing breath.

Laughing, Connor roared a primal challenge with a fury that joined the two of them, the war, the stand. Then with a dramatic scream Connor raised the M-79 as if he were about to fire and the Dragon reacted, lowered its scarred head. Its neck muscles tightened.

"HIT ME!" Connor screamed. "COME ON! HIT ME!"

Connor leaped desperately aside as the Dragon's fire extended.

Through pure oxygen.

Connor heard screaming, realized he was . . .

ON FIRE!

He roared and rolled wildly through the mud and water-soaked calcite, beating violently at the flames until he found himself smoldering and blackened, smoking, smoking . . .

Burned and dying . . . like the Dragon.

"Yeah . . ." Connor whispered, rising to his knees and forehead. "We'll both . . . die in this . . . Both of us . . ."

Connor made it to his feet, snarling like an animal to endure the endless, endless pain. He had never even heard the titanic blast created when the Dragon hurled flame through the oxygen. But Connor had felt the erupting roar that tore a white path through the space beneath the vault.

Staggering, Connor saw that the vault still stood. It had

somehow endured the terrific force of the oxygen. And a moment later Connor wondered if the beast wasn't dead before he felt or sensed the shadow approaching and then a batlike foreleg exploded through the stone at the vault to—

Connor shouted as the claws struck him across the chest, blasting a red-liquid path through flesh and rib bone to turn him away with the vicious velocity of the impact. Then Connor hit the ground hard, feeling dirt on his face, his eyes black with dust, black dust.

Blood . . . blood everywhere.

Connor moaned, rolled, trying to gain his feet, but he knew that he was hurt this time, something taken . . . from him. He pressed a dark red hand across his chest as he staggered up, weak, numb.

With a vengeful scream, the Dragon jerked its foreleg through the gaping hole. A second later the foreleg was slammed through the top of the vault, ravaging the brackets, preparing to defeat the barrier. Connor watched for a stunned second before he turned and ran, weary, weary now and losing whatever strength had been fired within him as he heard himself calling out to someone, his son his *son* and he was making promises, *I won't let you down, boy, I'll never let you down, not ever* . . .

Connor moaned and fell from fatigue. Blood beneath him, over him. He groaned and looked up, looked up to see . . .

Jordan . . . in front of him . . . Hand raised to the sky, the sky . . .

I'll always be with you . . .

"Jordan," Connor whispered, "I won't let you down boy . . . I won't . . . I won't let you down . . ."

A demonic roar thundered up the tunnel.

"Come on!" Connor cried out, rising on wounded strength. "Come on, don't let this thing beat you don't let it BEAT YOU!"

Connor roared in blinding pain as he reached the half-ton truck, still parked at the entrance of the power plant. He glared wildly as he climbed into the cab to see the generator mounted on the back and still running. He slammed it into gear and gunned it and then the truck was roaring down the passage on a collision course with the beast. The grill lashed to the front was charged with 25,000 volts. Twenty gallons of gasoline were roped to the hood.

Defiant, Connor screamed as the Dragon charged and some suicidal will almost held him in the cab until the last second but then something primal *because that was all there was* drove him out and Connor found himself sprawling across the rocks and dust with pain in his face and eyes as a wild and hoarse noise roared away from him . . .

Broken . . .

Bloody, dying . . .

Connor cried out, staggering to his feet, running.

The Dragon collided with the truck and Connor whirled against his will to see the electric bolts thrown from the grill racing over the beast and then the truck exploded in a mushrooming, smothering firestorm that became white air. Connor didn't know what he was doing in the holocaust until he saw the power plant entrance approaching . . .

Running!

I'm still running!

"Thank God . . ." he moaned. "Thank you . . . Thank you, God . . ."

Leviathan roared and Connor heard a crashing, rending attack, somehow realizing that the unstoppable beast was ravaging the truck, relentlessly tearing its hell-born path up the passageway.

Always, always coming had *always* been coming.

At the thought Connor met something else inside himself, a rage to defy, to defy even to death and he drove himself savagely forward. He was dazed and numb and dying as he came down on each stumbling stride, pushing himself mercilessly toward the entrance of the power plant.

And his last hope.

Chapter 40

Connor staggered blindly into the power plant, finally gaining the door in gore and pain and rage, his shirt burned from his body and his body black with wounds.

"Get cover!" he screamed, tearing the M-79 from his back. "Barley! Get ready! It's cooooooming!"

High on the dais Connor heard a terrified scream and glanced up to see Beth and Jordan. And somehow the image brought back to life what had been destroyed by his pain and wounds and fear. Connor's face tightened, eyes tearing. He spun to glare down the tunnel, seeing in the distance the demonic beast.

Leviathan focused on him, growling.

Connor snarled, lowering his head. Then he glanced up to see the severed sections of the Norwegian power line, poised above his own head. The bare copper coils, each one as thick as his leg, were bright with a billion volts of power. He focused again on the beast.

"Come on! Come on let's finish this!"

Leviathan leaped violently forward, landing well into the tunnel and charging. Connor screamed at Barley.

"Three seconds!"

"Bring it on!" Barley shouted, raising the LAW. Connor didn't turn back but he knew the beast was coming, coming, always coming. He staggered forward, falling . . . A black roar rushed over him, hot and hating. Ablaze beyond all feeling Connor instinctively spun to see a black monstrosity hurtling up the tunnel, all caution forgotten and he fired the grenade launcher from the hip, turning into the thrust with a yell.

Exploding in a mushrooming white blast the grenade hit high, phosphorus blazing off the ceiling of the corridor to hit the beast in a firestorm. A twin concussion, something Connor didn't understand and didn't try to understand rocked the entire cavern and he fell back, yelling incoherently at the echoing shock wave that thundered across them, the entire cavern alive with the trauma of the conflict.

In a breath he had staggered up, somehow clutching the grenade launcher. He heard Barley shouting, sensed the big black man running forward, still holding the LAW.

Leviathan came over them, blazing in flame.

With a savage roar it charged into the cavern, in their midst almost before Connor could react. The Dragon hit the power plant in a rush, blasting forward in a haze of black that was over Connor in a thunderstorm of fangs and claws. Then Connor heard Barley's shout and dropped as the air shattered with the colossal concussion of the LAW.

Connor sensed something black and bestial roaring over his head, sailing aflame through the air. And in a daze he saw Leviathan's monstrous head whirl to lock savagely on something and then its long foreleg had lashed out wildly toward . . . *Jordan!*

Yet the devil-claws missed the child to strike a maze of cables and the gazebo was torn violently from the ceiling, Jordan and Beth screaming together as it descended with a rending crash to the floor.

"NO!" Connor screamed, reaching out as the walkway slammed against the cement.

A wounded roar struck the opposite wall of the power plant far behind them but Connor didn't turn to it, had all but forgotten the Dragon as he gained his feet, running forward. He saw Beth pitch forward, unconscious but still holding Jordan tight and secure in her arms and with a terrible cry Connor leaped over shattered steel to catch them in his arms.

"Beth," he gasped, crying out, on his knees. "Oh, darlin', darlin' . . ."

He cradled his wife gently in his arms and hugged Jordan close. And then by some savage survival instinct he turned his head to see Leviathan on the opposite end of the cavern, on fire from the impact of the LAW. Ravaged, the beast was galactically enraged.

Hell on earth, it rose roaring, raging.

Barley was running to the middle of the cavern, waving. "Frank!" he screamed. "Get 'em out of here! Forget the plan! Forget the plan! I'm gonna blow this place and bury this thing! Get out of here all of you get out of here!"

Leviathan screamed and lashed out, shattering a support beam. Faintly Connor leaned forward, clutching Beth and Jordan close in his arms. It was a single moment of bright, shining hope in utter blackness, a moment of holding his wife and son close as a pure hell-born beast of unstoppable strength rose before them, gathering itself to kill them, to kill them all.

"Beth," Connor gasped. "Come on, darlin', . . . Come on, baby . . . We've got to . . . We've got to get out of here . . ."

Beth pitched forward, blood on her shoulder. Connor cried out, holding her closer. "Oh, Beth . . ."

And then Frank was there, yes, Frank. The scientist bent quickly over her, taking her firmly and gently from Connor's arms. And Connor leaned back, staring in shock and tears, kneeling as he held Jordan tight.

As calm and blessed as a surgeon, Frank touched Beth's neck, his hands so calm and confident, so gentle. Then he did something sensitive and caring and touching that Connor didn't understand before he reached under the railing to lift Beth effortlessly in his strong arms, turning.

"She's alive, Connor!" he gasped, his eyes bright and loving. "Come on, buddy! We've got to get out of here! Barley's going to—"

"Look out!" Barley screamed, and Connor whirled.

It was too late.

Leviathan lashed out, smashing its tail against the far end of the gazebo and together they were sailing through the air, struck by the near end of the railing and Connor lost it all in the roaring madness, charging all his soul to hold Jordan close. Then he struck a steel girder with a mind-shattering collision, and he was spinning to fall to the ground with his son slung far from him.

Connor landed screaming, reaching for his son and not knowing where he had gone even as he heard the reptilian roar and somehow in his mind saw the Dragon rising above them, so close.

"Jordan!" he screamed.

And then he saw Jordan. So close!

The child cried out in pain.

Leviathan stood high on its hind feet, glaring, savoring the moment. It took its time to strike terror and remorse and whatever else could be struck in the hearts of its helpless victims. And Connor knew with finality that this was far, far more than a beast could ever be.

It would be the end of the world. If it could be.

Then Barley was before it, in its teeth, screaming suicidally and firing up with a continuous stream from his blazing M-16 that Leviathan all but ignored until it suddenly glared down, irritated, fangs parting. It swiped out with a contemptuous foreleg, and Connor saw the lieutenant blasted wildly to the side. Barley was hurled incredibly high and hard across the cavern to smash into a broken stand of girders, spinning off the heap to crash with bone-shattering force.

Connor cried out, hurt by the sight. But almost instantly, incredibly, Barley was on his feet again and Connor wasn't even surprised. The lieutenant rose, staggering forward, always *always* back into the fight but Connor understood somehow that not even Barley, as much a man as he was, could stand after that, not after that. Barley took two staggering steps, screaming in rage and drawing a pistol to fire a full clip, firing until he fell heavily onto his face, silent, deathly silent in a silence that reached fully across the cavern.

Connor moaned, bowing his head.

Leviathan stared, unconcerned, until Barley collapsed. It

swung its ravaged serpentine head toward Connor, and Connor somehow felt the impact of the Dragon's unearthly hate. With a horrified shout Connor surged forward, trying to gain his feet. But he couldn't move.

Shocked, Connor glared down to see that he was pinned solidly to the ground by a steel girder. And fired by desperation, Connor cursed and tried to scramble out, shredding his legs on the steel. But his bones were held solid. And with a wild cry he searched for a weapon, saw the M-79 close.

In a breath Connor snatched the weapon up and cracked the breech, tearing out the spent round. He fumbled frantically through Jordan's hysterical screams for the remaining grenade.

Couldn't find it. It was gone, gone . . .

Connor's hands scrambled over all that he could reach.

Leviathan roared, stepping closer. And then Connor saw the grenade on the floor. It was lying cleanly on the cement, in clear view . . . between Jordan and the Dragon.

Leviathan's next shriek propelled Jordan hard into Connor's arms and Connor dropped the M-79 as he caught his son. The four-year-old was terrified and hysterical, and Connor frantically took a moment to hold him close, and closer. Then he pushed his son back, glaring with a father's dying, desperate love.

Leviathan lowered its head and growled, fifty yards away. The Dragon twisted its demon head, as if laughing, and Connor saw with a shock it would have to walk directly between the severed sections of the Norwegian power line to reach them. Jordan saw the beast and screamed, and Connor realized with horror what he had to do.

"Jordan!" he screamed, pointing frantically at the phosphorous grenade. "Listen to me son! Listen to me! Get that grenade for Daddy! Please! Get it for Daddy!"

"No! No!" Jordan screamed.

Jaws gaping, Leviathan approached the severed sections of the Norwegian power line.

Stunned by fear and hope, Connor grasped his son by the

shoulders, pointing frantically. "Jordan!" he screamed. "Please, son! Get that for Daddy! Please! Get it for me! *For me!*"

But Jordan only leaped and crawled farther into his arms and Connor groaned in utter pain as he pushed him back, knowing that everything, everything had come down to this single moment in time.

"Jordan!" he cried, eye to eye and heart to heart. "Do you remember how I *promised* you I'd kill the Dragon for you? Do you remember?"

Jordan shook his head. "No! No!"

"Yes!" Connor shouted, bringing their heads together as he *had* to bring their hearts together in order to survive. "Get that for me Jordan and I promise you I'll kill it! I promise! I promise!"

Leviathan opened its jaws, drawing breath.

Took another step.

"God help us!" Connor cried, throwing his face to the ceiling before looking down again. "Jordan!" he shouted. "Get that grenade for me now, son! *Get it for me! For me! And I promise you I'll kill it!*"

Shocked and crying, Jordan stared into Connor's eyes. And, as if he'd been touched by a force even more powerful than his terror, he suddenly turned, gazing in utter fear at the beast. And then with a child's purest love and trust and essence, the boy tore away from Connor and leaped onto the walkway, running helplessly and screaming toward the Dragon.

And the grenade.

Leviathan's dark eyes blazed with inhabited hate as the child approached and then Jordan bent to snatch up the grenade. And for a stunning, frozen moment the child stared up, up into the face of the Dragon. And the Dragon glared down, fangs gaping, hating and threatening.

Connor gasped, shocked at the moment of unearthly stillness. But Jordan somehow held his place as the Dragon hovered before him, colossal and satanic and monstrous but somehow . . . afraid . . .

Jordan stood, motionless.

Then Leviathan shrieked, staggering forward.

Instantly screaming in horror Jordan turned, leaped into Connor's arms with Leviathan following in his steps and Connor roared with love as he caught his son from the air, turning him away. Then in the next blinding split second he caught the grenade from the boy's hand to slam it into the M-79, snapping the weapon shut and raising it simultaneously.

The Dragon roared, bending over them.

It stood solidly between the severed sections of the power line.

With savage love Connor desperately pulled his son's face close into his chest, aiming the grenade launcher dead-center between Leviathan's demonic green eyes.

They glared, face to face.

Leviathan snarled, jaws twisting.

Connor frowned.

"You're *extinct*," he rasped.

And pulled the trigger.

The grenade struck Leviathan's hell-born face to mushroom instantly over the severed sections of the supercharged power line. And as the chemical cloud hit the copper coils a blue-white bolt of lightning leaped instantly across, hurled over their heads like the Wrath of God to strike the Dragon hard in the chest and blast a hole through its monstrous form. The air coruscated white with the firestorm that continued, continued through galactic reptilian pain that raged across the cavern, raging until it was itself overcome by the white fire that surged over them in a God-roar that finally tore the Dragon's shriek to shreds in an amazing, blazing blast of unearthly power and justice and wrath . . .

Chapter 41

Holding Jordan in his arm, Connor stood over the Dragon. It was finished. All that remained of Leviathan's gigantic, reptilian form was a charred mass of blackened bone and flesh. The serpentine neck and forelegs, once hard with muscle and tendons, were withered ash. Even the proud armor that had defied the might of an army was finally defeated, overcome by a force far more powerful.

Staring down, Connor saw that almost nothing remained of the Dragon's gigantic aspect. Leviathan was twisted and contorted with a savagely charred hole blasted clean through the center of its massive body. There was simply nothing there—no heart, no blood, no life. The Dragon was an empty husk. And the glowing green eyes were burned black, empty and dead.

Connor said nothing, hugging Jordan close beneath the emergency lighting. And then Beth was beside them, wrapping her arms around them both. Her forehead was bruised, but the blood was already stanched by Frank's bandage. Gazing down, Connor kissed her softly and held her.

It was a moment of silence, but of a rumbling silence, like the silence cloaking a low, lightning-torn sky. And then Frank was also beside them, staring down coldly. His face was empty, his pose solemn.

Connor turned to him. "Is it dead, Frank?"

"It's dead," the scientist said somberly. "Forever."

Raising his face, Connor gazed across the cavern toward Barley. "Is Barley going to make it?"

"Yeah," the scientist nodded, looking at where they had laid Barley on a stretcher after Frank had helped free Connor from the girder. "He's a strong guy. He'll make it. But he's going to be laid up for a long time. He's got a lot of broken bones." Frank stared tiredly. "Not that he really cares that much."

An interrupting voice came over the surface link radio and Frank instantly picked it up. With the calm thoroughness of an emergency room surgeon, he gave terse instructions for necessary medical assistance, along with their location in the cavern.

"It's the Sea Patrol," he said, turning to them. "They've arrived with a representative of Stygian Enterprises. They said that they can get to us in about an hour. And they're going to bring a couple of stretchers."

"Good enough," Connor said before he sensed Jordan staring up at him, quiet and still. With a gentle smile Connor gazed down. "You're a good boy," he whispered. "You're a real good boy."

Jordan smiled, wrapping his arms around Connor's neck.

"Are we going home now?" he asked. "Like you promised?"

Connor nodded, closing his eyes.

"Yeah, boy. We're going home. Like I promised."

It took EMTs three hours to haul Barley through the cavern, and then they were finally on the way to the surface. But Connor had been given an injection of morphine for his badly bruised leg and other wounds, and he insisted on walking the full distance, making a slight detour when they passed the Matrix to retrieve something he could not leave behind.

Then they reached the elevator and began to rise to the surface, but halfway up the ascent Connor curtly ordered the lift stopped. Then he opened a trapdoor and crawled beneath the cage, working quietly for a few minutes in the shaft.

When he crawled once more through the trapdoor he was bathed in sweat, and fresh blood gleamed through the bandages over his wounds. Beneath Beth's concerned gaze Connor rolled, exhausted, to a wall.

"Did you do it, Connor?" she whispered.

Connor nodded wordlessly and motioned for the confused rescue personnel to proceed with the lift.

And the elevator began to rise.

Toward the sun.

Connor gently placed a hand on Barley's shoulder.

"You're not going to die on me are you, Barley?"

Barley grunted, almost pale from blood loss. "No, Connor. I think . . . I think I'll stick around for a little while. Might even . . . might even take a vacation." He stared, lowering his voice. "Did you do it?"

"Yeah," Connor nodded. "It's done. A few more seconds."

"Good. Then it's almost . . . almost over."

Eyes narrowing, Connor turned to stare at the cavern shaft. The blackness of the abyss was completely isolated, the elevator itself anchored solidly on the surface. He knew that no rescue personnel had descended into the cavern since they had reached the surface. The United States government had ordered the facility secured. No one else was going in.

Frank walked up.

"Beth and Jordan are in stable condition. They've been airlifted out on the Sea Stallion," he said. "It's a fast-flight helicopter, so they should be at a hospital inside an hour. Jordan is dehydrated and suffering a low grade infection, but he'll be okay."

With a nod Connor focused on the scientist's youthful face. "I appreciate you taking care of them for me, Frank. I had some things I had to do."

"I know. But you need to get to a hospital, too, Connor. Those cuts on your chest are infected. And you've got a bad bone-bruise in your leg. You're not going to be standing when that morphine wears off."

Connor nodded. "You know what I've done, Frank?"

"I know."

Connor felt a sadness. "I'm sorry, Frank. I know that . . . the computer was more than just a machine to you."

"GEO was never a living thing, Connor." Frank's face brightened, stronger. "No. It was only a machine."

"But it was part of Rachel," Connor replied.

A pause, and the scientist blinked.

"Remembered love is enough, Connor," he said finally. "It has to be."

They nodded together.

And as the Sea Patrol lifted Barley's gurney, the C-4 that Connor had strapped to the limestone walls of the elevator shaft detonated like a volcano. And, awakened from his morphine stupor, Barley shouted at the thunderous blast, shouting to violently lift a hard fist in the air. His bellow of victory carried strongly across the compound.

Connor laughed, knowing that the C-4 had completely closed the shaft by sending over a million tons of granite and stone and dirt thunderously to the bottom, where it buried the vault in a mountain of stone. In moments, the cavern was completely sealed from the world—the computer, the dead, the Dragon, and the heroes who had defied it.

Startled by the explosion, a representative of Stygian Enterprises, someone Connor didn't know but recognized by his air of authority, ran up. The little man staggered to a halt beside Connor, staring in horror at the sulfuric dust roiling from the exit of the shaft. He glanced to the side and seemed to catch something in Connor's haggard, angry face.

"What . . . what happened?" the man whispered.

"I blew it," Connor said. "I buried it."

Pandemonium roars echoed from deep inside the cavern, and the thunder continued a long time until silence finally overcame all there was—a sea of silence that left the shaft as dead and buried as hell itself.

"Mr. Connor!" the man shouted. "I represent Stygian Enterprises, the company which owns that facility! I want to know immediately who gave you the authority to destroy the elevator shaft!"

Connor stared. "Nobody."

The company man staggered.

"So . . ." he gasped, ". . . so how could you destroy it? It's . . . it's going to take years . . . it's going to take a fortune to dig it out!" He stepped back, pointing a finger. "You're in big trouble, Connor! Big trouble! That was a billion-dollar facility!"

Connor laughed, turned away.

"Send me a bill," he said.

Epilogue

In ice-light, the tower stood.

Connor stared at the fortress that forever conquered and commanded the wind and sleet and snow. But he had finally come to understand, and with a strange contentment, that it had never truly been the man who inhabited the tower. It had been the tower that inhabited the man.

Connor moved slowly through the frost-framed doorway, glancing sadly at Tanngrisner's empty stable, for the proud stallion had been set free to roam the dark nightvales of the island, now that his beloved master had passed. Connor had personally seen to that.

Carrying the large, heavy object in his hand, Connor slowly ascended the steps toward the large, upper chamber where the white stone portal stood open, as it had always stood open, shrouded in light.

But across the circular stone room the deep fire hearth was filled only with gray ash and cold blackened iron, a reminder of death. Connor paused, staring as his hand tightened painfully on what he held. Then he limped slowly across the chamber, finally halting before the hearth where his gaze locked on the thick iron hooks, deep in stone.

Empty. Waiting.

It was an unknown and uncrowned king, old guardian of the people, who stood here last, reaching up with his strong arm to call down the strength to slay the Dragon. And yet now, Connor knew, Thor's great strength was gone, and gone forever. Just as he knew that one day, in some way, the Dragon would return. As it always returned.

With a grimace Connor raised the battle-ax, laying it to rest. Then he stepped back and stared a moment at the weapon, gazing at the image of cosmic battle etched upon the steel—the angelic warrior battling the Dragon, driving the beast down from the stars. And Connor once more saw Thor, wounded and dying and hurling the battle-ax through flame, fighting forever, defying the Beast to the last.

Connor stared, remembering, and remembering more. Then he reached up to gently touch the battle-ax again, searching for the faith and love and strength and life to defy the Dragon.

Connor searched a long time, and then he smiled.

Yeah, he thought, understanding . . . at last.

It was worth dying for.